TEXTBOOK OF STATISTICS, PSYCHOLOGY AND EDUCATION

TEXTBOOK OF STATISTICS, PSYCHOLOGY AND EDUCATION

By

ROMESH VERMA

ANMOL PUBLICATIONS PVT. LTD.

NEW DELHI - 110 002 (INDIA)

ANMOL PUBLICATIONS PVT. LTD.
Regd. Office: 4360/4, Ansari Road, Daryaganj,
New Delhi-110002 (India)
Tel.: 23278000, 23261597, 23286875, 23255577
Fax: 91-11-23280289
Email: anmolpub@gmail.com
Visit us at: www.anmolpublications.com

Branch Office: No. 1015, Ist Main Road, BSK IIIrd Stage
IIIrd Phase, IIIrd Block, Bengaluru-560 085 (India)
Tel.: 080-41723429 • Fax: 080-26723604
Email: anmolpublicationsbangalore@gmail.com

Textbook of Statistics, Psychology and Education

Reprint 2007, 2014

PRINTED IN INDIA

Printed at Balaji Offset, Delhi

Dedicated

to a noble friend

Dr. Suresh Sharma

Contents

Preface xv

SECTION 1

Chapter I. Educational Psychology **1**

I.1 Meaning of Psychology 1
I.2 Nature of Psychology 4
I.3 Branches of Psychology 6
I.4 Meaning of Educational Psychology 8
I.5 Aims of Educational Psychology 9
I.6 Scope of Educational Psychology 10
I.7 Limitations of Educational Psychology 11
I.8 Relationship between Education and Psychology 12
I.9 Significance of the Knowledge of Educational, Psychology for a Teacher 13
I.10 Learning Exercises 16

Chapter II. Methods of Educational Psychology **17**

II. 1 Introspection Method 18
II. 2 Observation Method 21
II. 3 Experimental Method 24
II. 4 Psychoanalytic Method 25
II. 5 Developmental Method 31
II. 6 Testing Method 32
II. 7 Clinic Method 33
II. 8 Learning Exercises 34

Chapter III. Psychology of Growth and Development **35**

III. 1 Meaning of Growth 35
III. 2 Meaning of Development 35

III. 3	Principles of Development	37
III. 4	Difference between Growth and Development	39
III. 5	Importance to knowledge of growth and development for a teacher	40
III. 6	Stages of Development	41
III. 7	Different Aspects of Growth during infancy	44
III. 8	Development of Social Life during Infancy to Childhood	48
III. 9	Different Aspects of Growth and Development during Adolescence	60
III. 10	Growth and Development during Adulthood	
III. 11	Role of Teacher and Development	
III. 12	Learning Exercises	
Chapter IV.	**Psychology of Emotion**	**67**
IV.1	Meaning of Emotions	68
IV. 2	Development of Emotions	71
IV. 3	Nature of Emotions	72
IV. 4	Diminutions of Emotions	74
IV. 5	Theories of Emotions	77
IV. 6	Types of Emotions	81
IV. 7	Effects of Emotions and Behaviour	83
IV. 8	Emotional Development and a Teacher	87
IV. 9	Instincts and Emotions	88
IV. 10	Role of Emotions in Life	91
IV. 11	Training of Emotions	92
IV. 12	Emotional Maturity and a Teacher	93
IV. 13	Learning Exercises	94
Chapter V.	**Memory and Forgetting**	**95**
V.1	Meaning and Nature of Memory	95
V.2	Types of Memory	99
V.3	Signs of Good Memory	107
V.4	Factors responsible to improve Memory	108
V.5	Methods of Memorising	109
V.6	Forms of Memory	111

V.7	Memory Problems	112
V.8	Treatment of Memory Problems	113
V.9	Role of Teacher to improve Memory	113
V.10	Meaning and Definitions of Forgetting	117
V.11	Theories of Forgetting	118
V.12	Causes of Forgetting	122
V.13	Differences in Memory of Adults and Children	125
V.14	Recall and Forgetting	126
V.15	Learning Exercises	127
Chapter VI. Learning		**128**
VI.1	Meaning and Definition of Learning	128
VI.2	Nature of Learning	130
VI.3	Types of Learning	132
VI.4	Learning Theories	133
VI.5	Difference between Classical and Operant conditioning	150
VI.6	Laws of Learning	152
VI.7	Factors affecting Learning	155
VI.8	Methods of Learning	159
VI. 9	Measurement of Learning	161
VI. 10	Learning Exercises	165
Chapter VII. Transfer of Training		**166**
VII.1	Meaning of Transfer of Training	166
VII.2	Types of Transfer of Training	167
VII.3	Theories of Transfer of Training	168
VII.4	Factors influencing Transfer of Training	172
VII.5	Methods of Instruction and Transfer of Training	174
VII.6	Suggestions for Improvement in Transfer of Training	175
VII.7	Learning Exercises	176
Chapter VIII. Motivation		**177**
VIII.1	Meaning and Definitions of Motivation	177
VIII.2	Significance of Motivation	180
VIII.3	Nature of Motivation	181
VIII.4	Motivation Cycle	184

VIII.5	Theories of Motivation	186
VIII.6	Types of Motivation	193
VIII.7	Effect of Motivation on Learning	194
VIII.8	Assessment of Motivation	199
VIII.9	Educational Implications of Motivation	201
VIII.10	Learning Exercises	204
Chapter IX. Personality		**205**
IX.1	Meaning of Personality	205
IX.2	Characteristics of Personality	209
IX.3	Dimensions of Personality	210
IX.4	Types of Personality	213
IX.5	Difference in Personality Patterns	216
IX.6	Meaning of Traits	218
IX.7	Methods of Assessment of Personality	220
IX.8	Types of Projective Tests	224
IX.9	Administering the Role of Rorrchah Ink Bolt Test	
IX.10	Thematic Tests	228
IX.11	Development of Personality	230
IX.12	Factors Affecting Personality Pattern	233
IX.13	Learning Exercises	240
Chapter X. Intelligence		**242**
X.1	Definitions of Intelligence	242
X.2	Concept of Intelligence	243
X.3	Nature of Intelligence	245
X.4	Theories of Intelligence	248
X.5	History of Intelligence Testing	253
X.6	Types of Intelligence Tests	256
X.7	Uses of Intelligence Tests	260
X.8	Distribution of Intelligence	261
X.9	Assessment of Intelligence	262
X.10	Intelligence Quotient	266
X.11	Advantages of I.Q	270
X.12	Limitations of I.Q	272
X.13	Difference between I.Q and Mental Age	273

X.14 Consistency of the I.Q 274
X.15 Educational Implications of Intelligence Tests 277
X.16 Role of a Teacher in Promoting Intelligence Tests 278
X.17 Learning Exercises 280

Chapter XI. Creativity **281**
XI.1 Meaning and Definitions of Creativity 281
XI.2 Characteristics of Creativity 284
XI.3 Principles of Creativity 288
XI.4 Theories of Creativity 289
XI.5 Assessment of Creativity 292
XI.6 Conditions Responsible for the Promotion of Creativity 294
XI.7 Role of a Teacher and Creativity 295
XI.8 Role of Community to promote Creativity 296
XI.9 Developing Creativity Environment 298
XI.10 Educational Implications of Creativity 300
XI.11 Difference between Intelligence and Creativity 300
XI.12 Learning Exercises 302

Chapter XII. Exceptional Children **303**
XII.1 Meaning and Definition of Exceptional Children 303
XII.2 Types of Exceptional Children 304
XII.3 Needs of Exceptional Children 312
XII.4 Objectives of Education for the Exceptional Children 313
XII.5 Creative Children 319
XII.6 Characteristics of Creative Children 322
XII.7 Assessing Creative Children 325
XII.8 Developing Environment for Creative Abilities 327
XII.9 Gifted Children 330
XII.10 Concept of Gifted Children 330
XII.14 Definition of Giftedness 331
XII.12 Identification of Gifted Children 336
XII.13 Assessment of Gifted Children 337
XII.14 Education of the Gifted Children 339

XII.15 Guiding Gifted Children and the Role of Parents and Teacher 344
XII.16 Learning Exercises 346

Chapter XIII. Mentally Retarded Children **347**
XIII.1 Meaning and Definition of Mentally Retarded Children 347
XIII.2 Identification of Mentally Retarded Children 349
XIII.3 Classification of Mentally Retarded Children 350
XIII.4 Causes of Mentally Retarded Children 351
XIII.5 Education of Mentally Retarded Children 355
XIII.6 Suggestions for Mentally Retarded Children 358
XIII.7 Learning Exercises 359

Chapter XIV. Learning Disable Children **360**
XIV.1 Meaning and Definitions of Learning Disable Children 360
XIV.2 Causes of Learning Disabilities 362
XIV.3 Characteristics of Learning Disable Children 362
XIV.4 Educational Provision for Learning Disable Children 371
XIV.5 Role of Teacher Promoting Learning Disable Children 379
XIV.6 Suggestion for Learning Disable Children 381
XIV.7 Learning Exercises 382

Chapter XV. Delinquency **383**
XV.1 Meaning of Delinquency 383
XV.2 Cause of Delinquency 384
XV.3 Remedial Measures of Delinquency 387
XV.4 Learning Exercises 390

Chapter XVI. Mental Health **391**
XVI.1 Meaning and Definitions of Mental Hygiene 391
XVI.2 Importance of Mental Hygienl 393
XVI.3 Criterion of Mental Hygiene 394
XVI.4 Factors Influencing Mental Hygiene 395

XVI.5	Mental Health and Teacher	398
XVI.6	Mental Health and Role of Family	402
XVI.7	Mental Health Hazards and Inadequate School and Family Climate	403
XVI.8	Role of Different Agencies in Promoting Mental Health	405
XVI.9	Learning Exercises	414

SECTION II STASTICS

Chapter XVII.	**Elementary Statistics in Educational Psychology**	**415**
XVII.1	Meaning and Definition of Statistics	415
XVII.2	Functions of Statistics	416
XVII.3	Importance of Statistics	416
XVII.4	Measurement of Statistics	418
XVII.5	Discrete and Continuous Series	418
XVII.6	Finding Mid point and Interval in a frequency distribution	420
XVII.7	Graphic Representation	421
XVII.8	Methods of Graphic Representation	422
XVII.9	Learning Exercises	429
Chapter XVIII.	**Measures of Central Tendency & Dispression**	**430**
XVIII.1	Mean	431
XVIII.2	Median	434
XVIII.3	Mode	436
XVIII.4	Importance of the Measures of Central Tendency	437
XVIII.5	Measures of Dispersion	438
XVIII.6	Calculation of Measures of Dispersion	439
XVIII.7	Condition Required for the use of various Measures of Dispersion	444
XVIII.8	Merits and Demerits of Dispersion	445
XVIII.9	Learning Exercises	446
Chapter XIX.	**Percentiles, Percentile Ranks & Correlation**	**447**
XIX.1	Percentiles and Percentile Ranks	447

XIX.2	Calculation of Percentiles	447
XIX.3	Calculation of Percentile Rank	450
XIX.4	Meaning and Definition of Correlation	452
XIX.5	Methods of Studying Correlation	453
XIX.6	Product Moment Correlation	454
XIX.7	Rank Difference Correlation	457
XIX.8	Interpretations of Correlation	459
XIX.9	Learning Exercises	460
Chapter XX. Normal Probability Distribution		461
XX.1	Meaning of Probability	462
XX.2	Properties of Normal Distribution Curve	463
XX.3	Application of Normal Probability Curve	465
XX.4	Learning Exercises	474

Preface

Educational psychology mainly concerns the promotion of learning environment by understanding the cognitive, connative, affective abilities, emotional equilibrium, interest, aptitude of the learner, to learn speedily, comfortably and accurately for better adjustment in the society.

Educational psychology in this scientific world is striving hard to work-out models facilitating comprehensions of content knowledge to develop the learner's personality. The explosion of knowledge has compelled to reconstruct educational psychological models for learning in this information and communication technological age. Therefore, role of educational psychology is to enshrine all what is good and noble, what is socially significant and what leads to emancipation and proper equipment of the learner to promote the well being of society of which he is an integral part. Thus, without a sound knowledge of educational psychology and human behaviour the society will remain an ideal dream.

Present book comprises two sections namely, educational psychology and statistics. Important postulates of educational psychology have been discussed in sixteen chapters and the statistical postulates have been explained briefly in four chapters. The book will prove useful for the teachers, scholars and student of B.Ed, M.A. (Edn.), and M.Ed., M.Phil. studying in various universities. The volume at hand will provide comprehensive knowledge in respect of human behaviour perspectives in the 21 Century.

— Dr. Romesh Verma

I

Educational Psychology

During our day-to-day life, we come across various types of people. As a matter of our experience, we react differently to different persons. This difference in our approach of reaction makes us understand that there is some force which regulates our responses. The discipline which enables us to understand the regulatory forces of our responses is known as psychology. Psychology is said to be the study of human actions and reactions, i.e., how people think, behave and why they behave in just the way they do. The main purpose of psychology is to know more about human nature and human activities. In the past, psychology was defined as the science of soul or mind, infact it is not possible to have direct knowledge of the soul or mind. While behaviour is subjective and can be observed both soul and mind which are just assumptions, and even if we agree that they are justifiable assumptions, they cannot be observed and are not proper object of scientific study. Now, psychology has taken a turn towards scientific dimensions; as a result, the concept of psychology has changed from soul to mind, consciousness to behaviour.

1.1 Meaning & Definition of Psychology

The term 'psychology' was derived from the two Greek words psyche and logos. By 'psyche' we mean 'soul' and by 'logos' we mean 'talk about or science of'. By combining both the words we mean that psychology is the science which studies soul. This was the earlier concept regarding psychology. Later different psychologists have tried to define psychology differently. For instance, psychology has been defined as the science of mental life, the science of mental processes, states, activities or functions, the study of behaviour in its mental and bodily aspects, a systematic inquiry into man's relation with his environment and the like. In fact, there are many definitions of psychology. But in spite of these differences psychologists agree that the chief purpose of the study of psychology is to know more about human nature and human activity. Let us study various definition of Psychology.

(i) Psychology as a Science of Soul

The term Psychology was first used by Rudolf Goeckle in 1590. This term is derived from Greek words 'Psyche' meaning the soul and 'Logos' the science. Thus literally, Psychology means the science of soul i.e., Atman. Old philosophers were more interested in the study of the soul. However, the term has very wide and comprehensive meanings and as such this term was widely criticised in the middle ages and the concept that psychology is the study of soul could not hold good. Then people started thinking that Psychology is related to one's mind.

(ii) Psychology as a Science of Mind

Studies report that some ancient Greek philosophers defined psychology as the science of mind. According to them it was held as a branch of mental philosophy. Though the term was a better substitute for soul, yet it was far from perfect. Modern psychology is a study of action and processes rather than of things. In other words, it is a science of mental processes rather than of mind. Moreover, even those who use the word 'mind' are not unanimous about its nature. The view that psychology as a science of mind does not include the overt behaviour of man and animal which forms a major subject of study in the present-day Psychology. Besides, the mind as a physical object does not exist in our body. So this concept again changed.

(iii) Psychology as a Science of Consciousness

At one time during the history of Psychology, it was felt that the main business of Psychology was to study the conscious experience. Various meanings were given for the term consciousness, the commonest being that of awareness. Consciousness makes us conscious or aware of the situation or things around us. This definition too is now obsolete and it has been rejected due to the following reasons:

1. Consciousness cannot be studied objectively as it is more personal and subjective.
2. Second objection came from the fast developing branch of the abnormal psychology which brought the study of unconscious part of our mind within the province of Psychology.
3. The term consciousness does not include animal or human behaviour.

4. The term consciousness also was supposed to have a philosophical.
5. The term is also not accepte by the modern scientific minded psychologists.

(iv) Psychology as a Science of Behaviour

Modern Psychology has been defined as a science of behaviour i.e., psychology has become behaviouristic. The leading exponent of this school is Watson. The behaviouristic psychology studied the mental life through observations and in a way confined itself to the description of the body or behaviour. By behaviour it is generally understood anything that a living being does. Behaviour involves all types of activities performed by a person in any state or condition. So all physical, mental, social, anti-social, moral, good or bad activities or actions performed consciously or unconsciously are included in the term behaviour. Talking, walking, sleeping, thinking, playing are different types of behaviour.

Psychology as a science of behaviour too has its own limitations. No doubt the physical and physiological conditions are concomitantly connected with our mental life, but these facts should not occupy the psychologist primarily but only secondarily. Behaviouristic psychology attaches too much importance to the bodily and physiological side and thereby undermines the conscious side of the mind and mental processes. So this definition too narrows down the scope of psychology and is, therefore, equally one sided and erroneous. Psychology is concerned both with consciousness and behaviour. To undermine the importance of either of these is to limit the scope of the subject.

(v) Accepted Definitions of Psychology

One of the most acceptable definition in contemporary psychology is that given by R.S. Woodworth. Woodworth says, "Psychology is the scientific study of the activities of the individual in relation to environment". The definition given by Dr Munn has equally stood the test of time. According to Munn, "Psychology today concerns itself with the scientific investigation of behaviour, including from the stand-point of behaviour, much of what earlier psychologists dealt with as experience." Both these definitions can be accepted as satisfactory, but the latter is better than the former in a certain sense.

Conclusion

From the above definitions, we understand that Psychology studies the facts about mind as well as behaviour. If we lay stress on the mind, we define Psychology as the science of mind or consciousness; and if we emphasize the bahaviour, we define it as the science of behaviour, but it is an error to emphasize either of them exclusively. In order to be complete, the science of psychology must combine the study of inner mental processes and outer behaviour. It is only by so embracing both of them that we can overcome one-sidedness and arrive at a comprehensive definition of psychology.

We may define Psychology as a *positive and empirical* science dealing with the process of the mind and the behaviour of the body. It is positive because it is concerned with mind and behaviour as they *actually are,* it is empirical because, like other sciences, it employs the *method of observation of facts.* We must not forget, however, that psychology has to build up its description by observing the mind and behaviour of animals as well as human beings and of abnormal persons as well as normal.

I.2 Nature of Psychology

The nature of Psychology is scientific. This fact has been recognized by various psychologists and thinkers. Let us, try to analyse why Psychology why has been called a science. In general a discipline is scientific if it:

1. Possesses a body of facts which can be supported through universal laws and principles;
2. emphasizes the search for truth;
3. does not believe in hearsay, stereotypes or superstition;
4. believes in cause and effect relationships;
5. adopts the method of objective investigation, systematic and controlled observation and a scientific approach;
6. stands for the generalization, verifiability and modification of the observed results or deducted phenomena;
7. helps in predicting future developments; and
8. is able to turn its theory into practice by having an applied aspect.

Analysising the nature of psychology in the light of the above-mentioned criteria. We find the following:

1. Psychology possesses a well-organized theory which is supported by the relevant psychological laws and principles.
2. It has its applied aspect in the form of various branches of applied psychology like industrial, legal, clinical and educational psychology.

3. It believes that every behaviour has its roots, and factors causing, influencing or nurturing it.
4. Subjective ideas and opinions are not considered significant in the study of behaviour in psychology. It emphasizes the search for truth by advocating objectivity, reliability and validity in the assessment of behaviour.
5. The methods and techniques employed in the study of behaviour in psychology are quite scientific. Steps like the analysis of behaviour, formulation of hypotheses, objective observations or controlled experimentation of hypotheses, objective observations or controlled experimentation, deduction, verification and generalization of the results etc. provide the solid base for the scientific method and approach in psychology.
6. The results of the study of behaviour are always open to verification under similar conditions by other experimenters and observers. These results may be accepted, modified, or altered in the light of the latest data and findings.
7. The established facts, principles and laws of behaviour in Psychology enjoy universal applicability in practical life, in other bodies of knowledge and future researches in its own sphere.
8. An appropriate description and quantification of behaviour is possible through Psychology. We may make dependable predictions about the organism in the light of its studie behaviour.

On the the basis of the above characteristics, it may be infered that Psychology qualifies as a science. Its nature is quite scientific and not philosophical or esoteric as it used to be earliar.

(a) Psychology as a Developing Science

We can divide all the sciences into two broad categories–the positive and the normative. While physical and life sciences are termed as *positive sciences,* subjects like logic, philosophy and ethics are included in the category of *normative sciences.*

In contrast to normative sciences, positive sciences study facts *as they are* and have little or no concern with what they *ought to be*. Psychology in this sense easily falls in the category of positive sciences.

Now the question that arises is that can we equate Psychology, the science of behaviour, with the positive sciences like Physics, Chemistry, Botany, Zoology, Astronomy and Mathematics? The answer lies in the negative. In comparison to these sciences, Psychology is not so perfect and developed science. In fact, it is a behavioural science which deals with the behaviour of an organism. Because behaviour is quite dynamic and unpredictable. Methods of its study are also not as absolute and objective as those adopted by the natural sciences. On the other hand, physical or chemical reactions studied by the natural sciences are always predictable on account of the nature of the material involved and the study processes. As a result, the studies in natural sciences are bound to be more exact, accurate and objective than the studies of behaviour in psychology.

It is, therefore, not correct to place Psychology in the same category as the physical and natural sciences because the tools used for the assessment of psychological attributes have no absolute zero on their scales, which we find in the tools measurements of physical sciences. Although constant efforts are being made to make its techniques and approach as objective, exact and accurate as possible, Psychology has not yet attained the position and status of these sciences. Thus it may, in the true sense of the term, psychology can be called a developing positive science rather than a developed positive science. Hence, in the ultimate analysis, for understanding the nature and meaning of the subject, we can define psychology as a *developing positive science of behaviour.*

I.3 Branches of Psychology

For the sake of convenience the specialised knowledge of psychology has been divided into different branches. The following list includes major branches/fields of psychology. These fields are not mutually exclusive. Broadly speaking, these various divisions fall under two groups viz. pure and applied psychology.

Branches of Pure Psychology

1. General Psychology. This includes a study of the basic principles of all aspects of Psychology. Usually this means a study of the normal human adult, though, of course, reference will have to be made to some other aspects also.

2. Abnormal Psychology. This includes a study of maladjustments among mental and emotional deviance. Abnormal Psychology deals more with the theoretical aspects to understand the nature of abnormal behaviour.

3. Child Psychology. This includes a study of the behaviour of individuals from the pre-natal period through the developing years to maturity. The study of the child has developed as a separate branch, because it calls for new and particular types of methods suitable to children.

4. Physiological Psychology. This includes a study of the physiological structure of the human being in relation to the working of his mind. It deals with the study of anatomical structure and organic functioning, especially of the nervous system.

5. Animal Psychology. This is concerned with the nature and reactions of animals. This has been done both for the sake of understanding the behaviour of animals and also for understanding the behaviour of man. There is a general measure of agrement that man is related to the infra-human animals in so far as we can discover in them traces of feelings, instincts and other processes which are similar to our own. Hence, our knowledge of the animal mind can throw much light upon the development and working of the human mind. The minds of some of the lower animals–monkeys for example–resemble our own minds so much as if they are our first cousins.

6. Social Psychology. This is concerned with the behaviour of individuals in group situations and of the inter-relationships among individuals or among groups.

7. Differential Psychology. Differential Psychology is concerned with individual differences. Strictly speaking, it forms part of general psychology itself. But in recent years psychological testing has developed sufficiently and the study of individual differences has become very wide in its scope.

8. Experimental Psychology. This is one of the most important branches of Psychology since it uses strictly scientific methods in its study. Only those phenomena fall outside its scope which cannot be studied in controlled situations. The scope of experimental psychology is gradually widening with the finding of new tools and instruments for experiments.

Applied Branches of Psychology

Applied psychology is the application of general psychology to a specific situation. It has been found that by an application of the principles of psychology, the general efficiency in various walks of life can be improved. The various branches of applied psychology are as under:

1. **Clinical Psychology.** This is concerned with diagnosis and treatment of mental, emotional and behaviour disorders. Application of Psychology to the understanding and treatment of mental disorders has made enormous strides during the 20th century.

2. **Legal Psychology.** Psychology has been used in the field of law and justice. This branch of Psychology has helped in the detection of crimes, false instances, etc.

3. **Industrial Psychology.** In industry people are brought together in very definite social relationships and given definite tasks. Psychology has

made a pronounced contribution to the various problems that arise in that particular setting. Practically every aspect and every department of industrial concern is using the findings of Psychology.

4. **Counselling Psychology.** This valuable branch of Psychology helps young men and women to choose their career according to their capacities and talents. Counselling and vocational guidance centres have been opened in universities, colleges, the industrial centres and in employment exchanges.

5. **Educational Psychology.** The application of Psychology to educational problems is known as educational psychology. Educational Psychology advocates that before teaching the child, his potentialities and basic nature must be understood. Hence, we could easily see how the principles of Psychology have a direct bearing on educational process. Actual teaching also must follow the principles of the psychology of attention and the learning process.

I.4 Meaning of Educational Psychology

The above discussion reveals that educational psychology is one of the many branches of applied psychology dealing mainly with the problems, processes and products of education. Educational psychology is an attempt to apply the knowledge of psychology in the field of education. There are various views about the origin of Educational Psychology. Credit goes to Rousseau for introducing the psychological dimension in education. psychologists like Thorndike, Terman and Stanley Hall, with their researches, furthered the cause of Educational Psychology. Its importance was realised and its study has become essential for a teacher.

Educational Psychology studies the problems of education in terms of psychology. It is a branch of Applied Psychology which applies the psychological methods and techniques in teaching. It is a study of child's mental growth in its various aspects with reference to its application to the education of the child. We may define educational psychology as the study of the psychological aspects of educational situations. It describes the behaviour of education and seeks to explain it in terms of his inner urges, motives and drives and the environmental influences to which he is subjected.

The child learns throughout his life and has to adjust his behaviour. Education helps to facilitate and further this process. Educational Psychology studies the way through which education has to take place. It thus plans for the all-round development of the child's personality.

Educational Psychology helps in understanding the capacities, potentialities and limitations of the child. It studies both Latin and John.

Latin stands for the mastery over the subject and John stands for the child. Educational Psychologist helps to know the child as he is. It is the study of learner and of the learning-teaching process in its various ramifications (branches) directed towards helping the child come to terms with society with a maximum of security and satisfaction.

Educational Psychology mostly deals with psychological problems involed in the process of education and also with practical application of psychological principles in this process. It has the following features:

(1) A study of human behaviour, specially the child is the centre of educational psychology.

(2) This knowledge is arrived at as a result of psychological *investigations* and *research.*

(3) This knowledge is presented in the form of *guidelines* for the teacher.

(4) It helps us in understanding the *problems of education* and *finding out their solutions.*

(5) It provides a knowledge to the teacher about the *principles and methods of teaching* which are used in the field of education.

I.5 Aims of Educational Psychology

Aims of educational psychology are in one to one correspondance with the aims of education. various views have been expressed by different thinkers about these aims:

Kelly has reported that educational Psychology aims at:

(1) giving an insight to the teacher about the nature of the child;

(2) enlightening the teacher with the growth and development of the child;

(3) helping the teacher in finding out ways and means of social adjustment for the child;

(4) imparting knowledge about the principles and methods of learning;

(5) Studying about the control of emotions and their educational importance.

(6) giving knowledge about the character formation of the child;

(7) a study of the techniques of evaluation of various school subjects;

(8) a study of the psychological methods of investigation used in the field of educational psychology.

Skinner identified general and particular aims of educational Psychology.

General aims are to provide a body of organized facts and generalisations that will enable the teacher to realize increasingly both culture and professional objectives.

Particular aims of educational Psychology include:

(1) creating confidence in the teacher to plan harmonious development of the child;

(2) approaching the problems of children in a sympathetic and impartial manner;

(3) planning education of children according to the age, ability and aptitude;

(4) understanding the social problems of children and planning for their total social adjustment;

(5) imparting the knowledge to the teacher about the latest developments in the field of child psychology and various methods of teaching;

(6) enabling the teacher to evaluate hiinself and his methods of teaching;

(7) helping the teacher to understand and analyse the behaviour of child; and;

(8) helping the teacher in solving the problem that may arise in the class-room.

I.6 Scope of Educational Psychology

The subject matter of educational psychology is of recent origin. The scope of educational psychology emphasizes important aspects which include:

(a) the learner;

(b) the learning process;

(c) the learning situation;

(d) the learning material.

(a) The learner. The major scope of educational psychology is to improve rather to modify the learner. For this purpose the concern of educational psychology is to examines the following dimensions:

(1) the study of the child, his abilities, aptitude and forces which motivate behaviour.

(2) the theory of individual differences among children.

(3) the various stages of growth which the children cross in their process of development.

(4) the influence of various social agencies on the personality of the child.

(b) The learning process. The scope of educational process is to study the process of communication, the process of reception, the process of codifying the information in such a way that the learner may decodify the information. The scope of educational psychology is to study the process of education in the following aspects are examined:

(1) the nature of learning and how it takes place.

(2) the various theories of learning and how the target of maximum learning in the minimum period of time can be achieved.

(c) The learning situation. The conducive learning environment. Besides, it tries to create adequate situation to foster the learning situation while doing so the scope of educational psychology to study:

(1) the nature of class-room management and discipline;

(2) the use of techniques and aids which facilitate learning in the class-room;

(3) methods of teaching children who have less than average intelligence;

(4) new techniques of evaluation and their effective use; and,

(5) a knowledge about educational and vocational guidance to be given by the teacher to the child.

(d) The learning material. The scope of Educational Psychology is to assess the quality and quantity of learning material to be offered at a particular age and stage of a learner. To identify logical sequencing arrangement, practical utility of the learning material for the learner falls in the scope of educational psychology.

It has been correctly said by *Garrison and others; "the subject matter of educational psychology is designed to enhance and enrich the lives of the learners and to furnish teachers with the knowledge and understanding that will help them to institute improvements in the quality of instruction."*

I.7 Limitations of Educational Psychology

Educational Psychology, as any other social and behaviour science, has the following limitations:

(i) psychology is a general study of the working of the mind. A branch of psychology which is known as child psychology is also a general study of the child's mind under certain situations. This does not mean that all the children will behave in the same manner. In fact, no two children are alike. There are individual differences among them. It is for this reason that the teacher should know the child thoroughly.

(ii) it is these individual differences in children which create problems for the educator. The teacher can be only successful if he knows the child and provides for methods of teaching accordingly.

(iii) human performance differs from one occasion to the other. We work more when we are hyper-motivated, whereas, we work less when we are in a state of mental depression. It is for this reason that the psychological results are more variable and less reliable. This however, is not the case with other physical sciences like physics and chemistry.

(iv) psychological experiments cannot be carried out on human beings. Generally they are carried on animals. Hence, the results arrived at are not reliable.

(v) the personality of the teacher plays a very important role in the learning process. A good teacher can achieve better results in a shorter period of time. Achievements in teaching depend on the aptitude, experience and personal influence of the teacher.

I.8 Relationship Between Education and Psychology

The applied discipline of educational psychology is based on the knowledge of education and psychology. In order to understand the relationship between the two, it is worthwhile to understand firstly, education and then Psychology. Now let us understand education.

Education. Education may be defined as the process modification of behaviour. The child is weak and ignorant, when he is born. He has no knowledge of the society, and he cannot control the environment. It is education that gives him knowledge and initiates him into the ways of the society and enables him to control the environment. Drever says "*Education is a process in which and by which the knowledge, character and behaviour of the young are shaped and moulded.*" Education therefore, gives knowledge to the child, builds his character and modifies his behaviour.

This modification of the child, is to be made according to specified lines. It is for this reason that the there are certain aims of education which guide the educator. It is the philosophy of education which lays down the aims of education.

Psychology. It seeks to understand and explain the why and how of the human behaviour. It is, therefore, known as the science of behaviour. This behaviour is a result of our physical and mental activity. It has its subject-matter as to how we think, feel and act. It also studies the conditions that underline human behaviour and why human beings behaves differently.

Relationship: The above explanation must have made it clear that both these subjects cover their own fields which are different from each other. Psychology is a phase of education and is quite different from it, in certain aspects. Here are some points to show how far they are related or are different.

1. Education is concerned with aims, ideals and standards of life which are determined by philosophy. These are beyond the scope of psychology. It is psychology that pronounces whether an aim is attainable or not.
2. Psychology deals with facts as they are. It studies the laws of child's nature as they are and as they operate. It has nothing to do with what ought to be. Education has got standards and advocates facts as they ought to be. Psychology gives an insight to the educator as to how to achieve these standards.
3. Education demands of teacher to know the child as well as the subject matter of instruction. The first demand is fulfilled by psychology. It enables him to understand the child and his problems. Psychology thus enables him to teach the child with maximum efficiency and greatest effectiveness. The teacher comes to know that every child has his own psychological make up and his teaching should be adjusted according to that mental make up.

In brief, it can be said that education attempt to modify the behaviour of the child/learner whereas, the discipline of Psychology helps us to identify the behaviour of the child/learner. By combining the acquired knowledge in both the disciplines we are able to start to make modification and refinement of mankind which is the real purpose of all education.

Significance of the Knowledge of Educational Psychology For a Teacher

Educational Psychology plays a significant role in the process of education. We see that the real purpose of our education is to bring refinement in behaviour. In order to bring refinement in the behaviour of a child, a teacher can use psychological principles during his teaching. Therefore, the knowledge of psychology can prove useful as psychology:

1. Understanding the child. Education is the modification of the native behaviour of the child according to a definite aim in view. It means the control and direction of his behaviour. The teacher ought to know about the conditions and forces which can bring the desired behaviour. This implies the study of the nature of the child by the educator. Psychology gives an insight to the teacher about the innate nature of the child. The teacher can educate successfully when he comes to have a detailed knowledge about the child's mind.

2. Designing child centred curriculum. The modern educators hold that the curriculum should be in accordance with the mental and physiological development of the child. If psychologisty attributes of a child is not kept in view, it will result in educational waste. Therefore, the educator should make use of the knowledge of the child's mental development provided by psychology while preparing the curriculum.

3. Planning for the education of the child. The teacher, before he starts teaching, must be certain about the educability of his pupil, He has to find out the learning capacity of the child. For the purpose he administers intelligence tests which have been framed by psychologists. Thus, a teacher comes to know the native endowments of the child and plans his education accordingly.

4. Identification of individual differences among children. In the field of psychology, the discovery of intelligence tests has led to the theory of individual differences among children. The theory that no two children are identical in their native intelligence. The theory has led the educators to believe that the methods of teaching should be according to the psychology of the child. The teacher in order to avoid educational waste should proceed from psychological order to logical order. He should start teaching keeping in view the psychology of children. He must vary his method from one child to the other depending upon his interests and capacities. This approach has brought a revolution in methods of teaching. Learning by doing, the project method, the Kindergarten system are some of the important contributions.

5. Developing teaching effectiveness. Above all the study of psychology enables the teacher to find out his own interests and capabilities as a teacher. Psychology enables him to know the qualities required for a successful teacher. He thus comes to know his own limitations and develops qualities required of him. Psychology thus enables him to become a better teacher.

6. Solving the problems of child and teacher. The study of psychology enables him to solve some of his day-to-day problems. He faces a large number of problems during the process of teaching and in a class-room situation. He examines them in the light of his knowledge failing which he refers them to the psychologists. The psychologist examines them and suggests solutions to the teacher. It is in this way that psychology helps the teacher to become a better teacher.

7. Meeting needs of children. In psychology the teacher studies something about the different phases of development of the child, *i.e.*, Developmental Psychology. This enables him to understand and appreciate the different stages in the development of the child. He also comes to know the peculiar needs of each stage. Thus, he is able to plan his educational programmes better.

8. Development of evaluation process. When we try to judge the achievement of a child we have to take him child as a whole. This is possible only when the teacher has a knowledge about the child. A study of psychology enables him to have this knowledge.

9. Gives a balanced approach to the teacher. A study of educational psychology enables the teacher to know that the behaviour of the child is a result of heredity and environment.

Heredity means certain qualities of head and heart which he inherits from his parents. Heredity goes a long way in shaping the character of the child.

He also lives in a social atmosphere. This goes by the name of environment. A good school enables a child to become a good child. There are, however, some dull children who cannot have all the benefits of a good school. In their cases, heredity plays a dominant role. The teacher has to plan his educational effort in such a way that every child gets what he wants and teach every child according to his needs.

10. Understanding the importance of play. Student, not only study in the school, they are also busy on the play-ground. Play is so natural to them. It is of great value to them. It gives them joy and pleasure. A good teacher, after studying psychology, always tries to make his work so interesting that the child takes it as play.

In brief, we can say that the knowledge of educational psychology helps a teacher to adopt better means and measures to improve the quality of the learner, the learning material, learning situation, evaluative devices. Besides, the knowledge of educational psychology helps a teacher to overcome the day-to-day problems of education in our fast growing society.

I.10 Learning Exercises

1. Describe the meaning and nature of psychology.
2. Define psychology and describe its branches.
3. Discuss the meaning of educational psychology and describe its scope.
4. Define educational psychology and describe the aims of educational psychology.
5. Discuss the relationship of education with psychology.
6. What is the importance of the knowledge of educational psychology for a teacher?
7. What are the limitations of educational psychology?

II
Methods of Educational Psychology

The possibility of studying human behaviour and experience through scientific methods, which have proven so valuable in other fields, was not formally initiated until the nineteenth Century. A major landmark in the history of educational psychology as a science was the founding of a laboratory of experimental psychology in 1879 at the University of Leipzig in Germany. Since that time, educational psychology has emerged as a science because it makes a scientific approach in arriving at its generalisations and laws. In order to study the behaviour, psychologists use different methods. The simplest method may be to see the type of interactions do we have with our fellows; what a man appears to his friends and vice-versa; A second may be the biographical method which gives the immediate picture of individual development in adding the pattern of growth and unfolding of personality of a person at home, school, and community and to see the type of resources and limitations each individual brings into each type of behaviour.

Third method of educational psychology is the biological method, which studies mankind, each one of us, as a living being that is an end result of the long series of biological changes which we know as evolution; it regards the individual as a system of life processes. The fourth, the clinical method, involves a study of those aspects of a person's psychological make-up on which his happiness and his effective adjustment to life's tasks depend; it studies his capacities and limitations, his successful or unsuccessful ways of meeting life's problems, the things which makes or breaks a person's life. This leads to a fifth method, the testing method, the use of carefully prepared tests of human abilities and traits. Besides, there is a large place for the experimental method in psychology–the method of the psychological laboratory–in which trained observers with suitable instruments observe and measure human responses. Laboratory methods are also available for the study of the emotions, learning, memory, thinking, imagination and many other psychological processes. Modern Psychologists also study the behaviour by the Psycho-analytical method.

In the light of the above discussion the method used by the psychologists in general, and the educational psychologists in particular apply these methods to study the behaviour of the teacher, the taught, as also the educational atmosphere in the school and the community. Reason being: The educational psychologists mainly feel concerned to maximize classroom conditions; to facilitate learning. But they are often more interested in the improvement of course planning and instruction methods for an entire school system than in the identification and assistance of individual child with learning problems. The educational psychology is also study behaviour of the teacher, the student and the teaching learning environment, and learning material. To maximize the teaching learning process. The educational psychologists use various methods for studying the behaviour:

(1) Introspection method,
(2) Observation method,
(3) Experimental method,
(4) Psychoanalytic method,
(5) Developmental method,
(6) Testing method, and;
(7) Clinical method.

II.1 Introspection Method

Introspection is one of the oldest methods of studying behaviour. By introspection we mean looking within i.e., looking into the working of our own minds and reporting what we find there. In other words, introspection is a method of "self-observation"—i.e., observation by an individual of his own mental state directly by focussing attention on a particular experience with a particular purpose. This requires a complete concentration of the individual on one's unexperiences. Such an effort requires a mental development.

Educational Psychologists while using the introspection method try to understand the potential level of the students and applied a suitable method of delivery of the knowledge/content for better understanding of the students. An educational psychologist while using the method of introspection tries to plan and organise the curricular and co-curricular activities in the school for the harmonious development of personality of the student. The introspection method in studying the problems of education has wide relevance as it can provide a glimpse of the problems of behaviour in advance. It helps towards the maximization of the learning outcome by eliminating the irritants held responsible for the minimal learning outcomes.

Suppose we have to study the problem of anger and we want to find as to what happens to mind and body in the state of anger. This problem can be studied by doing introspection in an angry mood. During introspection a subject is asked to note down his feelings, thinking and changes in body at that time. This process of watching one's own behaviour by oneself is known as introspection method. Thus, it is an armchair method of a philosopher which does not need any experiment or apparatus but involves only "thinking" about one's behaviour in a particular situation.

Advantages

1. The method is very simple and requires no apparatus or equipment. It is for this reason that it can be applied anywhere and at any time and only our consciousness is needed.
2. It is of great value when compared with data collected by other methods.
3. It is a very convenient and economical method.
4. It helps in comparing the reaction of different individuals on the same problem.
5. A teacher can benefit himself by introspecting his teaching methodology.
6. This method is very important in highlighting our own limitations.

Limitations

Introspection has been criticised as a method of Psychology on the following grounds:

1. In introspection the mind is asked to attend to its own working. The mind is the subject as well as the object. Mind acts and watches the same act at the same time. Two acts cannot be done at one time. If ever it can be, then both the acts of mind, i.e., doing and watching cannot be done accurately. If first act is done then the second work will suffer, if the second (watching) is attended, the first act (doing) will suffer. It means if we start analysing our anger, the anger will vanish. So this method is not accurate.

2. Introspection is completely a subjective method. Psychology is a science which is objective and experimental in nature.

3. Introspection is always retrospection as it desires memories or even happenings either past or current. Firstly an act is performed by the subject, then the same act is described. Therefore, introspection deals with passing events. Sometimes the memory fails, accuracy lacks.

4. Introspection cannot be done for every quick act. The mental state change so quickly or rapidly that only slower changes can be observed, the quicker one escapes introspective observation. For instance, nobody has been able to observe introspectively what really happens when we feel meaning of a word and then write it. What are my mental processes when I write a word is beyond introspection analysis. Thus, all the mental processes cannot be introspected.

5. Observation is not possible here. The essence of science is observation under controlled experimental condition. Scientific facts are always repeated and verified under the same conditions. In introspection, this is not possible. A mental state is a unique event. It changes very quickly. Thus, it cannot be controlled and introspected for the second time. Verification cannot be done under exactly the same conditions. The methods of comparing introspections of different skilled observations is of doubtful value. If one subject says, "When I am angry I feel so and so, No, your description is wrong; when I am angry I feel this and this. Who is correct? We do not know.

6. It is not an easy method. It is not given to everybody to introspect either easily or well. It is highly specialised and only very experienced philosophers can do so.

7. Introspection is solely with the mental states of normal or superior human beings. Children cannot express themselves. Moreover, it is extremely difficult to judge their own acts. Child Psychology is an important branch of psychology and it is very near to educational psychology. Similarly, the method of introspection does not hold good with abnormal persons. In abnormal psychology we have to deal with psychotics or insane persons who cannot introspect themselves. It is also not suitable for animal psychology. Animal psychology is very important as facts are tested on animals before they are applied on human beings. It is from the field of animal learning that a new world has opened up which is proving of the utmost importance for education.

Conclusion

Though introspection has several limitations as a method of psychology, yet it is used so often. No doubt, it is subjective but it is most easy and least expensive method. For certain problems, all other methods i.e., experimental, external observation and psycho-analysis fails and then we have to turn to introspection. Even in the experiments of psychology, the method which is regarded classical scientific one introspection on the part of subject is regarded and without report of introspection the experiment is not regarded as complete etc.

II.2 Observation Method

Observation method of studying psychological behaviour by which psychologists understand the external or overt behaviour is watched for interpretation. Essentially this is a method of behaviouristic school of psychology. This is a more scientific method than introspection as it does not depend on the subjective data. It is objective in its nature. Personal prejudice and idiosyncracies are checked and they do not enter here.

Observations are given for verification. In observation method the data collected by observation may be repeated several times under the same conditions and thus can be verified, which is an essential criterion of methods of science subjects. Introspection cannot be repeated in the same or controlled conditions. Not only can the verification be held by repeated observations but to make it more objective, reliable and valid, the same act of observation can be observed by different observers at one and the same time and the final result is obtained by comparing the notes of observations of different observers.

Advantages

1. This method is indispensable in the field of psychology because they serve as the proper background of our study of the child it is of great value in the classroom.
2. Observation is definitely a more suitable method of Psychology than introspection as it can be usefully employed in child psychology, Abnormal and Animal Psychology. Introspection method fails with these branches of psychology as children, animals and insane persons cannot introspect themselves.
3. Observation does not deal with past and passing events. It is not retrospective. It studies the situation at the time of action. Therefore, it does not depend on memory. The observer makes the records on the spot.
4. In the method of introspection, the same mind acts as subject as well as object. It has to attend two acts at one time, i.e., doing and watching it. Observation differs in this respect. Here, the observer and the object are two different individuals. Therefore, there can be more of accuracy.
5. In educational psychology, observation has higher value than that of introspection. In the class-room or in the play-ground a teacher reads the students by watching and observing their behaviour. Overt behaviour is the index of mind.

Precautions for Observation

Making observation correctly is not an easy work. It is hard task. Observation of today is a highly specialised field. It needs experience and good training. Faulty observation may give rise to far-reaching consequences. Therefore, before the actual observation is done, the whole scheme is pre-planned. First of all, it is decided whether observation will be controlled or uncontrolled. In the controlled observation, the situation is artificial and is planned by the psychologist's view-point. This type of observation is done in a psychological clinic where neurotic problem or deviated children are studied for diagnosis and treatment. Though it has got its own success and value yet the atmosphere becomes artificial and unnatural. Therefore, the response of the child under observation may not be natural as he may not feel at home in the presence of types of apparatus. The uncontrolled observation is in the natural setting as observing the child at play or watching the lesson of pupil teacher. The type of observation depends on the nature of problem to be investigated.

Method of observation

Having decided the type of observation, the observer will plan the time-table. How many sittings are needed? What will be the interval between the two sittings? Will it be once a day or twice a day or after a week? How to get and from where to get the subjects? How will the observer arrange for the apparantus?

Even in natural or uncontrolled observation some mechanical or electrical devices are used. Suppose we have to observe the children at play. In this situation, the children will be moving about in different postures and with different facial expressions. It will be useful to take their movies. The film can be seen again and again on the screen with the help of a projector. Its speed can be adjusted and thus the minute details be thoroughly studied. Similarly the sound-recording machine is used when the subject under observation has to speak something. As it is recorded in the same order and can be heard repeatedly interpretation will be more accurate and reliable. This will add to the objectivity of the observation. If the sound-recording machine is not available, then the responses of the subject are recorded by way of shorthand. As a matter of fact, the observer must know shorthand for quick recording of observed facts, which is an important feature of a good observation.

Conditions for observation

As far as possible the subject or subjects to be observed should not know that they are under observation, otherwise they will become conscious of it and their response may be affected. Their behaviour may change and thus observation fails. In clinics, this is overcome by suitable arrangements. The room has a partition of one way screen. The subject gets the instruction from the observer to play with toys, or to a set scene of dramatization by arranging toys or to do something else. The subject is left alone to do in this way and the observer sits in the other part of the room. The observer can watch the subject but the subject cannot see the observer as in one way screen. A device is to make partition with wire-gauze and to make one part of the room (where observer sits) dark but light is allowed in the portion where the subject is.

In order to make observation more objective, it is better to have more than one observer. Usually the number is three or five. All these observers confer before starting observation and decide the specific points of observation. While observing the subject, they watch and record their points independently. Later on, they may compare their notes and discuss them in order to give the final report.

Limitations

1. Observation is better than introspection as a method of psychology for the above mentioned reasons but it is not the best or perfect. It is very difficult to control all the conditions. Because, hundred percent control on human behaviour is impossible. Therefore, it has a limited value as a scientific method.
2. Secondly, in the controlled situation, the atmosphere is artificial and the subject may not feel at home. He/she may become nervous. Thus his/her responses are affected and observation becomes unreliable.
3. All the problems of Psychology cannot be studied by observation method such as dream interpretation. So this is not the universal method.
4. After all, observation is done by human beings. They may have their own prejudices and preconceptions and reflect or project them in observations. Likes and dislikes, level of knowledge, experience and training may affect the observation. The observation of two or more than two observers may differ and nobody knows who is correct. It may be possible that the points of observation made twice by the same observer at two different times of the same situation, almost under the same conditions, may differ much. This is due to subjectivity. It is like marking of essay type answers in examination. One and the same examiner may give two quite different scores when he marks and remarks after some time. This is a great drawback. Thus though observation is better than

introspection as a method of Psychology yet it is not perfect as it has its own limitations.

5. Teachers cannot use this method as they are not trained for the purpose in our training institutions.

II.3 Experimental Method

It is a classical method of the scientific age. Psychology has borrowed it from physical sciences such as Physics and Chemistry. This is the most objective and scientific method. Just as there are Physics and chemistry laboratories equipped with several types of apparatuses, similarly, there are laboratories of Psychology, where experiments are done and psychological facts are tested and verified. It is due to the use of this method that Psychology has attained the status of science.

In the experimental method, the hypotheses are verified. Hypothesis is an unverified and untested statement based on the same observation. It is nothing more than an opinion which needs experimental proof for its establishment. Hypothesis is a generalization based on specific observation. Suppose a teacher has been serving in public and government schools. His opinion is that students of Public schools are more social than those of Government schools. This is a generalised statement based on observation or experience. It can only be regarded as a fact if it is proved experimentally. Similarly, there are different hypotheses from different teachers for the same problem. Suppose some teacher say. "Reward is better than punishment in classroom teaching." Another hypothesis may be that 'Punishment is better than reward in class room teaching.' Thus the opinions differ. Both the statements are completely based on speculation. They are far away from scientific truth, as they have not been studied under controlled conditions. In order to reject or accept the above mentioned hypothesis, the following experiment may be done.

Method

Take two homogeneous groups of ninth class students. Each group consists of twenty students. Their chronological age, mental level, social background, habits of study, economic conditions and the standard of education are equated. It means that the two groups are parallel or similar in all the variables. If in group A, five students are very intelligent, then in group B there should five very intelligent students. If ten are of average intelligence in group A, then the same number (10) of average intelligence should be in group B. Five are below average intelligence in each group. This will assure us that intelligence level of both the group is the same. Similarly educational, social and economic factors are controlled. These students of the two groups are of the same sex.

In order to do experiments take one subject, say, History. Before starting the actual experiment, students are tested in History and experimenter sees that the average level of one group is equal to the average level of the second group. If this is so, the equated groups are ready. Precaution is, however, taken that students should not know that they are under investigation. The same teacher starts teaching history to both the groups by taking separate classes. Both the groups will be taught for the same period, say one month. Time table is also adjusted in such a way that time factor is equated. The teacher may teach one group in morning and the other in the evening and then change the time so that out of thirty days, each group gets morning coverage in one time for fifteen days alternately. The syllabus covered in one month is also the same. Only one variable will be changed. To one group, say A, reward is given with teaching the lesson and to the other group, i.e., B, punishment is given.

After thirty days, a test is administered in order to assess their achievements. This will be an objective test from the portion of syllabus covered during the experiment. As far as possible, it should have high reliability and validity. Answer papers of the two groups are marked and then the scores of group A and group B are compared. Suppose group A is better, then first hypothesis i.e. reward is better than punishment in classroom teaching is accepted, and the second one which is opposed to it, is rejected. Similarly, the value of different methods of teaching can be experimentally evaluated. Such are the educational experiments as are done in educational psychology.

Limitations

As already stated the experimental method the most scientific and objective in its nature, but it has also limitations.

(i) It is very difficult to perform the experiments on human beings. All the problems cannot be solved by it.

(ii) Complete control over the variables is not possible. Experiments of heredity cannot be done on human beings under controlled conditions.

(iii) Moreover, this method is very expensive and for certain experiments, there is need of highly sophisticated apparatus, which is not easily available. In addition to it, it takes a long time. The task mentioned is of one month but it takes several months to make equated groups.

II.4 Psycho-Analytic Method

Psycho-analysis is a school of psychology, which was put forward by

Sigmund Freud. The other exponents were Jung and Adler. All the three were Germans. Freud was a physician and became interested in mental diseases. His research in this direction resulted into a new school of psychology i.e. psycho-analysis. It is also known as Depth Psychology.

Literally psycho-analysis means analysis of psycho or mind. According to this theory the mind does not consist of consciousness only but there is also unconsciousness, Consciousness is comparatively a very small field or part of mind. At a given time, you can be conscious of only a few things. When I am writing these lines I am conscious of my pen, paper, ink-pot, table and chair in which I am sitting, there may be some more things or objects in the field of my consciousness but not many. The field of consciousness at one time consists of the objects which are attended to or which are in the focus of our attention. But we know so many objects and events. Our past is full of different types of experiences.

Right from birth to this time, we have performed various acts or activities. Out of these past experiences and activities some may be recalled. We can recollect our first day in primary school, transfer of father, some clothes of childhood, friends of childhood, certain important happenings at school or college. But all experiences of past cannot be recalled with the help of memory test in pre-conscious mind. It is just below the layers of consciousness.

Unconscious mind

All the experiences and activities of the past are not dead. They have their impact on mind. They can be revived but they have been buried deep in the deeper layers of mind. These deep layers of mind make the unconscious. It is believed with firm conviction by psycho-analysts, that all the completely forgotten happenings of past of life are present here and they can be brought to the level of consciousness by removing the resistance layers of mind above it. The unconscious consists of several layers. According to Jung, unconscious is not as old as an individual is, but it is as old as the race is. It means, that there is a racial unconscious also, which retains the experiences of race. Racial unconscious is the store of all repressed and completely forgotten wishes, desires, carvings and other experiences of past.

Super-ego, Ego and Id

There is another mechanism.of mind. In it there are two forces which are opposed to each other. Super-ego is one's own moral and social code of living. In simple words it is called conscience or esteemed self. Super-ego develops in the childhood. As the baby grows, it becomes conscious of the standards of family. He borrows the attitudes and values of life from his elders. In this way, super-ego develops at home. Similarly, school plays an important role in its development. Super-ego is always social and moral in its character. It may be known as good-self for moral conscience.

Opposed to super-ego there is 'Id'. It is animal in its character. It is infantile, immoral and unideological in its nature. Id does not care for the self respect. It is ready to break the rules and regulations. It has no morale and it is most selfish. Always it wants to get gratification. It is pleasure-seeking. At this moment, one is prone to do even anti-social or immoral activities. As it is to be guarded, it rests in the unconscious mind.

In addition to Super-ego and Id, there is Ego. Ego is focus of awareness. It is given to external reality. It makes compromise between super-ego and Id. Sometimes it is on the side of Super-ego and sometimes it favours Id and is against the rigid taboos and hard principles of Super-ego. If it is a success in making suitable compromise between Super-ego and Id, the personality is well adjusted. When it fails to perform its responsible duty, mal-adjustment starts. Sometimes the extreme rigid control of Super-ego on Id, with too much of suppression and repression on mind leads to neurosis and psychosis. Similarly, Id, at large, without any control of Super-ego on it may result into far-reaching consequences of natural diseases.

Mental Conflicts

In an individual there are numerous wishes, desires, cravings and needs. All these cannot be satisfied. Sometimes there are two opposite cravings in the same mind. If one is accepted, the other is rejected and so on. Suppose you have to buy a pair of shoes. For the purpose you go to a shop. After seeing several pairs of shoes, you select two, but you have to buy only one. At one moment you wish to buy the black and at the other you want to get brown. A conflict arises in your mind. After all, you decide to buy the black pair of shoes. As you are coming to your house, the brown pair comes in the conscious mind and you think that brown was a better one. Either you will bury the very thought of the brown pair with the help of your strong will or it will tease your mind from time to time and you will uselessly repent. This is external conflict. Such conflicts are very common, but at times there are serious internal conflicts, when it is extremely difficult for you to decide this way or that way.

There are also other external conflicts, Suppose you want to do something and you have mind for it, but the parents, your friends or social order of the day does not allow you to go in for that which result in conflicts and repressions. The conscious rejection of unfulfilled wishes is also known as suppression. When the process of supression goes on in the unconscious mind, it is called repression. Owing to rigid discipline at home or school or due to strong control of Super-ego, repression goes on increasing. These unfulfilled repressed wishes have some power. They are not impotent. From time to time, they try to come by breaking the resistance of upper layers or censor or super-ego. This is Id, which is responsible for the unconscious revolt. If the repression increases to a point—then that is a great force of pent-up energy and it breaks the resistance as the floods break the dams. The mind loses the equilibrium and balance and unwholesome personality results. The school of psycho-analysis deals with the analysis of mind, specially unconscious. Unconscious is a private domain which is hidden to oneself. An individual cannot know all about his unconscious mind. As already mentioned, the cause of mental derangement, i.e., psycho-neurosis or psychosis lies with the unfulfilled wishes of past, so the psycho-analysts try to dig out the unconscious mind inorder to find out the complex conflict or the repressed wish which is the cause of trouble. The principle of psycho-analysis is to dig out the unconscious and thus give outlet to repressed energy of unfulfilled wishes. The unfulfilled wishes are buried and curbed by the process of suppression and repression, which causes some form of complexes in mind. Complex is a small independent part of mind, which revolts against sane and healthy part of mind, and causes mental derangement. Psycho-analysis finds the cause of mental illness. In order to find the cause of mental illness, the Psycho-analyst traces back the past events and experiences, which are directly or indirectly related to the frustration of the patient. Correct diagnosis is half the cure. Knowing the complexes, the Psycho-analyst removes them by different techniques stated below:

a. Free Association Technique: This technique was used by Sigmund Freud. The subject is seated on a comfortable seat and he shuts his eyes or a piece of cloth is tied on his eyes, so that he may not see the objects around him, which may distract his attention. He is instructed to be in a light mood and free from serious thoughts. The vacant mood helps in unfolding the unconscious mind as the check of consciousness is the least. The Psycho-analyst speaks one stimulus word and the subject speaks whatever comes to his mind. He gives responses in a quick chain. He may speak different words, names, phrases etc. Care is taken that responses should come as quickly as possible. He is not supposed to think over and then give the response. If the subject thinks then his conscious mind plays a part and this prevents the unconscious to reveal it. The subject goes on speaking continuously for some time, say, two or three minutes. All the responses are recorded by shorthand writing or by a sound recording machine. The average reaction time is calculated. While giving the responses, the subject will take more time for speaking some words than other. If this time or reaction time of the specific word is more than thirty seconds, it is marked. As it shows more resistance in speaking this word, which means that consciousness does not want it (word) to be spoken. Such suspected words are noted and then studied. Often these suspected words give a clue to complexes. In addition to it, the nature of responses is determined, which reveals the hidden events with their associations.

b. Word Association Technique: This is a different technique put forward by psycho-analysts like Jung. This is not a continuous process of speaking out the responses. There is a list of one hundred selected words, which are connected with the emotional aspect of personality. The list is a standardized one and has got a key, with the help of which, we can know whether the response of a given stimulus word is normal or not. In the same way as in free association, a piece of cloth is tied on the eyes of the subject or patient and he is asked to give only one response in one word or phrase just after hearing the stimulus from the psycho-analyst. The response and its reaction time between getting stimulus and giving response is noted by using stop watch. In this way, all the words on the list are spoken, one by one, and the responses with reaction time noted down. The reaction time of each response is studied, and if it is more than thirty seconds, the same word is repeated again for the response. Such words may lead to find the complexes. The nature of all the responses is determined by comparing it with the key and thus abnormal responses are determined which may be the cause of trouble. The cause of the trouble also is diagnosed.

The two techniques mentioned above are the preliminaries of psycho-analysis as well as the method in themselves. As the hidden and repressed wishes of unconscious are spoken out, they get some sorts of gratification and the spent-up energy is puffed off making the person light. It is just like a angry person who gives to his anger by talking aggressively.

c. Dream Interpretation.Technique: This is another method of revealing the unconscious mind. Dream is a drama of unconscious. As the repressed wishes are not allowed in awakened state of individual to have their play and satisfaction, they make use of sleep, as thieves use darkness. In sleep the resistance of consciousness on unconscious is the least. This is a favourable time for the repressed wishes to crop up. So, dream is nothing but a manifestation of the unconscious.

The contents of dream are not always real elements of unconscious mind. In dream, there is censorship. The censor does not allow the undesirable elements of unconscious mind to play dramatic role in dream. The entry is forbidden as smugglers are not allowed to cross the border of a country. But the repressed thoughts are bent upon to satisfy themselves. Thus, they change their dress and come in disguised form. The Psycho-analyst records the dream and finds the real unconscious elements and interprets them to find the cause of mental illness and then the patient/subject is treated accordingly.

d. General Psycho-analysis: After getting the case history by doing dream interpretation and studying and word association, the psycho-analyst takes the patient/subject into a semi-dark room. The subject closes his eyes and is asked to go on speaking, whatever he likes or whatever comes to his mind. He must be free and frank in expressing himself. He would hesitate to speak out. Here sympathy on the part of Psycho-analyst wins him. It may be pointed out that the patient is a frustrated person. The affectionate and kind attitude of the psycho-analyst gains confidence of the patient and helps him to fight out the hesitation, as patient feels secure in the hands of the psycho-analyst. This stage is knows as establishing rapport.

Now the patient reveals his mind. He narrates his past hapenings and experiences. He will be touching his own pathetic tale of frustration. The psycho-analyst already knows about his complexes and cause of disappointment for free or word association and dream interpretation. At critical moments or stages, he (psycho-analyst) asks suitable questions to get the clear picture. At psychological moments appropriate suggestions are given to the patient. At times the psycho-analyst plays the role of the object which is the cause of frustration. In the conversation, the patient speaks out the hidden mind and thus feels better after it. Again, with the suggestions on the part of the psycho-analyst, the patient resolves his complexes, which is a cure in itself.

e. Hypnotic SuggestionsTechnique: It is an artificial, induced sleep by the psychologist. The patient is given the suggestion that he is going to sleep. After some time the patient feels he is sleeping comfortably. This is known as a process of hypnotism.

At this stage the patient is allowed to talk about emotional difficulties. The psychologists also give suggestions. The patient after some time comes to remember his forgotten events that have influenced his emotional behaviour. The psychologist, tries to cure the patient by explaining to him the right type of behaviour.

Importance

(1) It has brought a new approach into the field of education. We have come to know that actions of the child are governed more by the unconsciousness than by the conscious part of the mind.

(2) It has also provided a new approach to the various problems of children. We have come to know that delinquency and other problems are due to repressed desires working at the unconscious level.

(3) If we want to improve the child, we should try to identify the real cause of the trouble and should try to sublimate the instinctive impulses. The frustration of the child should be cures as far as possible.

(4) In the learning institution, equal opportunities of the development ought to be provided so that there is no frustration on the part of any child.

(5) The behaviour of the teacher should not be biased towards any child.

Limitations

(1) It is a very slow method and takes a lot of time.

(2) It is very expensive in terms of time and money.

(3) It is possible only with subjects of above average intelligence.

II.5 Developmental Method

In case of developmental method of studying behaviour, the psychologists lay much emphasis on the developmental tendencies of an individual, which seeks to find out the causes of that behaviour in its crude beginning. Developmental method requires psychologist to trace out the mental and behavioural development of an individual right from birth, or before birth up to maturity. In the regard, Woodworth and Marquis point our that there are many difficut questions here regarding the influences of heredity and environment, the conditions favourable to normal development, and the factors that produce such abnormalities as delinquency and insanity. Tests and laboratory methods can be used for measuring the stage of development reached at different ages and for determining growth curves. But to conduct a decisive experiment on development, one would need to have control over the conditions in which the child is reared and even to subject certain children to conditions presumed to be unfavourable, so as to make sure whether they are really unfavourable in any important degree. Such experiments might yield extremely valuable information. But the psychologist is not going to take it on himself to subject a child to unfavourable conditions. He will not, for example, stunt the child's physical development by an inadequate diet so as to determine whether mental growth suffers. He will perform such experiments on animals, or he will find undernourished children in the community and try to discover whether the malnutrition has had any demonstrable effect on their mentality. In the event, his results will not be so decisive as those of complete experiment.

Much can be learned, without such an experiment, by simply observing and recording behaviour up through childhood. We say 'simply' observing and recording; but the task is far from simple if dependable results are to be obtained. The child behaves *so much* that an observer cannot record more than small samples. Moreover, the records of a child's behaviour, though interesting, may not prove or disprove anything, unless the observer has had definite questions in mind, definite hypotheses to be checked by observation. When we know that some important development is about to occur, and the child will soon begin to talk, or that he is soon to have a baby brother or sister to whose presence in the family he must adjust himself, we can formulate specific questions to be answered from observations of his behaviour. The whole job of tracing child development is large and many-sided, but fortunately it is being seriously undertaken by many scientific observers.

II.6 Testing Method

The Psychologists while studying the behaviour apply standardized tests. The method which enables the psychologists to study the behaviour of an individual on the basis of psychological test reports/score is known as the testing method.

The testing methods comprise psychological tests, educational measurements, rating scales, checklists and questionnaires. Some writers characterise rating scales, checklists and questionnaires as field investigation methods as different from the testing methods. Rating scales and checklists are often used as important devices of observing and evaluating personality or behaviour traits. In *rating scales* we rate or judge an individual on the possession or absence of certain traits. The individual is given a place on the scale or a score which indicates the degree to which a person possesses a given behavioural trait. For example, if we want to rate teacher trainees on their sociability, we might ask three or four supervisors to point out the place of each teacher-trainee on the scale which may be as follows :

Avoids others	Tolerates others	Likes others	Likes others well	Seeks others

This scale had five degrees of the trait to be rated: This is a five point scale. Some scales have three or seven degrees. The descriptive words or phases used in the scale may be also given marks or scores, from *zero* to *five.*

In a *checklist,* examiners may be provided with a list of traits or qualities and may be asked to point out or check up ones that apply to particular persons.

The psychological tests are carefully devised and standardised tests for measuring aptitudes, interests, achievement, intelligence and personality traits. *Intelligence tests* measure the intellectual capacity of an individual and *achievement tests* throw light on the achievement of students in various subjects they are studying. *Aptitude tests* enable us to evaluate the nature and degree of aptitude of a person for a certain subject or profession. In many teacher-training colleges such tests have been developed for selecting candidates for teacher training courses. *Personality tests* which are of various types shed light on general personality patterns, cluster of traits, moods, temperament, emotionality, interpersonal relationships, needs and pressures and other qualities. The results of these tests are generally reliable.

II.7 Clinical Method

The clinical method is also called case-study method. This method is used by the clinical psychologists, psychiatric social workers and teachers in child guidance clinics or mental hygiene centres or in ordinary school situations. The clinical method is used by a psychologist when we want to understand the causes and sources of people's fear, anxieties, worries, obsessions, their personal, social educational and vocational maladjustments.

The case study method of studying behaviour enabled Sigmund Freud to develop the psychoanalytic method of studying behaviour by making case studies. Similarly, Jean Piaget has used the case-study method to learn about the cognitive development of children. From thousands of hours of observing and playing with children, including his own, he has fashioned a view of development that has inspired hundreds of other psychologists to undertake experiment with children.

The clinical method of studying behaviour a psychologist has before him a genius, a criminal, a problem child, or a remarkably fine personality, and the question is how this individual comes to be what he is. The psychologist is forced to adopt a substitute for the true developmental method by reconstructing the individual's development history as well as can be done from the memory of the individual and his associates and from whatever records have been preserved. This *case history or clinical method* has obvious disadvantages, much like those of the anecdotal method. It depends largely on fallible memory of incidents that were not scientifically observed in the first place. But it seems to be the only way to make a start towards answering some very important questions.

The case history method, up to the present time, has been employed mostly with individuals whose behaviour is undesirable in some respect. When a person has broken down mentally, the psychiatrist with the assistance of a social worker obtains information on this person's heredity and family environment, noting such conditions as are believed to be important. The patient's own story is taken down and an attempt is made to get back to earlier emotional conflicts which may have a bearing on his present trouble. When a child presents a serious behaviour problem—such as stealing, over-aggressiveness, destructive 'meanness', or shyness and dependence—he may be taken to a child guidance clinic, where a staff of experts considers his history from several points of view, medical, psychological, and social. These experts approach the child in a friendly spirit, and make him see they are not trying to 'get something on him', but wish to help him by first understanding him. They need co-operation from him and from his parents, and their inquiries must be conducted with tact as well as skill. They work on the assumption that the child's misconduct has causes which should be discovered, causes lying in his environment and in his own limitations.

The guidance clinic does more than reconstruct the history of the case to date. In co-operation with the home and the school, it tries an experiment on the child, by way of treatment. Any treatment of such a case is experimental in some degree, since there is no certainty of success. The case history and present state of the child suggest some cause of the misconduct; and the treatment tests this hypothesis by altering certain conditions of the child's life. The abnormal behaviour of child can be attributed to seeking attention. Treatment in time seeks cooperation from parents and teachers.

All these methods discussed are used in various situations, depending upon the nature of the problems. The methods have different approaches and make use of various techniques for collecting different types of data, their analysis and interpretation. However, almost all the methods follow scientific method as the method of investigation.

II.8 Learning Exercises

1. What are various methods of investigation in educational psychology? Describe the oldest method of investigation and its merits.
2. "It is the experimental method which has made psychology a science." Justify the statement and discuss merits and demerits of experimental method.
3. Describe in brief any four methods of psychology which you know.
4. Describe observation method. How will you make observation objective?
5. Discuss Psycho-analytic school of Psychology. What is its contribution towards education?
6. Describe the clinical method and describe its advantages.
7. Describe the following:
   (a) Id
   (b) Ego
   (c) Super-Ego
   (d) Unconsciousness

III

Psychology of Growth and Development

In the earlier chapters we have discussed that the discipline of psychology is the study of behaviour. To study behaviour, different psychological methods are used. The use of different methods of psychology depends upon the nature of the behaviour to be studied at a specific stage of development. To some extent the stage of development of an individual is directly responsible to exhibit a particular type of behaviour. Therefore, for clear understanding of behaviour, it is imperative to understand the process of development, i.e., to know better the human behaviour. The branch of psychology dealing with the developmental behaviour is known as developmental psychology.

III.1 Meaning of Growth

The growth is the unifying scientific concept that is used by all students of child development whether they are anthropologists, sociologists, paediatricians, educationists or psychologists. In all the term growth has been defined by Gesell that growth carries a more dynamic connotation; which organically ties the present with the past and directs it toward the future.

III.2 Meaning of Development

The helpless baby of today, who will be adult of tomorrow, has to cross various stages in the process of his development. This also involves the development of his physical, intellectual, emotional and spiritual side of his personality. This is denoted by the word 'development' which is much more comprehensive in comparison to the word 'growth' used in the previous section. The word 'growth' is confined to the physical aspects alone, whereas development includes the entire personality.

The process of growth from all angles is known as development. The terms development and growth are often used interchangeably and regarded as synonymous terms. However, the term development differs from growth as the concept of development gives us a central idea of organisms as living systems changing with time towards greater complexity of organisation, including the relationships of parts to wholes and adult's status with some stability and self-regulation'. The important thing for us to determine is that the human organism is an open system which changes as result of changes which take place within the system and as a result of interactions with the environment. Thus, the child is an active system maintained both by internal and external stimulation and he grows through time, and many aspects of his behaviour become more and more specialized. Finally, behaviour becomes so complex that further development takes place only on the basis of symbolisation. The symbols function as means of communication as well as stimulus to further growth, particularly through problem-solving.

Another view regarding the process of development may then be reserved for the end-product of maturation and nurture. As we have observed above that full significance of the interaction between maturation and nurture is not realised in such areas of development as an increase in size, development of movement etc. It is only as a result of carefue studies that we are able to observe the actual stages in the development of sitting, walking, finger-thumb opposition, vocalization, speech etc. But the full significance of the presence or absence of highly variable amounts of experience and nurture are seen very clearly in such areas as learning to swim, to sing, to read, to write. On the whole, the process of development is an improvement, rather multifaced refinement. Therefore, development represents the finest improvement from all aspects in our life.

Characteristics of Development

Characteristics of development can be described as:

1. Development implies change in shape, form or structure resulting in improved working or functioning. Improved functioning implies a mature and a complex type of behaviour.
2. It implies the effect of development on the body as a whole.
3. It means a progressive series of changes in an orderly coherent pattern till the end of life.
4. Development is indicative of a clear logical perception by the individual of interrelationship between the past, present and the future.

In the case of normal children, both (growth and development) go together. However, in the case of feeble-minded children, growth of the body may be there, but there may not be development of intellectual powers. In the case of highly intelligent children, the development of intellect may be higher in comparison to physical development of the child.

Causes of Development

Development depends upon the following factors:

1. There are certain natural endowments of the child with which he takes his birth. According to Herlock, these constitute his maturation. They unfold themselves when the child comes in contact with the learning process. Thus, development is the result of interaction between maturation and learning.
2. Learning also determines development of the individual which is due to selective direct and purposive training. It is this training which modifies the behaviour of the individual and determines his development.
3. It may also be observed that maturation and learning are closely related. Maturation, according to Herlock, provides the raw material for learning. It is learning alone which gives a final shape to maturation.

III.3 Principles of Development

Development is a complex phenomenon of change. This phenomenon is governed by certain principles which can be described as:

1. Principle of continuity. Development is a never ending process. It starts with the conception and ends with death. The changes, however, small and gradual, continue to take place in all dimensions of one's personality throughout one's life.

2. Heterogeneity in the developmental rate. Development, though continuous, does not exhibit steadiness and uniformity in terms of the rate of development in various dimensions of personality or in the developmental periods and stages of life. In passing through the developmental stages, the changes are often so silent and gradual as to be almost invisible over a long duration but sometimes they are so fast as to be noticed quite easily. Thus, instead of steadiness, development usually takes place in fits and starts showing almost no change at one time and sudden spurt at another, as for example, shooting up in height and sudden change in social interest, intellectual curiosity and emotional make-up.

3. Principle of individual difference. Every organism is a distinct creation in itself. Therefore, the development which it undergoes in terms of the rate and outcome in various dimensions, is quite unique and specific.

4. Principle of uniformity of pattern. Although there seems to be a clear lack of uniformity in terms of the rate of development and also there are distinct individual differences with regard to the process and outcome of the various stages of development, yet it follows a definite pattern in one or the other dimensions which is uniform and universal with respect to the individual of a species.

5. The principle of proceeding from general to specific responses. While developing in relation to any aspect of personality, the child first picks up or exhibits general responses and learns to show specific and goal-directed responses afterwards. For example, a newborn infant cries, his whole body is involved in doing so but as he develops, it is limited to the vocal cords, facial expressions and eyes etc.

6. Principle of integration. By observing the principle proceeding from the general to the specific or from the whole to the parts, it does not mean that only the specific responses are aimed for in the ultimate consequences of one's development. Rather, it is a sort of integration that is ultimately desired. Throwing light on this principle Kuppuswami (1963) observes—"Development involves a movement from the whole to parts and from the parts to the whole" and in this way it is the integration of the whole and its parts as well as the specific and general responses that enables a child to develop satisfactorily in relation to various aspects or dimensions of his personality."

7. Principle of interrelation. The various dimensions of one's growth and development are interrelated. What is achieved or not achieved in one or the other dimension in the course of the gradual and continuous process of development surely affects the development in other dimensions. A healthy body tends to develop a healthy mind and an emotionally stable and socially conscious personality because of interlative development.

8. Principle of interaction. The process of development is based on active interaction between the forces within the individual and the forces belonging to his environment. What is inherited by the organism at the time of conception is first influenced by the stimulation received in the womb of the mother and after birth, by the forces of the physical and socio-psychological environment for its development. Therefore, at any stage of growth and development, the individual's a behaviour or personality make-up is nothing but an end-product of the constant interaction between his hereditary endowment and environmental set-up.

9. Principle of cephalocaudal and proximodistal tendencies. Cephalocaudal and proximodistal tendencies are found to be followed in maintaining the orderly sequence and direction of development.

10. Principle of predictability. Development is predictable, which means that with the help of the uniformity of the pattern and sequence of development, we can, to a great extent, forecast the general nature and behaviour of a child in one or more aspects or dimensions at any particular stage of its growth and development.

III.4 Differencc Between Growth and Development

As discussed earlier that growth differs from development. The term 'growth' may be limited to the changes in the quantitative aspect, i.e., increase in size, length, height and weight and expansion of vocabulary etc., the term 'development' implies the overall changes occurring in both the quantitative as well as the qualitative aspects. Therefore, development as a term carries a wider and more comprehensive meaning than the term growth.

Since, growth is limited to the description of quantitative changes, its scope is confined to those aspects or dimensions of one's personality in which quantitative changes occur. As a result, in dealing with those aspects or dimensions, of personality where both the quantitative and qualitative changes are involved, the term growth is not employed. On the other hand, development as a comprehensive term, related to all types of changes which can be employed to describe the change in all dimensions of one's personality whether physical, mental, social, moral or any other. That is why we come across descriptions like physical growth and development, mental growth and development in the titles of the texts, we seldom come across these in the case of the social, emotional and moral aspects of personality. Here, we usually drop the term growth and refer simply to social, emotional and moral development. Since the quantitative changes in these aspects are not as directly observable and measurable as in case of physical and mental aspects. Therefore, when we talk of development in one or the other dimension of one's personality, it is clear that we are describing and explaining the overall changes in the structure and functioning of that particular aspect. For example, when we study physical development we do not aim to describe the change in the size and proportions of the physical organs in a solely physical sense but also to point out the impact of these physical changes in terms of improvement in the working or functioning of the physical organs. The term growth, on the other hand, carries a limited and narrower meaning. It is a sub-system of the development as it is concerned merely with the quantitative changes in comparison to the overall changes described and explained by the process of development. This does not continue throughout one's life. It stops when maturity has been attained while development is a continuous process. Starting right from conception, it does not end with the attainment of maturity but continues throughout the entire life span of an individual.

Development is said to be a complex process in comparison to the process of growth. The results of growth in terms of quantitative changes are very specific, fairly easy to observe and measurable. The results of development, in comparison, are quite complex and difficult as far as their actual assessment and measurement is concerned.

Thus, the terms growth and development, both imply change in one's behaviour and personality make-up. Development related to the overall changes, structural as well as functional, carries a comprehensive meaning and consequently we would prefer to describe the trends of changes during the life span of an individual in various dimensions of personality as well as discussing the principles and theories to highlight the pattern and mechanism of these changes.

Importance of the Knowledge of the Principles of Growth and Development for a Teacher

The knowledge of the principles of growth and development may prove beneficial to teacher and parents in a number of ways such as:

1. Development is a continuous and non-stop process at all periods and stages of human life. Therefore, we should never give up our efforts to achieve perfection in terms of development in the different dimensions of our personality.
2. The principles and knowledge of individual differences reminds us to understand the wide individual differences that surface at all periods of growth and development among children. Each child should be helped along the developmental process within the sphere of his own strengths and limitations.
3. The principles related to growth and development suggest a pattern or trend for the advancement of children on the developmental path. This knowledge can help us to know as to what can be expected in terms of the proper growth and development at a particular developmental stage and we can then plan accordingly to achieve it by organising the environmental experiences.
4. Principles like "proceeding from general to specific responses", and the principle of "integration" help us to plan the learning process and arrange suitable learning experiences so as to achieve maximum gains in terms of growth and development.
5. The principle of interrelation and interdependence directs us to strive from the very beginning for the all round harmonious growth and development of the personalities of our children and cautions us not to encourage the development of a particular aspect at the cost of another.

6. The principle of spiral advancement of development helps us to make adequate arrangement for the subsequent progress and consolidation of the progress achieved during specific developmental stages.
7. The cephalocaudal and proximodistal tendencies as suggested by the principle of developmental direction help us to arrange the suitable learning experiences, processes and environmental set-up so as to accommodate and help the youngsters to grow and develop according to the trend and nature of these tendencies.
8. The principle of interaction reminds us to recognise the joint responsibility of heredity and environment in the development of personality. Accordingly, they can develop within the limits of their genetic make-up; yet to attain maximum development, we have to arrange for the best environmental settings and experiences for our children. The environment that we provide should always be conducive to developing their potentialities and never prove to be an obstacle in the way of the adjustment of their self with their environment.

III.6 Stages of Development

The Developmental Psychology tries to study human behaviour right from conception. The individual from conception starts changing because he is never static. He passes through a number of developmental stages from birth to death. For our convenience we divide the process of human development in to different stages which can be described as the process of the development of a human being as:

Table 1: Stages of Devlopment

Name of Period		*Approximate Age*
1. *Pre-natal*	—	From 0 to 280 days.
(*a*) Germmal	—	From 0 to 2 weeks.
(*b*) Embryonic	—	From 2 weeks to 10 weeks.
(*c*) Foetal	—	From 10 weeks to birth.
2. *Childhood*	—	From birth to 12 years.
(*a*) Infancy	—	From birth to 3 years.
(*b*) Early childhood	—	From 3 years to 6 years.
(*c*) Later childhood	—	From 6 years to 12 years.
3. *Adolescence*	—	From 13 years to 19 years.
4. *Adulthood & old age*	—	From 20 years and beyond.

1. Pre-natal Stage

Individual begins life at the moment of conception. At this time of conception there is a union of the nucleus of the sperm with the nucleus of the egg. These nuclei are the carriers of 48 chromosomes, half from the father and half from the mother. It is very important for us to study the behaviour right from the time of conception. As Carmichael writes, "A knowledge of behaviour in pre-natal life throws light upon many traditional psychological problems. For example, some of the old questions concerning the relative importance of heredity and environment in the determination of adult human mental life are answered by his study." It is now accepted that pre-natal stage of development can be studied in three phases of development such as:

(a) The Germmal, in the first two weeks after conception,

(b) The Embryonic, from 2 weeks to 10 weeks, and

(c) The Foetal, from 10 weeks to birth.

One of the significant facts in the growth of the organism in the womb is that initially the development of head starts and during the 2nd month the head is about half the size of the whole body, in the 9th month it is about one quarter. At the end of the second month cutaneous stimulation elicits response and at fourteen weeks a spontaneous reaction of the organism as a whole. By the end of the sixth month, the movements of the foetus become very powerful and complex.

2. Childhood

Childhood is the most effective period of development in the life of an individual. The childhood has span of 12 years. The period of childhood is further subdivided to infancy, early and late childhood. Infancy-childhood ranges birth to three years.

(a) The new born baby during the first month after birth is called a neonate. During this period, the child has certain physiological adjustments to make. He does not have the full use of his senses. His eye muscles are too weak and lack in coordination to allow his two eyes to work together. Child does not have much discrimination among sounds of different pitch. He responds to the stimulation of various odours. Skin sensitivity such as touch, warmth, coldness seems to be present from birth. The other activities of the neonate include crying yawning, sneezing and smiling. The neonate sleeps for about twenty hours a day. Although the organs of the new born are developed and ready to function, he needs the help and protection of his mother.

It has been observed that during the first year of child's life we find very rapid growth. This period is the period of stabilization and control of physiological functions. There is a marked advance in motor development. When the child is 9-10 months old he is able to give differential responses to different words spoken by others. By about the time of his first birthday, he will be speaking his first word. There is a rapid growth in respect of his social development. The most intense social relationship is that which he has with his mother. He reacts with pleasure to her approach and her attention and responds with displeasure when she goes away from him. When the child is about one year old, he is able to stand up with the support of a chair and he may also take a few steps.

(b) Early childhood. This period ranges from 3 to 6 years. Nursery schooling starts at this stage. The child is now able to mix with other individuals and engages himself in various kinds of activities. Growth is not simple progressive one during this period. There is insecurity, disequilibrium and incoordination. A child of three and a half years shows incomparison with the child of three years in some motor coordination. By the time he is four years old, he becomes more vigorous, biting, kicking, throwing and breaking. The child also becomes highly emotional with fits of laughter and rage alternating. During this period another significant point worth noting is that the child is unable to draw a line between fact and fiction. He is quite intellectual and philosophical. He is also interested in details. He becomes interested in letters and numbers.

(c) Later childhood. This period ranges from 6 to 12 years and these are the years of elementary schooling. This is the period during which it becomes extremely difficult to deal with children. There may be outbursts against the mother. During this period, the child learns to read, write and do arithmetic. The period between 6 to 9 years is the period of greatest social limitation.

At the age of seven years, the child is more moody and withdraws himself and likes to be alone. There is a big change by the time he is eight years old. At eight, he is very eager to try out and make new things and new friends. The building up of individuality proceeds with considerable tempo in the next three years between 9 and 12. The child insists on being independent. He becomes more interested in his friends than his family.

In physical growth, the girls have their growth spurt earlier, between the ages 9 and 12 while in boys it occurs between 11 and 14. Consequently, between 10 and 15 girls tend to be slightly larger than boys. These differences, as well as other factors, bring about certain changes socially.

3. Adolescence

Adolescence is the most crucial stage of development in the life of an individual. The scope of the chapter permits the author to discuss the phases of development during adolescence separately. However, the period of adolescence ranges thirteen years to nineteen years. This is the period during which the growing person makes the transition from childhood to adulthood. This period begins when young people begin to show signs of puberty and continues until most of them not only are sexually mature but have also reached their maximum growth in height and approximately reached their full mental growth. The adolescent is very badly adjusted physically and mentally and lives under the delusions that he is the focus of every one's attention. According to Keats, "The imagination of a young boy is healthy; the mature imagination of a man is healthy; but there is a space of life in between in which the soul is in a ferment, the character undecided, the way of life uncertain." That period of uncertainty is called adolescence. The physical changes which take place in this period and the quick growth of the body bring about moodiness, irritability and emotional tensions are described separately.

III.7 Different Aspects of Growth During Infancy

Since, we are discussing growth and development is imperative to describe different aspects growth right from childhood. It must, however, be borne in mind that these aspects are not exclusive or independent of one another. They are all inter-related.

1. Physical Growth During Infancy

(a) Growth before birth is very rapid. A fertilized cell at the time of conception has a diameter of 0.13 mm. By the end of the two weeks the size of the fertilized cell called 'Marula' is 6.0 mm an increase of 5 hundred fold in length. During the 8th week the foetus is about an inch long. The growth per week at first increases rapidly and then after birth slows down. If the rate at birth were maintained until maturity, a grown man would be 45 feet tall.

(b) In the earlier days of the embryonic period the heart and brain grow much more rapidly than other parts of the body. At about the fourth week, the head constitutes half the length of the embryo. Even at birth, the size of the head is comparatively larger in proportion to its body length.

(c) The average new born boy weighs about 7½ pounds and the average girl 7 pounds. According to Rothney, "We can say with a great deal of assurance that growth is very rapid from birth to the age of 2 years, that growth tends to continue at a diminishing rate until a period of approximately 3 years before the advent of puberty, rises rapidly until puberty is reached and then falls away quickly to end points at ages between 17 and 19 years.

(d) Glandular Development: One aspect of pre-natal growth, the development of endocrine gland is very important to the life and happiness of

the individual. The endocrinal glands are the main sources to produce hormones. The hormones mainly controls the body energy so it would suffice to say here, that by pouring their chemical secretions into the blood stream endocrinal glands not only set the pace for much of the growth process but also act as regulators of changes in the already chemically differentiated tissues. They bring about and control changes in the reproductive organs, in the breasts, and in the vocal cords of the speech mechanism, thus setting the pace for the sharp changes in the development and in behaviour that occur in adolescence. Endocrine glands exercise an important control over the development of the nervous system. They form in the foetus before the nervous system is complete and directly affect its growth.

(e) Eruption of Teeth. At birth, there is an absence of teeth. Gradually, the child's first set of teeth or the 'baby' teeth appear. As growth of the body increases, these give place during childhood to a second set of teeth.

2. Mental Growth During Infancy

(a) At birth, the weight of the brain in relation to total body weight is greater than it will be at any other time during the process of body growth. The rate of growth is greatest during the early years of childhood. Maximum brain development reaches at the age of twenty years. Significant changes in mental ability accompany these changes in brain weight.

(b) During infancy the child gives little if any evidence of what may be referred to as an intelligent behaviour. The infant is concerned almost completely with himself and the satisfying of his feeding and sleeping needs and physical contacts.

(c) During the period from infancy to 3 years of age, the child's behaviour begins to show evidence of the functioning of those mental traits that will be helpful to him during his later life. He becomes aware of thirst, hunger, sleep, temperature, and other bodily needs. At the age of one year, he normally begins to walk and talk. During the next two years there is rapid growth of ability in walking, talking and sensory exploration.

3. Language Development During Infancy

Language is the ability to communicate with others. Man's greatest achievement and the sign that first and foremost distinguishes him from the ape is language. It has been rightly said that language is a weapon of warfare more deadly than the atom bomb and an instrument of peace more effective than the United Nations. If this is such an important instrument available to mankind, it would be interesting to know the sequential steps in the development of language.

4. Stages of Language Development during Infancy

The development of language passes through different stages which can be studied as the pattern of language development such as:

(a) Crying. By the end of the third week, the child's crying and gestures begin to take on meaning. It is possible for those who are familiar with babies to know what the tones and intensities of the cries signify. The baby's cries may indicate watness, cold, pain, or uncomfortable position. Crying is most frequent in babies before feeding and before the baby goes to sleep for the night. Before the baby is three months old, he knows that crying is an effective method of getting attention.

(b) Babbling. The ages between three and eight months are called the babbling stage. The baby selects and repeats with no apparent reason except their satisfying sound, such as ma-ma, da-da, etc. These sounds may be thought of as the material of language. These sounds are unlearned and are universally found in all nationalities and races. They are found even among the deaf. With the increase in age the number of sounds not only increases, but there is an increasing definiteness of utterance of various sounds.

Babbling is a form of play speech in that the sounds are uttered for mere delight of uttering them. Babbling is not linked with specific objects, situations or people, and as such is not a real speech.

(c) Gestures. The baby knows his wants but the vocal organs and nerve centres have not yet reached the maturational level for meaningful vocalization. Hence, he uses body movements and gestures to make his wants known. At first, these movements are feeble. As he gains greater control of body parts, responses to environmental stimuli become stronger and more definite. He squirms and wriggles or holds out his arms. He closes his lips and puckers his face and sometimes he turns his head towards or away from a person or a thing.

With the increase in age, the use of gestures decreases, except as a means of emphasizing what he is attempting to verbalize.

5. Vocabulary Development During Infancy

The baby learns to understand the meanings of words if those are accompanied by appropriate gestures. He tends to repeat the simple words he hears with little understanding of their meaning. Gradually, he develops a vocabulary of his own. He usually begins with nouns and then comes to learn verbs. At the age of one and a half year, the child learns the adjectives and adverbs. The growth of vocabulary starts slowly during the first two years of age, increases more rapidly in the pre-school years and then increases rapidly after he enters the school. The following table will show the increase in size of vocabulary with respect to age.

Table 2: Development of Vocabulary Patterns

Age		*No. of Words*	*Gain*
Years	*Months*		
0	8	0	–
0	10	1	1
1	0	3	2
1	3	19	16
1	6	22	3
1	9	118	96
2	0	272	154
2	6	446	174
3	0	896	450
3	6	1222	326
4	0	1540	318
4	6	1870	330
5	0	2072	202
5	6	2289	217
6	0	2562	273

6. Speech Development During Infancy

Speech is one of the important skill of communication. God has gifted to man. The skills of communication passes through phases of development. The skill of speech is an acquired skill. During the stages of development most of the children follow relatively similar patterns of speech development. There are certain factors which help accelerate or retard sequential progress. These factors can be studied as under:

(a) Innate Potentialities. The physically and physiologically early maturing child tends to articulate more clearly. He is able to speak more fluently and correctly than do average children. Slow rate of maturation is accompanied by slow language development. Mentally alert young children usually are what is known as 'early talkers'.

(b) Physical Health and Organic Factors. Physical defect and poor health retard the development of effective self expression. Organic factors also play in important role in the development of speech.

A child may lack readiness to distinguish sounds correctly or the vocal organs may not have matured sufficiently to reproduce that which has been heard.

(c) Sex Differences. Girls have a slight edge over boys in language development. Even apart from length of sentence, girls seem to make more rapid linguistic progress than do boys.

(d) Environmental Factors. The socio-economic status of the family have a significant influence upon the progress of a child in verbal expression.

III.8. Development of Social Life During Infancy of Childhood

The development of the individual in different areas is an integrated one. It is difficult to separate social development from intellectual development. Similarly, it is different from language development. According to Powers, "Social development can be defined as the progressive improvement, through directed activity, of the individual in the comprehension of the social heritage and the formation of flexible conduct patterns of reasonable conformity with this heritage."

According to Freeman and Showel, "It is the process of learning to confirm group standards to modes and traditions and becoming imbued with a sense of oneness, intercommunication and cooperation." Thus defined, social development places emphasis upon the fact that the growth must be progressive. The individual does not remain socially static. As a result the social life of child passes through various stages of development right from infancy and childhood to manhood.

(a) Social Development During Infancy. In the beginning, the young infant is concerned almost completely with the satisfaction of bodily wants. But very soon he begins to respond to the behaviour of those about him whose responsibility is to satisfy his wants. At the age of one year he has developed a fairly satisfactory pattern of response to adults. Infants differ from one another in the rapidity with which they begin to exhibit the characteristics of social behavioural responses of the child towards adult as shown in the table 3.

Table 3: Responses of Infants to Adults

	Age in Months
Returns glances of Adults with smiling	1 to 2
Is quieted by touching	1 to 2
Cries when adult who is attending him leaves	2 to 3
Smiles back at adult	2 to 3
Disturbed when approached	2 to 3

Returns approaching glance with "Lulling"	3 to 4
Displeasure when loses glance of adult	3 to 4
Quieted by caressing	4 to 5
Disturbed by the sight of people	4 to 5
Striving for attention by "Lulling"	7 to 8
Stretches out hands toward adults	7 to 8
Cries when adult stops talking	7 to 8
Strives for attention by movements	8 to 9
Pulls on the clothes of adults	9 to 10
Offers adult an object	9 to 10
Imitates movements of adults with a playing	9 to 10
Organises play activity	10 to 11

Growth and Development During Early Childhood

(i) As the child grows, there is a progressive change in the social behaviour of child, i.e., from individualization towards socialization. The child of two years will play with his own toys, even in the presence of another child. The only awareness of the other child that is exhibited is his attempt to take the toy with which the other child is playing. As the child approaches the third year, he starts sharing his toys with others. He comes to realize that what is mine is yours also.

(ii) During the pre-school years social consciousness develops in the child. He responds to those who give him attention. However, his behaviour towards others is stimulated by self interest rather than by interest in them.

(iii) During the ages of 4 and 5 years, children learn to play together. During the nursery school period the children start choosing friends. Girls are more likely to form friendships with girls and boys with boys.

(iv) As the child approaches the elementary schooling he still is interested in the satisfaction of his own wants but he has learnt to seek their fulfilment in terms of social customs of his group.

Growth and Development During Later Childhood

During the later childhood period (6-12 years) a child experience the following changes:

(i) This is the period of formal schooling. Schooling not only increases the child's opportunities for furthering his social development but also gives rise to problems of adjustment. The enlargement of his social world exposes him to a multitude of social problems of adjustment.

(ii) During their early years in school children ten to form into groups of 4 or 5. They owe their allegiance to this group. As they reach the middle classes the size of their groups increases to 6 or 8 numbers. There is a beginning of the separation of the sexes. The boys join boy's group and the girls their own.

(iii) From the age of 12 to 14 years, children's group tend to expand and to become highly organized. This is the period of the 'gang' or 'club'. Loyalty to fellow members becomes more intense.

(iv) By the time the child reaches the end of his elementary school, he has achieved a fair degree of social consciousness as a result of his experience with his family, his school-mates, community and other socializing media.

III.9 Different Aspects of Growth and Development During Adolescence

A child after attaining the age of 14 years enters into the adolescent age. By adolescent age we mean that a child after later childhood begins to show signs of puberty and continues until most of them not only are sexually mature but have also reached their maximum growth in height and have approximately reached their full growth.

This period, i.e., adolescence is a period of rapid physical, mental, emotional and social growth—a period of growing up. Physically the boy becomes an adult. His sex organs matures. There is intellectual growth towards a more abstract and mature mode of thinking. Sex consciousness develops in this period and that influences the emotional as well as the intellectual activities of the individual. Biological changes lead to moods, convulsions, insecurity and worries of all types.

This period begins between 12 to 14 years of age, but there are considerable differences, in some cases beginning as early as 10 years while others as late as 16-18 years. Inadequate diet, severe illness and other unfavourable environmental factors tend to retard the growth and development.

Adolescence is a period of rapid physical, intellectual, emotional and social growth—a period of growing up. During adolescence we experience the following changes among adolescents during the physical, mental, emotional and social development:

1. Physical Development During Adolescence

Adolescence is a period of growth and growth is noticeable both in size and weight. The adolescence shows a spurt in growth. The child who has been growing at a fairly even rate may seem suddenly to shot up, and for a period of a year or more may show a remarkable increase in the velocity of his growth. This may be followed by a period of diminished velocity of growth followed in turn by gradually lower increments in height until mature height is reached.

The adolescent girl grows or looks to be growing more uniformally as compared with an adolescent boy. This is due to her soudness of form. Boys are superior to girls in height and weight on the onset of adolescence but in the next two years girls outpace them, and in the next years boys are again superior. Besides, the following development are noticed:

(a) Change of Voice. Another commonly recognised feature of adolescence is the change of voice. This change, like other changes, does not occur at any fixed age or even at any fixed time in relation to other pubertal changes. The voice of girls also usually deepens during this period.

This change in voice has a significant effect on the behaviour of the adolescent. Some boys go through a period when their voices shift in an embarrassing way from deep to high tones. Some youngsters drop out of the school music clubs or school chorus due to this sudden change.

(b) Breast Development and Increase in Size of Genital Organs. During this period there is an increased growth of the external genital organs in boys. The growth of the breasts and the increase in the size of the pelvis in girls are the physical developments of puberty in girls.

(c) Growth of Hair. Hair appear on the public area and also in armpits. There are also changes in the amount and distribution of hair on other parts of the body.

(d) The Gonads (Sex Glands) and the Adolescent Spurt. The physiological investigations have established the fact that the maturing of gonads plays a direct part in the growth spurt in an adolescent. For about ten years, the gonads lie relatively dormant. Then suddenly they appear to awaken and grow to normal adult size and functioning in a comparatively short time.

(e) The Pituitary, the Gonads and the Adolescent Spurt. The pituitary plays an important part in changes in structure and behaviour during adolescence. Pituitary is a sensitive regulator of the reproductive life of the individual and of the mammary glands in the nursing mother. The interconnection between the pituitary and other glands are mainly by way of the blood vessels which carry the secretions of each gland to all the cells of the body.

(f) Other Bodily Changes. Pulse rate shows an average decrease of about eight beats per minute over the adolescent period but the rate of girls remains from two or six beats faster than that of boys at each age. Blood pressure rise with age and after the age of thirteen the blood pressure in boys rises more rapidly than in girls and becomes significantly higher. The outline of the forehand of many boys begins in late adolescence show the reading hair curves

of the adult male. The nose becomes more prominent and the chin assumes its adult dimensions. Facial blemishes and spots are also commonly recognized in adolescent boys and girls.

(g) Adjustment to Bodily Changes. The youngster enters adolescence as a child and leaves as a person able to beget children. He acquires the dimensions and proportions of an adult. There may be an increase in height as much as 4 or 5 inches. His nose, hands and feet become much larger. He may gain 10-12 kilograms in weight in one year. His movements become awkward. It is likely that he becomes self-conscious, especially if he also had pimples, a voracious and much noticed appetite for food in general and sweets in particular, and a vague uneasiness about whether or when his body and its several parts would stop getting bigger. Both parents and teachers should help the adolescent to accept his body. He should be reassured that sexual sensations are normal and there is nothing nasty or sorrowful about them. Sex education given in a scientific and objective manner emphasizing the values of healthy sex will be a great help to the adolescent.

(h) Psychological Effects of Physical Growth

(i) Adolescents are physically in the process of being converted into young adults. The strivings for independence which began in infancy moves towards its climax. The process of being weaned from parental care is hastened.

(ii) The youngster enters adolescence as a child and leaves as a person able to produce children. The growth spurt may add as much as 4 or 5 inches to a youngster's height in one year. In the mean time his nose, hands and feet become much larger. He may gain as much as 25 pounds in weight in a single year. It takes time to get used to such changes. He becomes self conscious and has a vague uneasiness about whether or when his body and its several parts would stop getting bigger.

(iii) The central feature of physical growth is the development of sexual maturity. There are individual variations in the age of onset of puberty. These differences in sexual development and other aspects of growth have many social and psychological repressions. A girl who had grown fast and has become taller than her peers might become sensitive about this. Her group members also become indifferent to her. The fact that the average boy is slower in maturing than is the average girl also complicates matters.

2. Mental Development of Adolescents

The adolescent advances on many intellectual parts. He continues during the terms to gain in intellectual capacity and power. The adolescent grows in ability to learn. Innate intelligence is practically mature and perfect at the end of the stage of adolescence. The important changes in thinking and concept formation were observed and described by Jersild in his book "The Psychology of Adolescent' reveals the attributes specifying the development of mental ability of the adolescents in the following ways:

(a) Increased Ability to Generalize. A noticeable characteristic of the mental operations of an adolescent, as compared with a younger child, is the ability to deal with generalizations.

(b) Increased Ability to deal with Abstractions. Adolescents not only think in general terms but also in abstract terms to a greater degree. They are capable of a greater amount of learning involving symbols rather than concrete things.

(c) Ability to deal with the Concept of Time. The ability to anticipate future and to imagine what might happen in it begins to develop at a very early age but comes into play especially during adolescent years. It is not until the age of 11-12 years that the children grasp the abstract idea of the historical past.

(d) Ability to deal with Ideas without Immediate Personal Involvement. The young child is concerned with the things in which he is directly involved. As he grows in years, he becomes increasingly able to be concerned about conditions that do not directly or indirectly affect him in any obvious way. In his thoughts he is able to encompass not only about himself and his family but also the people of the whole country and then the world.

(e) Increased Capacity for Intellectual Communication with Other Persons. The adolescent boys and girls develop the increased capacity of carrying on a logical discussion and pursuing a contained theme.

(f) Ability to Make Decisions. The adolescent develops the capacity of arriving at decisions. The adolescent gains increasing confidence in his own opinions.

(g) Understanding of Moral Concepts and Values. The young child's ideas about what is right or wrong, depend on what his parents tell and on what they praise or reprove. But the adolescent, to a degree, becomes his own spokesman for what is right and wrong.

3. Emotional Development of Adolescents

The term emotion means to stirring up of action. Since, adolescence is the age of actions, actions of an adolescent, with an adequate rational thinking, ultimately leads an adolescent towards emotional development. Emotional development is based on the occurrence of emotions. Emotion occurs in the life of the adolescent when his desires are not fulfilled, or when he is blocked or thwarted in his efforts, or when he is harmed. The circumstances that are most potent in arousing emotion in him are those that collide with his pride in himself or the expectations he places upon himself or arouse misgivings he has concerning himself. Sanford writes, "When the individual has ended—or partially ended—the relatively uncomplicated years of childhood and when he has just entered—or partially entered—the role of self-sufficient adult, he is in a confused and precarious situation. His childish behaviours are no longer adequate nor are they tolerated. Secure and comfortable adult ways have not yet been learned. Life can be something of a mess, and heightened emotionality can be expected. Similarly, Hurlock, 1953, has described the emotional life of the adolescent as characterized by:

(i) Intensity.

(ii) Lack of control.

(iii) Inconsistency.

(iv) Prevalence of long drawn out emotions, or moods.

(v) The growth of such sentiments as patriotism, loyality, and reverence.

The following are the important emotions that play an outstanding role in the development of personality of an adolescent:

(a) Love and Affection. Love and affection is the dominant feature of the adolescent's emotional life. This is due to the ripening of the sex instinct. Adolescent love is of the most selfless kind. The adolescent is prepared to do service to another child for no other ulterior end but to gain his love. The adolescent is prepared for any sacrifice demanded of him for the sake of his friend. Similarly, he also expects love and affection from others. Even though the adolescent is moving into a larger world, there is still much of the child in him. In one way or another, he needs affectionate support at home, much as he did at an earlier age. Though the adolescent has so many resources within himself he cannot live happily and healthy in emotional isolation from others.

The adolescent which is loved and accepted is likely to be better able to face the demands of life outside the home than the adolescent who has been rejected.

In the early period of adolescence, love usually directed to a person of the same sex. Later it becomes directed to a person of the opposite sex. The change comes natural as the sex instinct ripens. Sometimes, however, the former stage may persist longer than what is natural. This results in maladjustment to social relationships. According to the exponents of psychoanalysis, one of the reasons of the tragedy of Hamlet is his strong love of a male friend. His love of Horatio was abnormal.

Task of the Parent and the Teacher. It is the prime duty of the parents and the teacher that this feeling of love and affection does not take some mischievous turn. Adolescent love is to be utilized in the service of the society.

The love impulse can be easily directed towards great men. In adolescent we have the phenomenon of hero worship. "Boys in their teens," says Hall, "have a veritable passion for the stories of great men." Through this spirit of hero-worship we can bring immense changes in the life of the adolescent.

The adolescent is most open to religious influences. If a man ever becomes religious, he becomes in his adolescence. This is due to the fact that love in all its forms is intense during this period. Religious consciousness psychologically is nothing but sublimated love.

The adolescent child has an immense love of poetry. This is generally admitted that the soul of poetry is love, and the subliment poetry is an expression of one's devotion to the supreme being. The adolescent love of music is proverbial. Through music and poetry, many good sentiments can be developed in the child's mind.

The adolescent child loves nature. To him the sun, the moon, the mountains and the trees all talk. We should not starve this love of nature of the adolescent by refusing his hungry soul the necessary food. The adolescent should be allowed to indulge in nature and give expressions to his feelings in words.

(b) Anger and Hostility. Anger is an important emotion that plays an outstanding role in the development of the personality. Anger is essential in the economy of life, for it is through his anger that a person most sharply voices his demands and asserts his interests. In trying to understand the adolescent, four basic considerations pertaining to anger are essentially important.

(i) The first one has already been mentioned and that is anger is linked to human being's striving to assert himself. In the adolescent anger functions especially in connection with his endeavour to protect his pride, to gain independence and to work out a satisfactory relationship between himself and those who are in authority.

(ii) By the time a child reaches adolescence, he is not subject tochange that flares and then subsides but is also likely to have attitude in which there is a residule of anger in the form of hostility. Attitudes of hostility may manifest themselves in grudges, grievances, prejudices etc.

(iii) Hostile attitudes may sometimes be concealed that is instead of seeming to be angrily against, an adolescent may seem to be eagerly for. This means that often anger is carefully concealed and so it appears in disguised forms.

(iv) A fourth consideration relating to anger is that it may be turned against the person himself as well as against others.

Conditions Contributing Anger

An individual is likely to be more susceptible to anger when he is physically below average, is fatigued, suffering from lack of sleep or is hungry. Anger also frequently arises by reason of a piling up of irritations rather than a single provocation. If a child is subject to conflicting or inconsistent demands, or if he is compelled to perform an act over and over again, cumulative imitations are likely to develop. Needlessly rigid suppression of an individual activities may also give rise to such an accumulation.

Emotional factor also to a large extent depends upon the person himself. The child who is zealous, on guard against any show of favouritism toward a brother, will be angered by a mild rebuke which another child would be able to tolerate quite calmly.

The expression of anger during adolescence is most common because during this stage of development an individual is supposed to make adjustments. The expression of anger is in direct and indirect forms.

I. Direct Expression of Anger. This can be observed in the form of Hitting, Biting and other direct forms of attack. Crying and Verbal Aggression.

II. Indirect and Disguised Expression of Anger. Adolescents learn a great variety of indirect means of venting anger and hostility. But often this success in curbing the anger is deceptive, and often it is gained at a high price. This is socially so when a person takes out his anger on himself instead of directing it against others. The price may be painfully high. The two most indirect expressions are as under:

(a) Fantasy. Anger frequently expresses itself in fantasies and day dreams of revenge, or of someone's coming to grief, or of scenes of personal triumph that put the offending person in his proper place.

(b) Displaced Hostility. When an adolescent does not feel free to express anger directly against an offender, he will frequently direct his anger at someone or something else. The adolescent may direct an anger against animals.

(c) Fear and Anxiety. All adolescents are more or less frightened at times. Some of them experience fear only on occasions while others have occurring fears that are touched off again and again by happenings in their daily lives. Some experience states of dread lasting days or even weeks at a time.

Fear embraces a wide variety of conditions, ranging from paralyzing terror to mild forebodings and apprehensions, is aroused by events for which a person has no immediate response other than to shrink, to try and avoid, or flee.

The adolescents have reported fears in one or more of the following categories:

1. Animals.
2. Painful situation.
3. Danger or threat of bodily accidents and injuries.
4. Fears arising during dreams.
5. Fears of ridicule.
6. Failure.
7. Bad people such as robbers and kidnappers.
8. Imaginary creatures such as ghosts.
9. Dangers associated with dark.

(d) Anxiety. It is difficult to give a precise definition of anxiety. This concept is not easy to grasp. Even the psychologists have delved into the subject of anxiety have not agreed on any single or precise definition. Dr. Arthur T. Jersild had defined anxiety "as a kind of uneasiness of mind or a kind of apprehension, irritability, forbidding, or distress arising out of disturbance within a person's inner life." He further writes, "We can assume that an adolescent probably is burdened by anxiety linked to some form of inner conflict or distress if he feels blue or depressed for no apparent reason; if he is bitterly angered by something that seems trivial, or feels guilty when there seems to be no reason to feel that way;...".

Growth and Development During Adulthood

Human growth and development do not cease at the end of adolescence. As people grow older they usually show different concerns and involvements and must eventually cope with declining strength and the recognition that they may have more to look back upon than forward to. Different psychologists divide the adult years according to varying schemes, but there seems to be a consensus that we can safely use three broad categories; young adulthood, middle adulthood, and later adulthood.

1. Young Adulthood

Roger Gould's (1975) reported the twenties to be fueled with ambition. Similarly, *Passages* Gail Sheehy (1976) labelled the twenties the Trying Twenties—a period during which people strive to advance themselves in their carriers.

Sheehy interviewed one hundred and fifteen people largely from the middle and upper classes, including many managers, executives, and other professionals. Her findings may not generalize to all Americans, but the young adults in her sample were concerned about establishing their pathways in life, finding their places in the world. They were generally responsible for their own support and feeling increasingly free of parental influences as they made their own choices.

Sheehy noted that during the twenties we often feel "buoyed by powerful illusions and belief in the power of the will [so that] we commonly insist...that what we have chosen to do is the one true course in life." (1976, p. 33). We shall see that this one true course has many swerves and bends.

A central task of young adulthood is the establishment of intimate relationships. According to Erik Erikson, young adults who evolved a firm sense of identity during adolescence are now ready to fuse their identity with that of other people. Erikson warns that we may not be capable of committing ourselves to others until we have established our own life roles. People who do not reach out to develop intimate relationships may risk retreating into isolation and loneliness.

The Challenge of the Thirties. Gould noted that the ages of twenty-nine to thirty-four were commonly characterized by self-questioning: "Where is my life going?" "Why am I doing this?" Gail Sheehy labeled the thirties the Catch Thirties—the first major period of reassessment in life, when we often find that the life-styles we adopted during the twenties do not fit quite as comfortably as we had anticipated.

"One common response," according to Sheehy, "is the tearing up of the life we have spent most of our twenties putting together. It may mean striking out on a secondary road toward a new vision or converting a dream of 'running for president' into a more realistic goal. The single person feels a push to find a partner. The woman who was previously content at home with children chafes to venture into the world. The childless couple reconsiders children. And almost everybody who is married, especially those married for seven years, feels a discontent".

The second half of the thirties, according to psychologist Daniel Levinson (Levinson et al. 1978) of Yale University, is characterized by setting down. Sheehy similarly, found that young adults who had successfully ridden out the storm of reassessment of the Catch Thirties began the process of "rooting" at this time. They felt a need to plant roots, to make a financial and emotional investment in their homes. Their concerns became more focused on promotion or tenure, career advancement, and long-term mortgages.

2. Middle Adulthood

There is some point between age thirty-five and forty-five when most of adults realize that our lives may be more than halfway over, that there may be more to look back upon than forward to. The dreams of youth will never be realized. We'l never be president or chairperson of the board. We'l never play short-stop for the Dodgers or dance in the New York City Ballet in Taj Hotel New Delhi.

The middle-level, middle-aged business person looking ahead to another ten to twenty years of grinding out accounts in a Wall Street cubbyhole may experience a severe midlife depression. The housewife with two teenagers, an empty house from eight to three, and a fortieth birthday on the way may feel she is coming apart at the seams. Both are experiencing the midlife crisis, a feeling of entrapment and loss of purpose that afflicts many and propels some into extramarital affairs just to prove that they are still physically attractive.

Erikson labels the life crisis of the middle years as generativity versus stagnation. If we come through this crisis positively, we may newly embrace family values, maintain our creativity, and enthusiastically pursue the Eriksonian ideal of helping to shape the new generation, which may involve rearing our own children or working to make the world a better place in general. For those who weather the crisis, experience combines with strength to heighten productivity.

Daniel Levinson and his colleagues (1978) found that the early forties represent a turning point for men. In their thirties men still think of themselves as part of the Pepsi Generation, the older brothers to youths in their twenties. At about forty some marker event—a physical illness, a change on the job, the obituary of a contemporary—leads them to realize they are a full generation older than twenty-year-olds. They mourn their own youth and begin to adjust to the spectre of old age and the finality of death.

The Dream: Inspiration or Tyrant ? Until midlife, according to Levinson, men may be under the influence of the Dream—the overriding drive of youth to become, to be the great novelist or scientist, to leave one's mark on history. At midlife men must come to terms with the discrepancy between what they have actually accomplished and the Dream.

The Dream, you see, may tell the author that the merely memorable novel is insufficient—it must be a masterpiece. The Dream may lead all of us, not just men, to belittle our accomplishments. Middleaged people who free themselves from the tyranny of the Dream find it more possible to enjoy the passing pleasures of each day.

The Empty Nest Syndrome You may think that parents, and mothers especially, give a sigh of relief when the last child goes off to college, moves into an apartment, or gets married. After all, now they finally have some time to devote to themselves. But it turns out that mothers who have allowed themselves to become too wrapped up in their children's lives often feel that there is not much left to live for when their children leave home (Bart 1970).

According to Harbeson. Too many married women arrive at middle age without having looked and planned far enough ahead, and experience difficulties in making the transition from motherhood to socially useful occupations...[There] are an appalling number of unhappy over-forty women [who] could be helped if they could find a sufficient purpose for their lives. These women are simply at a loss to know what to do with themselves when they reach the point where their children are no longer dependent on them. Usually, they are the ones who have been the most devoted mothers... Too often their only relief is in some form of occasional social diversion which provides them an escape. [1971, p. 139]. Such women are also said to be suffering from the empty nest syndrome.

According to Gail Sheehy (1976), mothers of grown children usually expect that the appropriate path for filling their lives with new meaning is the cultivation of interests and talents that had been allowed to lie dormant when their families came along. Slightly more than half the American women whose children have left the nest are now in the work force. Some return to college.

A recent study of life satisfaction among Americans by Angus Campbell (1975) showed some encouraging results. Men and women with children over seventeen reported more general life satisfaction and more positive feelings about life than parents of younger children. They were also much more satisfied than people who had never married.

3. Later Adulthood

'Most people say that as you get old you have to give up things. I think you get old because you give up things.' The idea that society can provide only a limited number of jobs, and that the elderly are the logical ones to be left out, is no longer tenable. There are unlimited goods and services needed and desired in American society. Among the greatest resources that could be channeled toward these ends are the experience, skill and devotion of America's elderly millions.

Later adulthood begins at the age of sixty-five, and one very obvious reason that developmental psychologists have become concerned with the later years is that more of us are joining the ranks of the elderly in our nation's population all the time. Improved health care and knowledge about the importance of diet and exercise appear to have combined so effectively that more Americans than ever before are aged sixty-five and over.

At the time of the first census, conducted in 1970, half of all Americans were sixteen or younger. In 1970 the median age was under twenty-eight, but it may well be thirty-five by the year 2000 and almost forty by 2030. At that time more than fifty million of an American population of some three hundred million will be sixty-five or above, as compared with about twenty-two million who are sixty-five or older today!

Ageing. A number of changes occur in the ageing process, which lead to many problems we see among the elderly. Changes in calcium metabolism lead to brittleness in the bones and thus an increased likelihood of broken bones as a result of falls and other accidents. The skin becomes less elastic, leading to wrinkles and folds.

The senses become less acute, so the elderly require more stimulation than younger people for hearing, vision, taste, and smell to respond. You may notice that older people tend to use more salt, paper, and other spices for this reason.

The elderly show a marked increase in the amount of time required to respond to stimulation—reaction time. The elderly may infuriate younger drivers by driving very slowly, both because of increased sensitivity to bumps and because of the increased amount of time it takes them to respond to traffic lights and the actions of other drivers. The young do not help matters by yelling at them and cutting them off!

The elderly also show some decline in general intellectual ability, as measured by changing scores on standardized intelligence tests. This drop-off is most noticeable on items in which solution to a problem must occur within a certain time limit, for example, some of the "performance" items on the Wechsler Adult Intelligence Scale (WAIS). Loss of sensory acuity compounds problems, and decreased interest in performing well may also result in lowered scores. But in jobs the experience of the elderly, combined with continued high levels of motivation, often makes forced retirement an arbitrary and painful penalty for no sin other than turning sixty-five or seventy. According to Kimmel, "Up to the age of sixty-five there is little decline in learning or memory ability; factors of motivation, interest, and lack of recent educational experience are probably more important in learning complex knowledge than age per se. Learning may just take a bit longer for the elderly and occur more at the individual's own speed instead of at an external and fast pace" (1974, p. 381).

Theories of Ageing. Although it may be difficult to belive that it will happen to us, so far everyone who has ever lived has eventually aged. Why? There are several approaches to understanding ageing.

It Takes a Long Time to Become Young. Is youth purely a matter of age, or does personal attitude have a great deal to do with it? In *it takes a Long Time to Become Young* film director and Garson Kanin (1978) argues that too many people are automatically tossed into the human wastebasket by forced retirement policies when they reach the age of sixty-five or seventy.

Kanin cites data from the U.S. Bureau of Labour Statistics showing that the mean life span among forced retirees is only thirty to forty months. One of three marriages breaks up after forced retirement, and the suicide rate among forced retirees is twelve times greater than the norm for others in this age group. Kanin argues that only personal choice or demonstrated inability to 2perform in one's work should lead to retirement—at eighty-two or forty-two. The older worker's experience often compensates for lowered stamina. Kanin tells the story of a Connecticut town that lost its electrical power. After several days of fruitless poking around, the retired engineer who had installed the system was called in. He studied the problem, tapped his mallet once, and there was light. He sent the town a bill for $1.000.02—$.02 for tapping, and $1,000 for knowing where to tap. Wisdom does not come cheap.

The opportunity for meaningful work throughout our years is a major aim of the senior rights movement and groups like the Gray Panthers.

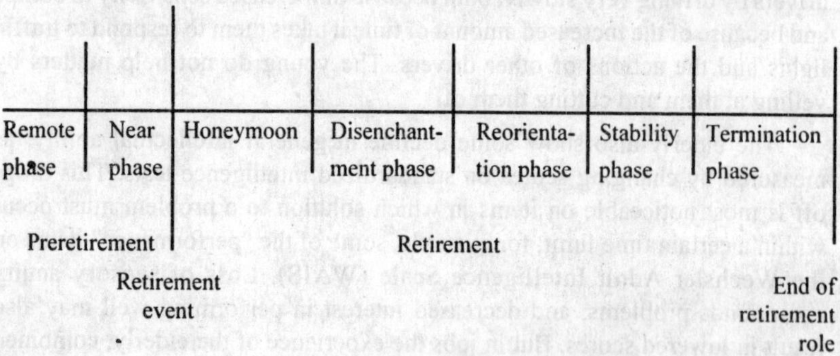

Fig. 1. *Phases of Retirement.* Retirement is not always smooth or straight-forward. We may not think about it much when it is remote, but we become more preoccupied with it and may make plans as it nears. At first we are often quite happy with it (honeymoon phase) but often become disenchanted as expectations are not quite met. We may then make some changes (reorientation) and enter a more stable period. Retirement can terminate with new work, illness, or death.

Heredity apparently plays some role. *Longevity* appears to run in families; therefore people whose parents and grandparents died in their eighties and nineties have a greater chance to reach these years.

External factors are also involved in the ageing process. For instance, it seems that people who exercise regularly tend to live some-what longer, and that disease, city life, overweight, and cigarette smoking are some factors that lead to an early death.

Other factors in ageing are more theoretical. The *cellular ageing theory* suggests that cells eventually lose the ability to reproduce, so that after a number of years human beings can no longer maintain the functions served by cells so affected. Another view is that waste products within cells may eventually accumulate to the point where many bodily cells are poisoned or no longer capable of functioning. Such views remain speculative at this time.

Living Arrangements for the Elderly. Since the aged may spend 80 to 90 percent of their time at home (Hansen 1975), living arrangements become extremely important. The elderly, also, prefer not to move, since moving requires adjustments.

About 25 percent of the elderly live in rural areas, 33 percent in inner cities, and 40 percent in older lower-middle-class neighbourhoods within cities (Hendricks & Hendricks 1977). The majority own their own homes. Mobile homes and senior citizen hotels are becoming more popular. Retirement communities, which began in Florida, have sprung up in most Sunbelt states, and the elderly feel that these communities provide protection from street crime and other city problems (Leslie & Leslie 1977).

Only about 5 percent of the elderly live in nursing homes and institutions, and despite the many problems associated with ageing, a survey of persons aged seventy to seventy-nine found 75 percent to be generally satisfied with their lives (Neugarten 1971). Senility was rather rare, and most retirees remained active to some degree.

On Death and Dying. Death is the last great taboo. In *On Death and Dying* psychiatrist Elisabeth Kubler-Ross comments on our denial of death: "We use euphemisms, we make the dead look as if they were asleep, we ship the children off to protect them from the anxiety and turmoil around the house if the [person] if fortunate enough to die at home, [and] we don't allow children to visit their dying parents in the hospitals" (1969, p. 8).

From her work with hundreds of terminally ill patients, Kubler-Ross found some common responses to news of impending death and identified five stages of dying that many patients pass through: *denial, anger, bargaining, depression,* and *final acceptance.* Others who suspect death is approaching may experience similar phases.

In the denial stage people feel, "It can't be me. The diagnosis must be wrong." Denial usually gives way to anger and resentment toward the young and healthy and, sometimes, the medical establishment : "It's unfair. Why me?" Then people may try to bargain with God to postpone death, promising, for example, to do worthy deeds if they are granted another six months, or another year. With the depression stage come feelings of hopelessness and loss— grief at the spectre of leaving loved ones and life itself. Ultimately an inner peace may come, a quiet acceptance of the inevitable that does not resemble happiness but is almost devoid of feelings.

The final hours pose a towering challenge, Kubler-Ross feels, that might be better met if death and dying were dealt with as facts of life rather than denied—and if the dying were helped to die in dignity in their own homes, not in an anonymous hospital.

Lying Down to Pleasant Dreams... The American poet William Cullen Bryant lived from 1794 to 1878, yet never in his maturity could he recapture the majesty of his poem "Thanatopsis," written at age eighteen.

"Thanatopsis" expresses Erik Erikson's ideal of *ego integrity* (rather than despair) during the later years: the possibility of maintaining a basic sense of trust throughout life and living in such a way that when it is time to "join the innumerable caravan"—the countless billions who have died before us—we can depart from life with dignity and integrity, accepting the inevitability of our own life cycle in the history of humankind.

Live, the poet writes, so that
...when thy summons comes to join
The innumerable caravan that moves
To the pale realms of shade, where each shall take
His chamber in the silent halls of death,
Thou go not, like the quarry-slave at night,
Scourged to his dungeon, but, sustained and soothed
By an unfaltering trust. Approach thy grave
Like one who wraps the drapery of his couch
About him, and lies down to pleasant dreams.

Of course Bryant wrote "Thanatopsis" at eighteen, not eighty-five. At that advanced age his feelings might have differed. But literature and poetry, unlike science, need not reflect reality. They can serve to inspire and warm us.

III.11 Role of Teacher and Development

The role of a teacher during our entire life-span cannot be over looked. The mother as a teacher guides a child to learn, to speak, crawl, walk and listen. Similarly, the role of the teacher in the healthy development is much more important in the early childhood when a child tries to develop a particular pattern of emotion and behavioural pattern. The role of the teacher even in the later childhood stage cannot be ignored because from late childhood a child enters a most crucial stage of development i.e., adolescent age. A teacher can help the adolescent smoothly and to adjust himself to the environment. For this, the following suggestions are made:

1. The teacher should make a thorough understanding of the general

characteristics of the period of adolescence, its stresses and strains, urges and cranings challenges and problems.

2. He should have a sympathetic attitude towards him.
3. He should set a good example of good conduct himself, and display his own emotional stability.
4. He should impart right information about sex.
5. He should redirect the energies of the adolescents to fruithful channels through sports and activities.
6. He should afford some freedom in organising and planning. He should not impose unreasonable restricitions. He should not force adult standards and curb his self-expression.
7. He should give applause and recognition to the achievements of the adolescent.
8. He should provide a variety of curriculum, in accordance with the diverse aptitudes. There should be special provision of music, art and dance for girls. A net-work of hobbies must be provided to cater to diverse interests.
9. Educational and vocational guidance should be provided.
10. Some programme of moral and religious teaching, accompanied by social service should be organised in the school.
11. Adolescent should be helped to control his emotions.
12. Patriotism, nationalism, citizenship and self-sacrifice are some of the essential ideals that must be interested in them.
13. Some freedom should be given to them, in all matters like selection of courses, selection of games and hobbies, and the daily mode of work. Adult standards should not be thrust on him.
14. Practical bias must be given to the curriculum. Work-experience and scientific enquiry are in consonance with adolescent psychology.
15. The Hadow Report in England sums up the above task so beautifully that There is a tide which begins to rise in the veins of youth at the age of eleven or twelve. It is called by the name of adolescence. If that tide can be taken at the flood, and a new voyage begin in the strength and along the flow of its current, we think that it will move on to fortune."

III.12 Learning Exercises

1. Discuss the meaning of growth and development.
2. Describe the principles of growth and development.
3. Differentiate between the growth and development.
4. Discuss the importance of the knowledge of growth and development for a teacher.
5. What are the characteristics of development and describe various factors causing development?
6. What are various sources of development?
7. Discuss the characteristics of development.
8. What are the various stages of child development?
9. How could you justify different curricula for adolescent boys and girls with respects to their growth and development.
10. Describe various aspects of growth and development of childhood.
11. Describe various aspects of growth and development of adolescents.
12. Describe important body changes during adolescence.

IV

Psychology of Emotion

Every body experiences emotions. You know that some of us react to a stimuli slowly and some react sharply. The difference in reaction to a situation is because of Psychology of emotional responses. For instance, the study of the behaviour of an individual reveals that there are some motivating forces which copel him to behave in the manner he does. The fear may be the cause of behaviour of one person, Jealousy of the other, anger of still another and so on. As usual, a person may not be aware of the instinct, instinctives, dirives, motives and emotions which cause his behaviour. The inner force of behaviour which motivates the behaviour is called emotions. The fact that instincts and drives also motivates the behaviour but the intensity of force to regulate the behaviour is different. The emotions are of different types, the difference of the emotional responses, has been categorically explained by different psychologists. However, let us study the existing body of available knowledge regarding the emotions, instincts, motives, incentives and drives.

Emotion is an intense feeling which causes mental agitation and excitement accompanied with some bodily changes. It is an affective experience. Emotion is innate but can be limited to a great extent. In other words, emotion is an innate response accompanied with excitement in mind and body and has intimate relationship with the preservation of the individual or species. The emotions, namely, the anger and fear are not simply feelings but they cause bodily changes such as clinching the fist, grinding the teeth, redness of eyes, more of heart beat etc. The word emotion is derived from Latin word "emovere" "which means to move out". This conveys the idea of an outward expression of something inside, which is one aspect of emotion. "To move out" also implies a second aspect of emotion—its motivational quality. Emotion supplies the motive power for a great deal of our behaviour. In brief, emotion is something we feel i.e., it is a physiological state that can be observed with the appropriate recording equipment.

Webster's dictionary, points out that emotion is "a physiological departure from homeostasis that is subjectively experienced in strong feeling (as of love, hate, desire, or fear) and manifests itself in neuro-muscular, respiratory, cardiovascular, hormonal, and other bodily changes preparatory to overt acts which may or may not be performed."

IV.1 Meaning and Definitions of Emotions

Definition: Emotion has been defined by different authors differently which can be studied as under:

1. McDougal defines emotion as a mode of experience that accompanies the working of an instinctive act.
2. Woodworth defines: 'Emotion is a 'moved' or stirred-up state of the organism. It is stirred-up state of feeling—that is the way it appears to the individual himself. It is a disturbed muscular and glandular activity—that is the way it appears to an external observer.
3. Crow and Crow define: "An emotion is an affective experience that accompanies generalised inner adjustment and mental and physiological stirred-up states in the individual, and at shows itself in his overt behaviour."

In brief we may define emotion as: Every emotional experience or reaction involves feeling such as anger or fear or joy. An emotional reaction is accompanied by marked physiological changes involving both visceral and peripheral areas. An emotional reaction or experience includes an impulse towards some kind of action. On the subjective side, emotion involves awareness or perception of what it is or what it might be, that causes the impulses and feelings.

In other words, emotion is the stirred up state of the individual. An emotional man behaves differently. His actions are gross and powerful. He manifests clear symptoms of internal physiological changes viz; flushed face, rapid breathing, restlessness, etc. Infact, the whole body is moved as we find in anger, fear, joy. Emotions are store house of great energies.]

Meaning: To describe the nature of emotions, psychologists, psychiatrists, and scholars studying human nature have made attempt to go even beyond verbal description for deeper understanding of emotions. They have tried to trace the origin and course of an emotion such as fear in a man's behaviour. Psychologists tried to devise ways of harnessing and controlling the effects of emotions i.e., why do children have temper tantrum? Can we do anything to eliminate such outbursts? All such attempts helps us to understand the fundamentals of emotions which can be studied as under:

1. Emotion is a Subjective Experience

Emotions are the conscious feelings. When a man is angry, he knows that he is angry. The knowledge of his anger is a sort of introspection ability. The introspection ability is a gift to human beings and not animals. Therefore, emotions can be studied from the outward behaviour or through physiological changes in one's body.

2. Emotion is a Response

The emotion is a sort of response exhibited by an organism towards any stimulus or a situation. The response may be internal or external. The emotion emerged out of the internal response reflects the disturbance of the internal environment of an organism that is why great physiological activity seem to occur. The response which disturbs the external environment of an individual is known as external response. All these disturbing responses of an individual explains physiological activity of an organism. The disturbance of internal and external equilibrium of an organism's physiological activities is due to the response of autonomic nervous system. The responses of autonomic nervous system affecting emotional expression can be studied as:

(a) Emotion as an internal response:

(i) Peripheral effects. Much of the work on the autonomic aspects of emotions has been done with anger and fear because they can be easily induced in animals. Under the emotional stress there is some sort of uproar in the sympathetic system. For instance; Salivation is stopped, movements of the stomach, secretion of gastric juices are inhibited—this may result in constipation. But the outflow of parasympathetic system may have reverse effects i.e., Defection and Urination. When you have caught a rat in a cage—you notice this time that it urinates again and again which is sign of emotionality.

Similarly, we find that there are changes in the circulation system. Heart beats faster, blood is taken away from the skin and viscera. The blood pressure goes up. These all are the signs of energy expenditure—because more energy is needed in emotion.

In answer to this the parasympathetic outflow may cause the dilation of the blood vessels in the body. The blood may suddenly leave the head and this may result in unconsciousness of the individual due to lack of oxygen supply to the brain. It also slows down the heart beat and reduces the blood pressure.

(ii) Chemical effects. Due to emotions, the sympathetic system influences the endocrine glands which further secrete certain hormones that have great bearing upon the whole internal environment of the organism. For instance,

the adrenal gland secretes adrenaline. It makes the glycogen stored in the liver to be converted into sugar thereby raising the sugar level in the blood and speeding of heart beat rate.

Thus, we find, that emotions bring great internal bodily changes. These internal changes further give rise to external responses which can be studied as under:

(b) Emotions as an External Response

By considering emotions as an external response, we mean that the external behaviour of an individual we may know about his inner emotional state and body physiology. For instance, if an individual is crying, laughing, trembling, it means that he responding to some of the external responses to certain specific emotions. The typical startle pattern of head and neck, is mostly seen after a sudden violent change in the environment —say after gun shot. There are studies about facial expression as index of emotions. In other words, typical emotions accompany typical facial expressions.

3. The Behaviour of a Man Under Strong Emotion is Mostly Unintellectual

As general experience, it has been reported that highly emotional man is confused person. His actions lack proper organisation and coherence. He appears instance.

4. Emotions are Fountain Head of Energy Over a Longer as well as Shorter Period of Time

Woodworth points out that emotional man has the force of a demon. The soldiers lay their lives fighting on the battle field, lover committing suicide, they are guided not by their mind but by their emotions. We have got finest work of art from poets and artists inspite of their very bad health. Not only that, an highly emotional state increases the indifference to pain. For instance, a boxer does not feel pain from his wounded face when actually on fight. The same we find in other games or similar situations.

5. Emotions Accompany Motivated Behaviour

Motivated behaviour tends to be tinged with emotions in all its stages. Rarely do human beings seek goals without fear or Joy, happiness or Jealousy. Emotions accompanying motivated behaviour may facilitate or in certain cases may interfere with that behaviour. For instance, a player who is emotionally involved in the game gives better performance than who is not, while an over-emotional player may spoil the game.

In brief, it can be said that emotions are the stir-up situation of an organism. The stir-up condition of an organism is because of external as well as the internal situations which acts as the stimuli to disturb the auto-nomic system resulting in the bio-chemical actions within the organism. Those actions of the organism which can be experienced outwardly are known as the external out burst of emotional responses and the stimuli which disturbs the inner organisation of an organism's functions are known as internal emotional responses. The internal and the external responses exhibited due to the action of auto-nomous nervous system within certain limits helps the organism to adjustment in life but the extreme responses by the autonomous nervous system hamper the physical, social and intellectual performance of an individual.

IV.2 Development of Emotions

Each individual has emotions like that of other behavioural responses and abilities. The emotional history of an individual begins with the hereditary differences that determine emotional tendencies. The development proceeds through a period of maturation during which the individual's emotional patterns of behaviour gradually mature in relation to his basic motor abilities. As the individual grows up, he learns to react emotionally to new situations and to modify his emotional behaviour. But question arises, what is the basic pattern of emotional development and how an individual modifies his behaviour by refining his emotional reactions.

To understand the pattern of emotional development one has to study the emotional reaction of a child right from his infancy. A sytematic study of emotional reactions makes us to understand the nature and type of emotions developing at a particular age. For instance, an infants come into the world crying, and they continue to cry periodically whenever they are hungry or uncomfortable. This is an inborn response to internal physiological needs or to discomfort. If we consider the responses to external situations, however, we find that almost the only emotional response that can be distinguished in the newborn infant is general excitement. This response consists of unconditional squirming, arms waving, kicking. It is not a specific response to any particular stimulus, but occurs whenever the external environment changes.

Sometime within the infant's first month or six weeks of life, this diffuse excitement, although continuing, begins to differentiate into more specific emotional reactions. The first reaction to appear has been called distress. This may or may not include the crying that has been going on since birth, but it is characterized by muscular tension and checked breath. Shortly afterward, something called delight is distinguishable. It is evident by smiling, gurgling, and muscular relaxation. Thus, by the time the infant is six weeks to two months old, the two general emotions—distress and delight, or call them what you wish—that will be felt and expressed throughout life have made their appearance. Such development is almost wholly, if not entirely, a matter of maturation.

As the infant grows older, he develops an increasing variety of emotional responses. At three months of age, for instance, an infant responds to unpleasant situations with general signs of distress, but responds to nursing, fondling, tickling, and rocking with smiles and general signs of delight. After that, emotional responses show rapid differentiation, and by the age of nine months the infant develops the emotion of delight into joy and the emotion of distress splits in to fear and anger. Gradually, the emotions by the age of two years, the child starts responding differently to the different situation because the negative and positive tendencies of the emotions start further splitting. Skinner has pointed out that the emotional pattern of development continue upto the age of 6 years. It has also been reported that the emotional development takes place even during the adulthood but it has been specified that no new emotion develops after the age of 7 years. It is the mere refinement of the pre-existing emotions which amounts to the difference in the pattern of one's emotions. Further, it has also been found that exact order and ages vary from child to child. However, general pattern of emotional development can be described in figure1 as under:

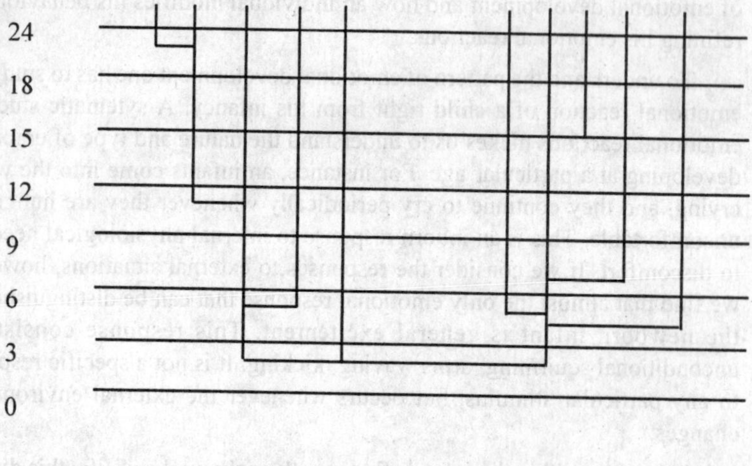

Figure 1: Showing the Development of Emotions

IV.3 Nature of Emotions

The Webster's definition of emotion gives us an idea about the emotion.

To understand the nature of emotions, it is essential to lay down certain criteria for distinguishing between emotional and non-emotional experiences such as:

(1) Emotions are the stired-up condition involving disturbance, excitement, conflict or tension in behaviour. In an emotional situation some stimulus arouses or stirs emotions into action.

(2) An emotion is brought into action by the perception of some stimulus. Psychologically it is a complex experience involving perception and widespread characteristic bodily changes in the action of muscles, glands and the autonomic nervous system.

(3) Every emotional state involves an impulse to action. There is a drive toward some kind of adjustment, to obtain satisfaction, to effect destruction or escape or to gratify a desire. The emotion subsides to the extent to which adjustments are achieved.

Bhatia describes that the importance of physiological changes has been variously interpreted by psychologists. James and Lange emphasize that bodily changes are a vital part of the emotional experience and if they were taken away the emotion as such would disappear. Furthermore, these physiological excitements precede, and do not follow, emotional experience, and they are the cause rather than the effect of emotional experience. It is difficult to accept this view. Not only popular thought is against it but experimental investigations also deny it. When adrenal is injected into the blood stream of subjects, it is reported that some subjects experience a variety of emotions, other feel no emotion at all. Therefore, it can be said that in addition to bodily changes produced by adrenaline, an appropriate situation is necessary to bring about an emotion.

Cannon W.B. argues that physiological changes prepare the individual to meet an emergency. The emotions represent increased and repeated efforts of the organism to make more effective adjustments to its environment, especially in a crisis. It may be true of the animal existance but in modern life human emotions are so overlaid with socio-cultural influences that the adaptive usefulness of some emotions may very well be denied.

Observation and experiments on the development of emotional experiences shows that emotions are subject to the general laws of development process. In the beginning there is a general mass of excitement, a sort of undifferentiated response, and it is only gradually that distinct and separate responses develop. The process of differentiation, elaboration and integration of emotional responses are the clear cut expressions such as anger, fear, Joy or disgust.

Emotions are spoken of as positive and negative. The positive emotions are those of Joy, exultation, hope, and they are aroused by situations which help and promote the satisfaction of needs and the realization of goals and purposes. Negative emotions are those of anger, fear, anxiety, and they are aroused by situations which hinder or threaten our welfare and happiness.

The emotions presuppose certain needs and motives is self-evident and many older psychologists like Mc Dougall connected them with instincts. Now it is difficult to list all needs and motives but some of the fundamental needs and motives may briefly be described. The foremost need is that of physical survival, bodily comfort and self-preservation. It includes the specific need for food, air and water, for shelter and protection from extremes of temperature and physical danger.

All human beings have a need of activity. In other words, we all desire to exercise our limbs and muscles, to enjoy sounds, sights and smells and use our intellect in finding, exploring and discovering, and the young people growing at a rate faster than that of adults need opportunities for free activity, fresh experiences and new discoveries. There is pleasure in activity, in manipulation and construction. The hunger of the hand and muscles has to be satisfied. Curiosity leads to inquiry and investigation, and heightens intellectual activity. Similarly, man has social needs which also need to be satisfied. To satisfy all such needs man acts. These acts performed by an organism to satisfy his needs are his emotional responses.

In brief, it is better to speak of emotional responses or experiences than of emotions. Emotional responses either precede or follow positive action. Every person has an emotional capacity, that is, he can learn to become emotional about objects, persons or situations. The learning of emotional responses is a function of the autonomic nervous system. So to learn emotion we need to understand autonomic nervous system.

IV.4 Dimensions of Emotions

Garrett (1975) reports that emotions can be studied from three behavioural dimentions such as:

(1) Emotions as Conscious Awareness,

(2) Emotions as Observable Behaviour or Emotional Expression,

(3) Emotions as A Physiological Phenomena.

1. Emotions As conscious Awareness

Mostly the emotions have been described as "stirred up" states of consciousness, a description undoubtedly often accurate. The expressions "up in the air", "lose one's head," "Out of control", "go to pieces", reflect the confusion often involved in emotional states. To support the above hypothesis William James held that the perception of one's bodily state constitutes emotion—that emotion is the way the body feels. This is the famous Jame-Lange theory of the emotions. In the words of James "we feel sorry because we cry, angry because we strike, flee because we tremble." In other words, it can be said that when the body is stirred up, our conscious awareness of these changes is also stirred up or confused.

The emotions are not always disruptive. Feats of strength and endurance performed under strong emotional stress, though tales of them are often exaggerated, do happen, and they show clearly the facilitating and bolstering effects which an emotion may have. For instance, students report that they do better in examinations when excited but not unduly apprehensive.

Emotions do not appear to be genuinely disruptive unless they are very strong and are initiated suddenly and without warning, and even then their disruptive effect is mostly at the outset. After the first shock, a strong emotion may be a help rather than a hindrance.

The emergency theory of emotions of Cannon an eminent psychologist points out that strong emotions such as fear and anger, have an emergency character in that they prepare the organism to fight or flee. Among animals and primitive people such defensive preparation often means the difference between survival and death. In modern life strong, unpleasant emotions may well be of service in the same way, but they ordinarily begin and end without physical exertion. We are often angry but are seldom forced actually to fight, often fearful but seldom forced actually to nun.

2. Emotions as Observable Behaviour

In order to study the genetic aspect of emotions, we need to study, the openly expressed emotional behaviour which usually begins with young children, before training and social pressures tuning to modify response patterns. For instance, the behaviour of the baby is at first largely in the nature of mass activity—a general excitement (threshing with the arms and legs, cooing and gurgling), from which specific elements of behaviour later become detached. Early experimental studies led child psychologists to conclude that there are three basic emotions:

(1) Fear, brought on by loud noises, hurtful stimuli (Pinches), loss of support;

(2) Affectionate or love responses, initiated by petting, fondling, and striking the sensitive zones of the body; and

(3) Rage or anger, arising when the child's activities are interfered with

or restrained. Some Psychologist believe that in addition to these three basic emotions we need to add further the emotion of Joy and grief. Thus, these five basic emotions are called as "Primary emotions" because they appear early in life, the stimuli which evoke them are relatively simple and dependable, and they are found in behaviour designed to lead to goal.

Studies on young children have demonstrated that, though the Primary emotions may be basically innate, their response patterns are by no means regular and invariable. Trained observers were shown motion pictures of babies reacting to hunger, a sudden dropping, physical restraint, being pricked with a needle, and so on. The stimuli themselves were not seen by the observers, only the responses of the child. Under these conditions, hunger was often called anger, and anger, fear. It was clear to the observer that the child's experience was decidedly unpleasant, but it was not at all clear just what emotion was being expressed. When these observers were shown the situations or occasions which led to the responses, their judgment was much improved. This means that we infer a child's (or an adult's) emotional state (for example, Joy or grief) from what we anticipate will happen under the circumstances rather than from actual observed behaviour.

This aspect of emotional expression indicates that emotional responses of an individual are observable under certain set conditions. The expected emotional responses are repeatable provided the stimuli remains the same. These emotional responses differ time to time in different forms such as fear, anger, Jealousy, Joy, Mirth, love etc. The difference in the expression of different emotions is observable with respect to variation in stimuli.

3. Emotions as Physiological Phenomena

You know the conscious awareness of an emotion is marked by disturbance, confusion, and at the same time the body is also upset or agitated. Common physical manifestations of emotions are trembling, tingling of the skin, tension in the muscles of the body and face, dilation of the pupils, and increased pulse and breathing rate. The skin turns pale or fiery red and may break out in a "cold sweat". Are there regular and measurable physiological patterns of body response which are characteristic of a given emotion? Or is the organic response much like the observable behaviour—namely, one of the general agitation, the specific emotion not being readily identified? In studying bodily upset, the physiologists uses the methods of expression to reveal and measure psychological changes. The main purpose of such measurement is to relate organic responses to the conscious report of emotion.

In many laboratory studies delicate instruments have been utilized to record the physiological upset caused by emotion—inducing stimuli. Records of breathing, pulse rate, blood pressure, and skin sensitivity during emotional stimulation may be obtained by means of the pneumograph, sphygmomograph, spygmometer, and galvanometer. The pneumograph consists of a coiled spring within a sealed rubber tube which can be strapped about the subject's chest. Rhythmic contractions of the chest in breathing cause the tube to stretch and relax. These changes are transmitted through a small rubber tube to a writing point or are electrically recorded.

Studying emotions in a variety of situations, some decidedly unpleasent, have been set up in an effort to induce genuine emotional states. The stimuli include sudden electrical shocks, loud noise, being told sexy stories of viewing sexy motion pictures, being thrown backward in specially devised chair, being forced to cut up frogs, decapitate rats, or go without food, and being angrily denounced by the experimenter.

Under these conditions, the subject presents a picture of general body upset—but no pattern of response with regularly characterizes reported emotional state. When the emotion is strong and unpleasant, as in case of anger or fear, pulse and breathing rate increase in rate and amplitude and both become irregular, the blood pressure goes up, stomach contractions (of digestion) decreases or stop entirely, the mouth goes dry, and there is muscular tremor. Soldiers who have experienced fear in combat give a report of general body agitation but no invariable response. The percentages of men reporting various physical manifestations differ from emotion to emotion. Besides, when the reported emotion is pleasant, as in love or joy, the body upset is less drastic and there is greater variation from person to person. In other words, the emotions effects the physiological functions of our body. The study of physiological responses resulting to cause emotional expression explains the physiological phenomena of emotions.

IV.5 Theories of Emotions

Strongman (1973) is of the view that the psychology of emotion has about twenty different approaches to understand the complex process of emotion. The general approach involves an aroused bodily state and a subjective feeling. Some theories elaborate emotions as the bodily changes that occur in emotions, while others focus on their subjective aspects. Keeping the difference of approaches in explaining the complex phenomena of emotions, it would be more advisable, if we classify the concepts into a limited number of approaches for convenience and better understanding. Keeping the above rationale in view. The theories of emotions are stated as under:

James-Lange Classical Theory of Emotions

James-Lange theory is quite opposite to the popular view-point—that is, if we see a tiger in the Jungle, after seeing the tiger we run in terror and fear. This theory explain, the phenomena in a different way. That is on seeing the tiger the autonomic nervous system comes into play and the effectors make us run. This running makes us afraid of the tiger. In other words, it is not that we run because we are afraid but we are afraid because we run. The physical changes precede the emotional experiences. It is the awareness of the physical changes which is called an emotional experience.

Specifically the classical theory of emotions can be explained when we say that emotions are the result of messages one receives from bodily changes while reacting to emotion producing aspects of environment. James (1980) states that "we feel sorry because we cry, angry because we strike, afraid because we tremble." In brief, the cardinal point of this theory is that the physiological changes do take place first and then one experiences the emotions. This may be diagramatically shown as under:

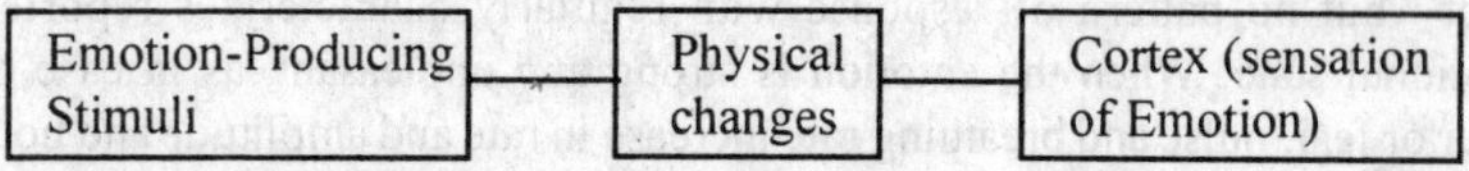

Criticism of James- Lange Theory

The James-Lange theory has not been supported by experiments. They are of the view that if theory is correct, specific emotion should follow a unique pattern of physiological changes. Physiological changes associated with Joy, for example, should have a different pattern from any other emotion such as despair. But most emotions seem to be accompanied by the same general pattern. Besides, same person shows different pattern of bodily changes while experiencing same emotion at two different occasions. James-Lange Theory could not hold its applicability as Cannon and his co-workers prepared cats—in which the sympathetic system was cut along the whole length of the spinal cord. Such animals thus cannot feel, yet they showed the signs of outword anger, when provoked through snarls hissing etc. This experiment thus striked at the very basis of James-Lange theory. Besides, we also find many cases in whom the expression of emotions is impossible due to paralysis and yet these patients/people feel emotions.

Cannon Bard Theory of Emotions

Cannon-Bard Theory is also known as emergency theory of emotions. Walter Cannon and his colleague Bard conducted various experiments on animals, mostly on dogs and cats, in order to find out centre of emotions in the brain. They removed certain areas of the brain and tried to find out how the absence of these specific areas affect the emotional experiences. During their experiments they found that the removal of cortical centres did not hinder much in the basic emotional responses but if the hypothalamus was interfered the animal was not able to show emotional reactions. Meaning thereby, that hypothalamus is the seat of emotions.

In other words, the theory advocates that the perception of external stimuli arouses the hypothalamus which in turn, simultaneously generates bodily changes and stimulates the cortex to produce the feeling of emotions. This way this theory tells nothing about any supposed stimulation by the bodily changes.

This theory further believes that neither the subjective experience nor the physiological reaction to a stimulus causes the other; instead, they are produced simultaneously as the nerve impulse from the thalamus which goes to the cerebral cortex causing the subjective experience of emotion and the other portion goes to the effectors resulting in physiological changes. This theory can schematically be presented as under:

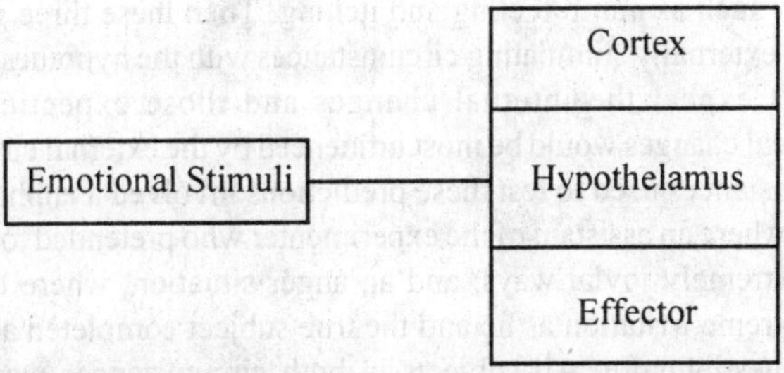

Criticism of Cannon-Bard Theory

Cannon-Bard Theory has the criticism of its inability to explaining the reason why the individual emotional responses differ when the emotions emerges from hypothalamus. Besides, this theory in most of human cases can not satisfy the results obtained on animal studies.

Cognition Theory of Emotions

Stanlay Schacter theory is also called as the Cognition theory. This theory is also known as arousal-cognition theory. This theory was given by Stanley Schachter (1971) which points out that emotions are generally physiologically similar and tend to vary along a weak-strong dimension that is determined by the level of arousal. The lablel we attribute to an emotion depends on our cognitive appraisal of the situation, we are in such appraisal involves recognition of external events and the ways in which others in the same situation appear to be responding.

In the arousal-cognition theory, it has been suggested that various states of arousal are labelled as per our knowledge or cognition of the emotion-producing situation. Experiences are labelled as anger or fear depending upon how we perceive, the circumstances of arousal. Suppose, for example, that an individual at one time narrowly escapes falling from a high building and at another time unexpectedly receives a very large sum of money. The two situations produce aroused states which are physiologically similar. In the case of the near fall, the individual may think of his injury or death and label his aroused state "fear"; he may label his feeling upon receiving the money as "Joy" or "happiness."

Another experiment offered support of cognitive theory in which male college students were injected with epinephrin, an adrenal hormone which induces an aroused state. Some subjects were informed that the usual effects of this injection include trembling hands, pounding heart, and a flushed face. The other subjects were told nothing about these reactions, believing the injuction to contain vitamin compound, the effects of which would be tested at a later date. Still a third group, was led to expect symptoms which would not appear, such as numb feeling and itching. Then these three groups were exposed to externally stimulating circumstances with the hypotheses that those who didn't expect the internal changes and those expecting different physiological changes would be most influenced by the external circumstances. The circumstances used to test these predictions involved a euphoric (happy) condition, where an assistant of the experimenter who pretended to be a subject acted in extremely jovial ways, and an anger situation, where the assistant showed extreme irritation as he and the true subject completed an insulating personal questionnaire. All subjects in both circumstances were observed through a one-way mirror and after the experiment they were questioned about their feelings during the incident.

Both the observations and self-reports indicates that the subjects without expectations about the physiological reactions to the injection were more susceptible to the assistant mood then the informed subjects. Furthermore, subjects with erroneous expectations were more susceptible to the circumstances created by the assistant experimenters having no expectation of their body states, have readily noticed, the mood which the assistant portrayed. These results were in essential agreement with the predictions, supported the basic hypothesis of the arousal-cognition theory.

The view of arousal-cognition theory has been supported in which the aroused state occured naturally rather than through drugs. All the subjects in one experiment received a place before an electric shock, but one group was told that tremors and heart palpitation would result from the pill. Both groups were naturally aroused by the shock and showed the symptoms just described, but the experimental subjects, believing that the state was induced by the pill, tolerated more electric shock than the controlled group of subjects and reported the shock as less painful. The results indicated that the emotional state was determined by both physiological arousal and the individual's interpretation of the situation.

In conclusion, the theories of emotion cited here range from the classical view points in psychology, presented forty to eighty five years ago, to the products of recent laboratory investigations. Our description indicate that contemporary views have received fairly intensive study. Neverthless, we are far from a full understanding of emotion, even with respect to brain localization.

IV.6 Types of Emotions

There are number of emotions which can be categorized into two types, the primary and secondary emotions. A child right from his early childhood develops primary emotions which are essential for our life and those emotions are:

1. Fear

Watson J.B. studied a large number of infants and found that originally infants are afraid of only two things, loud sounds and lack of support. Watson further points out that other fears are learned and acquired in the course of experience. For instance, an infant's pillow falls and he is frightened. If he is in a dark room the fear will be transferred to darkness, if he is alone fear will be transferred to loneliness. Loud sounds made when there is a cat or dog nearby makes the child fear cats or dogs. Most of our fears are acquired in this way, and from cats and dogs children begin to fear all furry animals like rats, rabbits. People are afraid of high places, snakes, lightening, of ridicule, disgrace and insults, of financial loss and failure. All these fears they have learned in the social and cultural environment in which they live.

Fear responses are marked by withdrawal and shrinking. Children may take to flight and adults may withdraw in fear. Children run and hide themselves when they see a bear, a policeman or a dog. A grown-up person may avoid attending a function or a party if he or she fears that people will not accept him or her or will laugh or poke fun at him or her. Fear of failure in examination or profession may make a person turn away from it.

2. Anger

Anger is a strong emotion which is caused by any type of obstruction, restraint or injury, and the person moves to strike or injure the source of that obstruction. Children get angry when parents interfere with their activity or force them to do things which they do not like. For many of them anger pays and by becoming angry they are able to make their parents agree to their demands. Grown-up young people get angry when they are teased, ridiculed, punished or unfavourably compared, and instead of hitting back they may criticize parents and teachers disobey them or develop a hostile attitude to all authority. Anauge makes a person sulky, quarrelsome and negative. Grown-up people may express their anger with their family because they cannot do it in the office. Such displaced anger is common in the lives of all of us.

3. Wonder

Wonder as an emotion makes one excited by anything new, strange or unusual and the individual is impelled to know more about it, to explore and discover its nature. Children break things to find out what is inside, older children ask questions to discover and explore things. Older people have goals and purposes which lead them to acquire more knowledge and when their interest and curiosity about nature weakens they are unduly curious about the personal affairs of others.

4. Joy

Joy is an undifferentiated emotion and we all seek pleasure, excitement and happiness without having any precise idea of what we want. Children seek pleasure in activity itself and indulge in all kinds of play just for the fun of being active. Emotion of joy in older people is observable as laughter which may be excited by a large variety of situations from the bizarre to funny. We try to prolong our delightful moments. Some pleasure may result from vigorous activity and some pleasure accompanies a state of relaxation and rest. Mountain climbing gives us pleasure and so does just reclining and dozing off after lunch.

Importance of Emotions

1. Emotions are the Prime Movers of Behaviour

Emotions are described as the prime movers of behaviour, these stirred-up states are store houses of energy which may work for both intense vigour and efficiency and strong disruption of mental life. Very often the story of a successful man is the story of effective and satisfactory emotional adjustments as that of an unsuccessful man is of gross mismanagement. Some very highly intelligent people fail because of their raw and disorganized emotions and some people of mediocre brains are able to get along because they are able to manage their emotions effectively and harmoniously. Therefore, significance of emotions cannot be ignored.

2. Emotions are Funds of Energy

The Emotions are funds of energy and prepare the organism for some emergency. The several organic and bodily changes have a purpose that they make the organism ready to meet the challenge of new situations. In the grip of strong emotions people have performed Herculean tasks which under normal conditions they could not handle. But modern civilized living does not need such energy-releasing aspects of emotions, and too much emotion and violent expression and behaviour may land us in trouble. Emotional gestures in anger, fear or love make for better adjustment in social situations. Angry sniffs help to intimidate, smiles help to ingratiate and the like.

3. Emotional Excitement Stimulates Bodily and Mental Activity.

The individual begins to think more rapidly and of other ways of meeting the situation. But though emotions stimulate the quantity of thinking they do not improve the quality of thinking. Emotions do not make thinking more trustworthy nor do they help better understanding which is the result of intelligent and logical approach to a situation. Emotions have a great value in liberating us from inhibitions. A slow and quiet person when roused to anger may act very energetically and quickly. That is why modern education insists on developing and expressing emotions rather than checking and controlling them

4. Intense Emotional Tenstion Impairs Adjustment

Emotions may be a great obstacle and handicap to adjustment. In the grip of emotions many adults behave like children, they break down and childish ways reappear. Emotions smother intelligence and confuse our understanding, they weaken our skill and obstruct close co-ordination between different parts and functions of the body. Sometimes intense organic changes instead of giving energy paralyse the organism for any activity. Many people become powerless to act in the grip of fear and anger. Many emotional responses last much longer and continue to thwart us for the rest of our lives. Many grown-up people are not able to get over their dread of the headmaster acquired in school days. Our phobias and fears, loves and hates continue in life and hamper adjustments.

5. Emotions are the Asset of our Behaviour

Emotions are the great asset of human behaviour. The emotions can be used to advantage or disadvantage of one's behaviour. Emotion helps the individual to enable him/her to manage relations effectively.

IV.7 Effects of Emotions and Behaviour

Emotions are the stirred up condition of human behaviour which influence our behaviour. You know that there are positive and negative types of emotions. The positive emotions viz, Joy, delight, love, affection etc., have one type of effect on the Physiology and Psychology of man. Similarly, negative emotions also effects the Physiology and Psychology of an individual. In this connection, it can be said that each type of emotion has its effect on human physique. Therefore, these bodily changes have, in fact, been widely investigated. By the nature of the problem, most of these investigations are properly conducted in the physiological laboratory. Some of the bodily expressions can, however, be profitably included in the investigation of the behavioural and judgmental components of emotional reactions. Most important changes due to emotional reactions have been reported are respiratory changes, changes in blood pressure and heart rate, and changes in the resistance of the skin which have been frequently measured in psychological studies of emotion such as:

1. Respiratory Changes

Emotional responses and reactions results two important phases of the respiratory cycle which are known as the inhalation and the exhalation of air. The temporal sequence of inspiration and expiration is described in Fig. 1. Inspiration is typically characterized by a rapid intake of air and is followed by more gradual expiration. Both the relative amplitude and the relative duration of these two aspects of the breathing cycle have been used in quantitative investigations. The amplitude refers, of course, to the height of the curve in Fig. 1. The temporal aspect has been quantified by the ratio of duration of inspiration to duration of expiration. This ratio, *I/E*, is called the inspiration-expiration ratio.

A device to record the durations of inspiration and expiration is called a pneumograph. This instrument consists simply of a rubber tube fastened around the chest of the experimental subject. This tube, through an airtight joint, continues to a small chamber of air. Stretched across this chamber is a rubber diaphragm. Movements of this diaphragm cause a lever to record on a revolving drum the rise and fall of the subject's chest. The combination of rubber diaphragm, attached lever, and chamber of air is known as a *tambour*. The lever is caused to move by chest movements because the system is an airtight one. The sensitivity of the *I/E* ratio can be demonstrated in many a variety of situations. Many sudden or tension-producing stimuli cause us to "catch our breath" and thus alter the *I/E* ratio. Similarly, an unexpected loud sound, a threat, the expectation of a noxious stimulus-all these produce measurable changes in the breathing cycle.

2. Changes in Blood Pressure

The emotional reactions are most commonly related to the problem of behaviour, behavioural reaction etc. therefore, the variations in blood pressure have often been reported as characteristic of emotional reactions.

Measurements of blood pressure are made by means of a sphygmomanometer. This instrument, shown in Fig. 2, consists of an inflatable rubber bag which is fitted around the subject's upper arm. This bag is connected to one side of a U-shaped tube which contains mercury. The upper portion of the other side of the U is evacuated. When the bag is inflated, it exerts a pressure in the U tube which causes the mercury to rise in the evacuated side. This pressure is increased until it exceeds that of the blood. In this way, the blood stops flowing through the artery.

Usually, changes in the systolic pressure are measured in emotional situations. The most general statement which can be made is that systolic pressure tends to rise during excitement. Our previous statement that specific bodily changes show little or no correlation with specific emotional situations certainly holds true in the case of blood pressure. Changes have been recorded in a large variety of experiments. It is not possible to state what specific emotional characteristics of a situation determine a rise in blood pressure.

3. Changes in Skin Resistance

Among the most widely investigated bodily expressions in emotional situations are changes in the electrical resistance of the skin. This change in the skin can be assessed by passing a weak current through the skin, it is possible to measure the level of skin resistance and the changes in this resistance.

For the purpose of measuring skin resistance, two electrodes (usually consisting of flat metal disks) are strapped to the subject's hand or to some other convenient part of the body. Although different types of instrumentation have been used, two items are essential: a source of current and a device for measuring resistance. Fig. 3 gives a schematic diagram illustrating the basic method of measurement. In Fig.3 the source of current is the battery, B. The circle indicates the subject's hand, and the e's the electrodes attached to it.

In brief, the tentative volts and accommodation helps to understand the passage oof electirc current helps in developing a method of assessment.

As our description of the apparatus has indicated, two types of measurement are made: measures of the general level of resistance and measures of rapid changes. As Fig. 3 shows, at the beginning of an experimental session, the skin resistance has a relatively high value. As the experimental session progresses and the subject becomes more apprehensive about the purpose of the electrodes, his resistance level less and less (Day 1). In the case of the experiment in which Fig. 3 was obtained, a "ready" signal was given near the end of the 6th minute and was then followed by a loud noise. The heightened expectancy induced by the "ready" signal and the startle caused by the loud noise resulted in a further rapid decline in resistance. That the subject becomes adapted in this situation is indicated by the curves for a subsequent day of the experiment. Fig 2, then, illustrates relatively slow changes in the level of skin resistance.

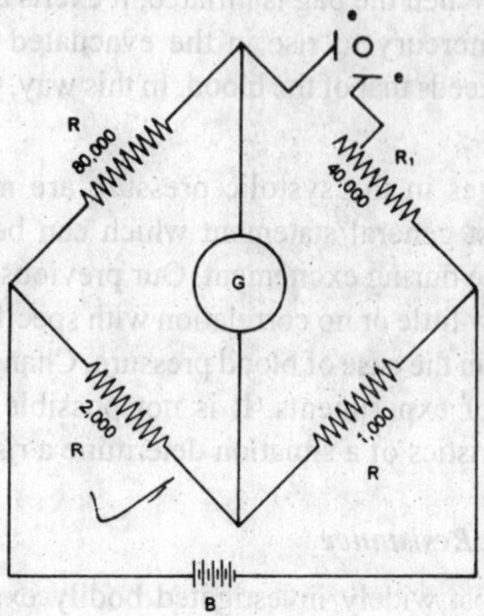

Fig. 2. Schematic Diagram of Apparatus used in the Measurement of the Galvanic Skin Response. B, battery; R, resistor; R_1, variable resistor; G, galvanometer; e, electrode; O, subject.

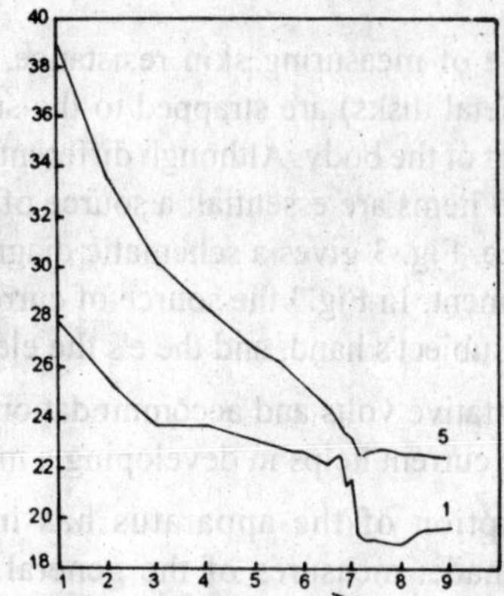

Fig. 3. Changes in Skin Resistance Observed During Experimental Sessions in which Startle Was Evoked by Means of a Loud Noise. As the session progresses and the subject's expectancy is building up, the skin resistance is lowered and drops further when the "ready" signal and finally the noise itself are given. The difference between the lower curve (day 1 of the experiment) and the upper curve (day 5 of the experiment) show the effects of adaptation to the situation. (After R. C. Davis, Modification of the galvanic reflex by daily repetition of a stimulus, *J. Exper Psychol.*, 1934, 17:510, by permission of the journal and the American Psychological Association.)

The more rapid change c in resistance which can be readily related to the presence of certain stimuli is known as the *galvanic skin response* (GSR). The more rapid change after the "ready" signal and in the presence of the loud sound represents such a GSR (Fig.4, Day 1). Such deflections may be elicited by a variety of stimuli. Electric shocks and loud noises are uniformly effective. The more general rule is that unexpected stimulation, even though not intense, results in the GSR. The more intense stimuli, however, elicit the GSR with higher frequency and with greater amplitude. The readiness with which the GSR can be elicited by a large variety of stimuli means that it cannot be used to distinguish one emotional situation from another.

Emotions and Facial Expressions

The effect of emotions can easily be understood by making facial expression derive. Facial expression derives its special importance from the fact that it is a sign of emotion continually used and reacted to in social relations. Experimental investigations have been addressed to two classes of problems: (1) Are specific facial expressions correlated with specific emotional situations, and (2) how well can individuals judge emotions on the basis of facial expressions?

IV.8 Emotional Development and Teacher

The study of emotions is also very important and for a teacher as he has got special educational significance.

Education is also known as modification of behaviour. You know that the emotions are very strong source of energy causing action/behavioural actions. The teacher has to make use of this raw emotional energy. This energy can be trained. Experiments of Watson on children clearly showed that the emotional behaviour can be destroyed as well as created by the process of conditioning. Thus, the teacher needs to suppress some of the undesirable emotions while utilize their energy by sublimating them for the achievement of higher social ends. Emotions can easily be conditioned e.g. some toy can give both joy and fear.

Human personality has three main aspects: cognitive, affective and conative. These three aspects of personality correspond to the three main aims of education given by Plato—Truth, Beauty and Goodness (to appreciate, sense of appreciation or aesthetic sense) depends on emotional development. No person can have a healthy body without well trained emotions. Thus, to develop harmonious personality of children, there is a need to make use of the good emotions and to sublimate the others. Emotions by themselves are no evil.

IV.9 Instincts and Emotions

An instinct is a negative tendency which is responsible for more or less fixed type of behaviour. As instincts are innate and given by nature, they form the basis of human behaviour. The whole future personality or character is built upon this initial equipment. These innate tendencies come into contact with environmental forces and are modified. The wholesome or unwholesome personality depends as to how the instincts are organised and adjusted in the life situations.

The word 'INSTINCT' has been loosely used in popular language and is associated with animals and considered as very low mode of behaviour. In laymans terms, instincts are nothing but very simple and mechanical patterns of human behaviour. Instincts are nothing but compound reflex action. No doubt, the instincts are innate and are the foundations of future behaviour, yet they are so simple as those of reflex action. Moreover, they are not mechanical because human being is not a machine. It is self-active organism which makes its own goal and acts depending upon one's own inner urge. His thoughts and actions are motivated by certain dispositions which are innate and are known as instincts.

Defination of Instinct

Instinct has been defined by different psychologists in different ways. According to Loyd Morgan instinctive behaviour has four characteristic features. It involves:

(i) The performance of complex traits of activity, engaging the whole organism;

(ii) Instincts are of biological value to the species;

(iii) Instincts are similarly performed by all members of the species, and

(iv) Instincts do not have to be learnt.

Instincts are performed perfectly or at least adequately at the first attempt.' Lloyd Morgan put this definition in 1896. It refers to the instinctive behaviour of animals, birds and instincts rather than of man. But human instincts differ very widely from animal's instincts. The definition given by Lloyd Morgan is supplemented by the definition given by W.Mc Dougall. His definition is particularly true in connection with the human instincts. According to Mc Dougall "An instinct is an inherited or innate psychophysical disposition which determines its possessor to perceive, and to pay attention to objects or ideas of certain class, to experience, on emotional excitement of a particular quality upon perceiving such an object and to act in regard to it in a particular manner or at least to experience an impulse to such action."

The analysis of the above definitions makes us to understand as under:

Firstly 'instinct is not acquired but it is inborn disposition or mental structure which is responsible for a specific action. It is neither purely mental nor purely physical. It involves both mind and body. Thus, it is psycho-physical in its nature.

Secondly, the above definition states that in the presence of an instinct, we undergo three types of distinct experiences. The first experience is mental. Here we perceive or know an object or idea. We see or hear something and give it to meaning. We are aware of a certain situation or an object and attend to it. Perception of the situation results into an affective experience. Here feelings and emotions are aroused and a particular type of excitement is experienced.

Lastly, we do or feel like to do some activity. It stimulates for some action. So in the above definition, there are three experiences in an instinctive behaviour:

1. Cognition 2. Affection. 3. Conation.

They are three main aspects of personality as cognition means to know or get knowledge, affection stands for feelings, sentiments, emotions and sense of appreciation. Conation means to do or strive.

The above explanation of the definition of an instinct will become more clear from this example. It is instinctive behaviour to escape or run away from a dangerous situation which destroys the very life of organism. On seeing a tiger the individual will be frightened and try hard to save his life. Seeing the tiger is cognition. Here the object is perceived and attended to and meanings are attached for its complete comprehension. As the individual finds that tiger is approaching towards him, he will undergo an emotional excitement. There is fear and the individual is frightened. The fear will have to lead to some action. Naturally the individual will do something to save him from the dangerous animal. He may hide himself under something, run away or face the tiger with his gun. These are conative experiences.

Nature of Instinct

The nature of instincts can be studied primary as under :

Instinct is purposeful direction. It is not vague in its action; it is meaningful. It represents the inner urge of an individual. Essentially, instincts fulfil the biological aims of life and have played important role in the evolution of life; as the purposeful and useful experiences are handed over to the next generation, in order to march towards goal.

Instincts is a natural tendency. It is inherited; it is not acquired. The instincts are not extremely rigid. Proper education and training can change their paths and modify them for higher social ends. They are known as racial habits.

Instincts are universal. They are present in all the human beings. They are even present in higher animals which are near man on the scale of evolution. All human beings have got them. But all instincts may not be at the same level of development. In some people, some instincts are more prominent and in others, other instincts are more marked. Even the level of development of all the instincts is not uniform or same in the one and the same individual. Social and moral environment plays an important part in their development. All the instincts are not present at all age levels. Some of the instincts are missing in children such as sex instinct.

Instinct is a psycho-physical disposition. It involves both mind and body. Instinctive behaviour is mental as well as physical.

Intincts are full of power and strength. As it is innate and may be centuries old, therefore it is very forceful. Its power may be compared with that of flood water. The whole of it cannot be suppressed and repressed. Its energy is raw and can be usefully converted into higher social ends.

Instinctive behaviour is permanent. It cannot be abolished altogether.

The secondary nature of the instincts is purposive. The purposive nature of instinct can be studied as under:

Self-presentation. Instinct is a purposeful tendency. It stands to achieve some interest. As instincts are basic tendencies, therefore, they are associated with basic interest. The first and foremost need of a living organism is to exist in the world. It is the life urge which is the basic and most strong. It is the inner urge to continue one's life. So, the first purpose of instinct is to safeguard the interest of life to save the life from the danger and to overcome the difficulties of life by adjusting with stresses and strains. So most of the instincts of an individual stand for this vital purpose. All such instinctive acts of animals such as the migration of birds, hibernation of frogs, withdrawing from enemies, are in the interest of self-preservation or preservation of species.

Race-preservation. The second main interest of an organism is to preserve one's species. It is, why the sex-instinct is a very strong one. Mating even in very low animals affords its example. Freudian theory of Psycho-analysis puts much emphasis on this natural urge.

Social living. Besides, the above mentioned two biological purposes of instincts in human beings, they are also beneficial for social behaviour. Gregarious instinct or herd instinct is very prominent in some of the animals such as sheep. Human being is bestowed with social instinct, which is the basis of all social rules and regulations and socially acceptable patterns of behaviour. The social instincts in children can be successfully used in making them good social beings.

Classification of Instincts

The widely accepted classification of instincts was given by Mc Dougall. He enlists as many as 14 instincts and gives corresponding emotions. The details of of few instincts are given:

Table Instincts & Emotions

No.	*Name of Instinct*	*Corresponding Emotion*
1.	Escape	Fear
2.	Combat (pugnacity)	Anger
3.	Repulsion	Disgust

IV.10 Role of Emotions in Life

Emotions add colours to our life. Adequate training of emotion develops maturity. Inadequate maturity of emotions effect the Psychological, Physiological and social dimension of our life. Therefore, we can study the effect of emotions in our life as under :

1. Emotions and Physical Health. Physical health is greatly affected by emotions. Because of emotional stimulation ductless glands become quick. Heart beating increases, along with the rate of respirations. Nerves get tense. Due to anger and fear our digestion is affected. Fear causes nervousness and confusion. Love and joy accelerate digestion and promote health.

2. Speech. Prolonged emotional strain may cause stammering. The cause of stammering of many children is their emotionality.

3. Attitude of timidity or of aggression may result from an emotional strain or frustration.

4. Learning. Emotional distress and frustration interfere with learning efficiency. On the other hand, joy, hope, encouragement, feeling of worth whileness and satisfaction at achievement help the student to concentrate better on the studies. Pleasant emotions, motivate learning. It is said that nothing succeeds like success. One's feeling of achievement gives rise to stimulation for better work. To be successful adds zest to living and affords emotional stimulation towards further successful achievement.

5. Emotion and social life. A person with good temper, moderate emotions control over anger is liked by all. He makes friends and wins social applause. Temper and temperament affect the social life of a person.

6. Emotions and social life. Situations may not be happy for each child. But the child who does not feel much frustrated, is able to adjust somehow to the unhealthy environment also. Emotional neurotics are the maladjusted pupils, and they become delinquents and problem children.

7. Emotions and mental health. It has been observed that same situation can arouse different degrees of emotions in different persons. Those who worry much, feel greatly frustrated, or rage in fury, disturb their own mental health. Persons who cannot control their emotions become neurotics and develop anxiety, hysteria, schizophrenia, mania, obsression and other mental diseases. If children are not guided properly to check their emotions, they develop excessive fears, anxiety, complexes and mental conflicts. All the exponents of the school of psycho-analysis attach great importance to the emotional experiences of children. Often the conflicts and complexes harboured in childhood also. Control over emotions is essential for mental health. Mental health needs peace, joy and self-satisfaction. Blessed is the person who can stand the stresses and strains of life. Modern life has become so complex that at every step we encounter unpleasant situations that may arouse unpleasant emotions and thus disturb our mental health. Hence, we crave for peace and calmness. One of the best means of controlling emotions and getting peace is religion.

8. Emotional maturity. One of the objectives of education is assistance to maturity. Besides, intellectual maturity, emotional maturity is very important for successful living. Every child must be made to lead to have consistantly in emotions, and to form definite attitudes.

It is not uncommon to find an adult with in consistency of emotional behaviour, who is nicknamed as childish. An emotional behaviour is indicative of maturity of a person. Emotional inmaturity is exemplified in a number of response patterns *e.g.,* attention getting, relationalisation, protection, and day-dreaming. Only those who out-grow such modes of behaviour are well-adjusted and socially competent men. Emotions are called the raw-material of character. They are the dynamic of all our actions and the teacher must take account of them.

IV.11 Training of Emotions

Emotions are the hidden energies in an organism. Appropriate regulation of energies helps to prove productive. To channelise energies of emotion effectively and productive requires training . The emotional forces of an organism can be controlled and regulated by training for the following reasons:

Personality Development. Emotions ought to be trained for various reasons: *(a)* Extreme emotionality injures the personality of the child. It disturbs the mental equilibrium. To have a balanced personality it is necessary that the individual ought to have control over his emotions. *(b)* a free play of emotions cannot be permitted by the society, *(c)* children are more emotional than grown up adults. If we want the child to have a balanced personality, then we should try to control the emotions in the early years of the child.

Repression of Emotions. Training of instincts may be applied for training of emotions. Repression of emotions will lead to mental disorders. Repressed fear may lead to some mental disease. Inhibition is not the remedy for training emotions.

Expression of Emotions. We should encourage children to express their emotions. If he is not allowed to express, the child comes to have a mental load. Consequently opportunities ought to be provided to him to express and satisfy his pent-up emotions. The training of emotions may start at a later stage.

Sublimation of Emotions. Sublimation is the best method of training emotions. They must be redirected to healthier channels. The emotion of fear in darkness may be removed by allowing the child to go to such places with the parents. For instance, the emotion of lust of a widow may be transferred towards the worship of God.

Mental Occupation. The children ought to be kept busy in some work. This will give them very little time for a free outlet of their emotions. It has been correctly said that an empty mind is a devil's workshop. Some activity will keep his observation, memory, imagination and the reasoning of the child well engaged. When the brain and the central nervous system are busy there is no scope for vulgar emotions to get a chance for their expression.

Catharsis. Children cannot always remain serious. There ought to be provision in the school for children to enjoy and to express freely their emotions, *e.g.*, festivals, fairs and social functions, etc.

IV.12 Emotional Maturity and Teacher

The teacher is a hero for children. Children imitate him. Therefore, a teacher needs to have an emotional balance and stability. A balanced state of emotions of a teacher will have a healthy influence on children.

A teacher should allow expressions of emotions by children. If they are excessive, he should not lose patience and should try to redirect them.

A teacher should teach to the pupils correct methods of appreciating the beauty of nature and works of art. The children ought to be encouraged by him to produce works of art.

The teacher should try to create a healthy atmosphere in the school. It should be one of sympathy and affection so that the child may feel secure and may not develop inferiority complex. He should look upon himself as an honourable individual capable of doing something worthwhile.

Emotions are of great value to the teacher. He can always appeal to the higher emotions of the child and make life worth living.

The heightened emotions of the child may lead him to do some creative work. The teacher should therefore, try to arouse worthy emotions of the child.

Strong emotions may improve the personality of the child. They may break down some other undesirable emotions.

The teacher while teaching should keep in view, the extent to which the emotionality of children can go and should adjust his behaviour accordingly.

Balanced growth of emotions leads to the formation of good character. Education should develop a fine pattern of emotions in the child.

IV.13 Learning Exercises

1. Describe the meaning and nature of emotion.
2. Discuss the development of emotions.
3. Explain role of teacher for balanced development of emotions.
4. Discuss different theories of emotions.
5. Describe different types of emotions.
6. Describe the effects of emotion on human behaviour.
7. What is instinct. How instincts differ from emotions?
8. Discuss the role of teacher inculca to emotional maturity.

V

Memory and Forgetting

In everyday speech we use the term "remember" in two different ways. We speak, the term on one hand, of remembering names or dates (i.e. word memories), and on the other, remembering how to ice-skate after a summer vacation or how to drive a car after an interval of ten years. While these two usages seem quite different (the first being verbal and the second muscular), functionally they cover essentially the same phenomenon viz; both describe the revival or reinstatement of certain responses acquired at an earlier time, meaning thereby that responses acqúired earlier are not obliterated from the mind with the passage of time but, rather, they remain in the mind permanently, at the sub-conscious stage and they come to the conscious level whenever they are needed or when there is the relevant context. The phenomenon of revival of previous knowledge and skills by an organism gives an impression of some power within our mind which guides our life to recollect, recognise people, places and things due to memory.

V.1 Meaning and Nature of Memory

The term memory involves several mental activities like recall,, recognition or retention. As a common experience we see indication of memory all around us. For instance, a person experiences ease in re-learning an activity which he had learnt earlier but had forgotten. This process proves very obviously that the previous learning had not been wiped out completely but had left an impression on the mind or a chance in the nerves which indicates re-learning. As an experience people do not completely forget the story of any movie they had seen but recount it with ease when they are requested to do so by a friend. If someone else takes on the tedious task of telling the story of the same film, they affirm it because they are reminded of it and if they hear any one from the film played anywhere they are easily reminded of that tool. Therefore, it indicates that there is retention, recall and recognition in the memory of a persons perceived experience, which make it a complete activity.

Woodworth describes that memory is often ascribed to the phenomena resulting from the retentive and reproductive function of the individual's mind. He further adds that we 'retain' the traces of past experiences for some time; and in many cases we can reproduce them with remarkable fidelity in the entire absence of the peripheral exciting conditions. In the same way we can notice, the phenomena of retentiveness in the physical material world "Impressions" or modifications imposed by the environment are often retained by the objects of mental organs that receive them. The retained impressions are easy to be reproduced because the process of retention, reproduction involves certain important mental activities viz, encoding, storage and re-travel process reflecting the memory. In brief, it can be said that memory is a complex phenomena of mental activities which enable an individual to receive messages in the verbal, non-verbal, symbolic form, through different sense organs to code, decode, store and retrieve the messages for cencious usage.

Nature of Memory

Memory is a complex mental activity effected by different mental processes such as:

a) Memory is a Physical Activity. Some Psychologists are of the view that memory is a physical activity, in the sense that experiences acquired by a person leaves impression on his/her mind, which are called memory traces. The memory traces are the basis of memory in the form of functional tendency. Because retention ends when these traces are wiped off. Besides, the psychologists have established by giving proofs that retention is a psychological process.

b) Memory is Psycho-physiological Activity. Bartlett, Piron and Libson advocate that memory is a mental activity independent of memory traces. To support this argument they have conducted experiments of stories and pictures, movies narrations. The results of these experiments shows that memory depends more on mental states like interest, motivation, basis etc., than on repetition of experience. This marks memory a mental activity. But just as every mental activity has psychological base, so memory has a psychological foundation. Meaning thereby that memory is a phsycho pysiological activity.

c) Memory as a Mental Process. As a common experience based on facts that memory proceeds from learning. Therefore, memory has certain psychological basis involving the following processes:

(1) Learning, (2) Retention, (3) Recall, and; (4) Recognition.

To understand the process of memory we need to know in detail the mental activities namely, the learning and retention because learning leads to recognition of acquired knowledge, experience and skills. It is also important for us to know that recall succeeds learning. Besides, learning and retention both recall and recognition are necessary for complete memory. Sometimes, recall takes place first which is followed by recognition. Therefore, in order to understand the memory as a process it would be worth to understand each activity involved in memory and it is described as under:

(i) Learning. Learning is a mental activity in which an individual acquires knowledge, experiences to derive principles to modify his behaviour. Thus, learning is a mental activity which make changes in the pattern of one's response by marking impressions on one's mind. These impressions developed by learning experience develops memory traces on one's mind on the basis of which recollection is effected.

(ii) Retention. Retention is another important mental activity to promote memory. By retention, we means making permanent the remains of experience. The remains of experiences are left on the mind in the form of memory traces. The retention involves the recollection, recognition and re-learning. Though recollection is a proof of memory, its absence is not the proof of absence of memory because a person often remembers something at a latter date which had eluded him at the earlier occasion. Same is the case with recognition because while its presence indicates memory, its absence is no proof that there is no memory. For instance, if we come face to face with a long separated friend and find ourselves unable to identify him, we cannot take this to mean that all the experiences related to that person have been obliterated from the memory because the next moment we might be astonished when at last, we succeed in identifying him. The most convincing proof of retention is furnished by re-learning in the absence of which retention cannot be accepted. If there is no progress in re-learning it will be concluded that there was no retention. After experiencing any thing the activity of its consolidation goes on for sometime. This is proved by the fact that a poem will linger for one time in one's brain for some time after one has learnt it, even though there is no effort to recall it. The students preparing for some examination would have experienced this activity.

(iii) Recall. The third mental activity involved in memory is recall. The recall is the activity by which the remains of experiences made permanent, are brought back to the conscious level. For instance, a student studies for his examination all the year round and a major part of his learning is present in a permanent and healthy state in his mind. While answering the question paper in the examination hall the student recalls this learning existing in the memory and puts it down in black and white. Though this recollection cannot be identical to the original learning, its matter resembles the original and a major part of the learning can be remembered in the same form if suitable efforts are made. Actually, recall is something novel and not just a more reproduction of the

past experience or perception. Inspite of the fact that it depends on retention, recollection is not fashioned entirely by it. It is not necessary that if retention is good, recollection will also be good.

(iv) Recognition. The fourth mental activity involved in understanding the process of memory is recognition. It has been observed that sometimes recognition comes before recall and sometime recall comes latter to recognition. For instance, when we recognise an old friend the moment we set eyes on him and then we are reminded of many things about him. On the other hand, if I am, travelling in a train and I am confronted with the embarrassing situation of some one asking me whether I had recognised him. I apologise doubtfully and confess my inability to recognise him. The person say," when ten years ago we lived in Srinagar, we were neighbours." And this statement starts a reaction, reminding me of my experiences of ten years ago. I then recognise the person, shake hands and start talking of this and that. The recognition is of two types viz, definite, indefinite recognition in which a person recognises a person, idea, thing or an experience exactly without any loss whereas, in indefinite recognition the things, experiences, ideas are recognised partially.

d) Memory as a Product. As discussed earlier that memory involves mental activities such as learning, recall, retention and recognition. All these mental activities work systematically in a cohesive manner. Therefore, memory can be studied as a product:

(i) Encoding Process, *(ii)* Storage Process and *(iii)* Retrieval Process.

(i) Encoding Process. Memory as an encoding process refers to the receiving of sensory inputs. All the informations that we receive are basically through one of the senses or through combination of some of them. When we listen to radio or lecture, the sensory input is in the form of sound or acoustic. We may read something and then the energy operates in light form and the input is visual. During the process of encoding some changes are made in the sensory input for facilitating the storage. So, the information is coded as well.

(ii) Storage. The storage process refers to the process of putting the coded information into memory. Unless the storage is proper, it would not be possible to get the information at a later period of time. The storage if done in a proper and systematic way—it would be easier to hold information for a longer period of time.

(iii) Retrieval. Later, when any information is acquired from the memory. The process of retrieval refers to the process by which is broadly similar to recall. Retrieval refers to the process by which the coded information is searched when required.

In brief, memory is a mental process which involves different mental activities such as learning, retention, recall and recognition. In this mental activity, the informations are recorded in codified form and used as and when required by decodifying the information to facilitate general and strennuous acts of our life.

V.2 Types of Memory

A number of memory theories have been proposed but majority of them are based on information processing approach. One of the most popular approach to describe the phenomena of memory has been proposed by Atkinson and Shiffrin (1968). This model has the following stages:

A) Sensory or Echoic Memory,

B) Short-Term Memory and Long Term Memory.

(A) Sensory or Echoic Memory

Sensory or echoic memory approach points out that the information perceived by our sense organs is registered on memory track. The process which passes information to our mind for storage, recognition and retrieval is known as sensory memory. For instance, while travelling in a fast moving vehicle you might have at times failed to read the milestone but you might have managed to read something from your memory even while you were moved away from the milestone. The image of milestone remain in your mind for a brief interval. This brief image of milestone gives an impression of sensory or echoic memory. The concept of sensory memory, can be verified while seeing a movie in a foreign language and trying to follow it as you might have wished at times that the sound would stop for a moment so that you could translate what was going on. This suggests that the words should remain for a brief period in the sensory memory where they are given some meaning.

As there are various senses so the sensory memories also differ. For example, when the input is visual the memory is called as iconic memory. While in the case of auditory inputs the sensory memory called as echoic memory.

George Sperling (1960) devised a new method for the experimentation of sensory memory. The experiment was so designed that it demonstrated the lingering of visual images. The material used for the experiment included three short lines of numericals and letters. These were exposed only for a very brief period of time. The subjects were able to recall between 4 to 5 times correctly. In the next part of the experimentation the subjects were shown similar material and soon after the material was exposed the subjects were presented with one of the three kinds of tones the high tone was an indication for the subject that he had recalled line while the medium tone indicated the middle line. Thus, after the tone, the subjects were supposed to recall the items contained in one of the lines depending on the tone. The results were quite striking. The subjects were able to recall 100% of the items in the line as indicated by the tone. This means that the subjects were having the whole of the material in memory but during the process of recall due to the passage of time they were lost and hence in the full recall their performance was poor. In the latter method, the subject had the full material in retention can be proved from the fact that depending on the tone which was presented after the material was removed, he could recall the whole line. This method is known as partial cued method.

The experiments showed that inputs presented remain in the memory for some time but during process of recall it is lost. So, when the partial cued method was used i.e., when after exposure of the material the subjects were given an indication (cue) to recall only a line, their performance improved this information was given only after the material was removed away. It indicated that soon after the exposure, all the information is available that is why depending up on cue any line is recalled in full. This kind of memory is known as sensory memory. In this particular experiment where the input is visual, memory is called as iconic memory.

The tone was made at different time interval after exposure, the result showed that if the cue presentation was delayed the subjects performance deteriorated considerably indicating that sensory memory and in case of Ikonic memory, memory has a very brief period of retention.

The duration of iconic memory has been reported to be 01 seconds while the echoic memory it is up to 05 seconds.

The sensory memory can hold up to 16 items but may be much more. The problem here is that most of the information is lost during the process of decay of memory traces. The memory traces soon fade away. It is believed that the information of the sensory memory are transferred to the short-term memory if attended to and recognised.

(B) Short-Term and Long-Term Memory

Some theorists have suggested that two separate memory systems exists, one of which controls memory for shorter periods (short-term memory STM) and one over longer periods (long-term memory LTM). In doing so, they have assigned differentiating properties to short-term memory and long-term memory. But have differentiating sets of laws have been empirically determined to justify the theoretical distinctions between short-term memory and long-term memory?

To understand the two types of memory systems, it would be convenient to study the characteristics of short-term and long-term memory in the following way;

Duration: The duration of short-term memory (STM) varies with different factors and is up to 30 seconds whereas, the long-term memory (LTM) has indefinite duration which exceeds from days to months and from months to years.

Capacity: The short-term memory can hold the information upto certain limits i.e., upto seven items or chunks whereas, the long term memory has unlimited capacity to hold the information.

Transfer: The transfer of information takes place in both the memory systems. In case of short term memory the transfer of information takes place from sensory memory to short-term memory through the process of attention and recognition whereas, the transfer in case of long-term memory takes place through the process of rehearsal.

Storage: In case of short-term memory the information is stored in terms of how inputs look like, how they sound etc., Whereas in case of long-term memory the inputs are organised in meaningful sentences and images etc.

Loss: The main reasons for the loss of information from short-term memory is interference, displacement of information by incoming information whereas, the main reason for the loss of information from the long-term memory is the faulty organisation which may make the retrieval of information difficult.

From the above discussion it is clear to some extent that short and long term memory has creative fundamental differences. One this is clearly that in short term memory the loss of received information is comparatively much more and faster as compared to the long-term memory. But we cannot deny that there is no loss of information in long-term memory system. To find out the reason behind the loss of information, experimental studies by Peterson (1966) indicate that the possibility of existence of two separate stores of memory namely: the long term and the short stores of memories. These will be discussed under following headings:

(i) Serial Position effect,

(ii) Semantic Vs Phonological Similarity, and

(iii) Neuro Physiological Evidence.

1. Serial Position Effect

In order to demonstrate the serial position effect the words are presented to the subjects in a particular serial order. After the learning trails, the recalls of the subjects are taken. The percentage of correct recall for each word is found out. At times the proportion of correct recall may be found. The percentage of proportion recall is put on the Y-axis of the graph while on the

X-axis of the graph serial positions are shown. The curve is drawn by meeting the points which indicate the proportion of correct recall for the words as per their serial order.

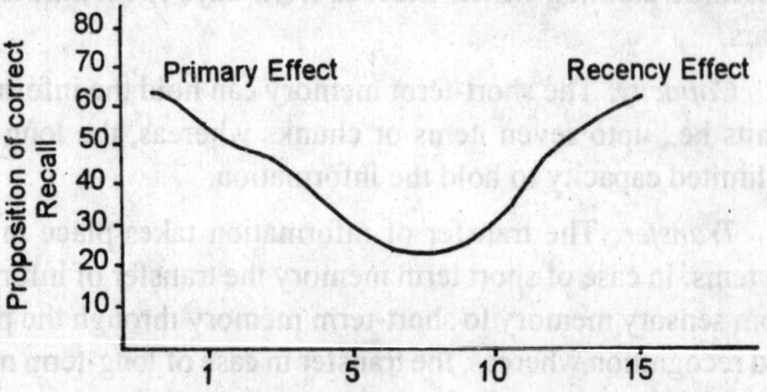

Serial Position Effect

The recalls are generally taken at various time interval after their learning trail is over. Glanzer and Cunitz (1966) conducted an experiment in which he took the recall at three intervals viz:

(1) After 0 seconds
(2) After 10 seconds
(3) After 30 seconds

The graph showed 3 types of effects namely:

– Primary Effect
– Recency Effect
– Asymptote Effect

Primary Effect. It was observed that the words presented earlier in the list were recalled better i.e., percentage proportion of correct recall was better for the words/items appearing initially in one list. This effect is referred as primary effect.

Recency Effect. The.recall percentage or proportion is also better for the words which came towards the end in the list. This is referred to as recency effect.

Asymptote Effect. The proportion of correct recall for items falling in between is generally poor in comparison to the items appearing in the initial or end portion of the list. This is known as asymptote effect.

When the interval between the end of learning trail and the recall trail is increased to more than 30 seconds, the proportion of correct recall is reduced drastically. This indicates that the recency effect is due to short term memory. Since the short term memory cannot hold an information beyond 30 seconds, there is deterioration of the recency effect.

However, it does not have any impact on the items learned towards beginning because the primary effect is due to long term memory.

2. Semantic and Phonological Similarity Effects

Kintsch and Buschke (1969) conducted an experiment to demonstrate how semantic and phonological similarities have differential effect on short term and long term memory. The two kinds of lists were taken which had the following composition:

List- I : 16 unrelated words (+ 8 pairs of synonyms).

List-II : 16 unrelated words (+ 8 pairs of homophones).

The list-I thus included words which had semantic similarity. The list-II thus included words which had phonological similarity. The example of pairs of words with phonological similarity would be rhyming words like rat and car, mad and sad etc. The example of pairs of words with semantic similarity would be palace, mansion etc.

Baddeley (1966) studied the influence of phonological and semantic similarity on secondary memory. Each presentation was followed by a task requiring remembering of a sequence of digits in order to destroy the short term memory.

The results showed that phonological similarity had little influence either it can delay retention test or learning. However, it is difficult for the subject to learn and recall semantically similar test. Thus, the two stores short-term memory and long-term memory can also be distinguished on the grounds that the short-term memory is influenced by phonological similarity, while long-term memory is influenced more by semantic similarity.

3. Neuro-physiological Evidence

There are some important empirical Neuro-physiological evidences supporting the existence of two process theory of memory.

Milner (1966) has reported of certain persons having bilateral surgical lessons in hyppocampal area who has their intelligence intact and their short-term memory is unaffected but no information is added to the long-term memory. This simply shows transfer from short-term memory to long-term memory which is somehow, disturbed due to the lesson and hence long-term memory does not function.

Another study by Narrington & Shallice (1969) it was found a patient who underwent hippocampus operation as a treatment for epilepsy was that though the patient's intelligence remained intact, even the events in the long term memory remained intact, however no new information was being transferred to long-term memory and as a result the family of the patient which has moved to new location face problems because he could not remember the new address and went to old one. Thus the neurological evidences with respect to the short-term memory and long-term memory are mixed. On the whole the evidences of empirical studies indicate that the two process theory is more or less correct but a further detailed investigation is required to produce a more, clear understanding.

Difference Between Short Term and Long Term Memory

The short-term and long-term memory can be differentiated on the basis of three stages of memory which can be categorically studied as:

	Sensory	*Short-term Memory STM*	*Long-term Memory LTM*
(1) Duration	Different for different types eg. vision ie. Iconic memory up to 01 sec. Audition ie. Echoic up to 05 secs.	Varies with factors upto about 30 secs.	Indefinite days months & years.
(2) Capacity	The capacity is large-up to 16 items but may be more.	The capacity is small-upto 07 items/chunks generally.	The capacity is unlimited-very large.
(3) Transfer process		From sensory to STM transfers—attention and recognition is a must.	From STM to LTM rehearsal is a must.
(4) Nature of information stored	Information stored in information sensory memory stored is copy of the input.	It may be visual images, sounds etc.	It is stored in LTM sentences, image, concept etc.

Contd.

(5) Loss of information reasons	Main reason is decay of memory traces	Main reason is displacement in info. by information.	Faulty organisation, interference the info. is there but inacessible.

Types of Long Term Memory

Studies reveals that long term memory is of two types which can be studied as under :

Tulving (1972) has proposed a further useful distinction out long term memory. He distinguished between two types of memory, each of which is dealt with a separate system viz., (1) Episodic Memory, (2) Semantic Memory.

The distinction between knowledge of personal experience and knowledge of the world forms the basis of episodic/semantic classification of long term memory. Semantic memory refers to an organised collection of knowledge about concepts. These are necessary for the use of language. A rough analogy to semantic memory would be the saurus which includes words verbal symbols, meanings and reference, relations etc.

Episodic memory is essentially autobiographicals in nature and holds information in the following form:

I Experienced...........At..........(place)

The episodic memory and semantic memory differs with respect to the type of information they stored.

The type of stored information for the two stores Semantic Memory : What is psychology ?

Episodic Memory

(1) Details of the episode were the stranger approached you and at what time-whether you were able to answer his questions.

(2) The two stores also differ with respect to the Conditions and Consequences of Retrieval. Episodic memory is the direct record of personal experience which is organised with respect to time and hence information can only be received if an exact record has been entered into the store on earlier occasion. However, information can be retrieved from semantic memory which has not been entered in exactly that form. For example you may have not specifically read whether psychology is a science. But if you know what is science and what are the characteristics of psychology

using your mind, you can answer the question.

(3) The episodic and semantic memory also differ with respect to the Susceptibility To Interference and Loss of Stored Information. This is partly due to episodic information to change and result of retrieval partly due to episodic information is always temporarily dated, episodic memory assumes to be more subject to interference and forgetting then semantic memory. The semantic memory is relatively stable because its rich and permanent structure of concepts protects the stored information from interference by other input.

Semantic Memory

The Semantic memory systems and the episodic memory systems are not completely independent of each other but they differ on the following basis :

(1) The contents of semantic memory must have been learnt at some point of time and at time the learning episode must have been part of the episodic record. In fact, the contents of semantic memory have to record. In fact, the contents of semantic memory have to be abstracted out of the contents of episodic memory; semantic memories are stopped of their autobiographical context. eg., Child learning first few words are context bound learning, so in learning in early stage of learning semantic memory must have strong connections with episodic memory. But over time and experience—it becomes more context independent structures. This achievement must be derived by abstract episodic record.

(2) We would not be able to interpret and store information about episodes unless we are able to make use of semantic information.

Thus, episodic memory and semantic memory systems, although clearly differentiated in terms of certain criteria, must be interdependent and operate in conjunction with each other in most memory activities. For example, the question—where is Taj Mahal? May have both episodic and semantic aspects. Mr. A may remember where Taj Mahal is because he has visited it while the other person may because he has read it. So personal experience may also relate to it.

The episodic and semantic memory are more conceptual in nature-there is no evidence for separate brain locations corresponding of the two systems. The distinction has been inferred rather than based on experimental considerations.

Keeping in view the above discussion the episodic and semantic memory can be categorically differentiated on the basis of the following characteristics:

Distinguishing Properties of Episodic & Semantic Memory

Memory System Property	*Episodic Memory*	*Semantic Memory*
Type of stored information	Personal experience	World knowledge
Storage reference of inputs signal	Personal past generally organised by time & space	Existing congnitive structure
Retrieval	Can only retrieve information which has been previously stored in the particular form.	Can retrieve information which has not been stored in form.

V.3 Signs of Good Memory

Memory is a complex mental process which depends upon number of mental activities. The most important mental activities which constitute a good memory can be studied as:

1. Rapid Recall. The first sign of good memory is a rapid recall. Quick recall means sharp memory. It is very serviceable as it takes no time to recollect the needed object or idea. It has got a special value for students who have to write against time, specially in the essay type examinations, where facts are to be recalled and written. In the same way, teacher who does not take much time to reproduce the facts or ideas in his lecture has a good memory. Teachers and students who can retain the facts but cannot recall them rapidly at the correct moment cannot impress much. So, rapid recall reflects sharpness of one's memory and which is essential.

2. Quick Recognition. The sign of quick recognition confirms the recall. It is very necessary for sure and certain memory. If recognition is poor, the recall will suffer as there will be doubt, whether the subject or face recalled is the same or not. Sometimes we confirm or verify the spelling by writing them. After writing the word, we identify it and remove the doubt of recall. So, recall supports the recognition.

3. Long Retention. The third sign of good memory is to retain the learned material for a long time without refreshing it. In other words memory should be a retentive one. The memory traces last for a long time. The person with retentive memory does not forget the learned material very soon. A student with retentive memory does not forget the lesson of a teacher and does better in the examination than other students who forget very soon.

4. Accurate Recall. The fourth sign of memory is the accuracy of recall. The recall should be complete and correct. Imperfect recall is likely to be distorted. It does not help in getting the complete recall but offers resistance to it. A good memory must be a serviceable one. A person should remember things which are needed and relevant. Many students are not to the point while answering a question so, they beat about the bush. The trouble is that they do not recall the relevant facts, a good debator, lawyer and teacher need serviceable memory.

V.4 Factors Responsible to Improve Memory

1. Attention. The students should be very observant in studies they should be mentally alert and make conscious efforts to organize the significant facts. They should be directly interested in the work and thus pay due attention. It is said that attention is a method of memory. Keen attention on the part of students goes a long way to memorize the facts. Attention can only be maintained if the students are well motivated. Motives supply the inner force to attend the subject of ideas properly.

2. Association. The principle of association is very useful in memorizing. It has been seen in the experiments that even in learning the list of nonsense syllables, there is tendency to make use of association. By association one idea leads to another. If the association is strong, the flow of idea will be a rapid one. Moreover, association gives the complete picture of past experience by filling the gaps. In our daily life we may remember our roll numbers of various examinations, number of car, cycle watch or important letters makes associations with the previously learned facts.

3. Learning. Learning is the first stage of memory. It is a base and should be very strong. All the laws of learning i.e., laws of exercise, law of recency, law of primacy, law of belonging and law of intensity are very useful. They also are very significant in memorizing, as memorizing is only a form or learning. We do not forget the names which we call daily but it becomes very difficult to recollect the name of person who met three weeks back and after that his name was never used. We can recall the recent and primary experiences with more ease than others. The important facts are retained for a longer time.

4. Healthy conditions. Good physical and mental conditions of the subject make the act of memorizing easier. A person who is physically fit has more favourable memory than the person suffering from stomach or other ailments. Similarly, a worried, emotional or nervous person cannot be very efficient in memory. After all, good memory depends on the strength of impressions or memory traces. If the person is physically healthy, the power of retention will be better one. This is the reason that first two school periods are better than the rest of school time as the students are fresh physically as well as mentally.

5. Quiet environment. Atmosphere should be calm and quiet. There should be least external disturbance. Rush of work and noise are unfavourable conditions. Last but not the least, the subject should have a strong will and the different sense organs may be used. If we see any object and hear about it at the same time i.e., we use ears and eyes at one and the same time, the learning will be better and the memory will be retentive and quick.

6. Practice & Drill. The practice and drill of a particular act helps in recognition of the skill performed in a particular manner. The texture of performing an act ultimately affects the neuromotors which ultimately change the neurons. The charged neurons releases the stored information of acts accelerates the memory.

7. Protest. The interest of a person ultimately prepares the mind of a person to receive a particular type of knowledge, skill or behaviour. The preparedness or the readyness ultimately helps in the storage and recall of the information as and when required. Thus, interest of a persons helps in memorising a thing or a process.

V.5 Methods of Memorising

The process of memorising is most important for human development. Effective development of a learner depends upon the method of memorising adopted by the learner. There are different methods of memorising but the most economic method of memorizing are: recitation, whole versus part learning, spaced and unspaced repetition. These are methods are discussed as under:

1. Recitation. Here recitation does not mean to speak out with rhythm. Here it means to recite oneself. The learner learns the lesson for some time and then he attemps to recite it to himself. He prompts himself whenever he is struck. Suppose a student has to memorize a lesson of chemistry. He learns it for some time. Then he speaks out the main points to himself. Whenever, he feels difficulty, he consults the books and goes further. It may be useful to recite the learned material by writing that on paper. Many experiments have been conducted which confirm the hypothesis that recitation helps in learning and economises the time. It has got a diagnostic value as it reveals to the learner his weak points. Thus learner can pay more attention and time to this unlearned material or weak points. The wastage of time on learned material is avoided and thus time and energy of learner is saved. Moreover, this methods of learning is more stimulating and encouraging. It tends to improve one's learning by affording a sense of self-competition which is very useful to secure better results. In addition to the above facts this method is very active. It makes the learner mentally alert. Continued reading and reading makes the tasks dull and boredom reached earlier. In this case the boredom does not reach so early and a change is provided which removes the fatigue also. It affords motivation. Further it favours permanent memory. Thus, in the school the teacher should ask the students, rather see that the school work is learnt by the students making use of recitation. To strengthen recitation a student needs to do recitation very soon, it means that the matter should be sufficiently learnt. Otherwise it will be mere wastage of time. Again too many recitations after very short intervals are not paying. The gap between the recitations depends on the material and the subject as there is no hard and fast rule for it. It is better to take it as a general and broad principle.

2. *Spaced and Unspaced Method.* An important method of memorizing the concept is spaced and unspaced method. By spaced and unspaced method it means whether the material should be learnt and mastered in one sitting, or it should be mastered in several short sittings. If there is only one sitting, it is known as spaced method. If the lesson is quite long, then spaced method is better than unspaced. However, for short lesson the unspaced method can do. The size of the lesson which is a deciding factor to adopt spaced or unspaced method depends on the degree of difficulty of task in hand and the capacity of the learner. A short lesson of 9th class may being one used for 6th and 7th classes. Similarly, the length of lesson for a very bright and very dull students may not be the same. The time should be distributed over the suitable number of stittings with suitable time Too many sittings having very short time for each, are not at all desired. Spaced method facilitates learning by fastness at every sitting. The problem of fatigue is also solved. It is very difficult to sit for eight hours continuously and master the material. It would be easier if the same material is mastered in three sittings of equal size. The school time table is formed by taking in view this fact.

3. *Whole Versus Part Method.* Another method of memorizing the subject is possible by whole method or by part method. Suppose there is a poem and we have to memorise it. We can read the whole of it i.e., we start from the first line and finish with the last. Again we give a second reading as a whole. Similarly, repetitions are made till it is learnt thoroughly. The other method which is called 'part method' will learn stanza after stanza. First stanza will be learnt, then the second is taken up and so on. It is not a piece of poetry, we can divide the subject matter in suitable units. Experiments revealed that whole method is better than part method, if the material to be learnt is not too long. It is an admitted fact that for short lesson while method is better. Even for long lessons it holds good. But if the size of lesson is very big, say it covers fifty units, the unit should be small and must be treated as a whole. It may be doubtful for a layman that whole method is better for considerable long lessons, but it is based on experimental evidence.

V.6 Forms of Memory

Bergson defines that memory are of two forms viz; Habit memory and True memory.

1. Habit Memory. Habit is mechanical and automatic. It needs the least attention. Thus the form of memory which is a mechanical one and has been learnt so much that it does not need much of the efforts, is called habit memory. Often this type of memory is not learnt intelligently with deep associations and insight into it. The mechanical repetitions are made without understanding. It is very specific in its nature and there is least transfer of training. It means that learning and experience of such memory cannot be carried over to another act of memory. There are several examples of such blind memory. The multiplication tables and the digits from one to hundred are learnt by the students of primary classes in typical Indian school. Some students use the method by committing the bookish knowledge to their memory word for word and put it in the same words in the examination hall. It is also known as rote memory or a learning by heart. Such memory is often used in certain lessons of history and chemistry. In Primary schools, the students of first standard, who to not know reading and writing are made to learn poems and songs to their memory. After several repetitions the facts are learnt with such a strength that they can be recalled at any stage of life. Rote memory is also useful in making prepared speeches and debates and lectures. Just like habit, the habit memory saves time as it can be recalled quickly and retention is long. No doubt, it is quite useful in certain situations, but often it is not appreciated as it is highly specific in its nature and does not help to develop the mind, as it often lacks understanding and there is not transference of learning from one act of memory to other. It has limited value and it holds good if it is taken for memory sake only for higher values.

2. True Memory. The true memory is a quality of mind. It does not have mechanical aspect. Sometimes there is no need to make several continuous repetitions. It is memorized at the first time, sight or first reading. Such memory makes use of associations. The new object or idea is associated or connected with elements of past knowledge which are in our retentive memory. Thus associations make it so strong that it does not need any blind repetition. The association make it a meaningful one and understanding gets in. This becomes intelligent memory and is very specific in its nature. There is transfer of training and the mind develops by it. It is not boring as habit memory is.

Most of the psychologists accept this division of Bergson but they are of the opinion that the distinction drawn by him is a psycho-physical problem. None says that according to Bergson, "mechanical association is an affair of the body, chiefly of the nervous system, while true activity of the spiritual force or entity uses the bodily mechanism for its purposes," and this means, "that mechanical association belongs to the "corpse" and true memory to the 'ghost in corpse'. This is too much. It separates body and mind whereas, they are not so.

V.7 Memory Problems

1. The student of class X who complains of poor memory in his lessons but who is alright in sport records and remembers vividly because he is *interested* in sports. The interest is an important word in learning. It gives the supply of motive or motivation. Without motivation learning is always weak and on low level. His interest is direct. He plays for play sake. This is no thrust on him whereas, he is lacking interest in studies. He takes the studies as task and not as play. Therefore, he makes complaints against memory in his studies.

2. *Secondly, he gives more time to sports* because he is interested in it. He might be playing much and thus quite fatigued. This physical fatigue causes mental fatigue which comes in when the lessons are learnt.

3. *Thirdly the trouble is due to habit memory.* In sports there is true memory. Here the associations are made. The new event or score of sport is connected with the past learnt behaviour, thus the apperceptive mass is made use of. The new learning is organized in the systems which are already there. There is assimilation of knowledge which involves understanding and insight. But in case of studies, it seems to be habit memory. As he is not interested, therefore, the new knowledge is not associated with previous one. It is not organized into system. It does not develop the mind as there is no transfer of training. Mere mechanical and blind repetition without understanding should not do.

4. The above mentioned facts seem to be the apparent cause of complaint. But it is only true in general. It has been assumed that there is nothing wrong with the memory of the student, only the method to use it is defective. But it is also worthwhile to note what the reason of his dis-interest in his studies is- there may be some emotional maladjustment. He might have developed hatred for the teacher, for books, for class-room and these may be the bases. These feelings would have been converted into complexes for studies. For this purpose the case history of the student should be taken and studied thoroughly. Special attention should be given to his school and studied thoroughly. Special attention should be given to his school or study experience. Thus, the cause should be determined and dealt with according to it. If the complaint is old, the teacher can reform the child by way of suggestions. If there are deep complexes, the help of psychological clinics should be sought.

V.8 Treatments of Memory Problems

1. If the case is not abnormal and our first diagnosis is correct, the method of learning should be improved. Interest in learning should be created. It is said that interest is the mother of attention and attention is the mother of memory. The curiosity of student should be aroused in order to motivate the pupil. The teacher should make use of illustrative aids which make the lesson interesting as well as concrete. The teacher should make use of audio-visual aids as there will be learning through ears and eyes.

2. Suitable association should be created by connecting the new lesson with the previous of one. The new material will be associated with the material which is going to be taught and the way in which all this is done, will merely remove his trouble. Whatever material is taught to him must have some meanings for him. It must be purposeful activity and satisfy the need of the pupil. He must understand it well and form suitable links in his mind. Blind and mechanical repetitions should be avoided and true memory should be used. This leads to conclusions: Firstly the law of association be applied as far as possible to facilitate the retentiveness of material on the part of pupil and secondly, the use of concrete methods to make the lesson clear and easy. Concrete material will remove the abstractness and will not hamper the apprehension. The moment the facts of studies are intelligibly grasped and assimilated, the complaint of retaining the lessons will disappear.

3. Special care should be taken so that pupil does not exert much while participating in sports. He should take rest and then he should sit to learn the lesson. Fatigued body causes fatigue to nervous system and brain. Memory is a higher mental process and fresh brain should be needed in order to achieve better results. Further the three main factors of economy should be clearly understood by student i.e., he should know the value of recitations, whole versus part method and spaced and unspaced learning. Information on types of memory and types of lessons may also be imparted to make him acquainted with elementary knowledge of memory.

V.9 Role of Teacher to Improving Memory

The question of improving memory by training makes us to understand that learning cannot be acquired without the active co-operation of the learner, the material to be remembered must be assimilated with previously known material and incorporated the interests of the person into an organised whole. Memory is not mere reproduction; for processes of condensation, elaboration and invention are happening in the interval, making the act one of reconstruction rather than the re-excitation of life less permanent trace. Memory, being a living process, also involves the general attitudes and interests of the person, which as they change from time to time also affect the manner and content of what is remembered. Various forms of reorganisation may happen as a result of this. The criterion of an efficient memory is, therefore, not exact reproduction (nor has this any educative value) but whether the reconstruction is appropriate to the changed circumstances has direct bearing on the memory training.

The memory training is a complex process which points out that it involves an act of memory which depends not only on our ability to retain, but also on our ability to record, ideas, i.e., to commit them to memory; and finally on our power of recovering what has been so committed.

It is a common experience that certain psychological conditions help in habit formation. Similarly, by education we can improve habits. The process which enables an organism to improve his habits makes the individual to utilise complex components of memory, meaning thereby that training exercises and adequate education effects the memory as a result habits are modified. The bio-chemical process involved in the modification of one's behaviour reveals that individuals native retentiveness is as much an unchangeable property of our nervous system as its chemical constitution, a doctrine which is based can the view that all association is due to the formation of traces of the brain, consisting of paths of low resistance between adjacent neurons which implies that all associations are of the mechanical habit type.

In addition to the above procedures applicable for the improvement of memory a teacher can make use of the psychological principle of association to gear up memory of his students for example, Carpenter says, the associations "which are most useful to us in the acquisition of knowledge, and over the formation of which we have the most power, may be distinguished as rational; being based on the fundamental relations of the ideas themselves, the perception of which gives to the new idea definite place in the fabric of our thought." Such connection as these between our ideas are the basis of all memorising that is truly educative and it is not necessary to invoke the central system in order to account for them.

For educational theory it is fortunately hardly necessary to consider whether retentiveness is or is not improvable, since pure tenacity of retention is not *per se* a valuable power of mind. If it is allowed to take the place of organised thinking, sheer retentiveness may be a barrier to progress. This is very aptly illustrated by Professor C. Lloyed Morgan in the following example: "I ask a boy who can readily learn a lot of dates when Jonson's Every Man in his Humour was published. He answer glibly 1596. I say: 'Was Shakespeare still living ?' He looks confused and I continue, 'Was Cromwell dead ?' To his still greater confusion. And yet he can give me pat, if directly asked, the dates of Shakespeare's death and Cromwell's protectorate. He does not think but trusts to parrot-like association." This unfortunate youth has had his physiological memory trained, to the neglect of a systematic training in relationships, which the result that what he knows has no education value. "Another body of whom the same question concerning Jonson's comedy is asked may reply: "I do not remember the exact date, though I have seen it stated. But it was after the publication of the Faerie Queene and before Bacon's Essays appeared. I happen to remember those dates, so every man in his, Humour must have been produced between 1559 and 1597." His answer is less exact; but it is more rational, and from the point of view of systematic knowledge of greater value."

There are of course, a number of facts which must be known by rote, such as the tables, but a rational procedure in explaining them is the best method for remembering them and for future advance, as the methods employed in the best kindergartens have amply shown. Some other things to be remembered have neither rhyme nor reason, such as English spelling; but whilst these must be learnt, they have in themselves no educational value, except as a means to some further end. Rational associations within an organised system of knowledge are the only kind of retentiveness worth educational consideration. It ought to be added that the systematic organisation of knowledge enables the material to be retained more readily, since each part of the system is retained by the combined suggestive power of all the rest. Moreover, as meaning is more readily assimilated than bare facts (as the work on retention of nonsense-syllables shows), and as the amount that can be retained in this way becomes incomparably greater, since a unit for meaning may contain many sub-units, the whole functioning as one without further effort; it follows that for practical purposes more complete organisation is equivalent to an increase of retentiveness. Every new generalisation or law increases one's power of retention, provided that it is arrived at by considering the particulars; for the mere statement of the law or rule implicitly revives all the particulars. The question of retentiveness has been much obscured by the false analogies used in discussing the subject, all if them drawn form the physical world, such as 'the store-house of the mind,' 'imprinting on the memory' and so forth. All these, which are comparatively innocuous when we are considering physiological memory, are apt to lead to erroneous implications when true memory is discussed.

When we turn to the other factors, namely the recording and the recovering, further light is thrown on the subject of the training of the memory. There is no doubt whatever that the ability to record is improvable by practice; this has been shown experimentally and indeed is obvious from general experience. For it depends on factors which are largely subjective and under our control;

namely on properly adjusted attention, rhythm, control of imagination, etc. and also on our acquired interests. A problem of considerable educational importance emerges at this point, namely whether the improved ability brought about in this way is purely specific, or whether it is of a general nature so that it can operate in spheres outside that in which the improvement has been acquired. As this question is not confined to memory alone, but concerns all the powers or the mind, it is considered in the next chapter on Mental Health.

Finally, we have the third factor, namely, the capacity to recall what has been learnt. The name recollect which is usually given to this power is significant, for it calls attention to the dependence of memory on the will to learn. Recollection is to be contrasted with the kind of reminiscence which takes place in reverie, where we are relatively passive spectators of the flow in ideas. When, however, voluntary attention is concentrated on the details of an organised system of knowledge, those associations are recalled which are relevant to the particular subject thought about. So that the condition of recollection, in so far as it is not subjective brings us back again to the organisation of our knowledge, which is likewise the condition of its retention. "Most men," said William James, "have a good memory for facts connected with their own pursuits. The college athlete who remains a dunce at his books will astonish you by his knowledge of men's 'records' in various feats and games, and will be a walking dictionary of sporting statistics. The reason is that he is constantly going over these things in his mind, and comparing and making series of them. They form for him not so many odd facts, but a concept-system—so they stick. So the merchant remembers prices, the politician other politicians speeches and votes, with a copiousness which amazes outsiders, but which the amounts of thinking they bestow on these subjects easily explains." It is evident that the real reason for the retentive memory in all these cases is the organisation of the facts brought about by an intense interest in them. Putting it briefly, we may say that in the will to learn, and in the systematisation of our knowledge, lies the secret of training the memory. In other words, there is no royal road to this goal, and instead of looking to specific exercises for this purpose we see that the proper methods is to stimulate a desire for what is to be acquired, and to make our studies systematic.

It is the universal custom amongst teachers to aid such systematisation by revising what has been taught. Without revision to consolidate and organise lessons there is little chance of remembering. An investigation has been made of the effects on retention of various methods of revision. A series of geography lessons was given to three classes of children of about eleven years of age whose school attainments and intelligence were about the same. One of the classes had a revision lesson at the end of the series, going over the notes, verifying places on maps and answering questions. The second revised their work by writing up their notes after consulting maps and asking questions of the teacher. In the third class some of the pupils prepared speeches after the manner of the Play Way and were cross-examined by their class-mates. A test, constructed on the lines of a mental test, which could be rigidly marked, showed that the last method was superior to the other methods of revision. This conclusion of the superiority of oral composition can only be accepted for young children, where no doubt the interest of the method combined with the free activity of the pupils serves to explain the result. A similar investigation for older pupils would throw further light on the question of training of the memory. Therefore, the memory can be improved if a teacher applies psychological principles which facilitates learning.

V.10 Meaning and Definitions of Forgetting

As a common experience it is observed that however, deeply a material is learnt, it is liable to be forgotten, if not in full, at least in parts. The loss of reproducing the material learned earlier gives an idea of forgetting. In other words, the difficulty, or inability, of a subject in being remembered on in coming to the consciousness in the mental activity, is due to forgetting. It contradicts remembering and it is the failure of retention. Sometimes, almost too often, the thought is retained even though it is not recalled. Its inability to come to conscious level can be attributed to a variety of reasons. Therefore, more failure to recollect is not the same thing as forgetting. But lack of progress in re-learning is definitely forgetting. Briefly, we can say that the failure of recollection is partial or temporary forgetting the failure of retention is complete or permanent forgetting.

Meaning: Ebbinghaus a renowned, psychologist describes that forgetting is a passive mental process. The activity continues automatically with the passage of time and the mind does not interfere with it. The activity of forgetting proceeds with good speed for some four to six hours after the learning of meanigless pieces but by the time 5 to 7 of days have passed, the enthusiasm dies out and the activity is very slow, so much so that the difference between the forgetting of the 10th and 12 days is almost impermeable.

On the other hand some psychologists contradict the views of Ebbinghaus and are of the opionion that forgetting is an active passive process implying that the mind too takes a hand that other being the passage of time, in forgetting. Forgetting is affected in no small measure by the mental processes which take place in the interval between remembering and forgetting. The least amount of forgetting takes place in sleep but if the person engages in some other activity forgetting is comparatively more.

V.11 Theories of Forgetting

The theories of forgetting can be studied under following heads:

(1) Consolidation Theory,
(2) Decay Theory,
(3) Interference Theory,
(4) Motivated Forgetting Theory,
(5) Forgetting Due to Retrieval Problems.

Consolidation Theory

Physiological Theory. Muller & Pilzecker (1900) have given a theory of forgetting which is a physiological theory. The theory assumes existence of memory traces. These traces take time to consolidate. If they are some how disturbed before consolidation, forgetting will take place. DUNCAN (1949) conducted experiment in which there was complete loss of memory of events taking place just before the electric shock was given. This is known as retrograde amnesia. Hebb (1949) also gave a theory of forgetting based on similar grounds. He has used the concept of electric circuits. These have been criticised on several grounds.

First, the physiological evidence of memory traces has not been proved. Their existence is only inferred.

Secondly, there are reported studies in which items learned long back showed impairment after and electro-convulsive shock. The theory fails to clearly specify the period of consolidation.

Decay Theory

The memory traces fade away with passage of time. There is common saying also that time is the best healer. This means that with the passing of time, we tend to forget even major events or set back.

The experiments of Ebbinghaus prove this point. According to the experiment, memory operates like a leaking bucket. The memory traces fade away over a period of time.

But this does not apply always. You must be very clearly remembering with even minute details some events of your childhood. Why this has remained so vivid after so many years ? This theory fails to explain even a slight variation of the theory i.e., *Disuse theory*. According to this theory, memory traces are lost because they are not in use. The same criticism applies here as well.

Penfield stimulated the brain electrically at various points. At one point, to the his utter surprise, he found that subject was able to give perfect detail of a scene from a play, she had seen years before. At another point she could see herself in an office she had worked years before. However, only a few of Penfield's subjects showed such memories.

Interference Theory

The theory of disuse and theory of decay of memory trace have been criticised on the ground that they have failed to take into account the various activities which may take place between learning and recall and prior to learning. These activities are very important, this was aptly demonstrated in a classic and heroic study conducted by Jenkins & Dallenback (1924) in which recalls were taken after various intervals of sleep after learning trails.

This is a matter of common experience that learning new things may be interfered by what we have learned already. Similarly, what has been learned earlier also is also interfered by what is learned later.

Let's take the example for the case where learning of new things is interfered by what has been earned earlier. Suppose you knew the telephone number of your friend as "A" 543809 later you learned the phone number of another friend "B" as 534072. Now when you are required to recall the number of B you may be at loss because the earlier number produces an interference for the later learning. This kind of interference is known as proactive.

Proactive interference refers to effect of previous learning on recall of later task. The design of an experiment for studying the proactive interference is as under:

Experimental Group

Learn Task A Learn Task B Retention interval Recall Task B

Control Group

Learn Task B Retention interval Recall Task B

The recall of Task B is measured for both the groups i.e., experiment as well as control group. If the performance of the experimental group is lower than the control group, it indicates that there has been a proactive interference i.e., the task A has interfered with the recall of task B which was learned subsequently.

Underwood (1957) demonstrated that as the number of lists learned prior to learning of the list. List increased, there was decreased percentage of recall.

The result that Ebbinghaus obtained in his experiment can be explained in terms of proactive inhibitions.

Retroactive Interference

Retroactive interference refers to effect of a later learning on the recall of previous learning. You go for a party you are introduced to number of persons. By the time the party is over and when you try to say good-bye to the individuals you may find that you do not remember half of their names. So the names that you learned later have had an interfering effect and caused forgetting.

The experimental design commonly used for the experiments conducted to demonstrate retroactive interference is as follows :

Group				
Experimental Group	Learn Task A	Learn Task B	Retention Interval	Recall Task A
Control	Learn Task A	—	Retention Interval	Recall Task A

If the performance of the experimental group is less than the control of group performance, this is explained in terms of the interpolated activity between learning of task A and its recall i.e., learning of task B. This is known as retroactive interference.

The interference has been tried to be explained in terms of a two factor theory. The two factors are:

(1) Factor 'X'

(2) Response Competition

Factor X is explained in terms of unlearning factor. When the learning is interfered by other learning it causes unlearning. The responses which are similar many interfere and lead to production of responses which are incorrect. By observing the responses and the errors in response, one can easily identify the errors resulting from response competition. This two factor theory owes its origin to Melton & Irwin.

Whatever may be cause and nature of interference, it has been generally considered to be one of the major causes of forgetting.

Motivated Forgetting Theory

Sigmund Freud has also discussed about the forgetting. This theory got its first explanation in his classic work "The Psychopathology of Everyday Life." Motivating forgetting theory advocates. That for learning fresh we need to forget. The motivating forgetting as concept is related to the process of repression.

Repression refers to a defence mechanism. It is an attempt to get away from the memories of events which are threatening to the ego. These are such events which produce anxiety, so avoidance of such events means safeguard from displeasure.

Repression operates at an unconscious level which suppression operates at a consious level. So in suppression a conscious effort is made to take away those events and things out of memory which are threatening to the ego.

Freud has given a number of examples for everyday life as to how memory lapses result from repression and how they are satisfying to the examples. Let us take some of the personal example which Freud have cited. Freud forgot the conversations he had with a man he disliked and also forgot names of persons whom he disliked.

These are, thus, examples of motivated forgetting. But these are instances both from our day to day life as well as experimental findings which put a question mark to Freud's explanation.

For example, we do remember very clearly some of the saddest incidents of our lives which when remembered at any point of time produces a lot of discomfort. These produce anxiety and are threatening to the ego. According to Freudian explanation it should not be.

Forgetting due to retrieval problems. Forgetting may occur due to retrieval failure. As discussed earlier that forgetting may be due to faulty organisation, faulty encoding or lack of retrieval ones. The information is there but due to retrieval problems one may find it difficult to reach at the problem.

The "Tip of The Tongue" phenomenon—you must have experienced a number of times. The word or information is there you know very well but its not coming out. It simply means that the information is available but not accessible.

Similarly, such problems may arise due to state dependent memory. The event may have taken place in specific state (say drunken) and when he is not in a drunken state, he may find it difficult to recall the event. This is due to state dependent memory.

Sometimes, memory of events may not be there and you may keep on searching for a book or some article suddenly this may come as a flash in a particular context and you remember where you have kept the book. This is due to the effect of the context in which one event had taken place.

Thus, there are various theories related to memory. Some have got experimental evidence in their favour than others.

But an important factor to be taken note of is that each theory may be applicable to some extent. For example, there is sensory memory where the decay theory may be. Interference theory, infact, has an overall high applicability. For the long term memory the retrieval problems pose important reason for forgetting.

V.12 Causes of Forgetting

Psychologists are of the view that forgetting is most essential for our further learning. By forgetting they mean that some irrelevant past of the learned material is forgotten by a normal individual. Now, question arises, how the process of forgetting takes place. To answer the questions we have two approaches to explain the phenomenon of forgetting which can be studied as under:

(i) Fading. We have already referred that in memorizing a material, the memory traces are formed in the brain. The main cause of forgetting is probably the gradual fading of brain traces that are not reactivated. Woodworth has described it as a return to normal, analogous to the healing of a wound. A trace that is too weak to produce recall may still suffice for recognition; but if it is not reactivated, it will gradually fade to the point at which it no longer under normal condition gives rise to any conscious experience at all.

It is the opinion of some psychologists that no brain trace ever fades out completely. This is the sort of statement that is impossible to verify. But it can be said here that there is sample evidence that brain traces outlast the stage at which they can give rise to conscious recall. The strongest evidence for this view is provided then we re-learn a matter which has already been forgotten. For example, we may have learned a poem by heart, and forgotten it so completely that we cannot recall a single line of it. Nevertheless, if we set ourselves to re-learn the poem, we find that we can do it in far less time than would be needed a memorize a poem of the same length that we had never learnt before.

(ii) Blocking. Fading is not the sole cause of forgetting. The other cause is referred to as blocking. You meet a person in the way and try to recall his name which you have learnt earlier and are unable to recall at the present moment, then you are forgetting on account for certain blocking in the way of its reproduction. In this case, the brain trace has not faded. In a sense, the memory is there but something gets in the way and prevents its emergence.

From the above discussion it is evident that the process of forgetting can be described by two approaches viz, fading and blocking of memory. To understand the phenomena of fading and blocking of memory takes place because of the following factors :

(iii) Lapse of time. All the activities and experiences learnt by any individual leave behind them their impressions. These impressions modify the brain structure which is called the memory trace. As long as the memory-trace of a certain activity is present, that activity can be recalled. With passing of time, these memory traces or memory impressions go on fading. The exact nature of these memory traces is not known, yet it is a little change in the basic

structure. If this structure change is durable, then there are less chances of its forgetting. If the memory trace is weak, then it may be forgotten soon. Just like organism, they have their life span. As the time passes, they go on fading and getting weak and weak, till they are so faint that they lose their energy to come in the conscious mind. It has been found after experimentation that 56% if forgotten after one hour 64% after nine hours, 72% after 2 days, 75% after a week and 80% after a month. It may be said that as the time passes we get new experiences and learn new activities. Thus, new fresh memory traces are formed, these new impressions push down the earlier images or traces in the lower layers of mind. The old traces are buried under the pressure of recent memory traces. Thus they are suppress and then repressed in the unconsciousness. According to this theory the memory traces do not die. They do exist but in the unconscious mind, which cannot be recalled by way of ordinary memory. So we forget them. School of psycho-analysis has shown that the experience of past which cannot be recalled ordinarily, can be recalled in the hypnotic state. This indicates that the memory traces do not perish but exists on lower levels.

(iv) Forgetting is due to use and disuse. The law of exercise holds good for the memory traces as it does with biological structure. The memory traces should be well nourished in order to keep it alive.

An organ of body loses strength when it is inactive for a long time, as happens when a broken arm is kept in a splint. Usually left hand is not so active as right hand, as left hand muscles do not get much exercise. Thus left hand becomes weak. Therefore, the use of exercise is essential to keep the organic body alive. Disuse leads to allotropy. The delegated memory trace should also observe this general biological law. It means that there is need to recall the memory trace or to get in field of consciousness, in order to avoid forgetting. If it is not remembered or used from time to time, it will lose its energy and it will be forgotten.

(v) Forgetting is due interference. Human being is evergrowing. It is ever-changing. Every moment we learn new things. The memory traces are not preserved in small separate compartments. Thus the new traces interfere and overlap the old traces. They are disturbed. Fresh learning disturbs the old pattern built up in previous learning. According to this view-point if learning is followed by another learning, it may be forgotten soon. If learning is followed by complete rest, such as-sleep, it will be strengthened. This is the reason that there is slow forgetting during sleep. If the memory trace is left undisturbed, it hardens or consolidates and can resist later interference.

(vi) Forgetting is due to fatigue and emotional disturbances. Without the cause of motivational objectives the learning is considered also the causes of

forgetting. In fear and anxiety, we are so nervous that we forget the experiences which can be easily recalled otherwise. Sometimes, students know the lesson or the answer of a question but the presence of harsh and hard teacher or in the examination hall they forget the learnt answer. They become nervous due to anxiety and fear. Poor mental hygiene may be another factor of forgetting, when there is loss of self-confidence, weak will and more of conflict.

(vii) Forgetting is due to painful experience and unhappy events. It is natural to avoid unpleasant experiences. They are suppressed with the great force and are buried in the unconscious mind by way of repression, from where they cannot come up in the conscious mind. This is an adjustment mechanism. Slip of pen or slip of tongue are also meaningful and their unconsciousness causes to forget one thing and speak the other. It is connected with the hidden and unfulfilled wish. Such forgetfulness is called morbid forgetfulness.

(viii) Forgetting depends on the learning stage. Weak methods of learning invite forgetting. Learning without association is forgotten soon, as there is no assimilation in this case. The meaningful material is not forgotten but the nonsense or meaningless material is forgotten very easily as it lacks association with apperceptive mass as said earlier, the loss of association is very important for the process of learning. It is therefore that the craft centred education provides greater chances of learning with full assimilation, and lesser chances of forgetting. All that is learnt, is learnt through concrete personal experience, and the learnt material has direct association with the activity in hand. The experience become meaningful direct and concrete. Apperception takes place more easily. Strong association leave hardly any chance for forgetfulness.

(ix) Forgetting is due to Lack of Interest. People forget the names, objects, ideas, or thing in which they are not interested. Pupils forget the topics which are dull and uninteresting. Learning without interest is a waste as it is prone to forgetfulness.

Distinction Between Natural and Morbid Forgetfulness

Morbid Forgetfulness. It has been seen that some people have very good retentive memory. They can learn quickly and can retain for a long time. Recall is very easy and comfortable. But for certain events, names and experiences they forget miserably. This type of forgetfulness is called morbid forgetfulness.

This type of theory of fogetfulness in explained by the exponents of psycho-analysis viz. Freud, Adler, Jung. In the mind there are several wishes, desires and carvings. All of them cannot be satisfied. If we do once, the opposite wish will be checked and rejected. Sometimes, the wish of an individual has clash with super-ego or with individual's social and moral code. Sometimes the wish of an individual cannot be satisfied as the social order does not allow. In order to adjust with the circumstances some wishes are suppressed and then repressed into the unconscious mind. If the event or face, name or experiences is related to these repressed wishes or cravings; the conscious mind does not allow then to come in the conscious level as it will remind the bitter experience of not fulfilling the desire. As this is associated with the repressed wish, which is opposed to conscience of the individual due to certain reasons, and is regarded somewhat harmful to the individual, so it is prevented to enter the consciousness and to forget it.

Thus there is underlying reason in forgetting these certain events or experiences. As some people avoid certain streets, rooms and certain types of faces where they had bitter experiences in the past, similarly, certain ideas or learning are avoided (forgotten) to prevent the unpleasantness. This is the reason of slip of tongue and common errors. In reality we wish to avoid them and we forget them.

The serious troubles of morbid forgetfulness are the cases of serious coflicts and complexes in the individual. This is due to pathology of mind.

V.13 Differences in Memory of Adults and Children

1. Memory of Children are in process of development. Children minds are on the way of development. Mentally they are not matured. Their learning is not the perceptual and not on the conceptual level as they lack concepts or at least their concepts are not as clear, defined and reliable as compared to the adults. Thus in children there is only perceptual memory. It means there is concrete memory or memory for concrete objects.

2. Children acquire fast. They learn new experiences very quickly. Upto the age of 25 the power to acquire experience is fairly great. After that it declines.

3. Children can retain more strongly than adults can. This is why the memory of childhood events is vivid. But in adult life, especially during old age, memory declines. Some old men cannot retain anything.

4. Memorizing methods are different in nature. Usually the children learn mechanically. There is rote memory. They do not make use of association. This is not intelligent method. They lack it because they are not intelligent as adults. On the other hand adults learn intelligently. They grasp it fully. They use their insight. They make use of associations and the new learning is assimilated with the already existing apperceptive mass. The child cannot do it because the quantity of apperceptive mass is less. He is not so rich in his past experience.

5. The memory of children has less transfer of training. Adults have a better ability memory transfer. The memories of the adults can be used for some other experiences of future. They can draw the conclusion from their past experiences and can use them to solve the present problems.

6. Children are better in general memory. Adults are better in specific memory. It means that as adults have different specific interest and aptitudes, their memory is better in these specific fields. But childhood is not the age of specialization. They are interested in the general environment by which they are surrounded. So their memory for the general environment is better.

7. Rote memory is decidedly better for children. They cram the subject matter efficiently and effectively. The adults cannot do so well. Perhaps it is boring for them or they lack concentration for such type of material.

8. The immediate recall is better in adults than in children. Both for nonsense and sensible material, the retention is better in children and it begins to decline with the dawn of adolescence. The memory does not go on increasing. After the age of twenty five (generally) there is decline for the power to acquire. In old age retention is lost to great extent. But this is now called law for all.

V.14 Recall and Forgetting

As said earlier, retention, recall and recognition are the three major factors of learning, and recall follows retention. Hence whatever is to be recalled must have retained properly. Generally good retention results in a good recall. However, there are certain factors that control recall which can be studied as:

1. Time factor. An idea is forgotten due to lapse of time and lack of interest. Hence if the incident is very recent, there are less chances of forgetting, and hence the recall will be better. Everybody can make use of his immediate memory, because due to recency of learning recall is easy. That is the secret of revision of lesson just before the examination.

2. Interest factor. The more interesting an incident or an idea, the stronger will it have the impression on the mind. Hence absolutely pleasant experience, novel things, happy incidents cause vivid impressions and strong engrams. Sometimes the first impression is the best, as it is novel. This is secret of love at first sight or strong impressions of the first day in the school, first sight of the cinema and first day in the office or profession.

3. Repetition. Recall becomes stronger when an experiences is repeated very often. A poem can be learnt by rote repeating it over and over again. Multiplication tables are recalled only after these are repeated often. A good number of revisions ensures better recall.

4. Association. Law of association works the best in recalling events. Difficult names, numbers or things can be recalled easily by association of these with something that is already assimilated. Here one impression stimulates another impression. Greater amount of apperception takes place through greater association and significance of associating assimilated experience with new experiences so as to bring about strong apperception, and consequently unfailing recall.

V.15 Learning Exercises

1. What do you mean by memory and discuss memory as a process ?
2. Describe different theories of memory and discuss any theory in detail.
3. What are the signs of good memory and how we can improve memory?
4. What are different methods of memorising?
5. Discuss the role of teacher for improvement in memory of a student.
6. What do you mean by forgetting?
7. Describe the theories of forgetting.
8. Discuss various causes of forgetting.
9. What is short-term memory and what is long-term memory?
10. Differentiate short-term memory from long-term memory.
11. What do you mean by forgetting?
12. Discuss the theories of values.
13. What are the causes of forgetting?
14. How we can improve memory?
15. How memory forgetting theories can help a teacher?

VI
Learning

Learning is a common term which are use in our day-to-day life. To understand the concept of the term learning, I would like to narrate an incidence. For instance, Rajat, a two year old child, made a number of visits to his uncle doctor's clinic. He took these visits as a matter of course. One day he was to receive his first three inoculations against typhoid. After the needle jobbed his arm, stimulating some pain receptors he showed alarm. His response was a mild withdrawal, a cry of pain. On the second occasion upon seeing the doctor preparing his needle he broke out crying and made movements to escape. On the third occasion, the mere sight of doctor's clinic was sufficient to set off the efforts to escape and the cries of fear. This little story illustrates many of the basic facts of learning as we find it in its natural state. Like the burnt child who often dreads the fire, similarly, Rajat learnt to try to escape from a needle, a doctor and his clinic and even his name. Before this painful episode, Rajat had reacted quite differently. These changes in his reactions are the reflections of learning. In the same way there is a vast array of behaviour patterns that is learned in the home, the streets and the playground which gives an impression that an individual has acquired is the net outcome of learning.

VI.1 Meaning and Definitions of Learning

The learning is the process by which the individual acquires different types of knowledge, develops beliefs, develops various habits and form attitudes that are necessary to meet the demands of life in general. Ultimately learning affects one's behaviour by producing changes that are suited to various situations. The changes in behaviour that may take place in the form of completely new patterns or may consist in the improvement of already existing basic responses. When complete learning takes place we can observe that the best way of responding to a situation becomes permanent. Thus, learning may be called as a process of effective changes in the individual's behaviour and making such changes permanent.

Most of our learning is purposeful. Because, the process of learning is directed towards end results which satisfy the organism by releasing the tension created by a particular need or purpose. The behaviour which fully succeeds in relieving the tension is accepted as the best possible solution and the learning process helps to make such changes in behaviour permanent, it is not meant that no further change in behaviour is possible. In the light of new experiences further changes can take place and what has been learnt is subject to the laws of remembering and forgetting.

In brief, learning can be described in a few bullet points which can be described as:

(1) Learning means modifying and changing one's behaviour with references to achieve a particular goal.

(2) Learning means establishing new relationships between a stimulus (S) and response (R), meaning thereby that learning helps in making new neural connection to bring out new responses. By learning we are able to change the neural responses to certain stimuli which are obtained because of our innate structure. Thus, learning helps us to react to the environment in more advantageous ways. Taking all these points into consideration, learning may be described as a process of effective change in behaviour which produces an important improvement in our relations with the environment effecting on us.

Definitions of Learning

Klein (1987), defines learning is a permanent change in the ability to exhibit a behaviour. This change occurs as the result of successful or unsuccessful experience. This definition of learning has three important components. First, the change in behaviour must be relatively permanent to be considered an example of learning. Secondly, learning reflects a change in the potential for a behaviour. Learning do not automatically lead to change in behaviour.

We must be sufficiently motivated to translate learning into behaviour. Thirdly, many examples of behavioural changes do not reflect the learning process.

Lornez (1966), defines many situations in which experience alters instinctive behaviour.

Skinner, defines. "The process of learning something more than acquisition of facts and skills through mechanised procedures such as repetitive practice. Instead, the learner organises and evaluates learning materials, endows them with many meanings and interpretations and becomes conscious of working goals."

Hilgard defines learning in the same way that "Learning is the process by which activity originates or is changed through reacting to an encountered situation provided that the characteristics of the change in activity cannot be explained on the basis of native responses, tendencies, maturations or temporary states of organism like fatigue or effect of drugs."

Garrett defines that the "Learning is that activity by virtue of which we organise our responses with new habits."

Woodworth and Schlosberg define the "Learning as a change that occurs in the organism during many kinds of activity. It shows later as an after effect of activity. A later activity is different from the earlier activity. We are tempted to say that learning is demonstrated whenever a later activity shows after effects of earlier activity."

Crow and Crow defines "Learning is the acquisition of habits, knowledge, and attitudes. It involves new ways of doing things and it operates in an individual's attempt to overcome obstacles or to adjust to new situations. Learning represents progressive change in behaviour as the individual reacts to a situation or situations in an effort to adapt his behaviour effectively as per the demands made upon him. It enables him to satisfy interests or to attain goals."

To my mind learning is a process by which an organism acquires knowledge, derive experiences, formulates certain principles which guide an individual to react to a situation more effectively to release tension for the gratification of particular need. Learning is a continuous purposive process of action and reaction while organising and synthesising the old and latest experiences resulting in a novel pattern of one's behaviour by an efficient utilisation of cognitive, conative and effective components of behaviour.

VI.2 Nature of Learning

Above definitions makes us to understand that learning is a change or modification of behaviour which takes place during our life for adjustment with the environment. Reason being an individual is ever growing and ever changing. Learning is not restricted to childhood but it goes with life. Death is its end point. But it is correct that childhood is the main period of learning and as the individual develops into adult, learning goes on decreasing, but the change in behaviour due to learning always takes place though the rate of change due to learning in advance/senior age group is negligible.

There are different view-points regarding the nature of learning and as such the nature of learning can be studied as per different schools of thoughts of learning:

1. Behaviouristic School of Psychology. Nature of learning as per behaviouristic school states that "Learning is essentially the attaching of a response to a stimulus which did not originally call forth that response." The school of Watson explains learning from Stimulus-Response theory. To understand this theory, we need to know What is stimulus? The influence which the environment exercises on the organism and rouses it to act is called stimulus. What is a response? The activity that is so aroused is called the response. If somebody pricks us with a pin, the pin prick is the stimulus. Owing to the pin-prick, we at once jump or try to escape it. The action of jumping or escaping is the response. Behaviouristic School of Psychology puts forth this theory. It takes human being just as a complex machinery and emphasizes the values of stimulus or environment. The weak point of this theory is that it ignores that living being is self-active, self-determining and self-resolving. It has inner urge to live and adjust with the external environment. On the other hand, there is too much emphasis on the part of environment.

2. Thorndike School explains the nature of learning by giving some objective laws of learning. According to his famous law of effect, learning takes place if the result of learning is satisfying and it does not take place if, it is not accompanied by satisfaction. The second law of learning is of exercise or use and disuse.

3. Kohler School of thought i.e., Gestalt School explains that learning takes place by insight. With the insight the learner perceives the different parts of the situations and connects them in a way so as to get correct view of the whole situation. This theory of insight learning opposes trial and learning theory of Thorndike.

4. The Latest is Field Theory describes the nature of learning as the exponents of this view-point hold that field (situation) is ever changing just as the field of consciousness. The choice of field depends on the motives of the learner. Thus, this theory explains learning from the view-point of motivation.

There are several theories of learning which explain learning in their own ways. Though all these theories defend themselves with experiments and logic, still no one theory is a success to explain all types of learning. There is no theory which is universally accepted. As a matter of fact, all these theories hold good in their specific situations and for different types of learning. Nobody can deny that all the factors *i.e.,* trial and error, insight, inner urge and motivation are needed for explaining different types of learning.

VI.3 Types of Learning

The fact that learning is a change that occurs in an organism during many kinds of activities. In other words, Woodworth says that learning is an after effect of activity. Since, man performs many activities. Therefore, on the basis of these activities learning take place in various forms : *(i)* motor learning *(ii)* perceptual *(iii)* conceptual *(iv)* associative learning *(v)* appreciational learning *(vi)* attitudinal learning *(vii)* verbal and non-verbal learning.

Let us study different types of learning:

(i) Motor Learning. The motor learning, trains the muscles of human body to control the environment to exhibit different responses of body. This is the first stage of learning. Bodily development occurs earlier than mental one. Therefore, bodily learning is the first to take place.

In motor learning body learns to handle the things. For instance, the child catches everything that is presented to him. Head and eyes co-ordination is perhaps the first to develop. There are also movements of legs. Gradually, the body begins to crawl. He is taught to stand with support. Then walking takes place. Similarly, the movements of mouth and tongue give rise to learning of language. Motor learning takes place before the mind is developed. Even the percepts are lacking in body. The method of all motor learning in the infantile stage takes place by imitation. The baby imitates his elders *i.e.*, mother, father, elder brother and sister. He copies them in their actions of involving simple movements.

(ii) Perceptual Learning. As the mind develops and child has his percepts, he gets sensations through the different sense organs and gives meaning to them. It means that objects around are meanigful for him and he perceives them wherever they are presented to him. For a very young baby all the objects are similar. He cannot differentiate between a toy and a biscuit but later on, when he learns the names of the different objects, he may differentiate a toy and a biscuit just at first sight. This is a great land-mark in the development of child and his learning process. Now, he begins to learn by percepts. In perceptual learning blind imitation is avoided. Trial and error is also rejected. Now, he uses his mind to solve the problem by his insight. He does not make any false effort but he chooses the correct response. For instance, Kohler performed various experiments on learning and showed clearly that the learning at this stage of mental development is more a question of correct perception than of motor activity and trial and error.

(iii) Conceptual Learning. Conceptual learning reflects the next stage of mental development of an individual. Conceptual learning develops thinking process. Therefore, thinking is an essential characteristic of conceptual learning. Thinking leads to abstract understanding and reasoning. The judgement,

another higher mental process develops through conceptual learning. When the individual is very well-equipped with these tools to form new responses and tackle more difficult and complicated problems and puzzles. These tools enable him to learn things quickly and retain for a longer time than young children, babies and animals. In other words the higher mental process *i.e.,* concept formation to solve the riddles. Man has most developed brain in which he excels the rest of the animal kingdom.

(iv) Associative Learning. The conceptual learning is helped by associative learning in amassing of knowledge. New concepts are tagged with the past concepts through association and as such knowledge and memory.

(v) Appreciational Learning. While conceptual learning is on the affective side, a child, from the very beginning, utilises his inborn trait of aesthetic sensibility, and acquires concepts of colours by appreciation.

(vi) Attitudinal Learning. Attitudes are the general dispositions for certain particular concepts, things, persons or activities A child develops an attitude of affection towards his mother, an attitude of reverence towards his teacher. His attitude towards play is most favourable. All this a child learns and adopts gradually which amounts Attitudinal Learning. Array of behaviour patterns that is learned in the home and the school, in streets and the playground, infact wherever the drama of life is being staged.

VI.4 Learning Theories

Historically speaking, formalized learning theory was developed in 1930 when proponents of various approaches attempted to build their own theory to explain the problems of learning. With the passage of time various theories to explain the phenomena of learning came into being as a result, it was thought to classify these theories into different categories. The latest classification of theories of learning can be studied as under:

A. **S—R Theories**

- *(i)* **S—R Theories without reinforcement**
  - *(a)* Conditioning learning theory Pavlov.
  - *(b)* Watson's learning theory.
  - *(c)* Guthrie's learning theory.
- *(ii)* **S—R Theories with reinforcement**
  - *(a)* Thorndike's theory.
  - *(b)* Hull's theory.
  - *(c)* Skinner's theory.

B. **Congnitive field theory**

- *(a)* Gastalt theory of learning.

(*b*) Field theory of learning (Lewin).

(*c*) Tolman's Sign—Gastalt theory of learning.

The above theories carries many names in psychological literature such as:

The connectionist theories are also called S→R theories; Behaviouristic or Mechanicalistic theories or Associative theories.

The congnitive theories are also known as purposive theories, S—O—R theories or organismic or Gastalt or field theories. In this book, we shall study only the selected theories as they represent all aspects of learning:

(1) Trial And Error Theory

(2) Conditioning Theory

(3) Watson Theory

(4) Gastalt Theory.

All these theories studies the different aspects of learning and for a successful educational psychologist, all these theories are useful. Reason being, the psychologists/educationists today are not much concerned with the theories of learning but they are concerned with the process and problems of learning and de-learning. In this connection, the knowledge of the theories of learning enables us to understand the behaviour of the students. Because, for an educationist the applied part of learning behaviour is most important. So, let us study each theory in details.

1. Trial and Error Theory of Learning

This theory of learning was put forward by an American psychologist Thorndike. This theory believes that we learn by making mistakes and errors. The solution of problems is obtained or the right responses are learnt by eliminating the wrong responses. In the process of learning, the learning takes place gradually. It is not quick and sudden. The exercise and practice help in acquiring the correct response. This theory does not believe insight. There are several examples of trial and error learning. When a beginner rides on cycle, he cannot control the handle, cannot have a balance, and free movements of feet on pedals are very difficult. He makes several attempts and loses the balance at the time and falls down. The handle moves against his wish and several minor accidents are repeated. But the efforts get fruit and after days he learns to run cycle smoothly on broad roads only. With a little more practice he may ride on cycle and move about in crowded streets. He can learn to control the handle with one hand and may balance himself even holding the handle. In the beginning, the new work (cycling) is very difficult, later on it becomes a very ordinary and simple act and is done with only a little attention.

Similarly, learning of a car driving, type writing and working on complex machines depends upon trials and errors. Gradually the errors are avoided and the correct responses are gained. This is not only true in case of working on machines. Even the child uses the method in motor and mental learning. Child does not learn to walk in one day. He takes time and makes continuous efforts in this direction. The movements of hands, head and the co-ordination of different muscles are learnt through trial and error process. Learning to talk, read and write are other suitable examples in favour of this theory.

Experimental evidence. This theory of learning is based on experimental evidence. Most of these experiments were conducted on animals like fish, rats, cats etc. by Thorndike, the exponent of this theory. The space does not allow to deal with several experiments. Only two typical experiments are mentioned below:—

(a) Cat experiment. Thorndike got a box for a cat. It was of 20" × 15" × 12" size and there were iron bars on the sides. Various forms of catches or fastening were used. In one classical experiment, the door of the box had a bolt and with it a string was attached. The other end of the string was tied to a wire loop which was bending above in the centre of the box. Thus, the door could be opened by catching the loop and pulling it. The cat was kept hungry for 24 hours. Then it was placed in the box and the door was closed by using bolt. Food (fish) was placed outside the box at a suitable distance so that the cat could not push a paw through the bars and claw it.

As the cat was hungry and confined to the box and the food was in its sight, so the situation was full of motivation to make attempts to get food. It pushed its paws through the bars. It moved here and there inside the box clawing the box, biting it or striking its head against the sides of the box. Thus various random attempts were made and during these trials, some-how the cat pulled down the hanging loop and the door was opened. It dashed towards the food and got it. The time taken by the cat in making all these attempts and getting food was recorded of this first attempt.

The same experiment with same apparatus and cat was repeated several times under similar conditions. The time taken be cut to perform successful attempt after the first attempt was recorded to be less meaning thereby that number of random activities were reduced which shows that stamping in and stamping out of useless efforts helps to learn. Besides, it also reveals that the rate of learning increases with attempt. For example, if it took 160 seconds for the first attempt but a few seconds for the last trial. Thus, as the number of trials increase, the time decreases or the efficiency of learning increases.

(b) Fish experiment. Thorndike did an experiment on a type of fish called Fundulus which lives in shade. It dislikes sun-light. A special aquarium was

prepared with a glass partition that divided it into two portions. The aquarium was placed in such a way that one end was under the shade and the other was in sunlight. To begin, with, the fish was placed in the shade. After some time, it was put in the portion of aquarium which was in the sunlight. As, by nature it dislikes sunshine, so it felt very discomfortable. It started making movements to escape from the annoying situation and rest in shade. The only way to shade was through a hole in the partition. It was striking its head to the partition, coming back, moving up, jumping on sides and making such movements at random. During the struggle, it found the correct path and went to the shade. After some rest (15 minutes) the experimenter again took it out and placed it in sunshine. It made effort and reached the shade. This was repeated several times. The time for each and every attempt was recorded and the learning curve was drawn. It was learnt that the fish very much profited by its experiences that modified its conduct to meet the situation. The time for the first trial was maximum and for the last one was minimum with much difference. Thus the attempts resulted into getting the correct response and eliminating the error or wrong responses.

Merits of the Theory. Trial error learning is present in animals and children. The movements of the limbs and the coordination of muscles are learnt gradually. Skills like walking, talking, reading, writing, swimming, running and cycling can be nicely explained by the theory.

It is also present in adults. They also learn by experience. The research for new machinery and invention is not the result of one effort. In every attempt and research on making better machines and other objects of this civilization the weak points or its limitations are removed. The rich experiences of human race and the empirical knowledge, which gives the ready-made solution to our general problems of life, are results of trial and error.

It is wrong to view that trial and error is only used for motor learning and it has no score for mental or higher learning. Refuting this objection of Kohler, Thorndike stated that trial and error may occur on mental level. Thinking, reasoning and viewing the situation critically may involve trial and error while solving the puzzles. Insight is the end-point of trial and error. The difficulty is only this that mental processes are so quick that it is very difficult to record them and their time. So, in mental learning, it (trial and error) plays hidden part, though very important one.

This theory explains the formation of habits and development of skill very nicely. Law of exercise holds goods in all the human activities. Nobody denies that practice makes a man perfect.

Educational Implications of the Theory. Students should note the mottos of "Practice makes a man perfect", "Work hard", "try, try, again."

Repetition of lessons and doing exercise in home work are good devices to learn the lesson efficiently. It stresses motivation which has great educational value.

Limitations. All the learning cannot be explained by this theory. Sometimes we get the correct solution in our first attempt and there is no need of other trial. Sometimes we get solution by insight. (This will be explained later).

It is wasteful to try at random. Committing the lesson to memory by learning mechanically and without understanding is not helpful. The transfer of training is least in such type of learning which is of great value in the field of education.

2. Conditioning Theory of Learning

The idea of learning by conditioning was put forward by Pavlov and Watson. Both were contemporaries. Pavlov was from Russia whereas, Watson was an American Psychologist. This idea was given in 1900 by them quite independently of each other's work.

According to this theory learning during life time depends on the innate responses. These are modified and the natural responses obtained by substituting the artificial stimulus for natural stimulus. This process of substitution of artificial or conditioned stimulus for natural or unconditioned stimulus is called conditioning. In this process, a new connection of stimulus and response is created. The connection in between the stimulus and response is known as conditioning.

Conditioning theory takes into account the fundamental concept as the basis of connectionism. This concept says that learning is the linking of a response to a stimulus (R—S) (S—K). The human organism as well as many other organism, have an innate fund of responses, tendencies, or reactions which are activated when appropriate stimuli are presented to them. For instance, the salivation is the natural response (NR) when an animal is hungry and food (NS) is presented to it, as fear and withdrawal are natural responses to bound noise. These reactions are natural because they have not been learned and are innate. But it has been seen that if another artificial stimulus (UNS) is presented along with, or shortly before the natural stimulus (NS), and if this association is repeated a number of times, the presentation of artificial stimulus is presented along with, or shortly before the natural stimulus, ultimately, causes the same response to occur. In this way, the response is often transferred to an artificial stimulus, and when this is done, the organism is said to have been conditioned.

The conditioning depends upon the situation keeping the situation in view we can categorise conditioning into four types such as: *(a)* classical conditioning, *(b)* operant conditioning, *(c)* cognitive learning, and *(d)* punishment and negative reinforcement. In the first two, positive, reinforcement (reward) is typically used to promote learning. In the third type of conditioning learning takes place without reinforcement. The fourth type of conditioning the learning type is somewhat like the first two except that negative reinforcement (unpleasant stimulation) is used to promote learning.

(a) Classical Conditioning

Classical conditioning gets its name from the fact that it is the kind of learning originally studied in the "classical" experiments of Ivan P. Pavlov (1849–1936). Beginning in the late 1890's, this famous Russian physiologist introduced the concept of conditioning and established many of its basic principles (1927 to 1960). Although classical conditioning, the term classical is used here.

The Basics of Classical Conditioning. Before we describe a typical Pavlovian experiment, here are some definitions. The essential operation in classical conditioning is a pairing of two stimuli. One, which is neutral at first in that it elicits only a general alerting, not a specific response, is called the conditioned stimulus (CS). The other, which consistently elicits a specific response, is called the unconditioned stimulus (US). The response elicited by the unconditioned stimulus is the unconditioned response (UR). As a result of the pairing of the conditioned stimulus (CS) with the unconditioned stimulus (US), the previously neutral conditioned stimulus comes to elicit the response. Then it is called the conditioned response (CR). Keep these terms in mind as you follow this experiment in classical conditioning.

Pavlov designed an apparatus, for measuring how much a dog's mouth waters in response to food. A cup attached to the dog's cheek collected drops of saliva flowing from the animal's parotid salivary gland, which had been moved to the outside of the cheek by surgery. The saliva ran from the cup to a tube, and the air driven out of the tube in turn displaced a coloured foluid in a calibrated instrument which looked somewhat like a thermometer. Thus, small changes in the flow of saliva could be read on this gauge. The dog was placed in a soundproof room equipped with a one-way vision screen through which the experimenter could see the animal. By remote control Pavlov could swing a food pan within the dog's reach, or he could puff some powdered food into its mouth through along with several other kinds of stimuli, including the sounds of a bell, buzzer, or metronome.

In a typical experiment, Pavlov trained the dog on sounding a bell the (CS), shortly afterward presenting food the (US), and then measuring the amount of saliva secreted the (UR). After pairing the sound of the bell with food a few times, the effects of the training were tested by measuring the amount of saliva which flowed when the bell was rung alone, without food Pavlov resumed the paired presentation of bell and food a few more times and then tested again with the bell alone. This shows, the amount of saliva secreted in response to the bell alone the (CR) gradually increased.

Over many test trails, this increase in the dog's salivation in response to the CS can be observed as a learning curve. Conditioning curve is typical of an experiment in salivary conditioning. It is drawn without specifying the number of trails or the amount of saliva, although on a graph representing an actual experiment, these measurements would be plotted. The conditioning curve, also called an acquisition curve, shows that the strength of the response on test trials gradually increases with more and more pairings of CS and US. Note that the curve gradually flattens; that is, each increase due to a trial is less than the preceding one. In other words, the curve is negatively accelerated; it is a curve of "diminishing returns."

The discovery of salivary conditioning was followed by many other conditioning experiments. Pavlov and others tried new conditioned stimuli and new unconditioned stimuli. They soon found that almost any stimulus which reliably produces a reflex response could be an unconditioned stimulus. The unconditioned responses are the basis of conditioning. For instance either a dog or human may be given a mild shock to the leg will reflexively pull the leg back in an attempt to withdraw from the object that shocks. In classical conditioning, the electrode that gives the shock is attached to the leg. Thus, the learner cannot, withdraw from it, but flexion of the still occurs reflexively. (What happens when flexion of the still occurs leg results in escape from the shock ? This will be described later.) Pairing of neutral stimuli CSs with the unconditioned stimulus of shock will result in classical conditioning. After conditioning, the learner will flex the leg when the conditioned stimulus when the bell was rung gradually diminished until it reached a level little different from its level at the beginning of the experiment.

If the scientists stopped experimenting at this point, he or she might conclude that the extinction procedure had simply erased what had been learned in the conditioning procedure. But this is not true. Extinction is a process of learning to inhibit the response acquired in conditioning. It is a new learning superimposed on the old without really destroying the original conditioned response. This can be proved in two ways.

One proof comes from a phenomenon known as spontaneous recovery. A conditioned response which has been extinguished may spontaneously recover some of the strength lost in extinction during an interval of rest following extinction. If, for example, a dog whose conditioned response has been extinguished is brought back into the experimental situation and the bell is again rung again without being followed by food), the amount of salivation is considerably greater than it was at the end of the previous series of extinction trails. This increase shows that, even after extinction, some degree of association remains between the bell and salivation. The conditioning has not been entirely lost.

Secondly, reconditioning is more rapid than original conditioning. To recondition, the experimenter is premanted. The shock in reconditioning experiment also results in bodily manifestations of fear and in the case of humans at least, the experience of fear. After pairing with shock, the CS now comes to elicit both the bodily responses associated with fear and the experience of fear. These conditioned emotional responses (CRRs), as they are called, may be a basis of some of the irrational human fears known as phobias.

Continuity in Classical Conditioning. Several points can be made about the pairing operation that is, the contiguity or closeness of the CS and the US. In classical conditioning, one concerns reinforcement. In classical conditioning, the conditioned stimulus is said to be "reinforced" by the unconditioned stimulus. Therefore, in classical conditioning the operation of pairing is itself the reinforcement.

Another an important condition considered essential for conditioning to take place is an optimal inter-stimulus interval in pairing. The inter-stimulus interval is the time between the onset of the CS and the onset of the US. The CS and US may be paired so that they occur simultaneously, but not much conditioning takes place if they do. The best interstimulus interval varies with the situation and the kind of response being conditioned. In general, short inter-stimulus intervals, ranging from 0.5 seconds to 30 seconds or so, are optimal (Kimble, 1967).

Extinction and Spontaneous Recovery. Once the conditional response has been acquired, and the CS is repeatedly presented without being followed by the US starts to occur. The response (say, salivation in the dog experiment) gradually weakens, or the frequency of responses (say, flexion of the leg in the experiment using electric shock) gradually decreases.

In another experiment Pavlov states that a conditioned dog was placed in the apparatus in the usual way. Then the bell was rung without being followed by food, on trial after trial, the dog heard only the bell and never saw or received food. The watering of the dog's mouth was measured in the usual way. As the procedure continued, the amount of saliva that the dog secreted gain pairs the US and the CS of the original conditioning. When Pavlov did this, he obtained the general results. The reconditioning following extinction occurred more rapidly than the first conditioning. Indeed, an experimenter can condition, extinguish, condition, and extinguish—and up to a certain point, the animal condition, a little faster each time and extinguishes a little more rapidly than the time before. Thus the original conditioning is not erased by extinction. Instead, learning both to respond and not to respond is taking place. The animal is learning when to do one or the other.

Stimulus Generalization. Pavlov discovered very early that if he conditioned an animal to salivate at the sound of a bell, it would also salivate, though not quite so much, at the sound of a buzzer of a metronome. The animal tended to generalize the conditioned response to stimuli that were different from, but somewhat similar to, the one to which it was specifically conditioned.

The example of stimulus generalization we shall use here comes from a study of the Galvanic Skin Response (GSR) in man. The galvanic skin response is usually measured as a decrease in the resistance of the skin to the flow of a minute electrical current. The mechanisms responsible for the skin is characteristic of alertness and arouses measured by the lie detector or polygraph. In the following experiment on stimulus generalization, the GSR was used as an unconditioned response to the unconditioned stimulus of an electrical shock (Hovland, 1937):

An electric shock was the unconditioned stimulus for the GSR. The experimenter began by conditioning the GSR of a person to the sound of a pure tone of a particular frequency. This was done by presenting the shock and tone (the CS) simultaneously, or nearly so. After the GSR had been conditioned to the tone, Hovland measured the strength of the conditioned GSR given to tones that were of frequencies different from the original tone (based on the conditioned stimulus shows the results. As you would expect, the tone, or CS, used in the original conditioning evoked the largest GSRs; tones similar in frequency to the CS evoked the next-largest GSRs; tones farthest in frequency from the original CS evoked the weakest responses. Thus a rough rule of thumb can be formulated. The greater the similarity between stimuli, the greater the generalization between them.

Many human responses and characteristics seem to be acquired through the processes of conditioning and generalization illustrated in the experiment with the GSR. There the shock was an unconditioned stimulus eliciting pain, and the conditioned stimulus elicited a fear of pain. This simple experiment serves as a model for the development of irrational fears. Such fears or phobias are irrational because people acquire them through accidental conditioning to some stimulus and then generalize them to situations that otherwise would not be frightening.

Higher Order Conditioning. In his pioneering work Pavlov discovered another conditioning process called higher-order conditioning. It involves several stages of classical conditioning which can be described in two-stage example: in the first stage, a response is conditioned as usual to a conditioned stimulus. In the second stage, the conditioned stimulus of the first stage (CS1) is paired with a new conditioned stimulus (CS2), and conditioning occurs.

In the Pavlov's first stage of the experiment, a dog was conditioned in the usual way to salivate to the sound of a metronome (CS1). After the dog was well conditioned, the second "higher-order" stage was began. A card with a black square on it (CS2) was thrust into the dog's view just before the metronome was sounded. No food was given during this second stage. In effect, then, the card was being paired with the sound of the metronome, the dog started to salivate when the card with the black square on it was presented. Thus, although the card was never paired with food, it came to elicit salivation.

The higher-order stage of Pavlov's experiment is not really different from any classical conditioning if you remember that an unconditioned stimulus was defined as one which consistently, elicits a reflex response. Higher-order conditioning works like this. As a result of conditioning in the first stage, the dog's salivation is conditioned to the sound of the metronome that is, the metronome now consistently elicits the response of salivation. In the second higher-order stage, the card with the black square is the conditioned stimulus, while the metronome, which consistenly elicits the response, acts as an unconditioned stimulus.

At first glance, you might think that higher-order conditioning has no limits that the second CS can be paired with a third, a third with a fourth, and so on. But in fact there is a limit and it is usually at the point of second order conditioning. The reason is that while the second-order CS is being paired with the first order CS, the first-order CS is being extinguished, because it is being presented without pairing with the unconditioned stimulus (US). Up to a point, such extinction can be prevented by interspersing trails in which the primary CS and US are repaired. By doing this and pairing another stimulus with the card, Pavlov was able to carry higher-order stimulus. But it was extremely difficult, whereas second-order conditioning is relatively easy, and possibly occurs in everyday learning situations.

Significance of Classical Conditioning. We have dwelt long enough on drooling dogs. Salivary conditioning was the first kind to be studied, and its study brought out many of the basic principles of classical conditioning as a form of learning. But of course these salivary responses have, by themselves, little significance in people's everyday affairs. It is the emotional responses which become conditioned to certain stimuli that are important in human life.

Many of our subjective feelings, from violent emotions to subtle nuances of mood, are probably conditioned responses. A face, a scene, or a voice may be the conditioned stimulus for an emotional response. Generalization, higher-order conditioning and the fact that we learned many of these responses before we could talk and label them, all make it difficult to trace such feelings back to their conditioned beginnings. No one can identify the origins of our emotional responses.

Although the sources of conditioned emotional responses often remain obscure, it is sometimes possible to discover their roots in ourselves and others. In the following quotation, the author describes the possible origin of a conditioned feeling in himself. Perhaps you can discover such responses and some of their beginnings in your own experience. The writer acknowledges a strongly warm, almost affectionate liking for pind willow-pattern dinner-ware, which he can trace back to childhood lunches eaten from a pink plate...In good contrast is the case of Arnold Bennett, who once wrote of a sudden ejection that came upon him whenever he saw anything pink; eventually he was able to the pink coloured alms houses of the English countryside. (Modified from Dashiell, 1949. p. 433)

Since some emotional responses to stimuli have been learned, perhaps other responses that are less disturbing can be associated with the stimuli that produce unpleasant emotional responses. The extinction and re-conditioning of disturbing emotional responses is one form of behaviour therapy.

Operant Conditioning

Let us come to another learning situation, operant conditioning, which is usually considered distinct from classical conditioning. The key feature of this learning situation is that some action or some behaviour by the learner is instrumental in producing reinforcement (or loosely speaking, a "reward") when it operates upon the environment. The behaviour is called a response by psychologists that produces the reinforcement which is strengthened and is more likely to occur in the future. The basic idea, of course, is not so strange; we expect people to repeat their responses and actions that are "rewarded."

The Basics of Operant Conditioning. Reinforcement is a key term for understanding operant conditioning. A reinforcer in operant conditioning is any stimulus or situation that strengthens the response which precedes it. Reinforcers correspond roughly to what we call "rewards." Many things can serve as reinforcement in operant conditioning such as food for a hungry animal, certain "pleasing" tastes, praise for a child, a well done from the boss, or escape from punishment.

In laboratory studies of operant conditioning, things are usually arranged so that a response actually produces the reinforcer. Thus the reinforcing event is said to be contingent upon, or to depend upon, the occurrence of a certain response. Now you can see why this kind of learning is called operant conditioning. The word "operant" signifies that when a response operates on the environment in the appropriate fashion, a reinforcer, or strengthener of the tendency to make that response, is forthcoming. Responses leading to reinforces are strengthened and are more likely to occur in the future. The likelihood of occurrence of responses which do not lead to reinforcement remains the same or decreases. We can now state the simple, but powerful, major principle of operant conditioning. If reinforcement is contingent upon a certain response, that response will become more likely to occur. Almost any response can be made likely to occur by following it with reinforcement; the behaviour of animals and people can be 'shaped' rather moulded by appropriate arrangement of responses and reinforcers.

An example, using the psychologist's favourite experimental animal, the rat, will help make things clearer. The apparatus for this demonstration is a simple box with a lever at one end. The lever is a switch that activates a food-delivery or water delivery mechanism or the lever may be wired so that it turns off a shock given to the rat through the grill floor of the box. In other words, reinforcement is contingent upon operation of the lever. Such a box, called a Skinner box was originally used by B.F. Skinner to study operant conditioning.

The first step in the operant conditioning of a hungry rat in this Skinner box is to get it to eat the food pellets when they are delivered by the experimenter, who operates the pellet-delivery mechanism from a push-button switch outside the apparatus. Pellets are delivered one by one; after a time, the rat eats each Pellet as soon as it drops. This first step in training is necessary for the food reinforcement to be effective later when the rat delivers food pellets to itself by pressing the bar. (of course, preliminary training is not necessary for reinforcers such as shock or stimulation of the brain.)

Next the experimenter stops releasing the pellets, and the rat is left alone in the box with the lever. After an initial period of inactivity, the rat, being hungry, begins to explore the box. Eventually the animal accidentally presses the lever. A pellet of food is released; that is, reinforcement is contingent the rat continues exploring, stopping to groom itself from time to time. After a while it presses the lever again, and again a pellet is released; then it presses the lever a third time. Usually after the fourth or fifth press, the rat begins to press the lever more rapidly, and operant behaviour is established which shows that operant conditioning is operated by external stimuli.

Watson's Theory of Learning

J.B. Watson an American behavioural Psychologist popularized the concept that nervous system can really explain all types of behaviour. He convinced the psychologists that for explanation of learning, understanding of brain and its functioning is very essential. Watson emphasized that all our behaviour is learned by interacting with external environmental stimuli. Watson's theory is based on the principle that stimulus—response (S—R) bondage which is the basis of learning. Watson advocated that all types of learning can be reduced to S—R connections. He further pointed out that the strength of connection between stimulus—response (S—R) depends upon the frequency of (S—R) repetitions. Watson's theory was like Thorndike's theory in respect of its claims that learning consists of strengthening S—R connections but there was one difference that Watson theory do not believed that there was no law of effect, there was no reinforcement but there was a very important law of frequency.

Watson theory can be better understood by his Rabbit—Baby experiment. Watson's Rabbit Baby experiment on human babies. A baby of 11 months was his subject. This baby was fond of furry animals and used to get pleasure by playing with rabbits. It was a pleasant act. Just as the baby was busy in playing with a rabbit, a sudden loud sound was produced at the back of baby (so that baby could not see it) by striking a hammer on iron bar. It is natural to

	Sudden Sound	Fear	R_1
	Natural S	Natural	R
S_2	Rabbit	Pleasure	R_2
In the beginning			
$S_1 + S_2$		$R_1 + R_2$	
After several days			
S_2		R_1	

get frightened when a sudden sound is heard. This was repeated several times and the furry animal and sudden sound *i.e.*, natural and non-natural stimuli were presented simultaneously to get the response of the act. After some days, only un-natural stimulus (rabbit) was given without the sound. The result was that the child was frightened. Some days back it (rabbit) was a pleasant object and now it became an annoying one.

Conditioning takes place as R_1 (natural response) was obtained by S_2 (un-natural stimuli). S_2 is known as conditioned stimulus and R_1 is conditioned response in the end. S_1 and R_1 in the beginning were unconditioned stimulus and unconditioned response respectively. Thus emotion of fear produced by artificial stimulus.

Laws of Conditioning

There are three laws of conditioning:

First law: "If the unconditional stimulus precedes the conditional stimulus, no new reflex is formed." It means if dog is fed before and the bell is rung after giving the food, there will be no conditioning. This is common sense that hungry dog has got the food and there is no reason that dog should take notice of it. There cannot be any association between ringing of bell and giving of food.

Second law: "If the conditioned stimulus is given just before the unconditioned stimulus, conditioning is sure to take place." It means that if the ringing of bell is presented just before the food, the association between bell and food will take place. In this case the ringing of bell will be meaningful for dog and it takes its notice.

Third law: "If the conditioned stimulus and unconditioned stimulus are represented at one time, the conditioning may take place or it may act." If it takes place, it will take more time than the situation of the second law, where the conditioned stimulus is given just before the unconditioned stimulus.

General Properties of Conditioned Responses

1. A conditioned behaviour, like other bare responses are more or less temporary and unstable. Conditioned response is not as durable as innate response. The conditioned response may be destroyed by law of forgetting of disuse. Therefore, in order to maintain the strength of a conditioned response, it must be regularly repeated.

2. A conditioned behaviour is highly specific, which has important bearing on the question of transfer of training.

3. Conditioned response obeys the law of summation. It means that if the same conditioned response is created by two different conditioned stimuli, then the application of both at time, results into a more powerful response.

4. A conditioned response can be destroyed experimentally. In addition to forgetting and disuse, it can be eliminated by deconditioning. Watson could remove that fear of baby by providing pleasant stimuli along with the unpleasant rabbit which was source of fear.

5. Conditioned reflexes may be more easily formed in children than in adults. It is due to the fact that adults have higher level of intelligence which resists it.

Educational implications

The educational implication of conditioning theories of learning for a teacher can be studied as:

(1) Reward and punishment should be given at correct time. The teacher should try to establish an association between giving of reward and good

work on the part of children. Some weak mothers wait for their husbands to come and punish the child for his mischief. This weakens the conditioning as the time spent during the act of mischief and actual punishment is much. As a matter of fact, punishment in school should be given there and then at the time of mischief.

(2) Likes and dislikes are nicely explained. If a teacher is somewhat rude and beats a boy, he develops hatred against him (teacher). Suppose the teacher teaches Geography. There is great association between this particular teacher and his subject as he teaches it daily. Therefore, the child may begin to hate the Geography subject and show his dislike due to conditioning.

(3) Similarly, some people avoid certain streets, corners of buildings, or cannot stand the sight of some other people as they happened to get some bitter experience in those streets or buildings or from such like people *i.e.* a burnt child dreads the fire.

(4) Child learns the names of various objects by conditioning. He hears their names and sees the objects and then slowly calls the name on seeing the object without having their names.

(5) This view-point of learning lays stress on motivation and repetition of acts, which are very useful in the class-room teaching. Habit formation is nicely explained and emotional responses can be created and destroyed.

Gastalt Theory of Learning

Gestalt Theory is also known as insight theory of learning. The exponent of this theory was Kohler, a German psychologist. He refuted the trial and error view-point of learning, stating thereby that a man has the highest developed nervous system and he learns the things while perceiving the situation as a whole Gestalt solved the problem with his intelligence using insight into it. The attempts are not at random, but based on thinking and other higher mental processes.

Gestalt is a German word which means 'Configuration' or 'whole'. According to this school of thought the data of psychology exists in wholes and not in parts. The minute analysis is meaningless and does not lead us to anywhere. Whatever we perceive, we perceive as whole. The object is not equal to its parts but it is something more than it. For example, the different parts of an object such as arms, legs, seat and back of a chair gathered together in a bundle do not mean a chair, but when they are organised in definite way, then only it becomes a chair. Thus, the correct connection between the parts of an object or of situation is very important in learning. If it is established, learning takes place.

Explanation of Insight Theory. The Gestalt theory of learning can be explained by describing the experiments performed by Kohler on monkeys and which are regarded as the bases of the theory. Kohler did several experiments on monkeys for instance:

Experiment 1. In one experiment Sultan (name of monkey) was the subject. Sultan was kept hungry for some time. Then he was shut in cage. The cage was of sufficient in size and on its sides there was wire gauze as to watch the behaviour of the monkey. From the ceiling of the cage bananas were hanging down. Just beneath the banana, there was a box.

Another box was placed in the corner of the cage. The height of the hanging bananas was so adjusted that the monkey could not reach them even by jumping from the box placed just beneath the bending corner on the floor of the cage.

As the monkey was hungry and food was in his sight, so naturally he would like to get it. The monkey made several attempts. He was jumping to get the bananas from the different points. He stood upon the box, extended his limbs but all in vain. Then he jumped several times from the box but could not succeed in achieving the goal. When Sultan was much fatigued, Kohler got into the cage. He took the box from the corner and placed it on the one in the middle of the floor and was able to reach the hanging food. Then Kohler stood upon the box to give the demonstration to Sultan. Kohler got down and placed the second in its original position and came out of the cage.

Seeing all this Sultan took the second box from the corner and placed it on the other. He stood on it and then made a jump and could get the food.

According to Kohler theory of insight learning took place as Sultan could connect the different parts of the situation *i.e.*, two boxes, their arrangement and bananas. As soon as Sultan understood that the second box can be made tool to get the food, learning took place. He viewed the situation as a whole or in other words he had the Gestalt's view of the situation. To connect the different parts into a meaningful whole, involves the play of intelligence. Thus learning is based not on trial or error but on insight.

Experiment 2. In another experiment, Kohler put the hungry monkey to the cage. There were two sticks, one was longer than the other there was a mechanism that one end of the shorter stick could be fitted in one end of the longer stick so as to make them into one still longer stick. Outside the cage, the food was placed. The monkey tried his best to get the food by pushing his limbs through the bars of cage. Sticks were also used. Even the longer stick failed to reach the food. Seeing this Kohler gave a clue by putting one of his fingers in a hole. Seeing this Sultan tried to adjust two sticks to make one long stick. He did so and could get the food by using it. The monkey viewed the whole situation and connected its parts in a definite way.

Educational Implications

Educational implications of insight theory of learning reveals that insight theory of learnings is very useful in classroom. It stresses to develop the intelligence of students. It does not believe at random efforts which are mere waste of time. The children should learn the lesson intelligently with full understanding. Blind and mechanical repetitions are very specific. Learning by insight leads to transfer of training. One intelligent learning makes room for the others. The difficult problem can only be solved by using insight and intelligence. For example, if a lesson is learnt by understanding it fully and by knowing its different steps, it can be retained for a long time. Learning insight saves time and energy. Insight learning is quick, efficient and permanent.

Gestalt theory of learning gives due emphasis on motivation. Sultan was kept hungry to motivate him to get food. The motives are very powerful. Teacher should form the desirable motives in students. They should be directly interested in their studies. The teacher can arouse the motivation of students at psychological moments in the class-room.

This theory is also used while teaching lessons. The teacher should always proceed from whole to part. While teaching about flowers in nature study, the teacher should show a flower as a whole. Then its parts are presented to class one by one in an order. The sepals, petals, stamens and ovary are shown. The lessons of Geography should also be taught by proceeding from whole to part. Now-a-days, the young children are taught first to complete words and then letters such as cat, rat, dog and then (c, a, t) it 'cat', (r, a, t) is 'rat', and so on.

Limitations of Insight Theory

Though the Gestalt (insight) theory of learning affords several examples to justify its stand and also is very useful in the class-room learning, yet it cannot explain all types of learning. Learning of children and of animals particularly is not due to insight but more due to conditioning, trial and error.

Still the different puzzles cannot be solved by the adults just in the first attempt. Trial and error is also used in mental learning. Even there can be trial and error on the mental level. Insight learning is only the end-point of trial and error learning.

Even the experiments of Kohler on Sultan, the most intelligent monkey of Kohler showed that there was much of imitation in his learning. Kohler gave the direct demonstrations. Before that the monkey did several trails. Only the easy and common behaviour is learnt by intelligence but the more difficult problems do need the trials before the success is achieved.

V.5 Difference Between Classical and Operant Conditioning

The theories of learning especially the conditioning differ from each other with respect to their approach. Depending upon the approach both theories can be better understood as complementary to each other and the differences can be studied as:

	Classical conditioning	*Operant conditioning*
1.	It was developed by Russian physiologist, Pavlov and is called Pavlovian or type-1 learning (respondent).	It was developed by B.F. Skinner and is called Skinnerian or type-2 learning (operant).
2.	In classical conditioning, the occurrence of Conditioned Response (CR) is reflexively forced by Unconditioned Stimulus (UCS).	In operant conditioning, the response is more voluntary and spontaneous.
3.	The Unconditioned stimulus (UCS) occurs without any consideration of the subject's behaviour.	The reward is contingent upon the occurrence of response.
4.	Classical conditioning is described as preparatory or anticipatory response and is also called signal learning.	Operant conditioning serves primarily to emphasize or guide an organism which already has certain responses available in its repertoire.
5.	In classical conditioning, the association between stimulus-response (S—R) is on the basis of law of contiguity.	In operant conditioning, association between stimulus-response (S—R) is on the basis of law of effect.
6.	It is related and controlled by autonomic nervous system in the organism.	It is controlled by central nervous system in the organism.
7.	There is pairing of UCS and CS.	There is no pairing of UCS and CS, but pairing

Contd.

Classical conditioning	*Operant conditioning*
	of a response and the reinforcing stimulus which follows.
8. Bondage between specific (UCS) unconditioned stimulus and (CS) conditioned stimulus is established.	Tendency to respond in a specific manner is developed.
9. Reinforcement comes first as in Pavlov's experiment food is presented first to elicit the response.	Reinforcement is provided after the response is made by the organism.
10. (CS) Conditioned stimulus and (UCS) can be placed in different temporal sequences close contiguity is followed.	Close contiguity is followed and R—S chain is formed.
11. Classical conditioning focuses on the single (S—R) stimulus response bondage.	Operant conditioning is concerned with sequences of responses. A chain of responses is formed which leads to the desired goal.
12. We present the (UCS) unconditioned stimulus regardless of whether the (CR) conditioned response occurs.	We present the stimulus only, if only, the organism makes the desired response.
13. Classical conditioning presents different pictures or behaviour and learning in which an arbitrary stimulus is associated with a highly specific, elicitable response.	The operant conditio-ning situation describes the differentiation and discrimination of a response out of a mass behaviour emitted in response to a complex stimulus field.
14. In classical conditioning stress is laid on time control.	Place of motivation and reward is stressed.

Contd.

	Classical conditioning	*Operant conditioning*
15.	The essence of learning is stimulus substitution.	The essence of learning is response modification.
16.	Classical conditioning is stimulus oriented.	Operant conditioning is response oriented.
17.	The classically conditioned reflexes may have zero strength initially.	The operant cannot have zero strength because it has to occur at least once before it can be reinforced.
18.	The classically conditioned response is correlated with and controlled by an antecedent event, an initially the UCS and subsequently the CS.	In operant conditioning, there is no antecedent, behaviour is controlled by its consequences.
19.	Respondent behaviour is internal and has a secret, personal quality about it.	Operant is external behaviour, it is the behaviour with which the organism operates on the environment.

VI.6 Laws of Learning

Learning is the after effect of doing. The process of doing activity helps to establish connections between the learning material, and learning situation. The process of doing a particular activity leads to learning. Since, learning is governed by some principles on the basis of job analysis, the experimental psychologists have derived basic principles of learning which can be summarized under four heads viz;

(1) Reinforcement, or Law of Effect;

(2) Repetition, or Law of Exercise.

(3) Initial Motivation, or Law of Readiness.

(4) Multiple Response, or Trial And Error.

These laws of learning first explain why the learner tries to learn; the second, how a learner gets the right responses; the third, why he retains and repeats the right responses; and the fourth, how a learner acquires habits and skill while learning.

In other words these principles of learning can be studied in the form of laws of learning as Thorndike formulated various laws of learning by doing experiments on animals. These laws are of great value to the teacher. The main laws are discussed below :—

1. Reinforcement or Law of Effect

This is also known as law of satisfaction and annoyance. In the words of Thorndike:

"When a modifiable connection between a situation and a response is made and is accompanied or followed by a satisfying state of affairs, that connection's strength is increased. When made and accompanied or followed by a annoying state of affairs, its strength is decreased."

It means that when modifiable bond or learning strengthened it, its result is pleasant one and it is weakened if it unpleasant. Thus we like the situations, the places and the persons which satisfy our needs. If they are bitter and make us feel unhappy, they are avoided. We like those class- fellows, who make us happy and avoid those who make us angry. These are likes and dislikes. Whatever is painful, is avoided. This is true in case of animals also. Without this the life is in danger, as painful in the first place is regarded as dangerous.

Experiment. Thorndike explained that it is the tendency of the learner to weed out those activities which do not give pleasure or success by performing an actual experiment on a rat and a maze was prepared. The path to the goal was complicated. At every turn there were two paths one leading to blind alleys and other was correct one. Rats were trained to get food placed in the maze. Arrangements were made that an electric shock was given to rat whenever it went towards blind alley or wrong path. In this way several attempts were made and every time the correct and wrong responses were recorded. It was found that wrong responses went on decreasing with trials. From these observations Thorndike stated that wrong responses are eliminated due to electric shock which was annoying.

It is very true that we always try to recollect the pleasant happenings of past. We do not touch the lamenting incidents and accidents of life. Generally we praise the past as we see all the good of it and forget its dark side. This is the reason that reward is better than punishment as reward associated with the school work with annoying situation.

Criticism. The criticism of the law of effect propounded by Thorndike can be described as:

(1) Generally we remember the pleasant days but incidents of horror and sorrow are always very permanent and we do not forget it. This picture will remain vivid. He will retain the day, date and period

and teacher along with other facts. A person who gets telegram about some loss will retain the actual wording of telegram with things. So it is wrong to say that unpleasant happenings are altogether avoided.

(2) Secondly, the process of learning is more important than its result, cause is the real thing that makes a man to learn. This law is associated or concerned with the end point.

(3) Thirdly, the result obtained by Thorndike in the above experiment on rat was very much doubted by Watson and Thomson. According to Watson, the same result can be obtained even the electric shock was not given to rat while following the wrong paths.

2. Law of Exercise

Law of exercise is also known as the law of frequency. Law of exercise is further sub-divided into two sub-laws *i.e.*, the law or use and law of disuse. The law of use help to identify the conditions of work activity identification of an activity helps to develop connections. Therefore, the modifiable connection is made between a situation and the response, and the connection's strength. It means that exercise strengthens the learning. Repetition is useful. It is correct that if we do a thing again and again, we will get mastery over it. In the beginning some works are very difficult but with efforts and attempts they become very easy. In all the experiments of Thorndike on animals, rate of learning increases with the number of trails. Practice makes a man perfect.

The second sub-law of law of exercise relates to the law of disuse is just the reverse of the law of use. It means connection between the situation and response of learning is weakened if it is not used at all. A good typist may not handle it properly or with much efficiency after ten years during which he never touched it. If we do not use our muscles, they become very weak.

3. Law of Readiness

This is the law of readiness that shows the individual is ready to learn, it is satisfying; when he is not ready to learn, it is annoying. Readiness for learning or action gives satisfaction and unreadiness leads to its dissatisfaction. In our common life, we see that we get better result of what we are willing to do and for which there is readiness for action. If there is no interest and subject is not in ready mood, then the achievement will not be so high. A student who is ready to show his knowledge is very happy if allowed to do so, and annoyed if the teacher does not give him chance to show his knowledge or ignores him.

4. Law of Primacy

This is the fourth law of learning. According to this law the learning that takes place in the beginning is best and lasting. This is why we say that the first impression is the last impression. We remember very vividly our first day in school or college, first railway journey, the first speech or the first cinema seen by us. Teacher should make use of it. His start should be very encouraging. The teacher must impress his students with his knowledge, personality and intelligence on the first day. Similarly, the students should have very pleasant and happy experience in the beginning of school career.

5. Law of Recency

Just as the primary acts are retained for longer time, recent acts are also lasting. We know the last days of our school, last working day of college or the last visit to a place. It is somewhat more vivid than others.

6. Law of Belongingness

According to this law, if the connection between stimulus and response is natural, the learning will be more effective. It will be more permanent than otherwise. On the other hand, if the relation between stimulus and response is not natural but artificial, the learning is weakened. Therefore, the teacher should create a natural atmosphere in the class-room and make use of natural tendencies.

7. Law of Intensity of Stimulus

If the stimulus is strong, the response will be healthy. If the stimulus is weak, the response will be weak. Thus learning depends on the intensity or strength of stimulus, such as, the students do not work as hard for home examination as they do for annual examination. Annual examination has more stimulus value than home examination. The students of first year and third year of college are not very serious about their studies as there is no university examination but they work very hard in second and fourth year classes. Some students attach more importance to studies, whereas, others do not consider school studies so important. It depends on the strength of different stimuli.

VI.7 Factors Effecting Learning

Learning is an active process in which learner interacts in a given situation. Learning can be made effective by observing certain conditions. Some important conditions which influence learning can be categorized into the following categories:

(A) Physiological factors.

(B) Psychological factors.

(C) Environmental factors.

(D) Methodology factors.

(A) Physiological Factors. The physiological factors are : sense perception, physical health, fatigue, time and day of learning, food and drink, age and atmospheric conditions.

(i) Sense-Perception. Sensation and perception are the basis of all cognitive learning. Weaker the power of perception, lesser the amount of learning. A blind man learns far less than a normal person. Impairment of sense organs is a handicap in the process of learning.

(ii) Physical Health. Bad health hampers learning. Sound mind and sound body are helpful in learning. Sound physical health gives vigour and vitality to pursue learning activities for a longer education. A diseased person is handicapped by the normal physical strength necessary for any mental activity.

(iii) Fatigue. Muscular or sensory fatigue causes mental boredom and indolence. Number of factors in the home and school environment may cause physical and mental fatigue such as lack of accommodation, bad seating arrangement, unhealthy clothing, inadequate ventilation, poor light, noise, overcrowdingness, and malnutrition. Longer hours of study also cause fatigue which affects the learning capacity.

(iv) Time of Learning. Morning and evening hours are the best period of study. During the day there is decline in the mental capacity. Experiments on children have shown that there are great variations in learning efficiency during the different hours of the day.

(v) Diet. Nutrition is responsible for efficient mental activity. Poor nutrition adversely affect learning. The type of food also has some effect. The alcoholic drinks, caffeine, tobacco and such addictive items have adverse effect on neuro-muscular system, and consequently upon the learning capacity.

(vi) Physical Conditions. High temperature and humidity lower the mental efficiency. Low ventilation, lack of proper illumination, noise and physical discomfort (as we find in factories and overcrowded schools) hamper the learning capacity. Distractions of all sorts affect power of concentration and consequently the efficiency of learning.

(vii) Level of Age. Learning capacity varies with age. Some subjects can better be learnt at the early age, and some during adulthood. On the evidence of experiments conducted. Thorndike says that mental development does not stop at 16 or 18 but increases upto 23, and halts after 40. Learning proceeds rapidly between 10 and 18, remains stagnant till 25, and declines upto 35. Age accompanies mental maturation. So some complex problems cannot be solved till the person is sufficiently mature.

Children learn the school subjects more easily than uneducated adults can learn. This is perhaps because the children's minds are not burdened with worldly problems, and they have more flexible nervous system as a result age level helps learning faster. But the speed of learning reduces with the age level.

(B) Psychological Factors. Psychological factors which influence learning can be discribed as:

(i) Mental Health. Mental tension, complexes, conflicts, mental illnesses and mental diseases hamper learning. A maladjusted child finds it difficult to concentrate. Concentration needs mental poise and absence of mental conflict or complex. Some pupils find it difficult to prepare for the university examination, simply because of fear of the examination and anxietic neurosis. A calm, serious and balanced mind as the power to concentrate and learn better.

(ii) Motivation and Interest. No learning can take place unless it is motivated. Purposeless learning is not learning at all. Every child is impelled by some motive to learn new things. In the absence of motivation, he does not feel interested in the act of learning. A child's behaviour in learning is energised by motives, selected by motives and directed by motives.

(a) Motives energise behaviour. Hunger and thirst induce acquisition of food. Reward induces further success. Punishment or failure induces action for achievement.

(b) Motives select behaviour. Only those acts of learning are selected which are supported by some motive. A boy visits a village fair. He sees only those toys, objects or things that interest him.

(c) Motives direct behaviour. These activate the person, enthuse him and impel him to do the desired action. These direct his energies to reach the desired goal. Sultan of Kohler was directed by hunger to reach the bananas and that way he strived and learnt the way.

Psychological phenomena of motivation play important role to learn. Inadequate level of motivation makes the children to find their studies dull and boring without motivation. Hence, learning should be made purposeful and meaningful. In words of Gates "Learning experiences are meaningful when they are invoked in his living when they not only contribute to the purposes at the time but enable him to more intelligent adjustments in the future, when they invoke discovery and problem solving rather than formal drill or mere memorisation and when they result in satisfying social relationship." It does not mean that the teacher should always present false incentives for learning. False incentives prove harmful in the long run. What is needed is presentation of motives at the right moment and in the right way.

(iii) Success, Praise and Blame. Nothing succeeds like success, Thorndike's law of effect, is applicable most commonly. Experimental evidences show that praise stimulates small children to work and learn although

it does not produce much effect on superior and elder children. Elder children are more sensitive towards reproof and blame, than younger children are.

(iv) Rewards and Punishment. Rewards of all sorts are powerful incentives to learn. But these days in India school rewards are more abused than used properly. A first division or distinction in the examination is a false reward. Work is its own reward. Pupils forget this point. They become over-dependent on rewards. They refuse to work without any incentive of reward. All learning should not be and cannot be rewarded immediately.

Punishments arousing fear in anticipation, may influence the pupil to work and learn, but not in all the cases. Sometimes punishment creates bad reaction, retaliation, hatred and disgust. Experimental studies show that punishments interfere with complex learning activities, when punishments become frequent. Absence of punishment becomes a basis of low activity on the part of the pupil. In the absence of fear, they disobey and waste time.

(C) Environmental Factors. Adequate Environment play an important role in learning. Adequate environment effecting learning can be studied as—

(i) Working Conditions. Learning is hampered by bad working conditions such as distraction, noise, poor illumination, bad ventilated, overcrowding, bad seating arrangement, and uncomfortable stay both at home and school. The location of the school, the internal set-up, the accommodation, decoration and healthful and sanitary conditions are very important for efficient learning.

(ii) Organisational Set-up. The organisational set-up of the school also influences learning:

(a) The time-table must be drawn, in accordance with the psychological principles. It should avoid fatigue and boredom. Difficult subjects should be taught in the morning. There should be interval after some periods.

(b) The democratic organisation promotes as healthy atmosphere for learning.

(c) The teacher-pupil relations should be healthy, so that there is mental cooperation and the pupils are motivated to learn.

(d) There should be some sort of competition. The inter-class or inter-house competitions will stimulate the pupils to work more in order to outshine others. Rivalry and jealousy should however, be avoided. Group emulation should be strengthened.

(e) The participation on the part of the pupils should be active. The pupil should not act as a passive learner.

(f) Guidance in the selection of subjects and activities in accordance with age and ability and aptitude of the pupils should be provided. Unguided children may oscillate from one subject to another, and thus gather no mass.

(D) Methodology Factors. The effect of instruction of learning can be studied as :

(i) Presentation and Organisation of Material. The learning material should be properly planned and organised. It should be graded to suit the mental level of the pupils. It should be presented in a meaniguful and interesting manners.

(ii) Learning by Doing. Practice makes a man perfect. Repetition and practice is important for learning. The pupils must be encouraged to learn through activity. Theoretical teaching should be replaced by practical application of knowledge, experimentation and personal application. Children learn better through personal experience. Verbalisation should be reduced to minimum.

(iii) Special Methods of Learning. It has been found that some special methods give better results. In learning a piece of poetry, learning by the whole method and by the part method have been advocated. Sometimes it is helpful to recall what is learnt and to recite by memory. Gestalt and other psychologists do not approve of trial and error learning. They advocate learning by insight. They discourage mechanical repetitions without understanding.

(iv) Timely Testing. Through tests, the learner knows his exact achievement and there is no scope for over-estimation or under-estimation. Occasional and periodical testing motivates the pupil to be regular in his studies.

(E) Knowledge of Result. Another factor in effective learning is knowledge of results. If in course of learning young people are told from time to time about the progress they are making and how satisfactory it is they do better, "Knowledge of what they have achieved spurs them to strive harder.

(i) Intelligence. Intelligence also affects learning, the more intelligent learn better and quicker. *Maturation* and *interest* are also important factors. An older, more mature person learns sooner and better and it is an obvious fact that those who want to learn and have a very strong interest do better."

In brief, the above factors effect the learning. In addition to the above said factors, the author is of the view that learning is influenced by the type of seriousness of the learner, the learning material, learning situation and learning teaching technology and learning culture.

VI.8 Methods of Learning

Psychological studies point out that despite the individual has strong motive to learn, adequate learning material and suitable learning atmosphere and individual cannot learn effectively because learning also depends upon the method of learning. Studies reports is that there are two methods of learning such as:

1. Massed or Spaced Learning. Suppose you have to learn swimming, cycling, skating or typing, should you go on practising till you have learned the skill ? Or should you take rest in between and practise for short periods ? Continuous learning is called *massed learning* and learning with breaks or rest periods is called *spaced learnings.* Several studies made with groups of children of the same age and intelligence show that those who distributed their learning surpassed in achievement whose learning was more concentrated. Spaced periods of practice are more economical than unspaced periods. This means that if you have to learn an assignment it will be better to study it a short time on several days than to attempt to learn it at one sitting.

The reasons for this are not far to seek. In the first place the spaced learning is more advantageous because it rules out fatigue and interest is maintained. In massed learning continuous effort tires the individual, lowers his efficiency and reduces his interest. Therefore, the individual has to make greater effort to learn and put in more practice. Secondly, spaced learning helps to drop wrong associations and strengthen correct associations. The rest periods give time and opportunity to make such corrections as well as to strengthen correct associations. In continuous massed practice there is no such opportunity. Thirdly, in spaced learning memory traces get opportunity to firm up during the rest periods. In continued massed practice there is no time and opportunity for consolidation, for allowing memory traces to settle down. Rest periods help such consolidation. Fourthly, a mental process, once started, continues even though our attention is directed to other things. This especially true if the final goal has not been attained. Once we accept a task, a state of mental tension persists until it is finished, whereas when a task is finished we tend to forget it. When periods of study are distributed mental tension persists between them; we learn not only during periods of study but also during the intervals. Moreover, the interval between study periods gives an opportunity for growth.

But we should note that such studies and experiments show that we should distribute and space our study and learning but they do not show that we should give up study or learning on the first sign of fatigue or we should never work when we are tired. In all learning there is a period for optimum efficiency and there is as much danger in making learning periods too short as in making them too long. A person who gives up as soon as he feels tired does little to develop his stamina.

(2) Whole or Part Method. Should a student read his lesson from beginning to end again and again till he has mastered it or should he break it into parts and learn the parts one by one thus learning the whole ? The former is the whole method and the latter is the part method. In committing to memory a poem of 300 lines one may go on repeating the whole of it or spend some time

on memorizing its several parts and then reciting the whole of it. Some people advocate the whole method others consider the part method more economical. A number of experimental studies have shown that when one has to memorize a long list of meaningless words the part method is more effective, when a short poem is to be memorized the whole method is more useful, and when long poem like the Ramayana is to be learnt only part method is practicable. But one must organise the material to be learned into large units and study it as a whole. In this way one can reduce the material to a few meaningful units, each one of which is easily learned as its component parts would be if taken separately.

By learning things as wholes we understand the material better and see how the different parts stand together in a general pattern. But there is a disturbing factor that the learner may lose confidence in the face of a longer assignment. However, much depends on such factors such as intelligence and experience, and individual differences are large.

VI.9 Measurement of Learning

The fundamental attribute of man is to develop a tendency to learn. The tendency to learn varies from individual to individual. Some learn only for a short period, while others function again and again and may do so throughout the life of an individual. *Learning* and *retention* are key concepts in the analysis of behaviour. Try to imagine an organism without the capacity to learn and to retain what it has learned. Such an organism would be for ever doomed to repeat the responses with which it was natively equipped, without the benefit from experience and teaching, reward and punishment.

The influence of learning is universal. If we consider any area of behaviour—motor and verbal skills, problem solving, attitudes and values—we find that they all reflect past learning in countless ways and are continually modified by new learning. Not only is learning uiquitous, but it manifests itself in many forms of behaviour changes and at many levels of complexity. Because of this variety and complexity of learning, it is necessary to study it analytically under controlled laboratory conditions. Through experimental analysis, some of the basic variables and relationships of learning have been isolated. With this knowledge and insight gained in the laboratory, it has been possible to apply principles of learning to many types of behaviour, from simple motor performances to the socialization of the child in a specific culture. To assesses the quantity of learning occurred there are different methods for the measurement of learning by measuring the strength of association.

1. Associative Strength

(i) Frequency of Response. A strong association is inferred from the fact that a response is given on nearly every occasion that the stimulus is presented. By this measure, a scale of strength is established in terms of the proportion of the total number of stimulus presentations which evoke the response. Complete absence of association in defined by 0 per cent evocation; full strength of association, by 100 per cent evocation; 100 per cent evocation, however, does not necessarily denote the greatest possible strength of association. Thus, two associations may both yield 100 per cent responses but turn out to be of different strength when tested by more sensitive indices. Moreover, the meaning of any proportion varies with the number of trials on which the proportion is based. Thus, the associations established by learning a list of nonsense syllables to a criterion of two perfect repetitions will not be as strong as the associations resulting from learning the same list to a criterion of five perfect repetitions. In general, the larger the number of trials yielding 100 per cent response evocation, the greater the inferred strength of association.

(ii) Resistance to Forgetting. As we have seen, per cent response evocation is not an unequivocal measure of strength. This frequency measure may be made more sensitive by introducing varying time intervals between the end of practice and the measurement of associative strength. Differences not apparent at the end of practice may be measurable after a time interval. For instance, if an individual after attempts is able to learn list of words after two or five perfect repetitions where both the repetitions results at 100 per cent strength at the end of practice. Differences in their strength would become apparent on a test a week after the end of practice. At that time, more items would be recalled from the list learned to five perfect repetitions. In this way, resistance to forgetting provides a measure supplementary to frequency of response evocation.

(iii) Ease of Relearning. When a time interval intervenes between the end of practice and the test, the associations are weakened by processes occurring during that time interval. After a given interval of time, an initially strong association is still stronger than an initially weak one. Clearly, a greater amount of practice will be required for the weaker association than for the stronger one if the two are to be brought back to the same strength. Hence, the number of trails for learning to a given criterion provides another measure of the relative strength of associations. Let us return to our example of lists learned to two and five perfect repetitions. If both lists are relearned after one week, the list originally learned to a criterion of two repetitions, will require more trials to yield 100 per cent evocation again than will the other list.

(iv) Latency. Latency refers to the amount of time which elapses between the onset of the stimulus and the beginning of the response. A strong association

implies a high degree of readiness to give the response under appropriate stimulus conditions. Experimental investigations have, indeed, shown that the more frequently evoked responses are also the quicker ones. Sometimes latency measures will detect differences which are not easily measured by the frequency method.

2. Learning Curves

Another way to assess learning is through learning curve. So, on the basis of associative strength we can assess the learning by using learning curve. Learning curve is a scale of associative strength, we can proceed to plot it as a function of number of practice trials. Such a plot is called a *learning curve.* Strength of learning can be measured in various ways and the particular units employed will help to determine the characteristics of the learning curve.

When the performance measure is the number of responses acquired, we obtain a rising curve. When the performance measure refers to the elimination of wrong responses or the time required for the completion of the task, we obtain a falling curve. For example, when a maze is learned, the number of correct choices per trial as a function of practice would show a rising curve. On the other hand, either the number of errors or the time per trial as a function of practice would yield a falling curve.

Whether rising or falling, learning curves may develop differently in time. The amount of change in performance between two successive measurements may keep increasing or keep decreasing over a certain number of trails. If each successive change is greater than the preceding one, the resulting curve shows *positive acceleration.* Such a curve is the one labelled 2 in Fig. 1. On the other hand, if each successive change is smaller than the preceding one, the curve shows *negative acceleration* (Curve 1 in Fig. 1. Some curves show an initial period of positive acceleration followed by a period of negative acceleration. Such curves are designated as *S-shaped*).

There is no simple rule for predicting the form of a learning curve in advance. Certain general relations between learning procedure and the form of the resulting curve have however, been established. For example, if the material consists of some parts which are easy and some parts which are difficult to learn, a negatively accelerated curve is typically obtained. The easier parts are quickly learned at the beginning, with the harder parts being acquired more slowly later on. Positively accelerated curves, on the other hand, are typically obtained for learning tasks which become progressively easier as practice continues. Since the S-shaped curve is a combination of the two other types, a proper combination of factors leading first to positive and then to negative acceleration yields such a curve. Even though such general relationships hold up fairly well, the particular shape of a learning curve is always jointly determined by the particular materials, the characteristics of the learner, the learning procedure, and the methods and units of measurement.

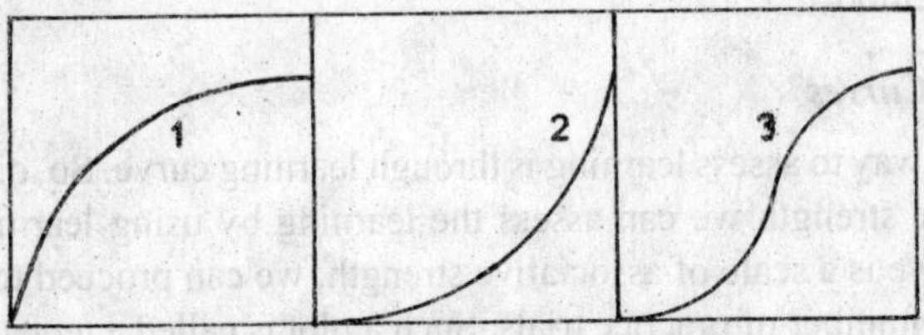

Fig. 1. Typical Learning Curves. Curve 1 Shows Negative Acceleration; Curve 2 Shows Positive Acceleration; Curve 3 Shows An initial Period of Positive Acceleration Followed By Negative Acceleration (s-shaped)

3. Vincent Curves

A learning curve describing the performance of a single subject is usually quite irregular, probably because it is not possible to control adequately many of the factors which contribute to fluctuations in performance from moment to moment. For this reason, it is necessary to average the performances of many learners in order to obtain a good picture of the general relationship. The averaging of learning data, however, poses a special problem. Different individuals enter the learning situation with different capacities to learn and with different preparations for the task. Therefore, different states of acquisition will be represented by different subjects performances on any given trial. Suppose a group of subjects has the task of learning a list of ten words. Some are fast learners, others are slow learners. On a given trial, say the fifth, the fast learners will have nearly achieved the goal of a perfect repetition while the slow learners will have learned only a few items. To average the raw data trial by trial in order to obtain a composite curve would introduce a serious distortion. To do so would mean to combine the data for individuals at different ages of learning.

One method, which at least partially takes this difficulty into account, is the construction of a *Vincent curve.* This method consists of dividing each individual's total learning period into a given number of divisions. The number of divisions is the same for all subjects, but the size of these divisions will vary from subject to subject depending on the total length of their learning periods. The performance at the end of corresponding periods are averaged to obtain the composite learning curve.

Limitations: There are certain dangers in the use of Vincent curves which should be mentioned. Such average curves should be computed only if there is reasonable assurance that each subject begins the task at the same level of performance. Thus if one subject enters the learning situation with one-third of the learning already accomplished while another subject starts from the beginning, we are averaging together different segments of the total learning curves. We assume when we use the Vincent method that each subject would give the same *form* of the curve even though some subjects take more trials than others. Unless all subjects start at about the same level, the method is likely to be misleading.

VI.10 Learning Exercises

1. Describe the meaning and definitions of learning.
2. Discuss the nature and types of learning.
3. Describe the theories of learning.
4. Differentiate between classical conditioning theory and the operant theory of conditioning.
5. Describe the laws of learning.
6. What are the factors which influence learning?
7. Describe different methods of learning and how do we measure learning?
8. Discuss the education implications of the knowledge of learning for a teacher.

VII

Transfer of Training

The process of acquiring knowledge and skill under a formal situation is called training. The process with which an already learned knowledge is made applicable for further refinement is called transfer of training. Transfer of training is of different types. The transfer of training is helpful for a trainer or a teacher to develop competencies. In this regard various efforts are being made to work-out the essential pre-conditions which can optimise transfer of training for better teaching-learning process.

VII.1 Meaning of Transfer of Training

The assumption underlying the educational process is that the knowledge skill acquired at the school and college level will not only be available in future, but will be applied in some measure for the solution of new problems as they arise in life. This process or carry-over of knowledge and skills from one learning area to another, usually is referred to as the transfer of training. In other words, the effect of past learning by an individual over the new learning is known as transfer of learning.

For instance, by studying Economics, Sociology, Social Studies, Psychology etc., the student is expected to gain the ability to interpret intelligently the social problems that will arise in the future. Similarly, teaching of mathematics makes us logical and the teaching of science enables us to be good observers and objective in outlook. If, the facilities of mind can be trained through various activities it means there is transfer of training. Prof. Dutt points out that transfer of training is a process in which something learnt in one situation is used in another. He further points out that the process of transfer of training takes place in different areas just as:

(a) *Transfer from Knowledge to Knowledge :* The arithmetic learnt in the school is applied in the grocer's shop.

(b) *Transfer from Knowledge to skill:* The technique of preparing oxygen gas learnt in the classroom can be applied in the laboratory where apparatus in fitted and chemical are used as per instructions.

(c) *Transfer from Knowledge to Behaviour :* We learn principles of ethics from books and the teachers and apply them in our day-to-day life.

(d) *Transfer from Skill to Skill:* If in an experiment the left hand is conditioned to withdraw on the ringing of a bell, the right hand is automatically conditioned.

(e) *Transfer from Attitude to Attitude:* Transfer of an individual's attitude in one situation affects the attitude in similar other situation. For instance, I believe in the following attitude.

"All men are equal as ends, though they may be different as means." This will automatically lead me to believe in the following attitude as a teacher—"The individuality of every student is to be respected."

(f) *Transfer from Attitude to Behaviour:* Often we notice a sort of conflict, a Psychological disorientation in people around us (including ourselves). This is due to the variance in 'attitudes' and 'behaviour.' But if the attitude is strong enough it is likely to motivate the behaviour in its own way. If my attitudes are favourable towards Marxism, I am likely to stand up against any exploitation.

From the above discussion it is evident that transfer of training is a process in which an individual learns the use of previously learned knowledge and skills for his behavioural furtherance in life. It has been observed that in some situations the previously learned material helps in certain situations and the previously learned skills sometimes impedes the further learning. But in some situations the previous level of knowledge and skills neither helps not impedes further learning. The effect of previously learned knowledge and skills causes difference in the levels of one's further learning which indicates that transfer of learning is of different types which can be studied as types of transfer of training.

VII.2 Types of Transfer of Training

The transfer of training is of three types viz, Positive, Negative and Zero transfer of training:

(a) Positive Transfer of Training: When the "past learning" of one subject or activity facilitates the learning of another subject or activity the process which facilitates learning is called positive transfer of learning. For instance, a sportsman playing football plays volley-ball nicely. A bus driver can drive a truck also equally nicely and efficiently.

(b) Negative Transfer of Training: Negative transfer of training indicates the learning of one task makes the learning of second task harder. Learning shorthand by Danton method may cause interference in subsequent learning by Pitman's method. The negative transfer is also called habit interferences.

(c) Zero Transfer of Training: The transfer of training is called zero transfer when the previously learned skill neither helps the further learning nor interferes with the further learning.

VII.3 Theories of Transfer of Training

The concept of transfer of training has been worked out by various psychologists which can be categorised into five types of transfer of training theories which can be studied as:

1. Theory of Mental Discipline. General transfer of training through mental discipline is the oldest theory. The principle feature of the theory of mental discipline advocates that the mind or its faculties such as memory, reason, will and perseverance are the "muscles of the mind" and like muscles of the body they are strengthened through exercise and later on function automatically in all situations and areas in which they are involved. Thus, the training of the faculty of memory through memorizing nonsense syllables is supposed to improve one's memory for dates, names, figures, facts, and in fact for anything and everything which involve memory. In the same way it is supposed that the rigrous study of geometry can train the faculty of reasoning and once it is so trained in a person, he can reason well in realms of mathematics, social issues, philosophy and business.

Mental discipline as an educational doctrine and as the basis for transfer of training was first seriously challenged by William James. He wanted to see whether daily training in the memorizing of poetry of one author would affect the learning of slightly different poetry of another author. He memorized 58 lines from Victor Hugo's *Satyr* in 131.5 minutes spread over 8 days. He then worked for about 20 minutes daily memorizing all of the First Book of Milton's *Paradise Lost*. This required 38 days. After this period of memory training he returned to the situation and memorized 158 additional lines. But now he could do so in 15½ minutes instead of 131.5 minutes in the first instance. James therefore, concluded that memory was not affected by training as claimed by the faculty psychologists.

In a more controlled experiment Sleight studied the effect of practice in memorizing poetry, tables or prose substance on memorizing nonsense syllables, dates, poetry verbatim prose substance and consonants arranged in haphazard order and came to the conclusion that mental discipline theory does not hold good for the transfer of training.

2. Theory of Identical Elements. The founder of the theory of identical elements in transfer of training was Thorndike. The theory of identical elements implies that learning is facilitated in the new situation to the extent that identical elements which occurred in an earlier situation are present in the new situation. This means that transfer takes place from typing to playing a Piano to the extent that such skills as eye-fingers co-ordination are identical to both activities. However, elements of similarity between two situations are not only confined to skills. They might take the form of information, procedures, or attitudes. Thus identity of elements can be either in subject matter or in procedures, or in attitudes.

The theory of identical elements grew out of several experiments conducted by Thorndike and Woodworth to study the transfer effect of improvement of the power to estimate areas, lengths and weights of certain shape and size upon the ability to estimate areas, lengths and weights, similar in shape but different in size, different in shape but similar in size and different in both shape and size. For example, one of the sets of material consisted of areas of different sizes, training in estimation which might have transfer effect upon estimating areas of other sizes and shapes. The effect of training in discriminating differences in areas of 10 to 100 square centimetres upon areas of the same size but differing in shape was 44 percent as such gain had appeared in the original areas. When the size was changed to 140-300 square centimetres, the improvement was 30 percent as great. When both sizes and shapes were changed the improvement was 52 percent as great as in the 10-100 sq. cm. Similar results appeared when the effect of practice to the discrimination of the weights of 40-120 grams was transferred to the discrimination of the weight from 120 to 1800 grams. The experiments attributed the transfer effect to ideas of method and habits of procedure. We came to the conclusion that training is transferred when there are identical elements.

The limitations which challenge the theory of identical elements appeared from many experiments. Ruger, for example, in a study of puzzle solving in adults, found that practice in a specific portion of puzzle did not necessarily aid in the solution of the puzzle as a whole. He concluded that presence of identical elements as such did not ensure transfer. He even found some evidence of negative transfer when identical elements hindered the solution of puzzles.

The difficulty with the theory of identical elements is that it considers transfer as an automatic process which may be taken for granted in presence of identical elements. In fact, the amount of transfer is influenced by many factors which depend upon the learned as well as the learning situation. The learner's factors include age, mentality, personality, attitude towards learning situation, efficient use of past experience, sentiments and ideal. The situational factors include meaningfulness, organised presentation of material and provision for continuous reconstruction of experience.

3. Generalization of Experience. Judd advocated that transfer of learning takes place through generalisation process. For instance: Judd conducted a dart throwing experiment to test the transfer value of generalization. The purpose of the experiment was to study the effect of instruction in the principle of refraction of light upon the ability of boys in the fifth and sixth grades to throw darts at targets placed under water. The boys were divided into groups. One group got careful instructions in the scientific principles of the refraction of light when it passed through water. The other group got no such instruction. Both groups of boys were then asked to throw darts in such a way as to hit an under-water target with them. In the first instance the target to be hit was placed 12 inches under water. Both the groups did not do well in hitting it. The boys who had theoretical instructions in the principle of refraction had to get some practice in throwing darts before their training in theory could be of use. Once they could get some practice, the target was moved to a position of 4 inches under water. Immediately the experimental group showed much better performance than the control group. Their understanding of the principle of refraction had helped them as to where to aim the darts in order to hit under-water objects which appear to be little nearer the water surface.

On the basis of his experiment Judd emphasized that the most effective use of knowledge is assured not through acquiring specific items of experience but only through establishing its principles so that it has general value. To prevent ineffective school teaching, the learner should be helped to see the broad situations of items of experience.

Similarly, the study repeated by G. Hendrickson and W. H. Schreder (1941) revealed similar results except for two additional and significant findings. In this study, eighth-class boys were employed, who shot with an air gun at bull's eye type of target submerged in water at depth of 6 and 12 inches. They took three groups of students. One group was maintained as a controlled group and was given no theory. The second group was explained the theory and principle underlying refraction. Third group was not only told the principle of refraction but were also had additional instruction "the deeper the lake, the farther the real rock will be from image rock."

The practice without theory increased the difficulty of task and more complete the explanation, easier was the initial task. In adopting a new task all groups showed the benefit of transfer while the experimental group receiving the most complete explanation benefited the most. To sum up, knowledge of refraction principle enlightened the pupils with general understanding. They could transfer knowledge easily to different situations. The understanding coupled with experience permitted to pupils to gain insight into the problem.

4. Theory of Ideals. W. C. Bagley gave an explanation of transfer of training in terms of ideals and asserted that generalisations are more likely to transfer if they are regarded as of same value, as desirable. He said that generalisation in transfer of training is not the whole story but it must be given an emotional sanction, or be elevated to plane of an ideal, worth striving for. There are two experiments on transfer of neatness which support Bagley's assertion. The first one was conducted under the direction of C. R. Squaire. The test consisted simply in insisting on neatness in the preparation of arithmetic papers by pupils in the third grade. Nothing was said about neatness in the rest of the school subjects. Language and spelling papers were then compared with arithmetic papers for improvement in neatness. While the arithmetic papers showed clear proof of neatness, the language and spelling paper rather showed decrease in neatness. It was concluded that specific training in neatness in one area did not transfer to other areas.

However, there is a different story to tell when neatness is developed as an ideal. Ruediger in a carefully planned experiment insisted upon neatness in written papers, in dress, business home, etc. Great effort was made to develop ideal, of neatness. The result showed an over all improvement in neatness in all subjects. The conclusion was that ideals do transfer. Thus, the teacher should consciously seek maximum transfer values by emphasizing ideals of neatness, of love learning tolerance for difference of opinion and so forth.

5. Relationship Theory. Gestalt a field psychologist advocates that the transfer of learning means the generalizations of concepts or insights which are developed in one learning situation which is employed as a whole in other situations. However, the transfer of generalizations or insights does not occur automatically. The transfer of learning to occur, the student must *perceive* the relationship between the two situations, must understand that the generalizations gained through past experience are appropriate to the new situation; and must have the desire to use the generalization and to benefit by the perceived commonality.

To prove that transfer occurs not through the presence of identical element but through perception of relationship e.g., Kohler experimented with hens. He taught hens to expect food only from the darker of the two papers placed side by side. For the lighter paper he then substituted one even darker than the original dark one. In 70 percent of the trials the hens changed their preference from the originally preferred dark paper to the paper which was still darker, suggesting that it is not the identical element in the two situations to which the hens responded but to "darker than" relationship.

Kohler conducted similar experiments with chimpanzees and a three-year old child and got the same result. Two American Gestalt psychologists—Raymone H. Wheeler and Francis T. Perkins experimented with goldfish and discovered that even the fish respond to relationship of lights for receiving food.

VII.4 Factors Influencing Transfer of Training

The studies reveal that learning is transferable. The teacher, the parents and the general practitioners in different fields of arts and craft are mainly concerned to optimise the transfer of training and skills. In doing so it is believed that there are certain factors which play vital role. All the factors which play the role of transfer of training depends on major conditions such as:

(I) Intelligence. The amount of transfer is closely related to the intelligence of the learners. Thorndike's experiments give clear evidence. Brighter children transfer their experience more effectively in different situations than average or dull children. The intelligent pupil comprehends the subject-matter more efficiently, masters it, remembers it and *over-learns* it. Overlearning helps greater transfer.

(II) The positive self-confident attitude. Attitude influences greater transfer when the pupil knows that a particular subject is to be learnt not for the sake of examination but for its intrinsic work, for its applicability, when he is confident of its utility in varying situations, he is bound to apply the knowledge in as large extent of the field as possible. The teacher and the pupil should be conscious of the goal.

(III) Generalising affects transfer. Transfer of training depends upon the extent to which principles are developed and experiences are made more meaningful. The common elements, common principles and common ideals in different situations, affect transfer. All these three conditions help transfer of training. But the transfer of training depends on the following factors:

1. Meaningfulness of the Content

Firstly, the purport and meaning of the subject-matter taught should be explained fully and in minute details. It is not enough to dole out some geographical facts to be mugged up. Thoroughness and details will stimulate the pupil to think more and apply the knowledge in different situations. The paragraph in a language lesson could be explained with all its details—grammar, spelling, pronunciation, idiom, etymology, beauty of thought etc. This will ensure maximum transfer.

2. Real Life Situation

All learning should take place in living and concrete situations. Thus all unreal problems in arithmetic, useless items in grammar, memorisation of dates and names in history and geography which have no utility in life situations should be eliminated from the curriculum.

3. Nature of Practical Experience

Practical experience affects significantly transfer of training in this connection, for transfer of learning a student should be given as much of practical experience as possible. The curriculum should contain subjects of practical nature, which are applicable in vocations or life situations.

4. Nature of Curriculum

Nature of the content. Transfer of training depends upon the nature of the curriculum. The theories and experimental evidences regarding the transfer of learning provide us with certain broad principles on the basis of which we can remodel, overhaul or reorganise the present curriculum in order to secure greater transfer, through:

(i) Disciplinary value of subjects. As the theory of formal discipline is no longer acceptable now, there is no reason for inclusion or rejection of any subject in the curriculum simply for its disciplinary value. We can easily dispense with theoretical grammar, include logic (in geometrical theorems) and classical languages which were thought to be of disciplinary value.

(ii) Varying Importance of the subject. All subjects in the present curriculum do not have equal value. Some subjects are least connected with life situations (like ancient history), and these have the least transfer value. The present approach is the *social-utility* approach in including a subject or a topic in the curriculum.

(iii) Subject-matter Vs Experiences. Thorndike and Wesman have experimentally proved that it is not the subject matter but the experiences gained in the study of the subject that is important and useful for future applicability. The transfer value of all the subjects for any trait (say improvement in reasoning) is almost equal. But the experiences gathered by the pupils differ, and that accounts for greater or lesser positive transfer. Hence an attempt should be made to provide superior *experiences* leading to greater transfer rather than teach subjects in a theoretical manner. Mathematics enjoys no monopoly for developing reasoning ability. There are no less opportunities for the same in the teaching of other subjects, say geography or history or physics. All subjects can be taught in a manner that they encourage raising questions and offering answers.

(iv) Classical Languages. The old belief that classical language should be taught for its disciplinary value is no longer tenable. Even its linguistic value is questionable. Experiments on transfer value of Latin by Thorndike do not give credit to Latin beyond 10% transfer. In India we may teach Sanskrit

not for its transfer value for Hindi or modern Indian languages, but for its literary importance.

(v) Grammar may be taught only for its practical use and application. In the present grammar teachers get lost in details of parsing, tenses, moods analysis, transformation and etymology, which have no bearing upon the real objectives of teaching the subject, as these do not help correct expression or smooth communication. The transfer is to take place from expression to grammar, that is, expression and communication is to take place first and then correct grammatical usage is to follow.

(vi) Subjects related to life. Subject and topics which are directly connected with our vocations, physical environment, social environment, social living and life situations have great transfer value. Hence, stress should be laid on those subjects which bear daily needs and help in solving life problems. Diversification of courses, and presenting groups of subjects directly connected with future vocations of the pupils or certain areas of life, will help the pupils in gaining appropriate knowledge of maximum utility which have transfer value for vacations and life-activities.

VII.5 Methods of Instruction and Transfer of Training

For optimum level of transfer, the present methods of instructions shall have to be modified and overhauled, on the evidence of experiments (cited above). There is no 'best method' but there are varying approaches to instruction in accordance with varying situations. Such as:

(i) Importance of goals. Firstly goals and outcomes of each subject should be clearly stated. It is only recently that attempts have been made in analysing a particular subject in terms of *objectives, behaviour patterns* and *learning experiences*. Much of what is useless and unrelated to the objectives of a subject is being discarded. The awareness of goals both on the part of the teacher and the pupil will lead to devotion to work, habits of thoroughness, exactness, accuracy, sound attitude to work and consciousness of the utility for future occasions.

(ii) Understanding of Individual Differences. The teacher should study each pupil and his credit side and debit side, so as to vary with great flexibility his teaching methods, illustrating material and emphasis on the subject-matter. Approaches towards bright and dull pupils will differ, otherwise the same approach might cause negative transfer.

(iii) Integrated Approach. Herbert tried to emphasise first the need for correlating various school subjects, and further upon concentrating upon subject as a centre of study for many other subjects. Ziller and Colonel Parker actually put this idea into practice. Froebel kept play as the centre of all study. Transfer

from one central subject to many others was considered possible. Dewey gave the integrated approach, and propounded the problem and the project method through which a number of subjects could be introduced in an integrated manner, with their common elements emphasised at one place. Modern experiments on transfer, the Theory of Common Components, vouchsafe the fact that maximum transfer can be procured by integrating different subjects and emphasising their common elements, principles or generalisations.

(iv) Attitude Towards Work. The value and importance of attitude towards work and study has already been explained above (develops attitude). Healthy attitudes and worthy-ideals get integrated into the mental and moral make-up of the pupil, and thus these ensure greater transfer. The pupils should study with a spirit of enquiry, desire to know, love for wisdom and hunger of the soul. All scientific discoveries have been preceded by this attitude. Such an attitude will be transferable from one subject to another.

(v) Practical Application of Knowledge. The earlier learned knowledge and skills are helpful in assimilating the core of a particular subject, which can help transfer. Every subject, including the sciences should be taught intelligently with the scope of practical application. Mursell remarks in this regard,

"When any ability is most intelligently taught and organised for its own sake, it is thereby taught and organised in such a way as will facilitate transfer, and its converse; When we deliberately work for the transfer of some ability, we facilitate its acquisition in its own right."

We may conclude that securing of maximum transfer depends solely upon the teacher. It is he who can inculcate worthy ideals and attitudes which secure maximum transfer in all situations. It is he who can find out that he wants to teach, and for what goal. Transfer can take place, if the goals of teaching are known, and the appropriate methods are used.

VII.6 Suggestions For Improvement in Transfer of Training

Curriculum construction is the first step. It should be highly efficient, diversified and connected with the present needs of human beings. After deciding the curriculum, the syllabi of different subjects and for different standards are formed. A good syllabus chalked out after great discussion and construction on the part of educationists will be very helpful. As far as possible it should be very specific in its items. Mere theoretical syllabus is not good. There should be due emphasis on practical work. In addition to it, the value of cocurricular activities should be evaluated and they should be encouraged accordingly.

The method of teaching and learning should not be mechanical. The machine like repetition should be avoided. All the class-room activities must be saturated with purposes. The motives should be created. The students learn lesson intelligently by using and understanding. Learning by doing, is another factor to promote the transfer of training.

There is also negative training which influences the other activities adversely. Such activities should be avoided.

The student should get various situations in and outside the school to practise their learning on the everyday problems of life. This will help the transfer of training.

VII.7 Learning Exercises

1. What do you mean by transfer of training?
2. Discuss the types of transfer of training.
3. Describe different theories of transfer of training.
4. Discuss various factors responsible for the transfer of training.
5. Discuss important factors responsible for transfer of Training.
6. Suggest means and measures for the improvement in the transfer of training.

VIII
Motivation

The term "motivation" has been defined by different Psychologists. Etyomologically, the term motivation has been taken as: to motivate, is to induce movement. From this point of view the term motivation would include the explanation of all behaviour, i.e. simple or complex, voluntary or involuntary, natural and acquired. In broader sense every activity or response is motivated, because a response is, after all, an observable change in behaviour. When an individual seems to be doing "nothing", his behaviour is merely relatively stable—he is breathing regularly, he is in attentive to the world around him (even though he may be awake), and his body processes are functioning smoothly. But if he stands up or reaches for a book or merely looks at something in the room his behaviour has changed and his "response" can be attributed to some change within him which may also reflect a change in the immediate environment. The factors that caused the response and determined its form and direction are what we call motivation.

VIII.1 Definitions and Meaning of Motivation

Moskowitz and Orgel (1969) define motivation as the initiation and direction of behaviour. In the same way Guilford defines, motivation as a motive/force which is internal factor/condition, that tends to initiate and sustain activity. In the words of *Morgan* and *King* (1966) motivation is a general term referring to states that motivate behaviour, to the behaviour motivated by these states and to the goals or ends of such behaviour. *Coleman* (1979), defines the term motivation which includes any inner condition of the organism that initiates or directs its behaviour toward a goal.

In broader sense, motivation is a broad concept which includes the inner needs, desires, and purposes of the organism. Specifically it helps us to understand by approaches viz;

(i) The directionality of behaviour,

(ii) The activation or energizing of behaviour, and

(iii) Individual differences in striving behaviour.

(i) Directionality of Behaviour

This approach advocates that every response in each species has built-in response propensities which tend to :

(1) bring the individual into contact with stimuli relevant to its survival—approach behaviour, and

(2) remove the individual from stimuli which are threatening to its survival—avoidance behaviour.

As the complexity of an organism increases in the evolutionary tree, the process of motivation also become complex. The major changes that occur are: *(a)* behaviour itself become less stereotyped and more variable and flexiable; *(b)* The control provided by external stimulation become less specific and less automatic; *(c)* The influence of temporary or short-term physiological conditions become both more complex and important; *(d)* The unique experience of the organism assumed a larger role in the determination of behaviour because, the higher species of course, become increasingly dependent on learning rather than built-in guides for their approach and avoidance responses. Through experience the individual learns to make fairly accurate appraisals of the reward or punishment aspects of objects and activities and on this basis buils a pattern of values, or preferences, which guides his choices. Thus we find, within the broad categories of approach and avoidance behaviour, that the directions of our strivings are as varied as the things we have learned to value. Curiously enough, we can learn to value that which is actually harmful to us—as in drug addiction—as well as that which meet our biological and psychological needs. Sometimes our value changes which ultimately redirect our behaviour.

From the *above discussion*, it is apparent that directionality makes our behaviour selective. For instance, motives make us selectively sensitive to environmental stimuli which are perceived as relevant to the meeting of our needs or wants. Thus, a hungry man is more sensitive to stimuli associated with food than is the man who has just eaten: The person striving for social acceptance may be more sensitive to his effect on others than is the person who has no worries about his popularity.

(ii) Activation of Behaviour

The activation approach of our behaviour advocates that though stimuli can trigger behaviour or act as cues in our search for particular conditions to meet inner needs, it is clear that stimuli do not provide the increased energy needed for goal-directed behaviour. The mechanisms of activation advocates that the amount of energy that is made available, and hence the vigor and persistence of the behaviour, depends on the importance of the goal to the individual. For instance, we all tire quickly for effort toward a goal we care little about, whereas, we will work long and tirelessly for something we see as crucially important. Thus, the strength of an individual's motivations is often gauged by the amount of effort he is willing to expend to achieve his goal, and stronger motivation give him a better chance of reaching it by making more energy available to him.

Although motivation helps us account for the direction and selectivity of behaviour as well as its vigour and persistence, it is not the sole determinant of what we do ? Motivation is not enough to put a football player on the team : he must also have the requisite health standard, skill, intelligence, and opportunity. And field forces, too, help to determine what he does at a given moment. If not receiver can get clear, the would be passer runs with the ball and if he is knocked off his feet by a hard tackle from an opposing player, his fall cannot be explained solely in terms of his motives. Although motives are key determinants of behaviour, they are always part of a large pattern of inner processes and outer conditions which together determine what we do.

(iii)Individual Differences in Striving Behaviour

Some motives, like hunger, start with a "wired-in" need; others, such as the desire for financial success, may be entirely learned. Since, we can acquire almost any motive as a consequence of learning, it is inevitable that our motivational patterns should show almost infinite variety. Thus again we are confronted with the problem of finding order in the diversity of human behaviour.

At first glance human motives appear to defy classification. Yet if we look closer, we see some common denominators. People everywhere are concerned about such matters as food, clothing, shelter, medical care, education, work, marriage belonging, security, and approval. And if we look still closer.

We see that common to man's activities everywhere are striving toward self-maintenance or survival and toward the actualization of potentialities— of both the individual and the group of which he is a part. In fact, all our specific strivings—toward food, shelter security, and all the rest—are variations on these two basic themes.

Although man shares these basic strivings with all living creatures, there is an important difference. The strivings that subserve maintenance seem less important to man than do the strivings that subserve actualization—at least under reasonably favourable conditions. For example, the college freshman is likely to be much concerned about getting good grades, having fun on dates, and improving his social skills than he is about his diet or his hours of sleep. Infact, it is in his attempts at creative expression, in his deliberate effort toward increasing his knowledge and ability and in his quest for values and meaning that man reveals himself as most human and most distinct from other species.

The concept of basic strivings toward maintenance and actualization also give us a basis for evaluating behaviour. Just as the efficiency of a machine can be evaluated in terms of how well and at what cost it achieves the purposes for which it was built. The behaviour of an individual is evaluated in terms of his efficiency in fulfilling his basic purposes—achieving his maintenance and actualization.

VIII.2 Significance of Motivation

For every activity of our life motivation occupies an important place in human affairs. Such familiar proverbs as "You can lead a horse to water but you can't make him drink" and "It is hard to teach an old dog new tricks" assign to motivation a key position. The horse does not drink for the simple reason that he does not *want* to drink, and the old dog's poor performance is due not so much to lack of ability as to fact that he has become too well satisfied with the tricks he already knows. Similarly, every teacher of experience has seen pupils of mediocre capacity succeed because of interest and enthusiasm, while others of more promise have failed utterly because of lack of motivation.

From these observations growing out of day today experience the views of psychologists and other keen students of education are in complete accord. Book, for example, asserts that "motivation is the central factor in every learning process." From a careful study of high-school pupils Turney came to the conclusion that the two major factors in school achievement are intelligence and motivation and that the latter is the more important.

Morrison makes the same point in explaining poor performance as due to a lack not of IQ but *want to*. Thorndike's statement is still more inclusive: "Thought and action occur largely in the service of wants, interests, and attitudes and are stimulated and guided by them". A similar view has been expressed by Einstein, one of the most eminent of modern scientists:

But behind every achievement exists of motivation which is at the foundation of it and which in turn is strengthened and nourished by the accomplishment of the undertaking. Here there are the greatest differences and they are of greatest importance to the educational value of the school. In brief, motivation is an important force which activates an individual. The degree of activation depends upon the quantity of motivation. The level of motivation and success has direct influence on our life.

VIII.3 Nature of Motivation

Psychologists differ considerably in their views regarding motivation. Thus, before attempting to make a systematic analysis of the concept of motivation, if will be helpful to consider four divergent viewpoints to study the current thinking about concept of motivation which can be described as under:

(i) *Motivation As Primary & Secondary Motives*

Morgan and King; described that by motive we mean the motion. Since, motion means movement, and motive means to move in the sense of incites to action. Besides, they points out that there are different kinds of motives, the primary and secondary. The primary motives are inborn, biological drives with which every member of the species begins life. The diversity of the motives in everyday behaviour is regarded as the result of the conditioning of our inborn biological drives to new goals which amounts to secondary motives. Such conditioning is to occur as follows:

The mother is usually present when the infant is fed; and she removes his cold clothing when he is wet. Thus she becomes a conditioned stimulus associated with relief from distress. And when she is not present, his distress is likely to continue. Because her presence is associated with relief of distress, he will learn many responses for which her presence is the only reinforcement. Then, as he discovers that her approval also signals rewards as well as relief from distress, he will learn to seek her approval. Later, seeking approval may come to be associated with honesty, academic achievement, athletic prowess, or whatever from of competence is valued by those around him.

Granting the reality of this conditioning process, it becomes apparent that a wide range of social behaviour could be based upon motives developed in this way.

Thus, proponents of this view regards motives for affiliation, for power and for achievement as extensions of more primitive physiological motive states. Any motives except the primary, physiological ones are considered secondary motives. Such a position has tended to be little the relative importance of psychological and social motives in human behaviour because of the assumption that behaviour apparently powered by "higher" motives was, in fact through conditioning, "really" still powered by hunger, sex and other biological drives.

This position seems plausible but two of its assumptions are open to question: (1) That our only inborn motive states are those powered by hunger, thirst, sex and other biological drives, and (2) that conditioning can in fact account for the diverse motives, that seem to power human behaviour.

The first assumption is open to question as a consequence of increasing evidence that whatever the neurological mechanisms may turn out to be, there is a substratum of in born psychological needs and strivings comparable to the biological substratum. For example, no child must be taught to be curious. Nor does a child have to learn to need love in order for a deprivation of love to distort his psychological development.

The second assumption is open to question because there is nothing in conditioning theory to explain how a supposedly conditioned derive could become stronger than the original one or one antithetical to it. Monkeys can be taught to work for tokens which they can then exchange for food, but never come to prefer the tokens to the food. Yet a man can choose to die rather than recont his beliefs. The truth may be sought even though it leads to no biological satisfactions, and the striving to preserve one's self-esteem may take precedence over any and all biological needs.

(ii) *Motivation As Tension Reduction*

To understand motivation as a tension reduction phenomena the approach points out that an organism has social, psychological and physiological needs which act as stimulant to make an organism to move. The deprivation of these needs amounts to pleasant or unpleasant tension. When the deficit is remedied—as when the hungry organism obtains food—the tension is relieved and the organism returns to the state of equilibrium. Thus, motives are viewed as devices for satisfying needs by reducing tension and restoring equilibrium.

Much of our biological and psychological functioning does obviously follow this pattern, and our homeostatic drives goad us into action when action toward maintenance is necessary. But human beings clearly are not concerned solely with removal of tension and restoration of equilibrium. We may put off eating and sleeping while we finish reading a book or watching television; and we may undergo a great deal of physical hardship and social disapproval in pursuing courses of action that we consider important for the maintenance of our freedom. Few people are content to live like vegetables. Instead they go out of their way to create, to explore, to build—to increase the complexity and meaningfullness of their lives. Such activities are often tension arousing rather than tension as a matter of satisfying needs, reducing tension, and maintaining equilibrium is incomplete.

A variation of tension-reduction model is the pleasure-pain model. Need deprivation and tension are unpleasant or painful, while the gratification of needs is usually pleasurable, and it has long been observed that man tends to seek that which is pleasurable and to avoid that which is painful. In recent years, techniques making possible the stimulation of specific brain areas have revealed so-called "pain" and "pleasure" centres-regions in which electrical stimulation seems to be unpleasant or pleasant and is actively avoided or sought by the subject. Such findings as these lend support to the old hedonistic doctrine that pleasure and pain—or in more modern terms, reward and punishment—are the key facets of human motivation.

The above approach of motivation as achievement of pleasure and avoidance of pain is no longer considered the key to human behaviour. Rather they are viewed chiefly as reinforcers of behaviour directed towards other goals.

(iii) Push and Pull Model of Motivation

The pull and push model of motivation emphasizes man's inner purposes, strivings, and essentially active nature. Rather than being an inert protoplasmic mass whose actions are controlled by environmental stimuli, he is viewed as an active, purposeful agent who receives and deals with his environment in accordance with his motives and values. The environment may provide what he needs or put obstacles in his way, but the action is initiated by his inner strivings to meet his needs and to find a meaningful way of life.

The pull model of motivation emphasize environmental stimuli as the forces that induce and channel behaviour.

So, behaviour is conceived as a reaction to demands and pressures, rewards and punishments—in essence, the result of the patterning of stimuli in the environment. Society, by manipulating the rewards and punishments for given behaviours, can shape and channel the behaviour of the individual in the directions which the given society deems desirable. Whereas, the push model emphasize the purposes and strivings of the individual or provide him with some measure of choice, the pull models view man as a puppet manipulated by whatever incentives and stimuli are most potent.

In extreme form, pull models do not use the concept of motivation at all in explaining behaviour. The concept of drive is replaced by that of response repertoires and habits built up by past reinforcement and called forth under appropriate stimulus conditions.

In brief, it is evident from the above discussion that neither a push nor a pull view point is sufficient by itself. Man is both active and reactive. His behaviour, like that of other living systems, is the result of both: (1) his inner structural and integrative properties and (2) the conditions and forces of his field or environment. Some things we do primarily because of inner demands or conditions; others primarily because of environmental incentives and demands. So both the instigation of behaviour and the form it takes must be seen as resulting from both our own make-up and the field in which the action take place.

(iv) *Eclectic Approach to Motivation*

The eclectic approach to understand the phenomena of motivation makes us not to accept the motion of primary and secondary motives as a full explanation of our motivation, it is clear that learning plays a tremendous part in shaping human motives. An understanding of motivation must thus delineate the role of conditioning and other learning. Although we do not accept a tension-reduction view or a pleasure-pain interpretation as the whole story, we will apply both concepts to the kinds of behaviour where they seem to fit. For it is apparent that the individual does guide his choice of goals and activities on the basis of their anticipated reward or punishment value. And although neither push or pull models are complete by themselves. The insights of both will be needed to show inner striving and field forces together direct our behaviour.

VIII.4 Motivational Cycle

As discussed earlier that motivation is a general term referring to states that motivate behaviour, to behaviour motivated by these states, and to the goals or ends of such behaviour. In other words, motivation has three aspects viz : motivating states, motivated behaviour, and the conditions that satisfy or alleviate the motivating conditions. Each of these state (aspect) may be regarded as a state in a cycle, for the first leads to the second, the second state leads to the third, to the first.

Motive

Goal

Instrumental Behaviour

Motivational Cycle

To understand the cycle of motivation let us learn the terms motive, drive, and need which are commonly used in the first stage of the cycle. The term motive is the most general term. It is derived from the same Latin and French roots that give us the word "motion". Motion means movement, and motive means to move in the sense of inciting, impelling, or supplying the power for movement. A motive, then is whatever moves or incites to action. Drive is sometimes used in place of motive, for it has a similar connotation of being an impetus to behaviour.

A motive or drive may arise from several causes. First, it may arise from a need caused by a lack of something required for the survival, health, or well being of the individual. Physiological needs are due to lacks in the tissues of the body of such things as food and water. There are also needs for other things, such as companionship, prestige, and achievement. A motive or drive, secondly, may arise from a stimulus either inside or outside the organism. Hunger pangs, environmental temperatures that are too hot or too cold, painful stimulation, or even novel stimuli which may be motivating. In some physiological drives, hormones in the blood may also be motivating. The sex drive and maternal drives in animals, for example, depend in part on the presence of certain hormones. The hormones seem to activate regions of the nervous system and thus are not stimuli of the sort that activate sense organs. They nevertheless constitute motivating conditions.

The second stage of motivational cycle is the behaviour that is instigated by the motive or drive. This behaviour is usually instrumental, sooner or later, in reducing the motive or drive. For instance, a hunger drive motivates an individual to explore for food. His exemplary behaviour, therefore, is instrumental in satisfying or reducing the drive, but it is only a means towards the goal of satisfaction.

The third stage of motivational cycle is the reduction or satisfaction of the drive or motive. This is ordinarily achieved by reaching some goal. In the thirst drive, for example, lack of water in the body is a need (first stage) motivating the individual. This need arouses exploratory behaviour (second stage) to find water. The goal of drinking water when it is found (third stage) satisfies the thirst and terminates the motivational cycle untill the need for water builds up again.

Goals, naturally, depend on the drive that is active. If a person is motivated by hunger, his goal is food; if he is motivated by the sex drive, his goal is sexual satisfaction; if he needs affection or companionship, his goal may be marriage, joining a club, or going to local poolroom. These goals are positive goals—goals the individual approaches or attempts to reach. Negative goals are those which the person tries to escape from or avoid, such as dangerous or unpleasant situations.

The term incentive in our day to day speach is used which glimps us the third stage of motivational cycle. However, the term also implies that something is being deliberately used by some one to control motivated behaviour, or to exploit motives already in existence. For instance, an experimental psychologist who wishes to have a rat learn a maze used food as incentive for motivating the hungry rat to learn the shortest route through maze.

In brief, the phenomena of motivation of course, does not have an immediate physiological basis, and many needs, especially complex social needs, can go unsatisfied without resulting in death. Nevertheless, these three stages form the typical pattern of both simple and complex motivated behaviour.

VIII.5 Theories of Motivation

Although major approaches to the study of motivation have already been described, yet there are certain specific theories of motivation which need a specific mention. The following are its main theories:

1) Pawn theory
2) Energy theory
3) Instinct theory
4) Need theory
5) Stimulation theory
6) Behaviour or Learning theory
7) Social theory
8) Depth theory
9) Physiological theory

1. Pawn Theory

Pawn theory advocates that man is just a puppet, an instrument in the hands of Nature or God who knows the art of controlling our actions. Therefore, we do not act, rather we cannot act as per our wish. We feel free, but we are free to the end of our chain only. We are free to do what we will, but we are not free to will what we will ! (*Scheupenhauer*). We are exactly like a hackney-carriage horse with an invisible rider at the back who pulls the reins in the direction he likes

The moving finger writes, and having writ
Moves on: nor all they piety nor wit
Shall lure it back to cancel half a line;
Nor all thy tears wash out a word of it.

(Omar Khyyam)

This transcendal approach to a very practical problem may be soothing and at a highly developed spiritual stage, correct too—but it does not answer most of the questions. This pawn theory—where a man like an insect sitting on a wheel is revolving because it is the wheel which is revolving, not the insect—is comparable to Freud's postulate that Man is a pawn in the hands of his unconscious which is ruthless, illogical, dark, deep and stronger than, the conscious. Here the 'wheel' is the 'unconscious' and the insect is the 'conscious' sector of mind—a thin layer of ephemeral foam on the surface of the vast and deep sea water. This theory is direct offshoot of 'metaphysical determinism. Both classical Freudian Psychoanalysis and Behaviouristic theories of learning leave no margin for human freedom and creativity. If at one place one is slave in the hands of the unconscious, at another place, one is bound by S→R. There is no scope for choice making in any case. This Pawn theory passes on the responsibility or some 'mysterious power', 'nature' or 'something' intangible.

2. Energy Theory

This theory also tries at explaining motivation as a source of energy. You see we get energy from different sources. For instance; the Physical energy comes from food. The source of physical energy is Eros according to Freud and Libido according to Jung. This theory is unable to provide scientific justification as a result this theory has its limitations.

3. Instinct Theory

The first classic statement of the Instinct theory of Motivation was given by Macdougall who said that, "The human mind has certain innate or inherited tendencies which are the essential springs or motive powers of all thought and action, whether individual or collective and are the bases from which the character and will of individuals and of nations are gradually developed under the guidance of the intellectual faculties." Mcdougall Theory of emotions put forward very elaborate list of 14 instincts and attached 14 emotions with them, the most important instincts among them being self-assertion, sex, curiosity, aggression, gregariousness, acquisition, etc. Mcdougall's theory of emotion further explains that the emotions attached with the instincts are modifiable, under the influence of education, become organized into sentiments, or attachments to persons and principles, and that these sentiments bring order, integration and continuity into our emotional life and make for behaviour which is consistent or predictable. The Instinct Theory of emotions reveals that as the instinct are based upon the inner behaviour of man, the source of emotion are basically within the human body. Therefore, it can be said that the source of motivation was not longer above the man but within the man.

If we examine carefully the thesis propounded by Mcdougall, we shall see that the main stress is on Education. Probably the British empire was vast and they needed efficient men of character to maintain its colonies. This purpose could be attained most efficiently through education based on the above notion of 'Instincts'. The American psychologists have put forward four main arguments against this theory:

(i) Most of the so called innate tendencies in children have been shown and experimentally verified to be acquired in early life.

Naturally this has raised doubt about all other innate behaviour.

(ii) The various findings of the social anthropologists (Refer to an earlier chapter 'The Concept of Human Nature') have greatly diminished the concept of basic human nature. Instincts like aggression and acquisition are due to certain social institutions and structure and not due to heredity.

(iii) During our lives, we acquire new motives which are neither compounds nor derivatives of inherited tendencies, but are self motivating or functionally autonomous.

(iv) There are various Methodological objections too against this Instinct theory. It tends to substitute abstract tendencies for concrete causes. It makes its adherents blind to the evidence of learning, development and adjustment.

Though an outstanding psychologist Burt gave a rejoinder to these objections as such, but the social anthropology has undermined only a false, popular version of instinct theory, and not the theory as put forward by Mcdougall. Why have not social anthropologists shown total lack of aggression in children from peaceful homes and societies? How is it that only a few acquired habits and ideas remain powerful motives and others as simply mechanisms rather than drives? The Behaviourist opponents again reply to these objectives that no society is perfectly devoid of action of aggression; and the hierarchy of acquired habits develops as the new grow out of the latter.

Again Burt sees no harm in 'abstraction'. To reach at 'abstractions' behind the 'Concrete' is the spirit of science. But probably the generalizations in 'animate objects' is more arduous than in the case of 'inanimate objects', but it does not mean that psychologists and educationists should not attempt at generalization.

The zoological studies of Lorenz, Tinbergen and their associates have also led to a revival of interest in instinct theory. They call themselves 'ethologists' and according to them, there are in born or instinctive patterns of behaviour, elicited by highly specific stimuli acting on highly specific mechanisms in the central nervous system. Though the term 'instinct' has fallen into ill-repute, but it is still a burning topic in comparative psychology.

'Instinct' is not a dead topic. Whether we use this term instinct or substitute it with some more sophisticated term is of little importance.

4. Need Theory

Murray Theory of needs reveals that needs are the basic forces to regulate our behaviour. There are two types of needs *viz.* the physiological and psychological which controls our behaviour. For instance, the experiments on rats regarding their needs for food, water and sex, etc. show the patterns of motivations. The more intense the need, the more the motivation but beyond a certain point, the increase in the intensity of need causes decrease in motivation. The relationship between need and motivation tends to become curvilinear, *i.e.,* with increase in need, there is increase in motivation till a breaking point is reached where the increase in need brings decrease in motivation. We should clearly understand that by need here we mostly mean the primary or biological needs. There are two sets of needs :

(i) Primary or biological, *e.g.,* water, food, sex etc.

(ii) Secondary or psychological, *e.g.* recognition, curiosity etc.

Need therefore is a deficiency of some substance or function which further life processes. This is a negative view of growth and motivation. Maslow has offered a positive concept of growth and motivation too.

5. Stimulation Theory

Stimulation Theory advocates that stimulus acts on a sense organ or other bodily structures so as to initiate new activities in the living tissues, *e.g.,* pinprick, tapping below the knee, hunger, thirst, etc. These stimuli can be external or internal. If you touch a particular region in the cortex with an electric needle, it arouses abnormal hunger in rats and dogs. It is an over-simplification, of course to say that behaviour is determined by only one stimulus at a time. There are many stimuli, interwoven in a complex pattern at one and the same time. All inner and outer stimuli that bear upon a person at one time constitute his psychological field and determine his behaviour jointly through interaction. However, there is no mystical relationship between a person and his environment. It is all analysable and open to verification.

6. Behaviour Theory

Behaviour Theory was advocated by Hull and and his associates. The theory points out that motivational as a phenomena which is based on three behavioural forces *viz.,* needs, desires and tendency to accept rewards. The theory further advocates that:

1. All behaviour is motivated in the sense that all behaviour is based on needs and desires.
2. All learning involves reward in the sense that only those responses that reduce need or drive are stamped in.
3. Need may by biological or psychological, primary or secondary.

Behaviour Theory of motivation has been criticised by number of psychologists but important critics such as Maslow point out that all behaviour is motivated. He develops the distinction between 'Adaptive behaviour' and 'Expressive behaviour'. The adaptive behaviour (*e.g.*, depressed mood) is motivated but the expressive behaviour (leaving posture due to depression) is not motivate is not due to need reduction.

Tolman, Hebb and Mowrer also opine that all learning is not need reduction. Tolman says that learning due to need reduction may also occur, but all learning is not like that as learning is based on 'cognitive, conative and psycho-somatic changes in behaviour. Therefore, the learning can influence the deeply the cognitive behaviour in case the learning is need based while criticising this theory. Mowrer draws distinction between learning from motivation which involves improvement in performance arising from some form of *conditioning* and that which involves the *solving of problems.*

There is also much controversy about the role of punishment and anxiety in learning. It is not only the 'need-reduction,' but also 'avoidance of pain' that goads one to learn

7. Social Theory

Social Theory of motivation points out that motivation is mainly influenced by the culture and environment, meaning thereby that an individual is motivated from the environment and culture of which he is a member. This theory can be studied into two heads *viz*;

(i) Culture-patternist theory which lays emphasis on the influence of the culture pattern.

(ii) Field theory which lays emphasis on the immediate social field *vis-a-vis* the individual who is very much in the field.

The *culture-patternists* are mostly social anthropologists like Margaret Mead (1935), who has drawn attention to the differences in sexual behaviour and aggression among the inhabitants of Mundugumor, Arapesh and Tchamubli. Her thesis is that these differences are chiefly due to the different customs, standards, expectations and institutions of three societies. According to this view point, an individual is cast in the mould of culture in such a way that he becomes the true attested copy of his culture. The different cultures would, therefore, produce different types of personalities. Thus, Linton (1947) mentions two types of personalities within an individual, one 'basic personality' and numerous 'status personalities' which are generated by the various sub-groups to which he belongs. Thus variations within any culture-pattern makes chameleons of its members. Undoubtedly, the culture-patternists overemphasize the influence of culture. Kardiner reports that at least pugnacity is due neither to frustration nor experience of childhood but is simply the result of adult calculations.

The field theory states that behaviour is a function of interaction between a person and his environment. This much is very acceptable but its assertions that 'the individual is a myth—the persons is a set of social relationship, ... or, that the behaviour of a person or group is due to the distribution of forces in the social situation as a whole rather than to the intrinsic properties of the individual', are too much. The individuality of the individual is also important factor. Moreover, however important may be the present, the past cannot be ignored. Kurt Lewin insists that behaviour is to be explained by reference to a person-in-an-environment situation and to all the forces that are presently interacting within it. To point out the main shortcoming in this argument, Mowrer and Kluckhohn (1944) have shown it is impossible, even in experiments with rats, to interpret features of animals' behaviour satisfactorily unless we know enough about their previous life history to tell whether their present actions do or do not exhibit a tendency to regress to an earlier pattern of response.

8. Depth Theory

Depth Theory of motivation was propounded by Freud who pointed out that individual behaviour is governed mainly by the motive forces. Later the concept of depth theory of motivational was further explained categorically by Neo-Fraudians and the theory can be studied on the basis of its features as under :

1. The Post Freudian viz; Karen, Hornly, Maslow, Roger, Erichete, treat normal and abnormal on the same continuum. Abnormality is nothing but a quantitative divergence from normal idiosyncrasies.
2. The spring of action is unconscious which is dark, ruthless, very powerful and illogical. The unconscious consist according to Freud of repressed sentiments, to Adler of attitudes, and Jung of unrealized potentialities.
3. Special exploratory techniques are needed to dig out the unconscious, e.g., dream analysis, free association, controlled association etc. Only then we become conscious of our motives. Prior to that we were unconscious about them. This is a very significant fontribution of Freud.
4. Unconscious motives influence our conscious thought and conduct through identification, repression, suppression and other defence mechanisms, etc.
5. Infancy is a very important period in the development of personality.

But there has been some revolt against it from Post-Freudians on the following points:

(i) There is a doubt regarding the structure of unconscious. It is not all sex and aggression only.

(ii) More emphasis gradually put on social environment which was practically neglected by the senior trio.

(iii) There have been some successful attempts at Group Therapy as introduced by Ezriel. This is opposed to individual psychoanalysis.

Another advance, not so much within psychoanalysis as in relation to it, has been the greater use of experimental approach in testing its hypotheses. Thus experimental verification has been attempted to test such Freudian statement as 'the need to suck, the consequences of its frustration,' 'the operation of the defence mechanisms (especially projection, repression and regression), the interpretation of dreams, etc. Some of these experiments have yielded very interesting results. For example, under hypnosis, but not in the waking state, 41 out of 50 adults were able to give entirely accurate statements of the days of the week on which their birthday and Christmas fell in each of the three years when they were four, seven and ten years old.

9. Physiological Theory

Physiological Theory of motivation was advocated by Lord Rutherford who said that in describing the phenomena of motivation, we should try to use the physical terms. Similarly, Lashley, Morgan, Beach, Krestchmer and Sheldon studied the relations between personality and physique, in relation to motivation and have reported that physique is said to be indirectly concerned with the physiology of motivation at least in the sense that they were seeking to determine the ways in which needs, desires, interests and attitudes vary with different types of body build. Presently Hebb and Stellar are busy in structuring this theory. It takes its help from cybernetics with its electronic models and encephalography. Some recent experiments in America on de-motivating a bull going to attack, with the help of electric waves which are claimed to have affected the brain waves of the bull, have given an experimental and authentic support to this theory.

In brief, we have seen that all these theories should be taken to be complementary rather than contradictory. These are the various attempts to explain the riddle of life and motivation, which is a multivariate phenomenon. A day may come when a single theory will weave all these apparently divergent theories into one unified whole and explain motivation. That will be a step forward in the scientific pursuit. Some attempts have been made to synthesize these theories, *e.g.,* by Mowrer and Kluckhohn, but it looks it is too early. The readers must have realised by now that the theories of motivation are the theories of behaviour, which are practically schools of psychology.

VIII.6 Types of Motivation

Precisely speaking, the motivation is the stirred up condition of an individual which cause him to act or move. The stirring up of an individual causing one to act may be from the inner self and from the outside world. The conditions which forces an individual from the innerself is labelled as the intrinsic motivation and the outward conditions which compels as individual to act is known as extrinsic motivation. On the basis of these conditions motivation can be categorised as internal and external motivation.

1. Internal Motivation

Man is born with natural behaviour. The natural behaviour *i.e.* taking food, water, sleep etc. are controlled by internal forces *viz.*, needs, derives and urges. All these inner forces play vital role in making an individual to act. Therefore, a man possesses appetite for food, for water, for rest and sleep, for change for sake of variety, for play, for sex, etc. A great part of the life of man is spent in activities which are motivated by these appetites. One of the most important foundations of happiness, contentment, and mental health is a feeling of security in terms of the basic organic needs. When the security is threatened, one may become radical in thought, he may try to lay the blame on others, or he may do any one of a great number of things developing on his training and experience. Maslow has given it second place in the hierarchy of needs.

Natural motives can be classified into three categories:

(a) Motives due to Elementary Basic Needs and Wants Structurally Determined. By such motives, we mean motives provided by heat, flow of blood, secretion of glands, growth and maturation, digestive processes, elimination, reflexes, appetites (hunger, thirst, sex etc.), crying, smiling, functions of the sense organs, etc., which are standard equipments with every normal human-being.

(b) Motives due to Drives Containing More Social and Physical Factors. These are imitation, anticipation, impatience, exhaustive emotional reactions, sentiment, satisfaction of drives due to exercise of special gifts, exploitation, acting according to habit, aesthetic appeal, security, achievement, situations, status, happiness, manipulation of any of the incentive ingredients in these motives can changes the motivation in the individual.

(c) Negative Drives and Motives. They are listed as : pain, all unpleasant sensory reactions, being forced to do things, fatigue, exhaustion, despair, being

put in an inferior position, frustrating feelings of failure and helplessness, being forced to make a choice, loss of freedom of action, general fears and phobias. These are the motives which we usually avoid and as such are called negative motives. It is not always true that positive drives are helpful. It has been observed that at times negative drives also play useful role for the betterment of man.

The motivational forces which makes an individual to act are of two types *viz.* natural and un-natural—It has be found that natural motive forces play useful role. For instance, in schools, the natural motivation finds a very useful place. To secure this type of motivation, the subject-matter must be made significant or meaningful to the learner. The learner's interest in the activity should be aroused. The teaching should be within the range of interest and capacity of the pupil.

2. *External Motivation*

External motivation or the extensive motivation advocates that learning must proceed in the absence of internal motivation. External motivation is influenced by external forces. The external forces which motives an individual are many but most commonly they can be classified as the cultural and community atmosphere based. The level of motivation an individual receives from the external forces depends upon many types of abilities such as intelligence, maturity. If there is intellectual immaturity and lack of sensitivity to ultimate consequences and ideals in the individual, then internal motivations will fail. In such circumstance recourse is to be taken to external motivation. External motivation, however, is so called only because it is external to the learning activity itself. By external motivation it should not be considered that it is in any sense artificial. It has to be built upon the foundation of some existing natural response or tendency. It can be successful only when it is intrinsic to the nature of the individual. Thus, drives which are the main sources of spontaneous attention and painless effort and are enormous resources of potential energy at the disposal of the learner and teacher should be judiciously employed and wisely directed towards motivating the pupil.

VIII.7 Effect of Motivation on Learning

We all know that motivation is a stir-up condition of an individual which makes him to act. Action due to motivation effects an individual differently. In case, the emotional state of an individual helps an individual to perform a job accurately, speedly and effectively, it means that a particular emotional condition of an individual has affected him positively.

Similarly, if a particular situation of an individual behaviour impeed his performance. It means that particular motivational condition has affected negatively. Therefore, we can say that motivation affects the behaviour of the individual as motivation affects the learner to learn. The effect of motivation on the learners in the following ways:

(i) *Intention to Learn*

The simplest mo6tivation which we can give to a child is to ask him to learn. When a child will know that he is expected to learn he will make efforts to learn. The readiness condition of the child makes him to attempt to learn. The attempt of the child to learn signifies his intention to learn.

Here it is also necessary to say that many a time an individual learns when he has no intention to learn. You learn the telephone number or car number without any intention. Much learning takes place when an individual concentrates his attention on any thing but is not asked to learn.

(ii) *Ego-involvement*

Man is different from other animals. He can perform higher mental functions. He can do many such complex tasks which the other animals cannot perform. The psychologists say that the basis for these complex activities is provided by a mental element—self.

The nature of self can be understood by observing the experience and behaviour. First of all we can say that the self of an individual is all that which can be observed. Every individual has knowledge of his own personality. Secondly, the self is the organization of values and attitudes. Thirdly, self includes much that we call egoistic. For the discussion over here these three characteristics of self are important: (a) Self can be observed and can be known by the individuals, (b) it can be clearly demarcated from the other individuals and the external world, and (c) it involves acceptable to the person.

A person can react to his environment in two way. When we tie the laces of our shoe, or board a bus, or produce humming sound we react in an uninvolved manner. The second type of reaction takes place at the time when we do some work very carefully and attentively and involve ourselves completely in it. In the first type of behaviour the self remains aloof. In the second type of behaviour the self *i.e.* ego is involved. Sheriff and Cartrill call the second type of behaviour as ego-involvement behaviour. *Ego-involvement is a condition of total participation of the self as knower, organizer, observer, status seeker, and as socialized being.* Ego is involved in all those actions in which our ability is challenged.

Many a time in such ordinary actions like dressing, shaving, catching a train, there is an automatic functioning and so there is no ego involvement. Ego is involved when there is an obstacle in the successful functioning. If we catch a bus daily and reach our office in time there is no ego-involvement. In case the bus is late, the ego-involvement takes place as we are now afraid that we will be late for our office. The extreme form of ego-involvement is self-sacrifice. Whenever we are learning some new skill or getting some new knowledge our ego is then involved. Therefore, involvement of ego related how seriously we are ready to act which is due to motivation *i.e.,* involvement of self.

(iii) Praise and Blame

The motivation of praise and blame directly indicates that an individual is influenced to behave or act in a specified way because of his self-involvement. Because of the reason, the praise and blame of the learner directly effect the self of an individual. For instance, there is experimental evidence which tends to show that praise stimulates average and inferior children but has less effect on those of superior intelligence. It has also been noted that reproof is felt most by superior children; but girls seem more susceptible to praise than boys. Some studies indicates, however, that regardless of age, sex or initial ability, praise is the most effective of the incentives tested. Reproof seems to decline in effectiveness for all students. Among the experiments worth mentioning here are those of Chase who in 1932 reported 'praise' to be less effective than 'blame' with young children, and of Hurlock in the 1920's which have led to the general conclusion, still accepted by contemporary investigators that praise is more effective stimulus in motivating both immediate and long continued tasks. But it will depend on the teacher as to where he uses praise and where blame. A good teacher will be one who can use these incentives at a proper moment and in a proper manner. In brief, the motivation due to praise and blame affects the learner.

(iv) Rivalry

Rivalry is a negative form of motivational force which may develop undesirable behavioural tendencies. But rivalry if taken in the right perspective can help an individual to excel in certain fields. Generally, the rivalry between the individuals may leads to resentment, jealousy, etc., or the rivalry between groups which creates hatred are the least desirable types of incentives to be encouraged in the schools. Self-rivalry or rivalry in the form of competition with one's past record, is the most valuable type. This should be developed in the individual because it helps learning of the learner. Education will fail to develop proper social attitudes if it will put greater emphasis on competition and rivalry. Even though many experimental researches have shown rivalry to be a powerful motivating influence, yet before it is to be used in schools, its emotional and social consequences must be considered by the teachers.

(v) Punishment and Rewards

The reward and punishment are the extrinsic forms of motivation. The reward acts as positive reinforcer where as, the punishment acts as negative reinforcer. It is admitted fact that both these reinforcers effect the learner in the following ways:

1) *Punishment*, is the art of inflicting pain deliberately, with the avowed purpose of affecting the future conduct of one being punished. As a disciplinary and educative process, it is the most ancient and obvious method of restraining, coercing, and guiding the young. It is based on fear; the fear of physical pain, embarrassment and loss of status. Fear is a strong motive, and may elicit a type of reaction which makes the child behave in the right manner. But punishment that is too severe, or inflicted when the reason for punishment is not clear and acknowledged, may breed resentment, antagonism and desire to avoid the form of learning to which it is attached.

(2) *Reward*, in the form of money, exemptions and medals or badges, has been shown experimentally to be a powerful incentive. But it must be remembered here that they are hardly ideal forms of motivation. Hartshorne and May, in their study of honesty among school children, have made an interesting discovery that a certain group which had been artificially stimulated to honesty through rewards, was actually more dishonest than the average. The children were evidently so strongly motivated by the desire to win prizes for honesty that they adopted dishonest means.

The common practice of awarding pins, stars, cups and various marks and badges easily degenerates into motivation for those trinkets instead of creating a desire for the true objective. In Indian schools, the saddest example of this type of motivation is the system of divisions and degrees. It will not be wrong to say that an Indian students stud ies only for passing the examination or getting the degree. His main goal of learning degenerates into securing a good division by hook or crook. As a result student develop wrong tendency to copy, threaten the invigilators, approach the examiners or indulge in similar other undesirable activities just to obtain a degree or a certificate and as soon as his task is accomplished and he gets a degree, he will try to forget whatever he has learnt, as fast as possible. There will be left no further incentive for him to gain knowledge or to work. The universities are largely to blame for this extraneous importance of superficiality by awarding division on a none too scientific system of examinations. If a complete analysis of education system of our country is made, our examination system may emerge out to be the greatest contributing factor for the major evils inherent in it.

(vi) Knowledge of Progress

The knowledge of results and the knowledge of progress to a learner directly effect a learner because of the season that the relation of progress stimulates further efforts. It is on account of this that records of progress, etc., are invaluable for all the students. The teacher should also provide opportunities where the students can successfully accomplish their task. If there are too many failures, the students are disheartened and they develop a feeling of frustration.

It is also necessary that the children are aware of the goals. Purposive striving for goals is much more fruitful than groping in the dark. It may be noted that motives have goals. If the goal is clearly perceived, the act will be very strongly motivated. Thus, the work should be definite in aim, within the capacity and interest of the pupil, but difficult enough to challenge effort in accomplishment.

Studies by Judd, in 1905, were among the first to demonstrate that practice without awareness of results had no effect in certain type of learning. For instance, Judd found that if the children are asked to judge the length of lines and a practice is given to them in this respect without giving them any information regarding the progress made by them they hardly show any improvement in their judgement. But the correction of errors, supplemented by knowledge of progress, tends to improve the learner's judgements. Thorndike's experiments as reported in 1935, similar type of results both in the case of mental and motor behaviour.

(vii) Electronic Media

The use of audio-visual material such as T.V., Radio, Tape-recorder and Computers can facilitate the learner to learn. The learner while learning through media devices feels deeply involved in learning a concept which ultimately affect a learner.

Use of media enables the learner to see what is being done which saves time and energy, and makes the test more interesting and vivid. This takes advantage of the power of imitation to reinforce motivation. Movies, comics, radio, television, laboratory and workshop, etc., should be utilized in school learning in so far as they are practical. They are great aids to motivation.

(viii) Level of Aspiration as Motive

The level of aspiration of learning also affects the motivation of the learner. The concept of level of aspiration has been developed by Lewin. The operational definition of level of aspiration is that "it is the level of future performance of a familiar task which an individual expects to need." The level to which the individual believes that he will perform the task is defined as expectation. The success is defined in terms of the individual's surpassing the level he expects to reach and the failure is defined as his unsuccess fulness in reaching the expected level.

The level of aspiration with respect to a particular task can be considered to be due to the operation of such motives as anxiety. Previous failures establish low level of aspirations and previous successes high level of aspirations. A number of research workers have also noted that the level of aspiration differs with different persons so far as a realistic approach is concerned. Some people set a level of aspiration in keeping with their performance while others set a level of aspiration either much higher than they are ever likely to attain or very low. All those researches show that the level of aspiration is very complexly determined and if treated as motivation, quite a good complexity is brought about.

From the above discussion it is evident that motivation affects psychology of a learner in three ways viz.

(1) Motives Energize Behaviour. Motives release energy and arouse activity. Thus, hunger and thirst induce muscular and glandular reactions. Praise, blame, reward, punishment, etc., are powerful incentives for many of our actions. They make us react in a particular way and are helpful in the learning process.

(2) Motives are Selectors of Behaviour. They dispose the individual to reach to some situations and to ignore others; they determine in considerable part how he will react to certain situations. When a newspaper is given to different people it is seen that everyone reads that column carefully for which he has got incentives. For example, a person out of employment will look at the "Wanted" column most attentively and will remember many of the vacancies *verbatim;* on the other hand, a sportsman will read the sports news most carefully.

(3) Motives Direct Behaviour. Motives are not merely the selectors but also the directors of behaviour. They direct the behaviour in such a manner that the individual gets the satisfying feeling. It is, therefore, necessary that for improvement in his learning the individual should be made active and motivated to direct his energies towards well-defined and attainable goals.

In brief, motivation is affected by number of other. factors. The most effective among those are the factor of learning abilities of the learner, the type of learning material and learning situation. The motivation level of an individual also depends upon these factors.

VIII.8 Assessment of Motivation

Motivation is purely based on the basic need of the learner. The need of the learner act as prime force to learn a task. In this regard the need to achieve was first stressed by H. A. Murray in his list of psychogenic needs, but it was his student David McClelland who devoted his efforts to the development of methods of measuring the achievement motive and discovering its properties, the behavioural correlates of this motive. Two major assumptions are made by this research: one is, that motivation may have some effects on fantasy or imagery, and the other is that motives can be brought into play by suitable conditions and by altering these conditions, the degree of arousal can be varied. The motivation can be assessed by three methods *viz.* direct, indirect and experimental method.

1. Direct Method of Motivation Assessment

In this category we may include all those methods and techniques that permit the subject to express his motives through verbal or other overt behaviour. Here the required information about the motives and the natural behaviour of an individual is gathered directly from the primary source, the subject by asking him to account for his behaviour or through naturalistic objective observation of his behaviour. The major techniques of methods included in this category are questionnaire, inventories, motivation scale, checklist, naturalistic observation, interview, autobiography and other self-description measures.

2. Indirect Methods

In situation where the subject is either unaware of his motives or is determined not to reveal them, the use of indirect methods is recommended. The material to which the subject is exposed in the indirect measures of studying motives consists of fairly ambiguous or unstructured stimulus situations. Based on the mechanism of projection, the subject is expected to provide clues for his hidden or true motives by responding to these unstructured stimuli. The interpretation of these clues by the experimenter then, may help in the assessment of the subject's true motives.

All the projective techniques like the Rorschach ink blot test, thematic appreciation test (TAT), child apperception test, (CAT), the Blacky pictures, drawing completion test, sentence completion technique, word association technique, role-playing and socio-drama, etc., fall in the category of indirect methods of measuring motives.

These projective techniques provide full opportunity to the subject to project his motives and intentions in a structured form through responses in the form of writing stories about the pictures shown or completing a sentence, sketching or drawing, associating a word or playing a role. The interpretation of these structured responses would depend upon the reason for administering the test. For example, if the experimenter is interested in measuring the affiliation or achievement motive, the subject's responses are evaluated in terms of how much affiliation orientation or achievement orientation they display.

3. Experimental Methods

Experimental methods of measuring consist of measures involving objective observations under controlled conditions. For ascertaining the real motives, the experimenter first makes some tentative hypotheses and tests them in the laboratory or laboratory-like conditions to arrive at some objective, reliable and valid conclusions. In addition to the investigation for the origin and causes of a behaviour involving motivation, experimental methods also help in testing the various empirical predictions based on particular motivational hypotheses. For example, one may hypothesize that persons having a strong achievement motive must differ in a number of predictable ways from persons with a weak achievement motive. In experimental testing of this hypothesis, the experimenter may collect scores related to the achievement motive by introducing a projective test like TAT or Rorschach ink blot and subsequently try to demonstrate that subjects who score high in terms of achievement motive are also faster at solving mathematical problems, memorizing poems and performing some typical complex skills.

VIII.9 Educational Implications of Motivation

The role of teacher in motivating the student can hardly be ignored because teacher performs the duties as a manager of learnings activities. The teacher has not only to assemble materials, organize them into viable units and draw up programmes and plans for putting them across to his pupils, but he has also to devise strategies and tactics by which pupils may be persuaded to put their best foot forward and apply themselves whole-heartedly to the tasks he has assigned them in such a manner that they assume responsibility for their achievement and to arouse and encourage them to continue pursuing their learning goals effectively. Majority of the students who join school do so with the express objects of learning and achieving certain goals. These goals may not be very clear to good many of them but they are present nevertheless. The teacher's task is to clarify these goals for both pupils and their parents and then try to arouse their interest in their pursuit.

The commonest Indian practice is to make pupils learn and achieve through one or the other form of coercion, physical punishment or fear of failure. There is hardly any tradition of stimulating pupils who are not interested and at best the indifferent pupils are tacitly ignored. As a result we find that adequate training of teachers is required to maintain the interest of the student is learning in school.

Indian teacher tries to motivate students by holding periodical tests, examinations at the end of every term, awarding marks and prizes, passing judgements of "pass", offering temptations of a prize or scholarship or inducing fear of failure. These are some of the types of pressures which teachers use to drive students to work hard and harder to achieve better. Tests and examinations should serve as useful tools to pupils for self-evaluations and to teachers for assessing achievement and learning, but too often they are used to produce and intensify anxiety among pupils. Pressure is mounted every day as examinations draw near, fear of failure among pupils of above average ability and fear of losing status among pupils of above average rank creates undue stress and tension and often has a very harmful effect on academic achievement performance. The role of teacher is to observe the situations which cause tension among the students and the teachers needs to regulate rather defuse tension among students.

Hard attitude of the teacher to some extent is unwanted because it kills initiative and student's sense of responsibility. They are keen only to carry out the commands of the teacher and make no effort at self-direction and self-achievement. Their attempts are generally along the lines laid down by the teacher and their main concern is to escape the censure of the teacher.

Some teachers motivate their students by insisting or expectancies. They keep repeating that students attend the school to learn and achieve what is prescribed for them, they keep giving the advice and directions regarding the tasks to be accomplished and they expect students to comply. As their approach is always of hope and confidence, they do succeed in motivating young people. Most of the teachers who succeed are otherwise effective and pupils respect their wishes. The total effect on pupils is the strong feeling that both teachers and pupils are engaged in tasks which are worthwhile and of vital importance.

The success of a teacher in motivating the student can be assessed how a teacher is able to make the student to enjoy the task of learning or doing a job. Whatever may be the level of difficulty of the job, however, hard may be the task, if students enjoy doing it, if their experience is interesting and they expect to succeed, they will learn and achieve. These teachers rely mostly on praise and recognition by awarding higher psychological effect of rewards are more effective than punishments. Rewarding correct learning increases the prospect of its recurrence as has been indicated in earlier chapters. In a class in which the social emotional climate is healthy, mere commendation of work in a group makes for strong motivation for achievement.

Healthy relationship between the pupil and the teacher results in better understanding. Therefore, happy interpersonal relations between the teacher and pupils are a strong motivating force in achievement. Where the teacher and pupils are happy with each other, where the teacher has a deep interest in the welfare of his pupils and where both have confidence in each other's good will, affection and friendship, the pupils will always be on the look-out to please and win the approval and commendation of the teacher, to live and work up to his expectation and to enjoy doing what is expected of them. The teacher for his part must see that the tasks allotted to pupils are well within their capacity, that their previous interests form the basis of their new interests and that he himself not only feels but also shows himself involved in pupil's efforts and activities.

The secondary role of the teacher is to induce motivation among the students while inducing motivation a teacher has to adopt suitable means of motivation. For instance, Kurt Lewin distinguished between *inner* and *induced motivation*, and Lippit and White in their new classic experiment studied the effects of different leadership styles in children's tendency to develop their own motivation with regard to group achievement. The psychological process involved in inducing motivation among the students demand the following steps to be followed by the teacher:—

1. Creating Cognitive Structure. It is a known fact that a person's behaviour is guided by his perception of the world in which he lives. Action is taken on the basis of a person's view of the 'facts' of the situation and the facts are coloured by his beliefs and opinions, the private map, so to say, that he maintains of the world. The content and relationships among parts of a person's psychological world may be called his cognitive structure. Since this structure underlies all behaviour efforts to influence pupils; behaviour will succeed only if this structure undergoes a change. The prime task of the teacher is to make young people understand clearly what they have come to school for, what are the aims and the objectives of schooling, what is the programme for classwork in this term or month and what is expected of them. This knowledge and understanding will re-orient them cognitively to school work. Many students come to school or college because their parents want them to get out of their way, they do not care what their children learn or do not learn, and naturally, for such children the school may not be a place for learning and achievement. On the other hand, there are students whose parents send them to school with the express intent that they learn and achieve things and this intent is very clearly dinned into their ears. The understanding, opinions and thoughts of the latter will incline them more to accept the messages of the teacher because they are consistent with their cognitive structure.

2. Creation of a Motivational Structure. Creation of motivational structure means the teacher must create in the minds of pupils needs, interests and purposes which will energize learning and achieving behaviour. If the teacher suggests to them goals from among which they choose some and if they are persuaded to accept them as worthwhile and vital, they will work for their achievement and fulfilment.

But it is possible for a person to understand a goal and develop a motivation for its realization without actually doing anything about it. The needs of hunger and thirst are accompanied by a discomfort which energizes action but the motive for achievement does not carry with it any insistent prod within any clear limitation of time. Therefore, the teacher must see that achievement motivation gains control of pupil's behaviour at a particular point in time.

3. Creating Behaviour Structure. Creating behavioural structure is in the process of induction of motives. The teacher will have to keep other motives out of focus and assign specific tasks to be completed at a particular point in time. The goal and tasks should be concrete and specific and if a time limit is given for their fulfilment and completion, it will precipitate learning activity and achievement.

From the above discussîon it is evident that the role of a teacher in developing, regulating and maintaining required degree of motivation is essential. The teacher can help the student to induce the motivation on one side and can help the student to develop internal inspiration to learn a lesson or a skill.

VIII.10 Learning Exercises

1. Describe the meaning and types of motivation.
2. Discuss the theories of motivation.
3. Describe the factors influencing motivation.
4. Discuss the assessment techniques of motivation.
5. Describe the educational implications of motivation.

IX
Personality

The term personality is used commonly in our day-to-day life. The term has wider meaning reflecting the inner most behaviour of an individual. The term has been defined by psychologists differently.

IX.1 Meaning and Definition of Personality

The term personality has its origin in the Latin verb persona which mean to sound through. This term for the first time was used to describe the voice of an actor speaking through a mask. Later, the term persona was referred directly to the mask worn by the actors and then the term became applied to the actors themselves. During early Roman days the term 'personality' was regarded as constituting what a person seemed to be and as a result layman's concept of personality was developed as such personality can be described as:

(a) Physical appearance of an individual;

(b) Manners in which he talks and behaves; and

(c) Intelletual qualities of a person.

On the contrary the modern psychologists have tried to describe personality along threee dimensions which can be studied as:

1. Personality as Social Phenomena

Social phenomenal view advocates that the personality of an individual depends to a large extent on how he acts and reacts in a social group. The actions and reactions of an individual in a group reflecting his personality can be studied on the basis of the following dimensions of social phenomena such as:

(a) Personality as a social stimulus value: By social value of one's personality we mean how an individual can influence others and to what extent he is possessing social stimulus leadership qualities. It is said that personality

can not be completely understood only in terms of social stimulus value because it is very difficult to define clearly the term social stimulus value because it is very difficult to define clearly the term social stimulus values. Because the social stimulus value of an individual depends on the kind of relationship that one attempts to establish in a particular situation. In other words the personality of a person depends upon the ability of an individual who omits social stimulus to influence the others.

(b) Personality as a particular patterns of social response: This view advocates that behaviour on an individual can be better understood by studying the relationship between stimulus and response similarly, personality can be better understood by understanding social stimulus and social response of a person. In other words personality as a social stimulus cannot give us a complete picture of an individual's personality. Reasons being the social stimulus of an individuals is in form of responses like aggressiveness submissiveness, explosiveness and the descriptions based on facial expression and emotional outbrust which are called individual's social responses. The effective regulation of facial and emotional expression i.e. social responses, by an individual in response to social stimulus reflects the personality of an individual.

(c) Personality as a product of culture: The social psychologists who adopt this view study the human personality in terms of social environment and social stimuli. While studying personality of an individual, it is true that man is to a large extent the product of culture and his social environment. But the fullest dimensions of his personality can not be understood by taking this view into consideration there is a danger of missing the dynamic aspect of one's personality. As culture may shape him, but it is equally true that the individual also shapes the culture. Therefore, to much extent culture helps in shaping the personality in majority of the cases. But some personalities do help in changing the culture. On the whole personality is the product of culture.

2. Personality as Ontological Phenomena

Personality according to this approach is the uniqueness of inner organisation. This view emphasises certain particular qualities such as intelligence, temperament (viz. introvert, extrovert) or dynamic nature of an individual. The intelligence has generally been accepted by every one as an important characteristics and conditions of personality. These characteristics are arranged in a particular pattern among different individuals. Thus personality can be described as a phenomena of inner organisation of an individual characteristic which depends upon the environment and heredity of an individual.

The ontological approach helps to understand the concept of personality which advocates that personality is based on selfhood phenomena. The approach to study personality of an individual is based on self-hood which emphasise that from early childhood the individual's concept of self is an important factor in guiding both his immediate behaviour and the further development of his personality. He acts constantly in terms of the kind of person he believes he is loveable or unattractive bright or stupid, capable or clumsy. The nature of ones deeds reflect his personality.

3. Personality as a Psycho-analytic phenomena

Modern psychological approach helps to understand the concept of personality on the basis of psycho-analysis. The psycholanalytical phenomena enable us to study personality as stated by :

(i) Frued is of the view that individual personality is to be understood more in terms of the conflict between the reality principles and pleasure principles. This approach reveals that individuals mind has three levels i.e. Pre-conscious and Super-concious. The motive forces which controls the individuals behaviour are the 'Id' 'Ego' and Super-ego. The dominance of one motive force over the other with the active co-operation of any level of one's mind amounts to follow a principle whether the reality or pleasure. The dominance of pleasure principle gives one shape of personality whereas the dominance of reality principle in one's behaviour provides other shape of one's personality.

(ii) Adler point out that "Personality is the style of one's life." The style of one's life is mostly shaped in the early years in the milieu of the home environment.

The style of one's life depends upon the approach in dealing the life situation. The nature of adjustment with the situation enables an individual to form a style of life. The type of one's life reflects his personality.

(iii) Jung advocates that personality of an individual is the outward and inward expression of "libido". The "Libido" is storehouse of one's behaviour energy. The type of inclination of Libido decides the type of one's personality. In brief, we can say that various psychologists have tried to explain concept of personality but unfortunately none of the concept is considered final. However, psychologist belonging to different schools of psychology have tried to explain the nature meaning of the concept of personality and have put forth their view points in the form of definitions.

Definitions of Personality

Etymological Explanation: The word personality is a derivation from the Latin word 'Persona'. Persona means the mark of dress used by players in a drama. The word was used about a hundred years before Christ by Roman players.

Layman's point of view: Personality is concept of wide and varied meanings. To the man in the street it is special almost magical quality which makes it possible to make a sale, win a sweet-heart or convince an audience. This idea can be more objectively expressed by saying that "Personality is the stimulus value which one individual has for another", or it is the impression of individual on another." This view of Layman is rooted in behaviouristic school of psychology which is mechanistic in nature, stressing too much on outer or external environment and neglected internal aspects of personality.

Philosophical Explanation: From philosophical point of view personality is individuality which has become objective to itself. Some call it self-stood. According to others it is an ideal of perfection. There are subjective definitions of spiritual nature and so these do not fit in the world of science.

Sociological Explanation: From the point of view of sociologists in defining personality individual being is not sufficient but they include society at large. Sociologists consider that personality is a reflection of our depending. Upon the social background Fairs said that the personality is subjective side of culture. He ignored biological and psychological determinants such as intelligence and temperament.

In 1937, Allport identified in the literature almost 50 definitions of personality (2) Today there are doubtless more. Most of the early psychological definitions emphasized the expressive aspects of personality and ignored or only indirectly implied the interior organisation that is responsible for the observable aspects Woodworth for example defined personality as the "quality of the individuals total behaviour. According to Dashiell, an individual's personality is the "Total picture of his organised behaviour especially as it can be characterised by his fellow men in a consistent way. Munn gave a more comprehensive analysis, pointing out that personality is the "most characteristic integration of an individuals structures and activities." It is characteristic in a dual sense because (1) it is unique, thus differentiating the individual from all others, and (2) it is fairly consistent, representing the customary integration of a particular individuals structures and activities.

These representatives early psychological definitions stressed the manifest aspect of personality (i) What may be observed by others, (ii) though they implied that what a person is, how he thinks and feels and what is included in his total psychological makeup will be revealed through his speech and behaviour. Munn implied this concept especially when he referred to the "integration of an individual's structures and activities" None, however, spelled out the significance of fundamental and often unconscious drives and wishes stremming from what may be considered the real personality, (iii) the individual's evaluation of himself, (iv) what he wants to be ? (v) How he appears to himself and to others (vi) How he regards his relationship with others?

To fully understand what personality is, the intricacy of its structure, and its all pervasive influence on the quality of the individual's total behaviour," One must understand its motivational aspects. This becomes apparent when one considers what a false impression one often gets from judgement based solely on the manifest aspect of personality: the individual's speech, behaviour and appearance.

Allports reports the deficiencies in the early definitions led to attempts to define personality in such a way as to include its motivational aspects as well as some of its other outstanding characteristics. Of these definitions, the most widely accepted is the short but all-inclusive definitions proposed by the late Gordon W. Allport of Harvard University. "Personality is the dynamic organization within the individual of those psychological systems that determine his characteristic behaviour and thought. An analysis of the key words in this definition show how comprehensive it is and how much stress Allport placed on motivation.

Precise definition of personality as given by Allport and other psychologists can be enumerated the following dimentions:—

1. The bio-physical system i.e. the body, the complexion, the size, the physical feature, physical health and the nervous system, inherited from the parents, and partly modified by environment.
2.
   judgement, reasoning, memory and abstract thinking.
3. The emotions, the temperamen, the sentiments, the affective or the emotional aspect.
4. Inherited dispositions besides intelligence and emotions such as impulses, innate tendencies, volition, interests and attitudes.
5. Acquired dispositions such as interest, aptitude, habits, sentiments, which shape personality.
6. Social aspect i.e. adjustability and sociability and social behaviours.

IX.2 Characteristics of Personality

In order to understand the meaning and concept of personality the Knowledge of personality characteristics are essential to be studied as under:

Firstly personality is self-consciousness. For instance we attribute personality to a person is self-conscious being. Whereas we do not attribute personality to a dog or a child because they have no awareness of their own identity. It is only grown up people who through success or failure, praise or blame begins to take an objective attitude towards themselves, to different acts of behaviour if they harmonize with each and can be linked into the system.

Secondly, personality is through and through social. It is only in relation to others that we are usually judged and our consciousness of ourselves arises only in our interaction with other members of society. Our growth takes place through social experience, how other people react to our abilities, qualities, and actions.

Thirdly, a personality is continually making adjustment to environment and to inner life. Lack of adjustment means strain and tension and the individual is for ever acquiring new patterns of adjustment to meet the challege of new situations. Adjustment, makes the behaviour smooth, easy and efficient.

Fourthly, personality is always striving for goals. Our life and behaviour is purposive, and we are for ever seeking new ends and goals to meet our needs. Our needs define our goals, our interest and desires provide their basis and our behaviour is directed towards their attainment. Thus types of one's need reflects his personality.

Fifthly, personality functions as a whole. Different experiences and mental activities are joined together in unity. An individual is a creature of impulse, every passing fancy makes him act. The type acts reflect his personality. The difference in personality depends upon the types of variations in acts all his experiences and activities are now joined or integrated and some of the highly developed personalities like that of Mahatma Gandhi are highly integrated. The unifying force is provided by their ideals and standard of behaviour which they have acquired in the course of their life and experience.

IX.3 Dimensions of Personality

Psychologists suggests that there are four main dimensions of personality such as : physical, mental, emotional and social. Although they seem to be quite seperate from one another, yet they are closely related. All these dimensions work together to constitute personality. These are the different aspects of a personality. Such as :

(i) Physical Dimension : Physical body is inherited. The limits of size, weight and the form of features are also inherited. But the development of body takes place during life time and thus it is or it may be extremely affected by the environment. It is possible that the full growth of body is not completed or is related to suitable nourishment is not completed or is retarded if suitable nourishment is not given to children. The child has to exist and grow. His need of nourishment is double thathat of adult.

Good features, fair complexion, well built body, healthy muscular body accompanied by tall stature make a person attractive. It adds to his personality. Person with ugly appearance and weak or unproportionate body make poor personality. When we judge the person, first of all we see him physically.

No doubt, the physical body is inherited but environment can do a lot . Good diet and suitable physical exercise go a long way to build a sound physical body. Physical personality also owes to the dress. A smart dress changes the person. it makes him smart. Clothes of suitable size and of suitable type to match the body is a great contributing factor to make the personality impressive. Even the shade of clothes and their combination means a lot. Though it is a common point yet it is not commonly recognized.

Parents and teachers can do a lot to promote the healthy growth of students. They should take preventive as well as curative measures. Good nourishment and healthy habits should be provided. The suitable arrangment for games must be done in every home and school. Parents and teachers must know the simple rules of hygiene and these should be put in practice. Personal cleanliness should be taught and taste for good dress should be developed.

(ii) Mental Dimension: Mainly it refers to intelligence of the person. In our common life, there is a need to adjust ourselves to the new situations. To a great extent our adjustment depends on our general intelligence. This is the biggest and most powerful tool gifted by nature. Personality is judged from ideas, thoughts, activities or behaviour and all these depend on general intelligence of a person.

Like physical dimension, intelligence is also innate and grows during life-time of the individual. Full development is fostered if the needed facilities are provided. Sometimes, the mental development is retarded due to certain defects in body, specially in thyroid glands. The rate of growth diminishes and the child loses mental appetite. On the other hand, it is facilitated if there is intellectual environment at home and school. For this purpose the method of teaching in school should be such as to seek the active co-operation in the learning situation and students are to think over the problems. Individual attention should be paid.

Sometimes, the children are intelligent, still they are mal-adjusted. Especially, the gifted children have more chances to deviate from the average behaviour as they are very superior and their needs are more of diffeent type than those of a normal intelligent child. There is danger that their intelligence may not be perverted towards anti-social activities. Similarly, dull and feeble-minded children may become problems. They should be handled with due care right from the beginning.

(ii) Emotional Dimension : Emotions are the springs of actions. Emotions if trained and used properly are great assets otherwise they may block the

intelligence of person by dint of their strength. Personality report is incomplete if it does not refer to the emotional stability of the person. A person who has a nice temperament and is emotionally stable, is liked by all the persons. His manners are pleasing. The person who is emotionally disturbed or unstable may live in the extremes. His behaviour is childish. He is very sensitive for petty remarks. If he shows anger, he is out of range. If he shows affection, he will become very sincere and full of affection.

Most of the mal-adjusted children and un-wholesome persons have emotional problems. Their emotional difficulties are at the root of their trouble. Thus control over emotions is needed to become a well integrated personality.

Emotions can be modified and sublimated. The parents and teachers should make use of the technique to regulate such a powerful energy in educating their children and students. Energy is not released, it will upset the balance of mind. the best way to realise the pent-up emotional energy is to provide games and play. At the same time, children must get worthy emotional experience to their emotions in natural way, as complete sublimation of emotional energy is not possible.

(iv) Social Dimensions: Man is a social animal. But as child does not know the rules and regulations of society. He gets them during his life time. He has inherited only joy of company.

A person may be bodily very healthy, intelligent and emotionally stable but may not be socially accepted by others. The behaviour of a person must be approved by the society at large otherwise he will be rejected by others and may live his life behind the bars for his or her antisocial activities. All these things he gets from the society.

In the beginning when child is very young, home or family is the society, All the needs are looked after by mother, nurse, father or by other elder members of his family. In this regard, the child has to obey the code of family or in other words child identifies himself with his parents. He borrows the attitude of parents and thus makes his own social and moral code. We mean to say that basis of sociability is formed at home and much depends on the standard of family for its formation.

Social aspects of personality is not limited to extraversion. It does not mean only to mix up with other persons with ease and live comfortably,and behave nicely by showing good manners but also includes socially accepted behaviour. A smart thief can be a member of club and can impress other persons by sweet talks and pleasing manners. He may be well-dressed, physicaly healthy but he is not a social figure in the real sense because he is thief and does anti-social activities. This is an important criterion on a well-integrated personality.

Sociability cannot be taught with long lectures and big lessons. Development of social dimension of a society psychologists feel that there should be a favourable atmosphere in the school right from the peon to the principal. Let all the senior members of school show the model of social behaviour. The students themselves will catch it and learn it unconsciously. The school authorities should provide varied social situations, where children may participate.

From the above discussion, it is evident that in order to understand the concept of personality we need to study the physical, mental, social, and emotional dimensions of an individual. Further understanding of the concept personality make us to understand the physical trait, mental traits, social traits and emotional traits of an individual. The traits do not emerge as such in an individual but an individual during his development right from his childhood develops personality. The traits of personality, thus to understand the concept of personality, it is imperative to study the development of personality.

IX.4 Types of Personality

The people do differ in the type of responses to a particular situations. An individual behaviour reflects his personality. Since, every individual behaves differently. The difference in behavioural patterns makes us to understand different types of behaviour, the psychologists have tried to explain personality with different perceptions. Though we are not very sure about the types of personality an individual possesses. In other words, it is difficult to provide the exact classification of personality. It is not because we lack knowledge about personality but were not in a position to provide a simple comprehensive classification of personality patterns which is commonly acceptable. Keeping in view the divergence of view points to classify personality types, it would be advisable to study personality types in the following order:

1. Indian Type: Indian thinkers point out that there are three gunas which constitute one's personality. The gunas which constitute personality are like the strands of a rope. These gunas are Sattvaguna, Rajas Guna, Tamas Guna. The personality of an individual depends upon the domination of one guna over the other.For instance, "Sattava Guna" stands for which stands which has inclination write towards truth, purity wheras, the 'Rajas guna' the red strand is that which causes activity, restlessness and passion, the strand of energy, A person having the domination of Rajas guna would be more anxious, political and vigrous. The 'Tamas' or Tamo guna, representing the black strand is that which is heavy and dark and indifferent and inert." The manifold differences in character are caused by the interaction of these three gunas. This concept has also been associated with the original division of men into different types and castes.

2. Humourous Type: Hipocrat made an attempt to correlate character with psychological factors. His attempt make us to understand that peculiarities in one's behavioural temperament are caused by the pattern of humours adopted. In other words, the individuals on the basis of their humours can be categorised into following four types such as:

(1) Sanguine,
(2) Melancholic,
(3) Choleric, and
(4) Phlegmatic.

This concept could not be considered as the basis to understand the personality type of one's behaviour because people do bear number of masks in dealing with the people in day-to day life.

3. Physical Type: Kretschmer on the basis of his study pointed out that people can be classified into four groups in terms of their physical structure viz;

(i) Athletic
(ii) Aesthetic
(iii) Pynknic
(iv) Dyplastic.

The classification of Kretschmer could not prove useful and effective reason being the type of behaviour and the physical body structure differs from man to man.

4. Philosophical Type : The philosophical approach to classify personality represents the philosophical inclination of one's behaviour. The most commonly accepted classification of personality based on philosophical approach is the Sprangarian approach. Spranger in his study reported that people have differences in the affinities towards philosophical values. The difference in the inclination towards a particular set of values amounts to classify a person to a specific type of personality from the other. Spranger points out that we can classify the people into different types of personality on the basis of the following six values such as:

(I) Political
(2) Religious
(3) Economic
(4) Aesthetic
(5) Social, and
(6) Theoretical.

The Spranger's classification to some extent helps us to understand the personality patterns on the basis of one's inclination toward a set of values but it can not provide us the detailed information about one's personality.

5. Soma Type: Sheldon reported that the personality of individual can be categorised on the basis of one's body proportions. This classification on personality type is based on somatic attributes of one's body structure. To provide this classification, Sheldon collected photographs of the naked body of hundreds of young men and women from three different portions (front, back, side, upper part, middle part and lower part of body). On the bases of the observations he isolated three basic characteristics on the bases of which the personality can be assessed. These body characteristics differentiating are the different types of personality are:

(I) Proportion or the predominance of the abdominal region. (2) the strength and formation of the muscles. (3) The prominance of skin and neural structure.

On the bases of photographic observations Sheldon found that some people were very thick, some were very thin and some fall in between the two. He gave the technical name such as:

(I) Ectomorphic

(2) Mesomorphic

(3) Endomorphic.

The typology given by Sheldon could not prove significant in explaining the behavioural differences because of the reason the physical proportion or the body structure depends upon the diet, the nature of work, the genetic structure etc.

6. Glandular Type: Keniziologists made attempts to typecast the personality based on the scretional level of the glands. On the bases of the scretion they classified personality into the following types:

(1) Hypo Thyroid Personality

(2) Hyper Thyroid Personality

(3) Para Thyroid Personality

(4) Pituitary Type Personality

(5) Adernal Type Personality

(6) Hypo and Hyper Gonadal Type Personality.

7. Jung Type: Jung pointed out that Libido is the general fund of life energy. The outward expression of one's libido makes an individual to be free, frank, out spoken, expressive, whereas the individual whose libido is directed in ward result, to be shy, reserve, less social and would have his feeling confined to himself. To the persons whose libido is directed outward are extroverts whereas, the person where libido is directed inward are interoverts. Jung further reported that in some people neither the libido is outward nor inclined inward such people have the personality called Ambivert personality.

8. Freud Types: Freud's concept of personality types can be studies into the following paradigms:

Firstly, the personality of a person is the outcome of the conflict between the reality principles and the pleasure principles. The dominance of one principle over the other reflects the personality of person. To support his hypothesis he pointed out that the conflict between the reality principles and the pleasure principles reflecting one's personality are, governed by 'id', 'ego' and 'super-ego'.

The domiance of one over the other reflect the type of one's personality.

The second hypothesis, helps us in classifying the personality types is also based on the pleasure principle. The hypotheses of development advocates the personality of person depends upon the type of pleasure he derive from his body organs. The stages of development of personality are:

(a) Oral stage of development

(b) Anal stage of development

(c) Genital stage of development.

The tendency of a person deriving pleasure amounts to develop particular pattern of one's personality.

9. Modern Typology : Modern trends in classifying people into different types are based on bio-medical parameters such as:

The blood groups, enzyme levels may give us scientific approach to classify people. So, on the bases of the above classification, it can be claimed that all attempts to classify people into distinct types have failed. This is mainly bacause of the following reasons:

(1) The observed facts that all psychological characteristics follow in their distribution.

(2) There is no rigid consistency even in the same individual.

Although all the efforts at classifying people have definitely helped us to increase overall knowledge of the structure of human personality.

IX.5 Difference in Personality Patterns

Every individual is unique in his behaviour. This uniqueness refers to one's pesonality pattern. Each personality pattern is unique in the sense that it differs in many respects from other personality patterns. It is the uniqueness of the personality pattern that is reponsible for individuality. Colman reports that there are five common ways in which personality patterns differ from individual to individual. This difference is based on the following personality attributes such as:

(i) Differences in complexity. Between the simple personality pattern of the young child or the mentally deficient adult and the complex pattern of the intelligent adult there are noticeable differences in complexity of personality on the other. Gradients of differences in the complexity of the concept of self as well as in the number and complexity or traits are apparent in individual of different ages, intellectual levels and cultural groups.

(ii) Differences in fluidity. There are great differences in the rigidity of the organization of different personality patterns, ranging from markedly fluid to markedly rigid, but with most people falling between the two extremes. A fluid personality is characterized by the ability to adapt to new circumstances, by consistent attitudes and values, by social insight and self-insight, and by smooth adjustments to life. By constrast, the rigid personality is characterized by inconsistent or contradictory patterns of behaviour, of atitudes, and of values, by poor social insight and self-insight, by poor adjustment, and by a tendency to break under stress.

(iii) Differences in accessibility. Accessibility refers to one's "openness' to new stimuli and to the ability to communicate one's feelings to others. In the accessible personality, the real and manifest structures of the personality pattern are closely related.

A "closed' personality is characterized by relative inaccessibility to external stimulation, as shown by the individual's limited response to social stimuli, his rigidly restricted speech and behaviour,and his inability to relate freely to others. In the closed personality, the gap between the real and the manifest personalities is wide.

(iv) Differences in the resistance to change. In general, resistance to change increases with age. Within the personality pattern, the core, or concept of self, is more resistant to change than are the traits. Those traits which are most closely related to defending the ego against threats from the environment, however, are more resistant to change than those which are least ego -involved.

(v) Differences in centralization. The term "centralization" refers to the degree of ego involvement in the organized systems of syndromes that constitute the traits of the personality pattern.

The differences in the attributes of an individual behaviour resulting in a pattern helps in developing different patterns of personality. The differences in these attributes has its effect on personality.

Differences in personality patterns help to explain why each personality is unique. They also throw light on the degrees of stability of the patterns once they have been established.

In some personality patterns, a high level of integration results in all the person's acts being harmonized with his basic concept of self. In others, the integration is less complete, while in still others, the integration seems to be non-existent. In the extreme form, lack of integration results in "split personalities," the "Dr. Jekyll and Mr. Hyde" structure, where there are two mutully inconsistent patterns but where,within each, there is integration.

Very high or very low levels of integration are relatively infrequent. Between the two extremes are varying degrees of integration and varying degress of consistency in behaviour. It is a well-known fact that people behave differently in different situations and under different circumstances. This inconsistency has been described in the old folk saying that a person is "house angel and street devil" or vice versa. Allport reports,

"Every parent knows that an offspring may be a hellion at home and an angel when he goes visiting. A businessman may be hardheaded in the office and a mere marshmallow in the hands of his pretty daughter."

What is the ideal level of consistency? The question is still unanswered, but there is agreement that above-average consistency leads to better adjustment than below-average. Extreme consistency is likely to lead to rigidity, while marked inconsistency leads to excessive flexibility. The individual whose personality is poorly integrated is overly influenced by the opinions and actions of others. He changes with every wind that blows, behaving in such a way that people regard him as unreliable and unpredictable, As a result, they judge him as having a "weak" personality.

(vi) Personality Differences and Traits. The difference in personality pattern is also attributed by the type of personality traits a person possesses. The personality pattern of an individual is unified multidimensional structure in which the concept of self is the core or centre of gravity. Into this structure are integrated many patterns of response tendencies, known as "traits", which are closely related to and influenced by the concept of self.

The major function of traits is to integrate lesser habits, attitudes, and skills into larger thought-feeling -action patterns. The concept of self, in turn, integrates the psychological capacities of the person and initiates action. In this role, the concept of self is the true core of centre of gravity of the pattern.

IX.6 Meaning of Traits

Personality traits have been described and defined in many ways though most of the descriptions and definitions are similar in that they include certain common salient points. A trait has been described as an aspect or dimension of personality which consists of a group of related and consistent reactions characteristic of a person's typical adjustment.

All descriptions and definitions of traits emphasize that traits are learned tendencies to: (I) evaluate situations in a predictable way and, (2) react in a manner which the person has found more or less successful in similar situations and when similarly motivated. Since the person's characteristics ways of reacting are learned, each new reaction is influenced to some extent by the success the person has had in his previous adjustment to similar reactions. As a result, traits,while predictable, are not automatic acts which occur in exactly the same form every time they are aroused by the core of the personality pattern—the concept of self. Allport has stressed the role of learning in bringing about slight variations in the predictable manner a person adjusts to situations:

Traits, unlike the "faculties" or "powers" of earlier psychology, are not little men within the breast" who pull the strings of behaviour .Traits are looser tendencies, each expression of a trait being slightly different because it confronts other determining conditions. Furthermore, after an act takes place, there is "feedback" to the nervous system, and in the future a trait will never be precisely the same as it was previously. Thus continuous flow is the primary fact. yet we know that traits exist because, in spite of the continuous flow and change,there is considerable constancy in a person's mode of behaviour. We can say that certain acts are characteristic of him. Traits underlie what is "characteristic" in conduct.

While traits are the product of learning, they are based on hereditary foundations and these foundations influence the form the trait will take. There is some evidence that certain traits are actually determined, or certainly favoured, by hereditary predispositions. People who show the characteristic pattern of neurotic instability, for example, have various degrees of autonomic imbalance. The intellectual capacity of a person, determined by his hereditary endowment, influences the way he perceives a situation and how he learns to react to it.

Characteristics of Traits

Every trait has three characteristics: uniqueness, degree of likableness, and consistency. Uniqueness does not mean that a person has certain traits that are peculiarly his . It means that he has his own individual quantity of a particular kind of behaviour. As Woodworth and Marquis point out. "Traits are 'dimensions' of behaviour in which individuals differ".

A trait is not something that is either present or absent. Instead, like intelligence, it is distributed according to the curve of normal distribution.

This means that a trait is present in all or almost all people, but in varying degree. And in the curve of normal distribution, most people cluster around the mean or average in any particular trait.

The second characteristic or traits is likableness. Some traits, such as honesty, generosity, and trust worthiness, are liked by othei, while some are disliked-rudeness, cruelty, and egocentrism, for example, their attitudes towards traits result for social learning in a particular cultural setting and are almost universal within a culture. Traits are liked or disliked because they contribute to social harmony or disharmony and add to the satisfaction or dissatisfaction experienced from being with a person who has the traits. A person who is generous not only contributes to the social well-being of others but is also a pleasant person to be with. By contact an egocentric person makes others feel uncomfortable because he is constantly talking about himself; he is likely to contribute to social disharmony by being uncooperative and refusing to carry his load.

The third characteristic of traits is consistency. This means that a person can be expected to behave in approximately the same way in similar situations. Consistency, like uniqueness, is relative. A person may be self-confident in a situation because he has mastered the skills needed to adjust to it and experienced success in similar situations. But in situations requiring skills and modes of adjustment which he has not mastered so well or has had less success with in the past, he will show less self-confidence and may even show fear. Similarly, a person may be punctual in situations where punctuality gives him satisfaction, but not in situations where being on time is unimportant to him or regarded as socially incorrect. These examples illustrate what Allport meant when he said that "perfect and rigid self-consistency is not to be expected"

From the above discussion it is evident that trait has certain characteristics which differentiate individuals. The difference in traits helps to form pattern of personality,

IX.7 Method of Assessment Personality

We know that individuals differ from each other with respect to their behaviour. To understand the difference in personality pattern we assess by using different techniques of assessment.

The techniques most commonly used in assessing and judging personality are I. subjective techniques viz; Case history, Interview, Questionnaires, Rating Scales, Situation tests, Psycho-analytical tests. II. Projective techniques viz; Rorschol Ink Blot test and T.A.T. A brief description of these techniques has been described as:

Subjective Techniques

1. Case history. Case history technique of assessment of personality has its aim to get as much information as possible about the family history of the individual, the social environment in which he has been brought up and in which he lives, his physical condition-constitutional make up and health, his education and training, his habits, attitudes and interests, his social and economic status, his adjustments to things and people around him, and whatever else bears on his life and personality. In doing so the person compiling case history must seek the co-operation of all those who have dealt with the individual in an important way as parents, teachers, friends, colleagues, relations, doctors. The successful use of case history technique of personality assessment calls for specialized training. The method can be employed to study both normal and abnormal subjects.

2. Interview. Interview is a face to face relationship between the subject and the psychologist to assess the personality: There are number of interview techniques. Although the interview popular and handy method of judging personality is largely used by staff selection board and public service commissions. But an interview can be successful if the interviewer is trained and knows what he is looking for and testing. In the hands of psychologist the interview means that the person to be interviewed is encouraged to talk freely without any hesitation about his past experiences, what he thinks of them. What are his problems, how he proposes to tackle them. The psychologist simply listens to him and accepts all that he says. If he makes any remarks, it is only to encourage the person to speak out his mind more freely. All the time he keeps observing how the person behaves, what hesitations he has and what his emotional responses are. The interview and the observations made reveal a lot about the person. Most objectionable limitations of interview are that the technique is not scientific, it is subjective and the most successful interviewers are not able to tell what makes the interview most successful. It is not quantitative either and the results of different interviewers cannot be compared. Again some of the problems of personality are very complex and may not be reached by even the most skilful interviewer. A successful interview depends on the intimate rapport which the interviewer is able to establish between the interviewed persons and himself, but this is not always easy to secure.

3. Questionnaires. Personality is frequently assessed by using questionnaires or series of questions framed to test a particular trait of personality for instance, Woodworth was the first to use it and devised a "Personal Data Sheet" in 1918 to determine emotional instability or neurotic tendency among soldiers. His questionnaire had 116 questions, each answered by yes or no. His questions related to fears, worries, feelings and physical symptoms of mental disorders. Some of the questions are: Do you usually feel well and strong? Do you have nightmares? Have you often fainted? Do you worry that people are watching you?

On the basis of questionnaires attempts have been made to test extraversion-introversion, ascendance-submission, and sociability-solitariness traits of personality. This technique of personality assessment comprises of a series of questions, and answers are required in the form of yes or no. It is a self-reported type of instrument. By classifying answers, it is possible to find out the type of problems the subject is facing and what he is doing to face it. An important difficulty in this method is that subjects try to slant their answers in such a manner as to conceal some aspects of their personality. This method is more suitable for the study of groups.

4. Rating Scales. Rating scale is a tool of personality assessment. Rating scale comprises of sets of statements which a subject responds in the form of degrees of his choice judgement. In other words, by this method certaintraits of personality are divided into several classes on the basis of varying degrees of a trait and the individuals are ranged into these classes by people who know them intimately. Usually these degrees are indicated by numbers 1 to 4, or 1to 5 or 1 to 7, and then we have a four, five or seven -point scale. Generally a five-point scale is used indicating very superior 5, superior 4, average 3, inferior 2, and very inferior 1. And the question expressing varying degrees may be ranged as for example, is he honest ? may be divided into five point scale:

Very honest 5 Generally honest 4 Honest 3 Generally dishonest 2 Very dishonest 1.

The rater places a mark on the suitable descriptive phrase, and his judgement or rating is converted into a numerical score on a scale or 1 to 5. Or rating may be done by arranging a number of persons in the order in which they show a particular trait like dominance, self-reliance or honesty. The most dominant, self-reliant or honest are placed at one end and the least dominant, self-reliant or honest at the other, with other persons arranged in between.

These rating scales can be used only by those who know the person very closely and have observed him in respect of the trait about which they are rating him. It is always possible for the judges to make rating favourable or unfavourable; and the validity of this method of measurement can be demonstrated only when rating is done independently by a number of judges tally.

5. Situation tests. In these tests the behaviour of an individual in a particular type of situation is judged. These tests are usually employed for children. For example, situation study of personality is provided by May and Hartshorne. They gave children many natural situations wherein they could easily cheat. In writing meanings of a given list of words they could copy from a neighbour's paper, consult a forbidden dictionary, change answer when scoring their own tests. There were other situations in which stealing and lying was tested. These situation tests are very much limited in scope and validity.

Projective Techniques of Personality Assessment

Projective techniques are considered the most effective methods to assess the personality of an individual because the projective techniques are based on the psycho-analytical schools of Psychology. The word 'projection' as used in psyco-analytical literature as a defence mechanism, stands for the process whereby the ego transfers on to some external object. An office boss may find fault with his subordinates or a professor with his students if he had a quarrel with his wife at home. He projects his own feelings into the person outside him. As Frank S. Freeman says:

"Psychologically, projection is an un-conscious process whereby an individual: (1) attributes certain thoughts, attitudes, emotions, or characteristics to other persons, or certain characteristics to objects in his environment; (2) attributes his own needs to others in his environment: or (3) draws incorrect inferences from an experience. Projection is not recognised as being of personal origin with the result that the content of process is experienced as an outer perception and of external origin".

The basic idea underlying the projective methods is that no two persons perceive the world in exactly the same manner. Hence, in the projective technique, the subjects are expected to project their own "images" into the unstructured test materials. If the inner urges are blocked off through social pressure or by fear of punishment, the subject will project his feelings into some other subject or situation which is taken as a symbol.

The person is asked to be as subjective as possible. He is asked to behave in an imaginative way e.g. by making up a story, interpreting ink blots or constructing some object out of plastic, materials. Tests are interested to reveal the underlying traits, moods, attitudes and fantasies that determine the behaviour. Here the subject should have complete freedom from any sort of self-criticism. The freedom which an appeal to imagination permits often tends to favour the projection of the real personality. That is why, author reveals unconsciously more about himself in his fictional works than in his consciously written autobiography.

Projective technique is based on reading out the meanings which the individual reads in the world around him.

The Characteristics of the Projective Method

The projective methods have in common the characteristics which can be studied as:

1. The stimulus material is unstructured, vague, ambiguous and neutral. The subject is asked to supply meaning, significance and organisation and in doing so he unconsciously leaves the impression of his own personality upon the undefined stimulus materials. For such purposes ink-blots, incomplete stories, plastic materials, miniature life toys, meaningless auditory stimuli etc. may be used.

2. It stresses the inner psychology. The psychological reality, rather than the actual reality of the subject world or the phenomenological approach is more important in the Projective techninque, The facts of his life may not have been important, but the attitudes, opinions, ideals conflicts and fantasies which populate his private, unverbalized world are for more important in his present adjustment and it is to these aspects of psychological reality that the projective technique turns its scrutiny.

3. It has a special system of diagnosis. As implicit and unconscious aspects of personality are revealed, the psycho-dynamic principles play an important part in the interpretation. It is a system of diagnosis based upon signs rather than upon samples.

Limitations of Projective Technique. Abuse of these techniques is possible because projection is that tool which cuts both ways. Not only does the person who is observed, project his own inner feelings and attitudes upon the situation, but the person who observes him or interprets may do the same. Psychologists are human beings as such they are by no means exempted from the laws that govern their kind. So the examiner may project his personality upon the subject type of test.

IX.8 Type of Projective Tests

A number of projective techniques are available. Out of these, the important techniques are:

1. Rorschach Ink-Blot Test
2. Thematic Apperception Test
3. Word Association Test
4. Story Completion Test.

1. Rorschach Ink-Blot Test

This test was standardized by Herman Rorschach, a Swiss psychiatrist. In this test, the subject is required to interpret standard ink-blots presented in series. The test is constructed on the basis of four general aspects of the responses:

(i) Their location—large or small areas—whole or parts.

(ii) The determinants—three characteristics of the blot which seem to be mainly responsible in determining his perception e.g. shading and colour.

(iii) Contents—general kinds of objects named—animals etc.

Construction of the Test. Rorschach prepared several hundred inkblots of different size, type and colour. As these were given to mental patients, he found their diagnostic value.

The responses from different types of patients were almost the same .This led Rorschach to use these ink-blots to find the diseases of mental patients. Out of several hundreds of ink-blots, only ten were selected for the final test. Therefore, in the Rorschach test there are ten ink-blots. These ink-blots have serial numbers from one to ten. They are white papers fixed on card board pieces. The colour of ink-blots are various. Often it is dark-grey. But red, blue colours are also present in some ink-blots. As the number increases, the ink-blots become more and more complex and difficult. There is great complexity in card No. 1 and card No. 10.

All these cards have been well standardized. They have been given to hundreds of people of known and unknown groups and the responses have been standardized .We have got norms, and by comparing the score of the subject with the norms, the personality can be explored and interpreted.

Administering the Rorschach Ink-Blot Test

The psychologist must know very well that all the ink-blots before they are arranged according to serial number and one is given to the subject at a time. The examiner tells the examinee that people can see all sort of things-persons, objects, animals, etc—in these ink blots. He further adds as to what the examinee sees through it. The subject is free to take any view of the ink-blot. He can see it from any side and takes his own time. He is required to tell what part of the ink-blot suggests a certain object. As far as possible, he is to see the whole of ink-blot as some objects and later he should proceed to parts.

The psychologist is also there. He records the time as well as the responses of the subject. He must not interfere with the subject. Therefore, his seat is just at the back of the subject. He has to note the time, specially when the subject takes long time to give the response. Remarks and exclamations of subject are not to be counted.At times, when the responses for certain parts of ink-blot are not clear,the examiner can ask the subject to clear the point.

It is always better that the whole of the test is finished in one sitting. If the subject is bored or fatigued, then rest should be given after 5th blot and not prior or after it. It means that it is better to finish the test in one sitting. However, there can be two sittings. In the first sitting the first five ink-blots must be finished and in the second, the last or remaining five ink-blots should be finished.

Originally, there is individual test, but for normal literate persons it can be used as group test. In the group test, the ink-blots are projected on cinema screen one by one for a sufficient long time and all the subjects see it and go on writing whatever they see. No doubt, time is saved but it permits less adequate inquiry than the individual test, but otherwise it is satisfactory for intelligent adolescent and adults.

Scoring and interpretation of Rorschach Ink-Blot Test

Scoring and interpretation in Rorschach Test is based upon four major categories which can be described as under:

(i) *Location.* This means the part or the area that has been perceived by the subject. This may be the entire ink blot, a large portion, a small portion, or a part of the white background. The area may be well-perceived or the subject may only have the blurred or vague idea about it.

(ii) Determinants. This refers to the characteristics of the ink-blot perceived by the subject. The characteristics may be form, shading, colour, perspectives, or motion or a combination of them all. This means what caused the subject to see the ink blot as he saw it.

(iii) *Content.* This refers to the fact whether the subject saw animal, human shapes, plants or landscapes, sex or something else.

(iv) *Originals or Populars.* This means whether the response/ responses is/are the one that could be commonly or popularly given or the one that is uncommon or original.

Interpretations: Interpretations of the responses based on the above characteristics can be made with the help of the following table:

Catagory	*Indication*	*Interpretation*
(i) Location	(i) Sees the whole blot not in parts.	(i) Capable of intellectual organisation.
	(ii) Breaks the blot into unusual details.	(ii) Indicates preoccupation with the trivials.
	(iii) Same procedures with all the cards.	(iii) Indicates rigidity.

(ii) Determinants	(i)	Perception of form clear and accurate	(i)	Indicates control over intellectual processes.
Form	(ii)	Perception of form distorted.	(ii)	Indicates dis-organised intellectual processes.
Colour	(iii)	Perception of only colour without consideration of form.	(iii)	Indicates emotional intensity.
	(iv)	Perceives both form and colour, form dominating.	(iv)	Optimal emotional control and a capacity for social adaptability.
	(v)	Perceives both form and colour, colour dominating.	(v)	Suggests impulsive egocentric personality.
Shading		Subject responses to shading.		Suggests anxiety, depressed attitudes, etc.
Movement		Perceives movement, especially human movements.		Suggests the richness of the subject's associative life.
(iii) Content	(i)	Perceives human shapes.	(i)	Suggests a stable personality.
	(ii)	Perceives animal figures.	(ii)	Suggests an unstable personality.
(iv) Original and Populars	(i)	High percentage of original responses.	(i)	Suggests high level of intelligence.
	(ii)	High percentage of popular responses.	(ii)	Suggests popular level of intelligence.

The use of the ink-blot test. This test is widely used to classify abnormal subjects by finding their troubles. It is a great tool in the hands of psychologists for systematic procedure. So in mental hygine clinics and other reformatory institutions, this is commonly used.

Besides its diagnostic use in clinics and mental hospitals, it is very useful in making prediction for future. As such, this is a great valuable test on which the counsellors in vocational guidance programmes depend. This field of Rorschach Test to predict the academic and vocational fitness, and success of young person, is getting more and more importance.

This test is also used to supplement Binet's result or poor learners by suggesting them, whether low score or backwardness is due to lack of mental power or any inhibition which prevents the use of mental power. It is also useful to find the causes of anti-social activities or delinquent and other problem children.

IX.10 Thematic Appreception Test

'Thematic Appreception Test' (known as T.A.T) was designed by *Murray* and *Morgan*. The principal data of the test is a particular topic or theme which the subject projects into a vague picture. The subject looks at the picture and weaves a theme or a story round it, from this own subjective imagination. Thus he indirectly, indeliberately and unwillingly projects his own mind and his own feelings into theme of a picture. He perceives only what he subjectively feels. His perception is subjective, while the picture acts just as a stimulus. So the test is named as Thematic Appreception Test.

The T.A.T consists of a series of 20 pictures selected by Murray and Morgan. Each picture is presented to the subject. He is asked to look at the picture, think and imagine a story that is suggested by the picture. The subject weaves a story (fictitious one) out of the picture, creates characters as seen in the picture, explains their relationship to each other and states outcome of the story. One by one the pictures are presented in particular order. The psychologists go on recording what the subject says.Then he analyses the data and finds out the major theories such as the personal interests, attitudes, mental conflicts, ambitions, family adjustment, social adjustment, sexual matters etc. Common elements of the theme in all the 20 pictures are discovered. They reveal a wealth of information about the sub-scores and the total personality of the subject. The test as a whole throws light on the functioning of the mind.

Interpretation of T.A.T

The story of T.A.T may be interpreted in many ways, depending upon the view-point of the examination and purpose for which the test is administered. Murray has suggested following points for analysing the stories:

(i) *The hero:* the character in each picture with whom the subject identifies himself.

(ii) *Motives, trends and feelings* of each of the heroes of stories.

(iii) *Forces in the hero's* environment.

(iv) *Outcomes:* relation of the outcomes of the story to the rest of the plot.

(v) *Themes:* intersection of a hero's needs with environmental forces

(vi) *Interests and sentiments:* choice of topics and style of dealing with them, handling of sex relationships.

It may be cautioned here that the single response on a T.A.T has significance only as an element in the total pattern. It is the recurring themes and features that are significant.

On the model of T.A.T which are designed for adults, Children apprecepation Test (C.A.T.) has also been prepared by *Bellak* In India, some adaptations' of T.A.T and C.A.T. have been done, especially by the psychological Institute, Allahabad.

Difference Between and Comparison Rorschach and T.A.T Test

Rorschach and T.A.T are the two prominent projective techniques of personality assessment. Both have a completely different system of going to the depths of the unconscious mind, and both have gained widespread popularity. Rorschach throw light on the structure of the personality whereas, T.A.T. reveals the functions of personality. Let us discuss the difference between the two.

T.A.T It is an abbreviation for Thematic Apprecepation Test, designed by two psychologists—Murray and Morgan. The principal data of the test is a particular topic or theme which the subject projects into a vague picture. The subject looks at the picture and weaves a theme or a story round it, from his own subjective imagination. Thus he indirectly, indeliberately and unwillingly projects his own mind and his own feelings into theme of the picture. He perceives but what he subjectively feels. His perception is subjective while the picture acts just as a stimulus. So the test is named as Thematic Apprecepation Test.

The T. A. T. consisting of series of 20 pictures is presented to the subject. He is asked to look at the picture, think and imagine a story that is suggested by the picture. The subject weaves a story (fictitious one) out of the picture, creates characters as seen in the picture, explains their relationship to each other and states outcome of the story. One by one, the pictures are presented in a particular order. The psychologists go on recording what the subject says. Then he analyses the data and finds out the major theories such as the personal interests, attitudes mental conflicts, ambitions, family adjustment, social adjustment, sexual adjustment,. Common elements of theme in all the 20 pictures are discovered. These reveal a wealth of information about the sub-scores and the total personality of the subject. The test as a whole throws light on the functioning of the mind.

On the model of T.A.T which are designed for adults, Children Appearception Test (C.A.T) also have been prepared by Pellak (a psychologist).In India, some adaptation of the T.A.T and C.A.T. have been made, especially at the psychological Institute at Allahabad.

Comparison of Ink-blot test and T.A.T: Ink-blot test throws light on the structure of the personality, while the T.A.T reveals functioning of the personality. In this way, these are not supplementary but complementary. But ink-blot Test is too technical to be used commonly. We need highly trained personnel to give the test and interpret the data. Again it is time-consuming. Adaptation of this test to suit local conditions is difficult, as it is very difficult to construct new and standardise the same on a new population. Again, it is not specially meant for children. On the other hand T.A.T. is less time-consuming, less technical, more adaptative and more useful. This technique can be used for adults as well as children, separately. Hence, T.A.T. is preferable to Rorschach Ink-blot Test.

IX.11 Development of Personality

We all know that babies differ in heredity and environment. Therefore, it is not surprising that babies look different and behave differently. These differences are though small as compared with those of later childhood, but it is easy to identify that some babies are "good-looking" and others are "homely". The observer of a group of newly born babies may also see that some babies hardly emit a murmur, while other squawk during almost every waking moment. Further behavioural differences of these babies can be noticed such as some babies are active, kicking vigorously and thrashing their arms about, while others lie relatively still, and that some suck at the nipple tenaciously while others suck with seemingly indifference. From the above observations we can conclude that even at birth babies have behavioural differences which relate to their personality differences. Practically these differences remain stable with the development of their physique.

Broadly speaking the development of personality starts right from the time of conception but later in the post-natal development, the differences in the personality development of an individual are sharpened depending upon the circumstances and experiences of life. The development of personality can be studied in the stages of development such as:

I. Emotional Development

The development of healthy personality depends upon the balanced development of emotions. The emotional development starts from the birth and the maximum development of important emotions takes places in the beginning three years of our life. Sound and balanced development of emotions helps proper adjustment of an individual in our personal and individual child passes through the following stages of emotional development. The scheme of Watson's emotional development can be described diagramatically as ahead:

Munn is his book 'Psychology and Life' has pointed out that development of personality depends upon two aspects of behaviour viz, the general activity namely, the emotional expressiveness and the temperament. Further Mun reveals that the development of personality refers to the aspects of emotional expressiveness and the temperament which gets sophisticated with the advancement of age and experience.

Allport describes that the development of personality is reflected from the type of personality traits a person has. Allport while describing the concept of development of personality states that the traits are the reflections of an individual's inclination towards a particular type of behaviour. A group of traits also decides a type of personality. It has been found that the heredity and environment mostly play vital role in developing a particular type of personality traits among the children as environment plays effective role in developing the traits.

2. Psycho-analytical Approach and Personality Development

The personality development of an individual can be explained as per the Psycho-analytical school of Psychology. For instance, *Freud* advocates that the personality of an individual is developed as an outcome of a conflict between the pleasure principles and reality principles. The type of personality pattern of an individual depends upon his tendency to adopt the reality or pleasure principle. Freud further points out that the development of personality of an individual depends upon the dominance of id, ego and super-ago. He further reveals that the development of a particular pattern of personality helps to dominate the biological urges. The process to achieve domination over the biological urges takes place with the active involvement of conscious, unconscious and sub-conscious mind of an individual. Another approach high lighting the Freud's concept of personality development reveals that an individual child during his development passes through the oral, anal and genital stages of development. During these stages an individual derives pleasure. The tendency of seeking pleasure out of these stages affects the type of personality development of a person.

Adler points out that the development of personality depends upon the social interactions and social expression to one's behavioural tendencies, the tendency to express one's self development individual directly indicates that there are certain forces which control our social expressions. Those social forces directly influence the development of personality. In other words we can say that the development of personality is a conscious act in which an individual is aware of the reasons for his behaviour. A developed personality of an individual enables him to make suitable planning and can guide his actions with full awareness of their meaning for his own self-realisation.

Another psycho-analyist viz; Jung, advocates that the personality development is the net outcome of the forward looking tendency of a person. Greater the tendency of looking forward, greater will be the speed of personality development of an individual. Jung further believes that man is constantly progressing or attempting to progress from a class complete stage of development to a more complete one. He further reports that the goal of development is self-realisation. The self-realisation means the fullest, most complete differentiation and harmonious blending of all aspects of man's total personality.

Erikson's theroy of personality development advocates that the personality development can be treated as a series of turning points. These turning points, he describes in terms of dichotomies of desirable qualities and dangers. In the development of personality it is not necessary that only positive points or qualities may emerge, Sometimes some negative qualities are also essential for the development of personality.

The difficulties in development of personality arise only when positive quality is outweighted by the negative qualities.

Erikson further reports the following stages of development personaliy of an individual child:

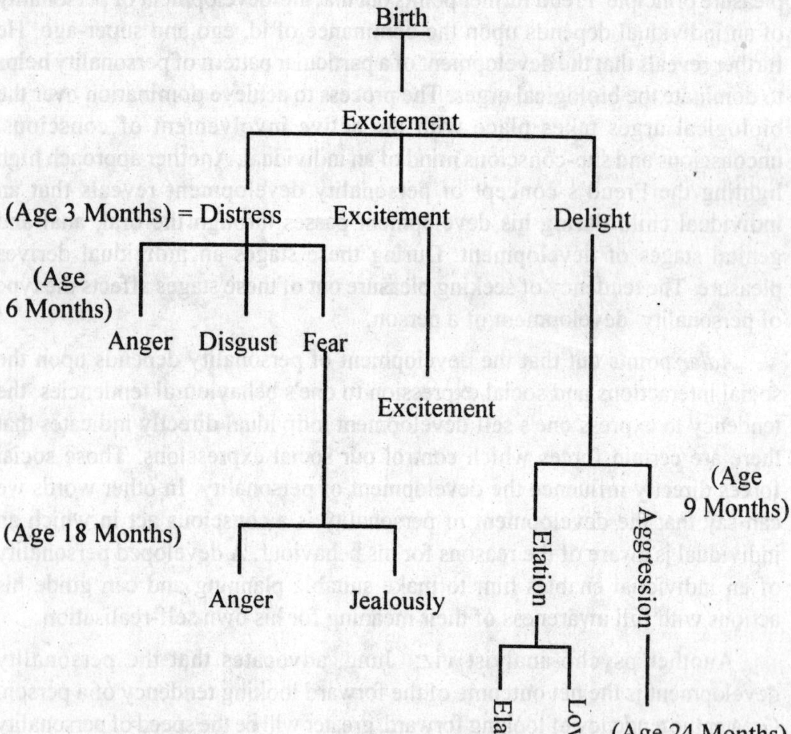

1. Trust Vs. Mistrust
2. Autonomy Vs. Shame and Doubt
3. Initiative Vs. Guilt
4. Industry Vs. Inferiority
5. Identity Vs. Confusion
6. Intimacy Vs. Isolation
7. Generativity Vs. Stagnation
8. Integrity Vs. Despair.

In brief, the above theories put forth the view points regarding the development of personality, but it is certain that these theories are unable to give true picture of the personality development of an individual.

Factors Influencing Personality Development

Development of personality depends upon number of factors. There are different views which advocate various possible factors influencing the personality development. Though scope of the book does not permit to discuss the factor for development of personality, however, we will try to point out most commonly accepted factors influencing personality development which can be described as:

(I) Parents, (2) Home Environment, (3) School, (4) Locality, (5) Exposure to Social and cultural interactions, (6) Socio-economic status of the individual, (7) Birth order, (8) Attitude towards life, (9) heredity.

IX.12 Factors Effecting Personality Patterns

Personality pattern of an individual is mainly based on certain determinants such as self concept, heredity, environment etc. However, the "core" or centre of gravity of the personality pattern is the individual's concept of himself as a person as related to the world in which he lives. The quality of his behaviour, expressed in the way he adjusts to people and things in his environment, is related to and, to a large extent, determined by his self-concept.

Effect of Heredity on Personality

The personality pattern is founded on the individual's hereditary endowment. But it is not inherited. It is the product of learning during the course of prolonged social relationships with people both within and outside the home. As Anderson has pointed out," Personality becomes organized around nodal points or experiences which have received particular emphasis and much reiteration".

Three major factors are at work in determining the development of the personality pattern: first, the individual's hereditary endowment; second, early experiences within the family; and third, important events in later life outside the home environment; (4). Thus the personality pattern is not the product of learning exclusively or of heredity exclusively. Instead, it comes from an interaction of the two. How different environmental influences affect personality development is illustrated in Figure 1.

The personality pattern is inwardly determined by and closely associated with the maturation of the physical and mental characteristics which constitute the individual's hereditary endowment. Although social and other environmental factors affect the form the personality pattern takes, it is not instilled or controlled from without but evolves from the potentials within the individual. The principal raw materials of personality-physique, intelligence, and temperament—are the result of heredity. How they will develop will depend on environmental influences.

The significance of the hereditary foundations in determining the personality pattern has been stressed by Rainwater.

Personality is formed from the interaction of significant figures (first the mother, later the father and siblings, later extrafamilial figures) with the child; The child brings to this interaction a certain biological constitution, certain needs and drives, and certain intellectual capacities which determine his reactions to the way in which he is acted upon by these significant figures.

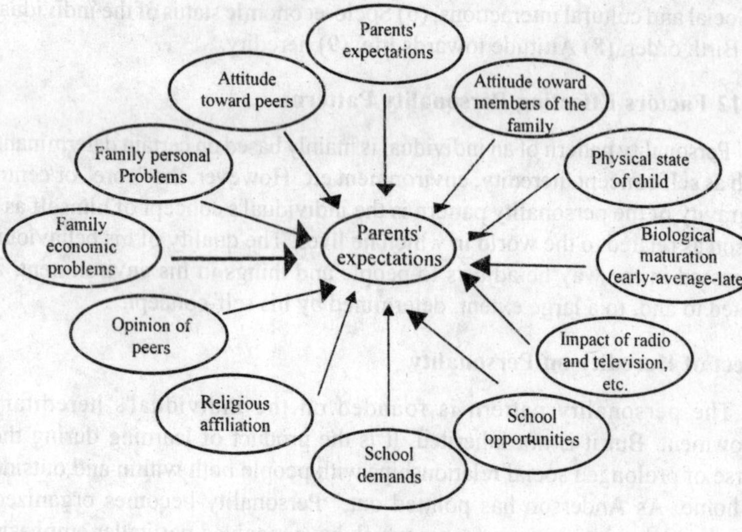

Figure 1. Different environmental influences, within and outside the home, that affect the developing self-concept.

In this interaction between hereditary and environmental factors, the individual selects from his environment what fits his needs and wants and rejects what does not. Therefore, the personality pattern develops from interactions with the environment which the individual himself has initiated.

One reason for stressing the role of heredity in the development of the personality pattern is to point up the fact that the pattern is subject to limitations. A person who inherits a low-grade intelligence, for example, cannot, even under the most favourable environmental conditions, develop a personality pattern that will lead to as good a personal and social adjustment as a person who inherits a higher level of intellectual ability.

Furthermore, recognition of the limitations imposed by heredity underlines the fact that people are not totally free to choose and develop the kind of personality pattern they want. Using intelligence again as an illustration: A person with a low-grade intelligence cannot develop the personality pattern of a leader even though he wants to do so and even though his desire gives him a strong motivation to try to develop the personality traits essential for leadership.

Effect of learning

Learning, in its various forms, especially conditioning, imitation, and training, or learning under the guidance and direction of another, plays a prime role in the development of the personality pattern. Attitudes toward self, characteristic modes of responding to people and situations,attitudes toward the assumption of socially approved roles, and methods of personal and social adjustment, including the use of defence mechanisms, are learned through repetition and are reinforced by the satisfaction they bring. Gradually, the self-concept is built up and the learned responses become habitual, constituting the "traits" in the individual's personality pattern.

Social pressures within and outside the home determine what traits will be incorporated into the pattern. If a boy is encouraged to be aggressive, for example, because aggressiveness is considered a sex-appropriate trait for males, he will learn to react to people and things in an aggressive way. If, on the other hand, aggressiveness wins social disapproval or does not bring satisfaction, the person will try out other methods of adjustment until he finds one that meets his needs. He will then repeat it until it becomes a habitual form of behaviour.

Knowing that learning plays a role in the development of the personality pattern is important for two reasons. First, it tells us that control can be exercised to ensure that the individual will develop the kind of personality pattern that will lead to good personal and social adjustments. This control will come from seeing to it that the person has learning experiences that will lead to a healthy self-concept and to socially approved modes of adjustment. As was stressed earlier, however,hereditary limitations must be considered in controlling the individual's learning experiences.

Second,it tells us that unhealthy self-concepts and socially unacceptable patterns of adjustment can be changed and modified. As in all learning,the sooner a change or modification is attempted, the easier it will be.

Effect Due to Self Concept

The personality pattern is composed of a core of centre of gravity, called the "concept of self," and an integrated system of learned responses, called "traits." These are interrelated, with the core influencing the traits, which are

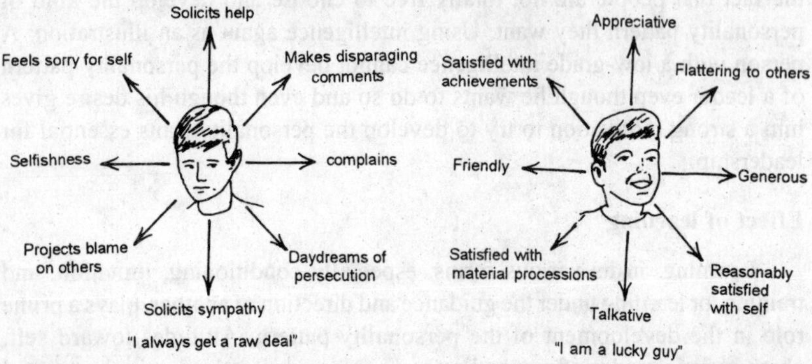

Figure 2. A person's concept of self influences his characteristic patterns of adjustment.

the individual's characteristic methods of adjustment to life situations. To show the interrelationship, the pattern can be compared to a wheel in which the hub represents the concept of self and the spokes represent the traits. Just as the spokes of a wheel are held in position and, thus, influenced by the hub, so the traits are influenced by the concept of self.

The interrelationship is illustrated in Figure 2. If a person sees himself as a martyr, his self-concept, whether justified by facts or not, will have a profound influence on his behaviour. In time, his behaviour patterns will become so well learned from repetition that they will constitute his characteristic methods of adjustment and occur in a predictable manner. Others will then judge him as "feeling sorry for himself."

How the personality pattern develops and how the interrelationship between the concept of self and the different traits function will now be examined in a detailed analysis of the two major elements of the pattern.

Many years ago, James called the core of the personality pattern, which provides its unity, the "self." Later, Freud referred to it as the "ego," and Sullivan used the phrase, the "self system". According to James, a person's self is the "sum-total of all that he can call his".

In recent decades, what a person "can call his" has been spelled out in more definite and specific terms. It has been referred to as his "attitude toward self", as an "organized configuration of perceptions of self", as "those perceptions, beliefs, feelings, attitudes, and values which the individual views as part or characteristic of himself", as the "organization of qualities the individual attributes to himself", and as a "system of central meaning he has about himself and his relation to the world about him".

Allport (5) has described the self-concept in this way:

The self is şomething of which we are immediately aware. We think of it as the warm, central, private region of our life, As such it plays a crucial part in our consciousness (a concept broader than self), in our personality (a concept broader than personality).Thus it is some kind of core in our being.

How broad and all-inclusive the concept of self is has been emphasized by Jersild:

The self, as it finally evolves, is made up of all that goes into a person's experiences of his individual existence. It is a person's "inner world." It is a composite of a person's thoughts and feelings,strivings and hopes fears and fantasies, his view of what he is, what he has been, what he might become, and his attitudes pertaining to his worth.

The importance of the self-concept in the personality pattern is evidenced by the labels usually given it. it is referred to as the core or center of gravity of the pattern or as the "keystone of personality". Its importance stems from its influence over the quality of a person's behavior and his methods of adjustment to life situations. As Lewin has pointed out, it gives "consistency to the personality".

Components of the Self-concept

The concept of self has three major components: the perceptual, the conceptual, and the attitudinal. The perceptual component is the image the person has of the appearance of his body and of the impression he makes on others. It includes the image he has of the attractiveness and sex appropriateness of his body, the impórtance of the different parts of his body, such as his muscles, to his behaviour and the prestige they give him in the eyes of others.The perceptual component is often called the "physical self-concept."

The conceptual component is the person's conception of his distinctive characteristics, his abilities and disabilities, his back and origins, and his future. It is often called are "psychological self-concept" and is composed of such life-adjustment qualities as honesty, self-confidence, independence, courage, and their opposites.

Included in the attitudinal component are the feelings a person has about himself, his attitudes about his present status and future prospects, his feelings about his worthiness, and his attitudes of self-esteem, self-reproach, pride, and shame. As the person reaches adulthood, the attitudinal component includes also the beliefs, convictions,values, ideals,aspirations, and commitments which make up his philosophy of life.

Kinds of self-concept—James was the first to suggest that a person has many "selves." The "real self," for example, is what a person really believes he is, his "ideal self" is the person he aspires to be, and his "social self" is what he believes others think of him and how they perceive him.

Recent studies reveal that the self-concept does indeed take different forms. Each form falls into one of four major categories which relate to the physical as well as the psychological self-concepts. The four categories of self-concept are the basic, the transitory, the social, and the ideal.

The Basic Self- Concept—The basic self-concept corresponds to James's concept of the "real self"; it is the person's concept of what he reallly is. It includes his perception of his appearance, his recognition of his abilities and disabilities and of his role and status in life, and his values, beliefs, and aspirations.

The basic self-concept tends to be realistic.The person sees himself as he really is, not as he would like to be. Sometimes the basic self-concept is to the person's liking. More often , it is not. The person finds flaws in himself which make him unhappy and dissatisfied and which he would like to change. Even when the treatment he receives from others would seem to encourage greater self-acceptance, a person may cling of his basic self-concept.

The Transitory Self-Concept—In addition to a basic self-concept, a person has a transitory self-concept. James first suggested this when he referred to the "self he hopes he now is" and the "self he fears he now is". This means that a person has a self-concept which he holds for a time and then relinquishes.

Transitory self-concepts may be favourable or unfavourable, depending largely on the situation in which the person finds himself momentarily. They are generally influenced by some passing mood or emotional state or by a recent experience. They are transitory and unstable because they lack the perspective found in the basic self-concept.

A person who is well and happy, who is accepted by others, and who achieves what he has set out to do may have a transitory self-concept that is more favourable than his basic self-concept. Temporarily, he sees himself as the "self he hopes he now is". Changes in circumstances, in mood, and in achievement are likely to lead to a less favourable self-concept and he will then see himself as "he fears he now is".

People differ in the frequency with which their behaviour is guided and influenced by transitory self-concepts. Some experience frequent and intense fluctuations while others experience only slight and occasional shifts.

The Social Self-Concept—The social self-concept is based on the way the individual believes others perceive him, depending on their speech and actions. It is usually referred to as a "mirror image". If a child is constantly told that he is "naughty," he soon develops a concept of himself as a naughty child. If the social group regards members of a gang as "tough," they come to think of themselves as tough and act accordingly. The child whose parents are always telling him how bright he is develops a self-concept that contains some elements of false pride. Social self-concepts may in time develop into basic self-concepts if the person believes that he is as other as see him.

Since social self-concepts derive from social interactions, whether the concepts will be favourable or not depends on how the social group treats the individual.A person who as a child or adolescent was discriminated against because of his race, color, religion, or social class will usually have a far less favourable concept of himself than the person who was not subjected to such discrimination.

In early childhood, before the child is capable of assessing himself in terms of his abilities and disabilities, his needs and wants, his aspirations values, he thinks of himself as he believes others think of him. His social self-concept is thus dominant It is developed earlier than the basic self-concept and is the foundation for the basic self-concept. Only after the child is mature enough to understand and interpret the speech and actions of others is he able to judge the accuracy of his social self-concept and develop a basic self-concept.

People build up different social self-concepts, depending on the kinds of social groups home, peer, or community—with which they are most often associated. A young child's social self-concept is influenced most by his relationship with his mother because he spends most of his time with her. How the different self-concepts are developed will be discussed later in the section, hierarchy of self-concepts.

The effect of the social self-concept on the behaviour of the individual will depend largely on how important the opinions of others are to him at that time and on what person or persons are most influential in his life at that time. Jersild (99) has explained the matter in this way:

If a child is accepted, approved,respected , and liked for what he is, he will be helped to acquire an attitude of self-acceptance and respect for himself.

But if the significant people in his life—at first his parents and later his teachers, peers, and other persons who wield an influence-belittle him, blame him and reject him, the growing child's attitudes toward himself are likely to become unfavourable. As he is judged by others, he will tend to judge himself.

Since the young child is most responsive to his mother, his social self-concept is largely based on her opinion of him or what he believes to be her opinion.His social self-concept may be transitory or permanent, depending on the consistency of the mother's treatment of him. In adolescene, the social self-concept is derived from the opinions of the peer group as a whole—the "generalized others". In adulthood the effect of the self-concept on behaviour is influenced by the strength of the person's desire to win the attention, approval, and acceptance of others. A man who is anxious to be a civic leader will be greatly influenced by the opinions of members of the community at large.

The Ideal Self-Concept is made up of perceptions of what a person aspires to be and what he believes he ought to be. It may be related to the physical self-image, the psychological self-image, or both. It may be realistic in the sense that it is within the reach of the person, or it may be so unrealistic that it can never be achieved in real life.

In childhood, the discrepancy between the ideal self-concept and the basic, the transitory, and the social self-concepts is usually large. Toward adolescence, the discrepancy normally diminishes as the other self-concepts become stronger and play a larger role in determining the person's image of himself. In adulthood, and certainly by middle age, the ideal self-concept usually has little impact on the person's concept of himself.

Almost everyone has an ideal self-concept in addition to his basic and transitory self-concepts.Whether the ideal self-concept is realistic or unrealistic is determined chiefly by whether the basic or transitory self-concept dominates. If the basic self-concept dominates, the ideal self-concept is founded on a more realistic appraisal of one's capacities and abilities. Whether an unrealistic ideal self-concept will be unrealistically high or low will depend on whether the transitory self-concepts are mainly favourable or unfavourable.

On the whole personal pattern of an individual is formed due to multiple factors interacting on an individual right from his birth.

IX.13 Learning Exercises

1. What is personality? Describe some of the major factors determining personality.
2. What are the characteristics of personality? Discuss the social and biological factors in the formation of personality.

3. What do you understand by personality "traits"? Discuss some of the main dimensions of personality and illustrate your answer.
4. Describe the different types of personality. How far is it desirable to classify people into types?
5. Explain the term Intraversion-extroversion and Ascendance-submission and describe the characteristics of individuals having such traits in high degree.
6. Discuss the nature of personality. Can we really measure personality? Describe some of the important methods of personality assessment.
7. Write short notes on: case history, interview, questionnaire, rating scales and situations tests, and give their value.
8. What is projective techniques? Describe some of the important projective technique and give details of their procedure.
9. 'Discuss the important factors of Personality development and describe Freud's concept of personality development.
10. Describe the significance of Projective Techniques as compared to Subjective and Objective Techniques of assessing personality.
11. What are the different projective methods of assessing personality? What method do you regard as most useful and why?
12. Why are projective devices called as such? Give details of any two such devices that you could use as teachers.
13. Write brief notes on:
    (a) Personality Inventories
    (b) Case History
    (c) Autobiography
    (d) Interview
    (e) Rating Scales.
14. Discribe the role of different determinents determining one's personality pattern.

X
Intelligence

As a matter of day today experience we find that some persons learn a concept easily, some persons learn the same concept with little more efforts and still some other learn the same concept with great efforts. This difference among the individuals in learning a concept enable us to understand that some mental force helps an individual to learn faster as compared to the other. The mental force rather the mental ability which enables to learn quicker, faster and accurately is also known as the mental ability. There are different type of jobs and each job requires different types of mental abilities. Keeping in view this problem the Psychologists have tried to explain the types of abilities working together to explain the concept of intelligence.

X.1 Definitions of Intelligence

The term intelligence is so commonly used and it is so widely associated with different meanings that there is a confusion among psychologists, educators and laymen concerning the precise meaning of the term intelligence. Inspite of many attempts by psychologists to agree among themselves upon a satisfactory definition of this term, there still prevails a controversy about its exact meaning. Various psychologists have tried to give definitions of intelligence as per their own view points and theories. Most probably of the psychologists believe that intelligence is applied to those activities that are associated with the higher mental processes. Among the various aspects of intelligence can be included power of attention, memory, imagination, reasoning and other forms of mental activity. Some of the definitions propounded by well known psychologist are presented as under:

1. Binet: Alfred Binet, a pioneer in the construction of intelligence test, considered intelligence as consisting of comprehension, invention, direction and criticism.

2. Wyate: Intelligence is the power of apprehending the relationship.

3. *William Stem:* He suggested that intelligence is a general capacity of an individual consciously to adjust his thinking to new requirements. It is a general mental adaptability to new problems and conditions.

4. *Carl Spearman:* He analysed mental ability and stated that all branches of intellectual ability involve two types of abilities viz; general ability and specific ability. He formulated his two factor theory.

5. *Thurstone:* He and many other psychologists assert that mental ability can be analysed into group factors which are quite independent of each other. His multifactor theory included thirteen factors. This list includes: 1. Verbal comprehension. 2. Word fluency. 3. Number facility: speed and accuracy in computation. 4. Associative memory. 5. Ability to visualize space. 6. Perceptual speed: speed and accuracy in judging differences or similarities. 7. Induction: ability to derive a principle from a given data. 8. Problem solving: deductive thinking.

6. *Termana:* He defined intelligence as the ability to carry on abstract reasoning.

7. *David Wechsler:* Defined intelligence as the aggregate or global capacity of the individual to act purposefully, to think rationally and to deal effectively with his environment.

From the above stated definitions or intelligence it can be safely concluded that the ability of an individual which reflects the power of a person to deal effectively, act purposefully and think rationally. The above mentioned definitions expounded by different psychologists can be summed up in the following words:

1. Intelligence is the ability of adjusting to a new situation.
2. Intelligence is the ability to avail of past experience.
3. Intelligence is the ability to do abstract thinking.
4. Intelligence is the conglomeration of many powers.

X.2 Concept of Intelligence

The fact that intelligence is a mental ability which enables an individual to learn quickly, easily and accurately. Intelligence is said to be an abstract mental ability which enables an individual to think rationally, deal effectively and act purposefully for suitable adjustment. The capacity of an individual to adjust, re-adjust as per the situation enable us to understand the degree of mental ability a person possess.

The concept of intelligence has been discussed by number of psychologists:

Binet: Points out that intelligence is a single mental ability of an individual which works at three levels such as:

(a) Ability to understand and maintain desired direction for a goal,

(b) Ability to make adaptations for goal,

(c) Ability to make auto-criticism for the attainment of goal.

Thorndike: Reports that intelligence is a mental process which works at three levels viz;

(a) Abstract Intelligence. The abstract intelligence makes an individual to understand and manage ideas, symbols to learn process.

(b) Machanical Intelligence. It enables an individual to manage and learn mechanical process.

(c) Social Intelligence. Social intelligence enables an individual to understand and maintain.

  (i) Man/woman (social relations),

  (ii) Wise actions in life,

  (iii) Regulate social actions.

Spearman : Reports that intelligence is the capacity of individual's constructive thinking. The capacity of constructive thinking works at two stages viz; general 'g' and specific 's'. Further Spearman reports that the intelligence as a capacity of constructive thinking works on these stages at three levels viz;

(i) Ability to understand mental process

(ii) Speed to draw relationships

(iii) Accuracy with which correlations among the things are established.

Thurstone: Describes the concept of intelligence as the ability rather the capacity of an individual to understand impulses and to regulate his behaviour.

Wechsler: Describes that intelligence is global capacity of an individual which enables him to:

(i) think rationally

(ii) act purposefully

(iii) deal effectively.

Keeping the above discussion in view we understand that intelligence is a mental ability which helps an individual to think rationally, act purposefully, deal effectively for suitable adjustment in his life by making speedy accurate and useful decision.

X.3 Nature of Intelligence

The nature of intelligence can be described into the following approaches:

1. Deductive Approach

Under this heading come all those view-points which have been arrived at as a result of arm chair thinking. There is hardly any attempt at quantitative analysis:

(a) Monarchic Doctrine of Intelligence. In the words of Spearman, "Now paramount among the lay beliefs is that which assumes mental ability to lie under the sovereign rule of one great power named 'intelligence'. This credence in a single power may be characterised as "monarchic". From the monarchic point of view intelligence is a single mental function.

(b) Oligarchic Doctrine. The failure of the monarchic view of intelligence led the psychologists to assume a few power like judgement, invention, attention, memory etc. to constitute intelligence. It was thought that each faculty has its own water-tight compartment and so the measurement of each faculty has to be done separately. According to this theory each trait was measured separately. The values were plotted on a graph paper and then they were joined by a line and this line was called a profile. This profile was taken as a mental measure of the individual.

The oligarchic theory contradicts the most essential character of the mind, that is, its unity. Also it requires separate measurements for each kind of faculty. For example, if we take the cause of judgement it is not one type of judgement. There can be various types of judgement, say judgement for science, humanities, arts and so on. The whole view about oligarchic doctrine is best summarised in the words of Spearman, "The oligarchic doctrine which takes ability to be constituted of some few great faculties, each functioning in a unitary manner, which would claim to measure each faculty by a single value, which puts together a set of such measurements into the so called profiles, which on the strength of these would dispose of the fate of thousands of persons, this doctrine would seem on close scrutiny to be fully devoid of foundations".

(c) Anarchic Doctrine. Anarchic approach to study the nature of intelligence advocates that intelligence comprises several mental faculties or types and every faculty was found to need a separate measurement, since each appears to be independent of the other. In opposition to the oligarchic doctrine, Herbart and his followers advocated the 'Anarchic Doctrine', that is, the doctrine of all round independence. He stated that ability or

intelligence was subdivided into innumerable independent parts and rejected the view that ability was tied up into a few great separate faculties. Thorndike advocated the nature of intelligence in the words: "The mind is a host of highly particularised and independent faculties. But to maintain that the abilities for different operations are independent of each other now be proved untrue universally".

2. Mathematical Approach

The deductive, oligarchic and the anarchic approaches could not explain the true nature of intelligence as a result Psychologists strived further to explain the concept and nature of intelligence and arrived at a conclusion that intelligence is the ability of an individual which can be analysed mathematically. The nature of intelligence as per the mathematical approach can be studied as:

(a) Doctrine of General Level. The psychologists felt that all individuals have certain level of intelligence. The theory says that intelligence is single mental ability.The quality of mental ability, generally called intelligence, has general level distributions of intelligence which can be calculated in order to measure intelligence, it was advocated that this could be done through sampling by the tests, and then the general level or average of the person's abilities could be calculated. But then to obtain a group fairly representative of the whole is usually a most difficult matter and further no sample can be a representative unless it contain cases in such large number as to smoothen away accidental errors. In the words of Spearman, "No genuine averaging or sampling of any ability is made, can be made or even has really been attempted." So even this doctrine could not help us much in solving the problem of measurement of intelligence.

(b) Electric Doctrine. Electric approach to study intelligence indicates that intelligence is composed of two factors. A general factor 'g' and a specific factor 's'. This approach was given by Spearman and was the outcome of a deep and thorough observation of a mathematical data of coefficients of correlation between different abilities. The correlations show a particular trend which could be expressed by the following equations:

The following stated equation reporting tetrad differences have been taken from the book " Abilities of Man" by Spearman:

a denotes 'opposites'
b denotes 'discrimination'
p denotes 'completion'
q denotes 'cancellation'

	Opposites	Completion	Memory	Discrimination	Cancellation
Opposites	—	.80	.60	.30	.30
Completion	.80	—	.48	.24	.24
Memory	.60	.48	—	.18	.18
Discrimination	.30	.24	.18	—	.09
Cancellation	.30	.24	.18	.09	—

From the above table it will be clear that

γ ap = .80, γap = .30, γbq = .09, γbp = .24 are the mathematical figures reflecting the differences in abilities among the individuals.

3. Factorial Approach

According to this approach, the intelligence is composed of a number of factors which have been arrived at as a result of highly mathematical and analytical techniques employed by various Factor Analysts viz;

(i) Guilford's 'Structure of Intellect' : Guilford classifies intellectual traits along three dimensions :

Operations : (i) Cognition, (ii) Memory, (iii) Divergent thinking, (iv) Covergent Thinking, (v) Evaluation.

Content : (i) Figural, (ii) Symbolic, Behavioural.

Products : (i) Units, (ii) Classes, (iii) Relations, Systems, Transforma-tions, Implications.

Guilford identified 120 factors.

(ii) Hierarchical Theories: These theories have been propounded by British Psychologists like Burt, Vernon and Humphrey in America. The factors have been organised in a hierarchical fashion as shown below:——

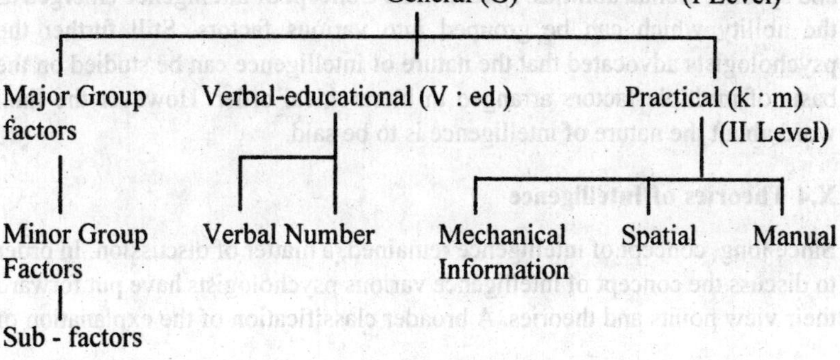

Therefore, the whole tetrad equation becomes.

80 × .09 – 0.30 × .24 = 0 Which is correct.

Now this will hold true in any table of actually observed correlations. Spearman showed a remarkable bearing of this fact. He said that whenever the tetrad equation is held true in any table of correlations then every individual measurement of every ability can be divided into two parts. One he call the " general factor" and denoted it by the letter 'g'. This 'g' according to Spearman is different from individual to individual but it remains the same for an individual in respect of all the correlated abilities. The second part he designated as 'specific factor' and denoted it by the letter 's'. This 's' varies not only from individual to individual but also from one ability to the other and even in the case of the same individual. So the number of 's' is as many as there are activities in the case of the same individual. The special feature about Spearman's 'g' are:

(i) It is merely a value of magnitude and not something concrete.

(ii) This magnitude does not measure something but merely tells us where this 'g' can be found.

From the practical point of view of testing, this doctrine is very helpful because it gives a method by which we can measure the intelligence of an individual.Suppose a person scores in a particular test Max. Now this Max contains two factors. An amount of 'g' that is, the factor common to all the tests say 'a' and 'x' which is specific (s) of this test. Similarly, others tests can be given and this value of 'g' which is common in all can be calculated. According to Spearman, this 'g' is an abstract factor and merely a statistical concept.

From the above discussion, it is evident that the historical development of the concept of intelligence reveals that intelligence was previously believed to be a general rather a single mental ability. This approach could not hold good as a result another approach advocating that intelligence is based on general and specific mental abilities. Further, The Concept of intelligence emerged as the ability which can be grouped into various factors. Still further the psychologists advocated that the nature of intelligence can be studied on the basis of multiple factors arranged in hierarchical order. However the final word about the nature of intelligence is to be said.

X.4 Theories of Intelligence

Since long, concept of intelligence remained, a matter of discussion. In order to discuss the concept of intelligence various psychologists have put forward their view points and theories. A broader classification of the explanation of the concept of intelligence reveals that we have four types of theories of intelligence viz;

(i) Single factor theory,
(ii) Two factor theory,
(iii) Multi factor theory.

(i) Single Factor Theory: It has been emphasized by Binet, Terman and Stern. Binet feels that intelligence can be fully described by one single factor. He gives this factor as the "ability to have good judgement." Terman advocates that intelligence is also based on a single factor. According to Binet, it is "the ability to think conceptually." Ebbinghaus regarded intelligence as being displayed in a power of synthesis i.e., the capacity to bring together a multitude of independent impressions into a unitary whole.

The single factor theories regarded intelligence as a single function. These theories are criticised on the basis of the fact that the various tests of abilities do not correlate perfectly with one another. There cannot be mentioned any one single factor which means intelligence.

(ii) Two Factor Theory: Spearman advocated this theory as early as 1904. This theory considers that intelligence consists of two factors: a general intelligence factor, 'g' and several specific factors, 's'.

The general factor 'g' is considered as playing some part in almost all human activities. In science, philosophy and similar other subjects and tasks success depends largely on the 'g' factor, while there are some special types of activities which are associated with the 'S' factor. For example, learning in certain skill, and crafts etc., the 'g' factor is not so important as the specific ability in the particular skill or craft, etc. Every individual has one 'g' factor and many specific abilities or many 'S' factors. In the every type of activity, one 'S' factor pertaining to that activity is necessarily involved while in all types of activities the necessity of 'g' factor is felt.

There are activities in which the 'g' factor is relatively important and also such activities where it plays only a minor role. In such case the 'S' factor or factors are prominent. 'g' can never be directly measured. It is measured indirectly the studying the correlation of many functions involving 'g' factor.

Spearman later on added a group factor to the two factors, 'g' and 'S'. By group factors he meant such factors which are less general, widespread and homogeneous than 'S' factor. For example, between the ability in addition (involving S factor) and general intelligence involving 'g' factor, there may lie an all-round numerical ability (involving group factor).

(iii) Three Factor Theory: As has been seen above, Spearman has added a group factor to the already existing two factors 'g' and 's' . His theory, thus, consisted of three factors at the later stage of its development.

This theory was opposed by Thorndike, who considered that there is over simplification of the facts in believing that there is a general factor which is homogeneous. His view was that the intellectual tasks are performed by a complex nervous system which operates in many different total patterns. Those patterns are too complex, and varied, to be described as mere mixtures of a 'g' and many 'S' factors, or a 'g' factor and some group factors and a few S factors.

(iv) Multiple Factor Theory: Multiple factor theories are based on elaborate statistical analysis. Thurstone, together with his pupils, developed a method on mathematical basis for the isolation and measurement of individual attributes which is known as factor analysis. On the basis of the factorial analysis Thurstone reported that intelligence is made up of nine primary mental abilities. These abilities are:

(1) Spatial ability, (2) Perceptual ability, (3) Numerical ability, (4)Logical or Verbal relations ability, (5) Fluency in dealing with words, (6) Memory, (7) Inductive ability, (8) Deductive ability, and (9) Ability to restrict the solution of a problem.

Thurstone considered that in performing any particular activity , such as, understanding a typical problem in mathematics, one or more of these nine mental abilities are required. There are some of these abilities which has greater utility in one type of activities than others. For example, in learning mathematics, numerical ability, inductive and deductive abilities, etc., will be required in much more degree than the other abilities.

Thurstone's theory of multiple factor is based on the principle that these mental abilities are primary and general, because, they enter in some degree into all complex intellectual activities. His view differs from Spearman's as his nine mental abilities are not the types of energy as conceived by Spearman.

(v) Guilford's Theory of Intellect: The lead given by Spearman and Thurstone to understand intelligence was followed by Guilford and his associates to postulate a theory of intellect that organizes the primary intellectual abilities into a structure of intellect. Guilford commences by defining a factor as 'a unique ability that is necessary to do well in definite tasks or tests'. Each factor is sufficientlly unique to be measured. However, three kinds of classification can be made because of similarities between various factors:

1. *Process or Operation*: It provides five main groups of mentalabilities viz;
   (i) Cognition, its refers to discovery, re-discovery or recognition.
   (ii) Memory, it implies retention of what is recognized.
   (iii) Convergent thinking, this is the type of thinking that results in the right or best answer.
   (iv) Divergent thinking, this is the thinking in different directions, or searching for variety about goodness, suitability, or adequacy of what we know, remember or think.
   (v) Evaluation, it is reaching decisions about accuracy, goodness, or suitability of information.
2. *Material or Content:* It involves four factors :
   (i) Figural Content. It is material perceived through the senses.
   (ii) Symbolic Content. It is composed of letters, digits and other conventional signs, usually organized in general systems (alphabet, number system).
   (iii) Semantic Content. It takes the form of ideas, to verbal meanings.
   (iv) Behavioural Content. It refers to social intelligence or knowledge and understanding of ourselves and others.
3. *Products.* They result from the application of operations to content. There are six general kinds of products:
   (i) Units. Comprehending visual, auditory, and symbolic units, plus knowledge of the meaning of words.
   (ii) Classes. The ability to classify into words or ideas.
   (iii) Relations. The ability to perceive relationship between objects because of their figural or symbolic properties, and the ability to discover relations in conceptual material.
   (iv) Systems. The ability to structure objects in space, to structure symbolic elements, and the ability to structure problems in the preparation for solution.
   (v) Transformations. The ability to visualize what would happen to objects if they were changed, or to suggest changes in existing circumstances.
   (vi) Implications. The ability to extend expectations and project present information into the future.

Guilford explains that each cell in the figure 1 is three dimensional since, it portrays the intersection of three variations : (i) operations, (ii) contents, and (iii) products. As described in the figure, there are five kinds of operations, four kinds of contents and six kinds of products. Therefore, there are 5 × 4 × 6 = 120 cells. Factors identified with 80 of the cells are known; thus, there are still 40 vacant cells. The view of Guilford is the most comprehensive view of intellect which has been presented so far. Guilford, however, feels that the model is purely theoretical and subject to change. This will depend on future researches.

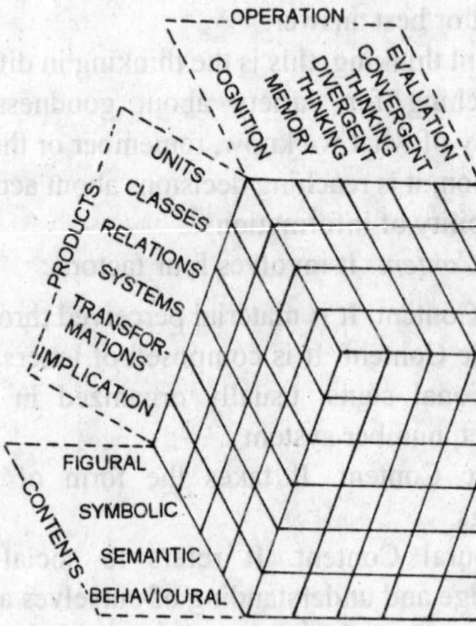

Figure 1 Guilford' Intellect Model

The theory described above may be briefly stated. Guilford believes that intellect is a logical structure composed of two main categories, memory and thinking. Thinking is subdivided into cognition, production and evaluation. Production is further subdivided into convergent and divergent abilities. In this way there are five groups of intellectual factors characterized by certain operations. Each of the five groups may be classified by two principles —the kind of product involved (the ability to know units, classes and the like), and the kind of content death with (figural, symbolic, semantic and behavioural). Guilford remarks that vacant cells indicate undiscovered primary intellectual abilities.

Guilford's theory has vast implications for education. He considers that the student is not simply a stimulus-response mechanism. He resembles a computer, who acquires, stores and uses information. This viewpoint stimulates many new ideas for the class-room.

In brief, depending upon the knowledge our psychologists tried to explain the mental ability i.e., intelligence in different forms of theories. These theories are still not able to satisfy us. However, today we need to see how valid and useful they are can not be clearly decided at present. Only future researches can lend us to get a correct notion about intelligence. In education we are concerned with the measurement of abilities which we can do by having reliable and valid instruments of measurement. Our task at present is to do that, rather than to indulge in discussion about the nature of intelligence.

X.5 History of Intelligence Testing

In the present day life, intelligence tests play a great part particularly in the life of the student and they have become an important tool in the educational system. In many countries the results of intelligence tests are considered for admissions to Universities and technical courses and also for selecting candidates for various appointments.Examinations mostly test the knowledge of a candidate. Success in an examination may or may not give an accurate indication of one's intelligence. To discharge our duties in life, a certain amount of intelligence is necessary. Because of these various practical implications a large number of psychologists have given their time and attention to the construction and development of proper intelligence tests during the last fifty years. To be precise, the history of intelligence and its testing has its origin right in the beginning of the 20th century when attempt to differentiate the slow learners from the fast learners were made.

Inspired on this rational Alfred Binet attempted to define intelligence by devising intelligence test. No doubt intelligence testing is a recent growth but attempts had been made from time to time to measure intelligence. The old methods were not so accurate, so valid, so objective and reliable.

Binet is the founder of modern technique of intelligence testing but he was not the only worker in this field. The work of Binet is very important and merits special consideration. His work has got a great historical importance as he gave a start in right direction howsoever humble it was.

Alfred Binet was a French subject, who was very interested in abnormal psychology. Before 1900 he did a lot of research in the field of psychology on topics such as 'The Psychology of Reasoning, Animal Magnetism, Alteration of Personality etc. Near about 1900 he became interested in the measurement of intelligence. He measured living heads to relate the results with intelligence. He measured the blind, deaf and abnormal children in way of head measurements.In 1903, he wrote a book 'Experiments on Intelligence .' In it he took broader sense of intelligence as equivalent to higher mental process.

In 1905, Binet and Simon began their work with feeble minded children who were released from the schools for their backwardness. For them the question was to know, to find, to differentiate between feeble minded children and normal children. Actually there was the need to measure the level of intelligence. Fortunatety, statistical knowledge was available and thus using the concept of statistics, they started their work and soon they prepared one intelligence scale in 1905.

First Intelligence Scale of intelligence was constructed which gave a clear idea of mental measurement. Binet and Simon prepared several questions out of which thirty were selected for the final scale. These thirty questions were simple, brief and general. They were not pedagogical and consumed a little time. They were of heterogeneous nature. The thirty questions were given to solve to different children of different age groups and thus from the data, they were arranged in order of difficulty. Thus continuous test was meant for all the ages and from the score the mental age was calculated. It was not a group test but of individuals. It could be given to one child at one time.

We may say that it was not fully standardized, valid and reliable test. Even then it contained idea of graded series, and concept of fundamental qualities of an intelligence test.

The 1908 Scale : Binet revised the 1905 scale in 1908. Now the number of questions was increased from 30 to 50. Several new questions were introduced in the scale. Some of the old items were deleted and they were substituted by new items. The concept of age norms was introduced. The list was meant for age group of 3 to 9. For every different groups there were different questions.

Another improvement in the scale of intelligence was made. The idea of mental age was given by Binet for the first time in the history. In order to find out the norms of specific age, he put the criterion in which 60-90% of children of same group passed. Hence, a good start was given towards standardization of intelligence test.

The use of mental age is undoubtedly due to Binet although the comparison of an individual in regard to knowledge or ability in the child of specific age was previous to the time of Binet. But it remained for Binet to get the credit of crystallizing the concept by making it definite and concrete.

.The 1911, further, Binet revised his 1908 scale. It differed from that of 1908 in arrangement of test and in the allotment of items in each age group. Several new items were substituted for old items. The total number of questions is fifty six. This scale is better standardized and the selection of test items is decided by superior to the first and the second scale. Perhaps Binet would have given more ideas about intelligence test but he died in the same year.

Goddard's Test: Goddard was the first psychologist who introduced Binet scale in America.In 1908 he began to use the scale at Vineland. He was very much impressed by its usefulness. He changed the items according to American culture, but he did not make many changes. Only a few items were changed to suit American children. Then he took the step of standardization on 2,000 American children. The test of Goddard was published in 1920 and is based on Binet's 1908 scale of intelligence. For some time, Goddard's revision of Binet's test remained very popular.

The standard revision in 1916. : In 1916, Terman revised Binet Simon scale. It has a great landmark in the history of mental measurement. Really it was a great advance in this direction. Terman and his coworkers spent about five years to put the revision in its final shape. The achievements justify the time and labour.

The revision is more thorough and more accurate. The standardization is very superior. There is uniform number of questions for each group. The number of questions was increased to 90. The calculation of mental age was better, as questions were given for months. For one age group, there are six questions. It means that if a child solves all the six questions of seven years age group and also solves two questions of eight year group, his mental age is equal to seven plus four months i.e.seven years and four months.

Stern suggested the term ' mental quotient'. Mental Quotient is the ratio between mental age and chronological age. Terman developed this idea, and multiplied the quotient by 100 in order to remove decimal fraction. He termed it 'Intelligence Quotient' or 'I.Q'. It may be put in the form of a formula :

$$\text{Mental Quotient} = \frac{\text{Mental Age}}{\text{Chronological age}}$$

$$\text{Intelligence Quotient} = \frac{\text{Mental Age}}{\text{Chronological Age}} \times 100 = \frac{\text{M.A.}}{\text{C.A.}} \times 100$$

The term I.Q. was used for the first time. Its credit was due to Stern who introduced this term in 1914.

After 1914, the numerous tests of intelligence were constructed. In 1915, Yerks, Bridges and Hardwick introduced new methods of scoring (percentile) for their tests. This was an important achievement in educational statistics.

The Pinter-Paterson Performance Test came out 1917. It is useful for children who are deaf and who cannot express themselves. Several other performance tests were prepared for illiterate people when there is need to do something practically and not to read and write.

Group Test: So far there were all individual tests. Individual test takes long time, as at one time only one individual is tested. A development of group tests was introduced by American army psychologist who prepared Army Alpha and Army Beta test during the first World War.These were originally meant to be used in selecting the soldiers and officers for American Army. These tests proved very useful and are also used in these days.

During the period from 1900 to 1920, great progress was shown in the field of intelligence testing as a result various types of tests were developed. Even now (1995) latest revision of Binet Test has been made.

X.6 Types of Intelligence Tests

Intelligence can be categorised into different ways.There are different types of tests. Each of these types has its own characteristics which can be studied as:

Individual Intelligence Tests: Binet-Simon scale and its revisions, such as Goddard Test and Stanfort Revision are individual's intelligence tests. Here the examiner can give test to one individual at one time. Perhaps such tests are superior to all other types because individual attention is paid to the examinee. Such observation on the part of examiner is extremely useful in clinical studies.Sometimes students do not follow the complete instructions. They are nervous or do not feel at home. How do they take the test, what is their attitude and such other things are very important specially when test is estimated from diagnostic purpose. No doubt, such test needs more time and effort on the part of examiner but its achievement justifies time and labour spent on it.

Group Intelligence Test: Group intelligence tests are those psychological tools which can be used to assess large number of individuals to assess their intelligence level at a time. Most commonly used group test is Army Alpha test used for the group testing of intelligence. In World War I Americans wanted such a test which could be given to a group at a time. This test was prepared under the guidance of Yerks. Such a test is very useful if we have a little time and more work. Such a test can be given to fifty and more children at one time. Thus, it saves our time. It is useful for normal adults. Even normal children need special attention. The instructions are to be carried out very strictly. If the instructions are not followed by the subject or examinees, the score of the test will not be valid. This is the main difficulty that it is very difficult to know whether complete instructions are carried out by the subjects or not.Such tests are more useful when we have to measure general intelligence irrespective of any diagnostic purpose.

Verbal Intelligence Tests: Both the individual as well as the group test can be categorised into verbal and non-verbal individual and group tests. The verbal tests of intelligence needs reading and writting skill. The exminees are to read the questions from the paper and have to write answers. Such a test is also known as paper and pencil test.Army Alpha Test and Wechsler Test are verbal tests of intelligence. These tests are useful for literate persons who have sufficient skill in reading and writing. Such test cannot be used with illiterate adults or children who have not sufficient practice in writing and reading.

Non -Verbal Intelligence Test: Here reading and writing is not required. The examinees have to do something. Sometimes they are also called performance tests of intelligence. Good enough 'draw - a - man' test is of non-verbal type. In this test, child is instructed to make the best possible drawing of a man. In scoring artistic ability is not connected but points such as indication of feet, ear, nose, mouth, number of fingers, clothes, hair etc. are counted.

Such a test is very easily scored and can be given to children of different states and nations.Moreover it is a group test and saves our time. At the same time its scoring is not objective, rather it is very subjective. Army Beta Test and Pinter - Peterson Tests are other examples of such types of tests where there is no need of much of reading and writing but some performance has to be done.

There are also other types of tests. Some tests are administered against time. Time is fixed. Some are power tests. There is no time limit, but in the end the questions are so difficult for the given age group, that all of them cannot be solved. Some are continuous tests and can be given to all age groups. The norms are prepared for the different age group. In the game some tests have separate sections while other are continuous. In this way there are numerous types of tests. Besides, all the different points , the scoring method may be different. Moreover, the norms can be represented in different ways, such as there are age norms, percentile norms, I.Q. etc.

Army Alpha Test: This is verbal group test. In April, 1947, a commitee was appointed by American Psychological Associations to construct Army Allpha Test of Intelligence which may perform the following functions:

Alpha test

1. It measures general intelligence.
2. It is a group test.
3. It is paper and pencil test.
4. It is useful for literate persons.

The committee met the following requirements by constructing this test:

1. It should be independent of specific school information.
2. It should be deeply graded in difficulty. It means that it should contain questions from very easy standard to very difficult ones, so as to measure all graded of persons who range from idiot to genius.
3. Scoring should be simple, rapid and objectives.
4. It should require minimum of writing.
5. Number of different forms of equal difficulty should be prepared to prevent coaching on particular forms.

Standardization: It was tried out on students in elementary and high classes, large group of students in schools, colleges and training camps. More than 5,000 enlisted men, inmates of different institutions for the feeble-minded children. So, it was very well standardized.

Validity of Test: Validity of the test was checked against several criteria:

(a) School grade criterion;

(b) Teacher's estimate;

(c) Against other test such as Stanfort Binet.

For soldiers, the following criteria were used:

(i) Officer's rating of soldiers.

(ii) Rank attained.

(iii) Ability attained.

(iv) Previous civilian accomplishments.

The co-efficient of correlation between alpha and various criteria ranged from 5 to 95 which means that statistically the test was reasonably a valid measure.

The reliability of test was measured in different ways and it was found that test scores were constant with high level of reliability.

The test consists of eight sections. In each there are several items.

S. No.	*Nature of Test*	*No. of Items*
1.	Following Directions	12
2.	Arithmetic Problems	20
3.	Practical Judgement	16
4.	Synonyms and Antonyms	40
5.	Dearranged Sentences	24

6.	Number Series completion	20
7.	Analogies	40
8.	General Information	40

Different duration of time is fixed for different sections. In all there are 212 questions. One mark is allotted for each. There are five different forms of the same difficulty. Score is represented in grades such as A, B, C + etc. The following tables makes it clear:

Grades	A	B	C+	C	C	D	D
	312	134	104	74	44	24	14
Score	135	105	75	45	25	5	0

Remarks very high, fairly high, average low, very low.

According to the Army Alpha test, Mental age of typical soldier was about that of an average first year high school boy.

The types of intelligence test can be presented diagrammatically as given below :

Classification of Intelligence Tests

Types	Individual	Group
Verbal	Individual verbal	Group verbal
Non-verbal	Individual Non-verbal or Individual Performance	Group Non-verbal or Performance

A. Criteria of A Good Test of Intelligence

There are several criteria of a good intelligence test. The important criteria can be discussed as:

1. Validity: The co-efficient of correlation of validity must be reasonably high. It means that the test should be valid.A valid test is that which measures the quality to a high degree of satisfaction for which it has been prepared.An intelligence test is valid if it measures intelligence only. If the intelligence test which stands for the measurement of intelligence means memory scholastic attainment or general knowledge, the test is not valid.

For this purpose, it should be very clear what intelligence is. According to the definition of intelligence, the item of tests will be prepared. If the subject is not clear then item selected for the test may not represent the real trait or quality which is to be tested.

Validity of test can also be viewed if the test can differentiate clearly between known, individuals or known groups. Suppose we have two subjects, one is normal in intelligence whereas, the other is dull. If the test scores of these two subjects are quite different and they also verify or confirm the truth which is already known the test is valid, otherwise it is not.

With the help of statistical knowledge we can measure the degree of validity. It is called co-efficient of correlation of validity.

Reliability: The second essential criterion of a good intelligence test is that it should be reliable or the co-efficient correlation of reliability should be high.A test is reliable or trustworthy if we get the consistent scores of a student. Just as a thermometer which gives different readings for the same temperature is not trustworthy, similarly is an intelligence test which gives quite different scores for the same subject when given to him twice or thrice within a short duration. The test is not reliable which tells that a subject is dull and next time its recording is different as it may indicate the student bright or normal. So reliability means consistency of score.

3. Objectivity: A good intelligence test is always objective. It can be objectively scored. The method of scoring is fool-proof. The marking does not depend on the subjective knowledge of the scores of examiner. If the answer is correct, the award will be in complete units. If the answer is wrong, there will be no award. Now-a-days, tests are so objectives that there is no partial award for the answers. There are scoring machines which can score the answer sheet at very rapid speed.

4. Practicability: The test must be practicable. It could be used under average conditions. It should not need much of apparatus. It must be simple and could be afforded by most of the people.It must be brief, to the point and exact. Very lengthy tests are discouraged.

X.7 Uses of Intelligence Tests

Intelligence tests have helped us to increase our knowledge of psychology. From what we have said so far we can gather a few of the uses of intelligence tests.

(1) These tests are very useful in the educational guidance of children. we can grade them properly and give them the proper quality and quantity of work. We can also use the tests to find out whether a pupil's failure is because

of a lack of reliability or because of lack of application to work. (2) For any programme of vocational guidance and proper vocational selection intelligence testing is a basic necessity. Different kinds of jobs require different grades of intelligence as basic qualification. Hence these tests become very useful. (3) For the study of personality also intelligence tests have contributed a great deal. Intelligence is an important component of one's personality. Hence without a knowledge of one's level of intelligence it is not possible to get an accurate picture of his personality structure. (4) Modern intelligence tests have helped us to discard old ideas that girls are less intelligent than boys and that a particular race as a whole is inferior to other races in intelligence. (5) With the help of intelligence test we have been able to study the different factors, particularly with reference to heredity and environment that affect development of intelligence. We have been able to discard the old idea that heredity and environment are completely independent and separate factors. (6) One more interesting use of the intelligence test may be mentioned. Intelligence tests were first constructed on the basis of the meaning of the term intelligence we had. But these tests have returned the compliment as it were. When testing became highly developed, these tests and the process of their construction have sharpened and made clearer the very concept of intelligence. It was the existence of intelligence tests that made it possible to develop the theory of factors and the composite nature of intelligence. Thus these intelligence tests have helped us to understand more fully the nature of intelligence itself.

X.8 Distribution of Intelligence

Studies reveal that there is a vast difference in the level of intelligence among the individuals and this difference is assessable. Normally we find that there are more people of average ability than there are very bright ones or very dull ones. On the basis of studies made, it has been found that 80 per cent of the total population has an I.Q. ranging between 85 and 115. They are the average and normal people and the finding of the psychologists accord with the general statement that God must have loved the common people because he made so many of them. The lower I.Q. is as low as 25. These people are very inferior, of low intelligence such as morons, imbeciles and idiots; they cannot look after themselves nor they able to learn a useful trade. The highest I.Q. is as high as 150. These people are very superior and make great success in life, their understanding and adjustments are of a high order. Studies reveals distribution of intelligence in any randomly selected group of people shows the below mentioned patterns:

I.Q	Percentages	Classification
150 and above	0.25	Genious or near genious
120 to 150	6.75	Very superior
110 to 120	13.00	Superior
90 to 110	60.00	Average or normal
80 to 90	13.00	Dull (backward)
70 to 80	6.00	Dull, feeble minded
Below 70	1.00	Definitely feeble minded

X.9 Assessment of Intelligence

As a common experience of our life that there are number of jobs which require different levels of our abilities. The difference of abilities required for a particular job make us to understand that some means and measures are required to assess the ability required for a job and the level of ability a person posseses. The whole process of abilities required for a job and the level of ability a person posseses, make us to work out for idea of assessment of intelligence.

Since, we have different types of tests available viz; the group, individual, verbal and performance tests, which can be used for the assessment of intelligence. It is the duty of the psychologist or an educator or, counsellor to decide which test would prove useful for the assessment of intelligence for a particular individual or a group.

For the assessment of intelligence we most commonly use the Binet's test and Wachsler test of intelligence.

Binet Test of Intelligence : Alfred Binet, a French Psychologist during the early twentith century got inspirations from the works of psychologist Withem Wundt, J.M Cattel, Hugo Munsterberg , Joseph Jastrow to devise a psychological tool (test) which may assess the mental ability called intelligence.

Alfred Binet is also known as the father of intelligence testing as he made a deep dent on the previously existing belief about intelligence as he disagreed with those who sought to measure general ability by testing speed of reaction, rote memory, sensory acuity or muscular movements. Intelligence can be estimated, according to Binet, only by tests of high faculties like reasoning, comprehension, judgement, adaptability, persistence and self-criticism.

In 1904 Binet was appointed to a national educators committee to investigate retardation in French Schools and to devise a way of distinguishing the bright pupils from the dull who could not benefit from the ordinary teaching of the schools. Is it possible to find out what children cannot profit by common school education and should be taught in separate schools? This was the problem posed before Binet. He saw that in solving this problem he must find out some means of measuring intelligence that no single test would so, and that children increase in ability as they grow up. In collaboration with Theophile Simon he devised a number of tests., graded in difficulty according to age and requiring information of a non-scholastic nature which every normal child of a particular age could be expected to possess. He has to try these tests on a large number of children of different ages to standardize them, that is to make sure that they suited children of a certain age level. Then these tests had to be tried again and again and revised frequently before they could be offered as an accurate measuring device. The scale is known as the Binet-Simon scale.

Binet-Simon scale consists of thirty items arranged in order of difficulty. Among them are: following a moving object with the eyes, recognizing simple objects in a picture, comparing two lines of different lengths, repeating spoken sentences, memorizing things in a picture, finding rhymes for a given word, completing sentences, defining abstract terms. Binet tried out these tests of children and in 1908 published a revised scale which divided the tests into age groups from 3 to 11 years. At some age levels only three questions were asked; at others, 5 or 5. In 1911 shortly before he died, Binet published a second revision of his scale. It omitted certain test items previously included, added others, and brought the scale to the adult level. In this edition Binet included five tests for each age, except the 4-year level. The 1911-Scale, validated and standardized, represented a great improvement over the earlier two series.

Binet observed that intelligence develops to certain level with the increase in age. Keeping this reationale in view Binet proceeded to find out what children of different ages can known and perform. As many as 200 children were studied in the first examination in order to get an idea of what children of a given age can do. Later these tests were given to a large number of children between the ages of three and twelve and a fairly satisfactory evidence was acquired about what the average child of Paris of any age could do. Now with a knowledge of the average it was easy to find out if a particular child was above or below it. The more widely these tests were applied, the more they were standardized.

Another revision of Binet test was made with the collaboration of Terman of the Stanford University. Terman tested 2000 school children to discover just what a normal child at any given age can do. He chose six tests for each year from 3 to 10, also for ages 12, 14, 16 and 18. His calculations indicate that an average adult has mental age of 16 years while a superior adult has one of 18 years. By using six tests for each year he was able to give two months and of his birthday of else to tell how many months of Binet's items, though some were shifted to higher or lower age levels according to Terman's findings on normal children. Several new items were added to that the Stanford Revision as it was called, had a total of ninety tests compared with 54 of Binet's 1911 scale. In 1916 his monumental work, *The Measurement of Intelligence,* was first published.

Intelligence tests

A few samples of tests are given below:

Binet Scale Tests

Three years

1. Pointing out nose, eyes and mouth
2. Repeating two numbers
3. Enumerating the objects in a picture
4. Giving one's own surname
5. Repeating a sentence like. "It is hot, let me go."

Five Years

1. Comparing two weights
2. Copying a figure, a square, for example
3. Repeating a sentence of ten syllabus
4. Forming a triangle from two rectangles
5. Counting four coins.

Eight years

1. Finding omission in a picture
2. Counting backwards from 20 to 1
3. Giving differences from memory
4. Repeating five digits
5. Giving the date, month and year.

Terman's Stanford Revision Test

Three years

1. Pointing to parts of the body
2. Naming familiar objects
3. Enumeration of objects in a picture

4. Repeating six to seven syllabus
5. Giving the family name
6. Giving sex.

Five years

1. Comparing weights
2. Naming colours
3. Aesthetic comparison
4. Giving definitions in terms of use
5. Putting 2 triangles together to make a rectangle
6. Performing a triple order: putting a key on the table, shutting the door, and bringing a book.

Eight years

1. The ball-and-field test
2. Counting backwards from 20 to 1
3. Comprehension e.g. what will you do if a playmate hits you without meaning to do so
4. Giving similarities
5. Definitions superior to use
6. Vocabulary, 20 words.

The Stanford Revision, first published in 1916, has been most popular. Again the Stanford Terman test was revised further in 1936 with the co-operation of Terman and Merill and brought out an improved richer sampling of abilities, and include non-verbal test situations, particularly at the lower ages. Many more test items were included in the scale, tests were made suitable from the age 2 to the age 14, two forms of tests were devised so that each form could be suitable checks on the other and the tests could be repeated and for each age test six to eight items were included. The ability to differentiate individual ability with respect to age level gave birth to an idea of Mental Age.

Mental Age

The usefulness of the method of intelligence testing is greatly enhanced by the concept of *mental age.* (M.A.) Tests were framed on the examination of a large number of children of different age levels, for example tests devised for five-year old children were those passed by a typical five-year-old child. If a test passed by 60 to 90 per cent of the children of a given age level, Binet assigned that test to that age level. A child who passed all the tests designed for children of six years and did not pass any test for the seven has said to have a mental age of six years, no matter what his actual or chronological age might be. If he is six years of age he is normal, but if his age is five, he is above normal having passed tests above his age, and if he is seven years he is sub-normal having passed tests must below his actual age and is judged backward. Thus an eight year old child may have the mental age of six or a six year old may have the mental age of eight. Mental age, often expressed symbolically as M.A., represents the level of mental development attained by a child, as expressed in terms of the average development of children of a given age. It is a relative measure of mental growth. If a child of 5 does as well on an intelligence test as an average child of 7, his mental age would be seven. It is the level of ability of a given child, expressed in terms of the age at which the *average* child attains that level of ability. The concept of mental age is an important contribution to the psychology of mental development and individual differences.

X.10 Intelligence Quotient

Intelligence Quotient (I.Q.) is an index of an individual intellectual development with respect to his age. For example. I.Q. can be easily understood if we consider three children whose ages are eight, nine and ten may have the same mental age of nine, and yet the first one is bright, the second one is normal and average, and his third is backward. How are we to distinguish between the three having the same mental age? This is done by obtaining the ratio of the chronological age to the mental age of the individual, that is, by finding the so called Intelligence Quotient or the I.Q. The mental age is divided by the chronological age or C.A. and the result is multiplied by 100 to avoid decimals and this gives us the I.Q. Thus the child who passed all the tests of the age group seven and two tests of the age group eight has a mental age of seven years and four months (two months for each of the six test items), that is, 88 months. If his chronological age is six years and three months, that is, 75 months his intelligence quotient would be

$$\frac{\text{Mental age (M.A.) } 88}{\text{Chronological age (C.A.) } 75} \times 100 = 117.3$$

The child whose chronological age is the same as his mental age has an I.Q. of 100. The child whose mental age is 9 but chronological age is 10 has an I.Q. of 90. As we shall see later, I.Q.'s below 75 are definitely inferior; those above 130 are quite superior.

The concept of Intelligence Quotient was devised by a German psychologist Stern, but its popularity is due mainly to its adoption by Terman.

Therefore I.Q. is an index of an individual's intellectual development, determined by dividing his mental age by his chronological age and multiplying the result by 100.

The concept of I.Q. can be further studied while knowing the process of computing the I.Q.

Wechsler Test of Intelligence

David Wechsler, an American clinical psychologist developed a scale measuring intelligence of adults in 1939. In 1949 he developed the Wechsler Intelligence Scale of Children (age to 15 years) commonly known as WISC and in 1955 he brought a revised version of his earlier scale. It was known as Wechsler Adult Intelligence Scale. The earlier scale for adult intelligence was very popular and the revised version began to be widely used. It could be used from the age of 10 to 60 years. Before this scale was devised there was no scale for testing the intelligence of adults.

The Wechsler Adult Intelligence Scale is an individual test. It consists of two parts, the *verbal* part which has six tests and the non-verbal or *performance* part has five tests which require minimum of language. The full scale is a combination of the two. The tests are outlined here:

Verbal:

1. *Information:* 29 questions graded in difficulty.
2. Comprehension: Fourteen questions requiring understanding.
3. *Arithmetical reasoning*: Fourteen problems in mental arithmetic.
4. *Digits Forward and Backward*: memory span for digits of increasing length.
5. *Similarities:* Thirteen pairs resembling each other in some way.
6. *Vocabulary:* A list of forty words of increasing difficulty to be defined.

Performance:

1. *Picture-arrangement*: Which would make a story.
2. *Picture completion*: An important part of the picture is missing and has to be identified.
3. *Block design*: Cubes to be arranged so as to reproduce seven designs indicated.
4. *Object assembly:* Jigjsaw-puzzle type test.
5. *Digit-symbol*: A test of association learning in which digits have to be matched with symbols.

The Wechsler-Bellevue scale does not provide for mental age as this concept is not applicable to adult intelligence but it does yield an I.Q. which is of value in comparing one adult with another. The I.Q. obtained in Binet scale indicates development ratio, that is how a child stands with others children of the same age and what his mental status at present is. Wechsler-Bellevue scale for children employs the same techniques as the Binet-Simon scale. Therefore, both Binet and Wechsler scales of intelligence are based on I.Q.

Calculation of I.Q.

Intelligence Quotient (I.Q.) is the index of mental age (M.A.) over chronological age (C.A.) I.Q. is calculated by the formula:—

$$\text{I.Q.} = \frac{\text{MA}}{\text{CA}}$$

That is, the I.Q. is the quotient obtained by dividing the mental age of the pupil by his chronological age at the time the test was given. As a matter of fact, however, the C.A used as a divisor in never more than the age at which the test maker assumes mental maturity is reached. Upon the basis of the evidence available at the time, Terman suggested that a divisor of 16 years be used for all pupils whose C.A. is 16-0 or above. Experience since that time has been somewhat contradictory. Wells, Pinter, and Boynton conclude that the evidence favours using 14-0, or 168 months, as the maximum divisor. Dearborn offers evidence to support 14-6 as the maximum divisor. In the Revised Stanford-Binet, Terman and Merrill suggest this rule: "Up to 13-0 the entire C.A. is counted; beyond 16-0, none of it.

The C.A. of subject who is between the ages of 13-0 and 16-0 is counted as 13-0 plus 2/3 of the additional months he has lived. This means that a true C.A. of 14 is counted as 13-8; a true C.A. of 15 as 14-4; a true C.A. of 16 as 15-0, which is the highest divisor used in the computation of the I.Q."

In calculating I.Q. maximum. Chronological age is kept in consideration because with the increase in age the individual when crosses 16 years mental maturity is reached gradually rather than abruptly. It is probably true that no test so for using MA and the I.Q. units has been adequately standardized for the upper age groups, and certainly none makes possible a final answer to the vexing problem of the age when mental maturity is reached. Mostly the psychologist favours using some unit other than I.Q. especially beyond the age of 13 years. The author favours retaining the use of I.Q. concept through the senior high school while making allowances for greater inaccuracies beyond the age of 13.

While calculating I.Q. we should prefer the sample group belonging to the lower grades this age score should be taken from the date of birth as shown on the school records. A young child is likely to put down 9 when he is merely "going on 9," for example. In the intermediate and upper grades it is usually safe to rely on the pupil's answer as given on the test blank. On most tests he is asked to give his age at his last birthday, and then to give the months and day of his birthday, or else tell how many months, it has been since his last birthday. The trouble usually comes with computing the months. This computation should always be checked, preferably by a simple table prepared by the examiner.

By careful calculation of C.A. and score on a test we are able to know the M.A. and C.A. When the correct M.A's and CA' are determined, the I.Q. values can be read from the Inglis or some similar table. If the I.Q's are computed by actual division, it is necessary to have the work done twice independently.

Interpretation of the I.Q.

The I.Q. is a measure of *brightness,* or of *rate* of intellectual development. Following the lead of Terman, many writers consider I.Q's of 90 to 110 as "normal," those below as subnormal, and those above as supernormal. According to scheme, I.Q.'s below 70 indicate feeblemindedness." Individuals in this group are often sub-divided into three types or levels of feeble-mindedness: idiots, below 25 imbeciles, 25 to 49; and morons, 50 to 69, inclusive. Most clinicians recognize these as rather rough and arbitrary groupings and attempt to apply other criteria, such as social sufficiency or success in school. In any case, an individual test would have to be given by a competent person to warrant even a tentative classification of feeblemindedness. Terman has suggested that a minimum I.Q. of 90 is required for success in the ordinary high school.

It will be noted that there are no distinct groups. There is a continuous distribution from the idiot to the genius, and the various degrees of brightness shade into each other until they are as indistinguishable as the colours of the rainbow. It is easy to see that red is different from violent, or to see the difference between red and yellow; but it is hard to tell where orange leaves off it becomes red on the one hand or yellow on the other. The concept of "genius" is worthy of further consideration. Following the lead of Terman, it has been common to interpret any I.Q. of 140 or above as indicating "genius or near genius." Evidence is accumulating that this limit is much too low. In an illuminating discussion of this problems Mrs. Hollingworth comes to the conclusion that a minimum I.Q. of 180 is more defensible, and that works of genius conditioned by high ability when combined with ze2al and the capacity for hard work. Terman supports the conclusion that "*above the I.Q. level of 140, adults success is largely determined by such factors as social adjustment, emotional stability, and drive to accomplish.*"

X.11 Advantages of the I.Q.

The identification of various degrees of brightness is one of the advantages of the I.Q. Moreover, many studies have shown the I.Q. to remain relatively constant under ordinary conditions from year to year, although radical changes in the home and school environment, which rarely occur, are likely to be reflected in larger changes in I.Q. when they do occur.

Nemzek summarized 97 studies which used the Stanford-Binet test and 27 studies which used group tests. The median correlation coefficient by the test and retest method was 832 for the individual test and 846 for the group tests. The corresponding range of the middle 50 per cent of the coefficients was 760 to 889 and 779 to 885, respectively.

The similarity of results for the individual and group tests is remarkable. But these correlations permit considerable variations, which apparently are more likely to occur at the extremes of the distribution than near the centre. There seems to be a tendency for the lower I.Q.'s to decrease somewhat on later tests, while the evidence for the higher I.Q.'s is somewhat contradictory. After six years Terman found that 73 to his "geniuses," still below a C.A of 13, had lost in Stanford-Binet I.Q. the boys 3 points and the girls 13 points on the average. On the other hand, Cattell at Harvard found that children with I.Q.'s above 120 gained approximately 8 points in three to years. Most studies have noted a regressive effect, however. But, of course, most cases tend to cluster closely about the centre of the distribution, where the I.Q. is "fairly stable." After a summary of the experimental evidence, Cattell arrives at this practical conclusion:

The results are reported as evidence of the large changes in the I.Q. which do occur in ordinary school practice and to emphasise the caution with which the results of a single intelligence test must be interpreted, even though it be an individual examination made by an expert.

Since the I.Q. of the average pupil is likely to be relatively stable, if originally computed for C.A's between 6 and 13 years, his M.A at any later age can be estimated with considerable assurance from his C.A and his I.Q., no matter when the latter was computed. For example, suppose that a pupil who had an I.Q. of 95 when in the third grade is now in the fifth grade. His present C.A is 10.2 is 10.2 or 122 months. His estimated M.A in months is 122 × .95, which is 116 months, or 9.8. Comparisons with achievement test scores expressed in ages can, therefore, be made wherever such comparisons are thought desirable, without the necessity of repeating the intelligence test at the same time.

Although it is desirable to repeat intelligence test until at least three tests have been given during the pupil's educational career, the tests need not be given at the same time as the achievement tests in order to make comparisons. The I.Q. from a test given by an expert to pupils in the public school may be regarded as sufficiently constant to make adjustments for a different date fairly safe.

X.I2 Limitations of the I.Q.

In common with all units in which test scores are expressed, the I.Q. suffers from two limitations. The zero point is arbitrary rather than real, and the various units are an unequal length or value. The difference between 60 and 70 is not equal to the difference between 90 and 100, or to the difference between 130 and 140. In the same way it is absurd to say that a pupil whose IQ is 120 is twice as bright as one whose I.Q. is 60, or half again as bright as one whose I.Q. is 80, such interpretations are meaningless. But in this regard the I.Q. is no worse than are all raw scores and practically all other derived scores. For example, it is obvious that when the thermometer registers 10 degrees below zero it is not twice as cold as when the thermometer registers 5 degrees below.

There is also another serious limitations of the I.Q. Many studies have shown that the I.Q.'s on one test are not comparable to those obtained on another test. Table taken from Gates, illustrates this problem is the first grade. Pupil A, for example, would be classified as just average or "normal" on one test and as a "genius" on another. Not only do the scores for the various individual pupils vary, but the average for the class varies greatly. One test would indicate that the class is just an average or normal class with a mean I.Q. of 119, whereas, another test would indicates that the class is "very superior", with a mean I.Q. of 129.

The remaining seven tests indicate that the class is "superior" with a mean I.Q. of 113 to 118, depending on the test. That these discrepant results are the rule rather than the exception is corroborated by other studies. Sangren reported similar results for first-grade children in Michigan. Boynton gave 14 different tests to several sixth and seventh-grade classes within a period of two weeks. Out of a typical class of 24 pupils he found that 6 pupils each received more than 50 points on these test, on one test a pupil would be classified as practically a moron, and on another test this same pupil would rate a near genius. In a study by Miller, already discussed, similar variations were found in the high school. It would appear, therefore, that the makers of intelligence tests have not agreed very much better upon the norms for interpreting their tests than have ordinary teachers upon the values for interpreting essay examinations.

All these studies are agreed that the I.Q.'s from different tests must be equated in order to make them comparable for even when average I.Q.'s on different tests are close together the extremes are likely to vary widely. One solution which has been proposed is to equate all tests in terms of some widely used test. Kefauver has prepared such a table in which ten tests have been equated in terms of the Terman Group Test of Mental Ability. Kefauver, gives an example, that pupil who gets an I.Q. of 60 on the Terman Test would have I.Q's ranging from 31 to 77 on the other tests. I.Q. values comparable to Terman I.Q's of 75,100, 125, and 140. It is worthy to note that the I.Q. values of different tests by the same author are by no means equivalent. The implication for test users is to record the name of the test and form with I.Q.

Doubtless the fundamental solution is for all test makers to standardize their tests, whether they aim to measure intelligence or achievement, on a national population so chosen as to conform fully to the mathematical theory of sampling. As long as tests continue to be standardized on samples chosen primarily upon the basis of convenience, even when they involve large numbers and wide geographical areas, there is still no assurance that the samples are truly representative and thus comparable with each other.

Miller shows the value of equating I.Q.'s in terms of a single test. The records and standard deviations before and after equating value in the I.Q. Table shows that the data are for 160 pupils tested annually over a six-year period with various forms of the Otis group tests. Although the tests were scattered over six years, the variation in terms of equated I.Q.'s is practically the same as that of the I.Q.'s of 160 first-year high-school pupils on five group tests administered within a period of three hours. The first study involves 2,400 differences between pairs of scores, and the second involves 1,600 differences between pairs of scores. It is clear that equating I.Q.'s in terms of a single test greatly reduces the variability ordinarily found when different tests are used.

All things considered, the author is disposed to agree with Terman and Merrill that the sensible thing to do under the circumstances is to "employ the simplest indices available and as rapidly as possible acquaint teachers, school counsellors, social workers, and physicians with their significance and their limitation." The M.A and the I.Q. are examples of such "simple indices."

X.13 Difference Between I.Q. and M.A.

The most commonly used units in which to express the results of an intelligence test are mental age and intelligence quotient, usually abbreviated

MA and I.Q. It is important to understand the distinction between them. M.A is a measure of *mental maturity* and "indicates the level of development which a child has reached at a given time," to use the words of Terman.

This degree of mental maturity of level of development is expressed in terms of that "*possessed by the average child of corresponding chronological age.*" For example, a point score of 75 on the Terman Group Test of Mental Ability is equivalent to an M.A of 13 years and 2 months, usually written 13—2.

This means that when the Terman Test had been given to hundreds of children in various parts of the country it was found that the average score of a child with a chronological age (C.A) of 13 years and 2 months was 75 points. Any child who makes a score of 75 on this test is said to have an M.A of 13-2. But pupils of various C.A's make scores of 75 on the Terman Test. It is clear, therefore, that a 10-year-old child with an M.A of 13-2 has matured rapidly, whereas a 14-year-old child with an M.A of 13-2 has matured at a much slower rate.

In other words, M.A is measure of *stage* or *level* of maturity but *not* of *rate.* Rate is measured by the I.Q. which is obtained by dividing the M.A by the C.A. In the preceding illustrations the I.Q. of the 10-year-old child would be 158 ÷ 120 = 132. It will be noted that the quotient is carried out two places but that the decimal point is omitted. In reality, the I.Q. is the per cent that the MA is of the CA. In like manner, the I.Q. for the other pupils is 158 ÷ 168 = 94. The I.Q., then, gives us a different interpretation of a score on an intelligence test from that afforded by the MA. The I.Q. is a measure of rate of maturity, whereas the MA is a measure of level or stage of maturity.

In both cases rate and level are relative to the standardization group. If a child has matured rapidly, he is said to be bright; if he has matured slowly, he is said to be dull. A fuller interpretation is to be given a little later. For the present, it is sufficient to note that ordinarily both the M.A. and I.Q. of a pupil should be recorded, for each has its distinctive values and limitations.

X.14 Constancy of the I.Q.

A careful reader could note that the I.Q. of an individual must always be constant. If a boy has a mental age of eight and his chronological age is six, his I.Q becomes 8/6 × 100. This would mean that this particular boy is very bright. He would continue to be bright. The IQ which is an indication of his brightness should always be 133.3. At the chronological age of ten his mental age will be 13.3 making the I.Q. 133.3 again. Thus it will be seen that the mental age will be increasing every year with the chronological age but not the I.Q. This fact is called constancy of I.Q'. However, some psychologists have questioned this concept seriously and have conducted experiments to find out whether the I.Q. cannot be increased by giving special attention to a particular child by giving him favourable learning facilities. The intelligence testing movement true to its origin, has thrived in the classroom situation. Thus most of the experiments related to intelligence tests and the testing of intelligence have been conducted on school pupils.

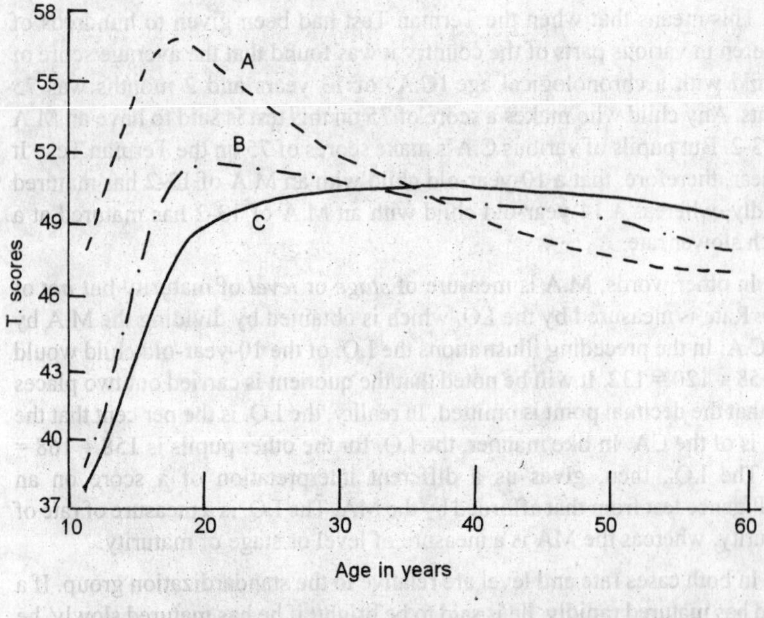

Fig. 2. Showing declince of ability in different tests as age advances. A—Verbal analogies. B—Arithmetic reasoning. C—General information.

Some experiments have shown that if a child from a poor environment is given special training and education quite early in life. It is possible to increase his I.Q. by a few points. In one study the gain was slightly more than ten points. In some cases retests showed even a loss up to about ten points. But these experimental results were not sufficient disturb the general acceptance of the hypothesis, *viz.,* the constancy of the I.Q. In any testing and retesting programme certain other factors disturb our results. It has been observed that some boys blossom out rather late and in any single case the tested I.Q. largely depends upon when he is tested. Our tests themselves are not always perfect in the sense that they often involve items which might only test the individual's knowledge of the environment. In such cases, even accidental contacts with different kinds of elements in the environment may increase the score in the intelligence test. In spite of these difficulties the concept of the constancy of the I.Q. has been generally accepted.

This concept of the constancy of the I.Q. has raised another interesting problem, *viz.,* the limits of the mental age. Binet's assumption is that intelligence keeps on growing as the child advances in years. This increase in intelligence is indicated by the increasing mental age. Physical growth and development stop mostly by the time the individual reaches the late adolescent stage. The question arises, does mental growth also stop around that time. Various studies have been made on this problem. It has been suggested that mental growth stops somewhere between the ages 16 and 20. This does not mean that the adult above 20 in intellectully the same as the boy of 16. Their innate capacities may be the same but their actual achievement will naturally vary because of experience and learning. This has a practical bearing on testing the intelligence of an adult. It would be unfair to divide the mental age by his chronological age. His chronological age may be 50, but according to our assumption already made the mental age cannot be numerically greater than 16 according to some and 20 according to some others. So, as a practical device in computing the IQ of an adult, chronological age is always taken as 16 by some people and 20 by some others. Of course, this will also depend on the nature of the intelligence test used.

Measured IQ is constant because intelligence improves with chronological age. It is agreed that mental age reaches its maximum limit by about the age of 20. Thereafter it remains more or less constant for a period of about 10 to 20 years. Most investigators have observed that thereafter there is a decline in mental age. When we refer to the development, the constancy and the decline of intelligence or mental age, we must always remind ourselves that we are only referring to intelligence or mental age as measured by our tests. The typical curve obtained in most studies showing the changes in achievements in intelligence tests as age advances can be seen in fig. 2

In a similar manner the question has also been asked by psychologists as to when intelligence begins to function. Is there intelligence even before birth or at birth or how long after birth? Various answers have been given to these questions. Arnold Gesell and Thurstone are the two people who have done the maximum amount of work to answer this question. The former gathered extensive data regarding the motor performances of infants and attempted to formulate a scale of intelligence for young infants. The latter used mathematical principles with the results obtained from grown up children. From these he suggested that intelligence begins to function at about the sixth month after conception. However, these attempts have only theoretical value. We have not yet been able to devise sufficiently accurate testing devices to measure the intelligence of new born babies.

We started by saying that intelligence testing is becoming very popular. The concept of IQ was held as a great boon to teachers and employers. Since the results of ordinary school examinations depended upon a number of factors, the IQ came to be accepted as a true mark of one's intellectual capacity. In the assesment of the abilities and difficulties of school pupils, IQ came to be used very freely. It almost became a fashion to speak of one's IQ. However, it should be mentioned that the modern trend in intelligence testing does not lay so much value on the IQ as such. As said earlier, psychologists have begun to realise that one single score as the IQ does not really give a good and complete picture of the assets and liablities of the individual in the school situation or in other situations. The abilities in different aspects of mental function should be known before we can form a useful idea of the capacities of a boy. Even for giving training and education, such an analysis is necessary. Thus is addition to the IQ, a short pen picture or a profile giving the individual's differential capacities and various abilities is more advantageous (fig. 3).

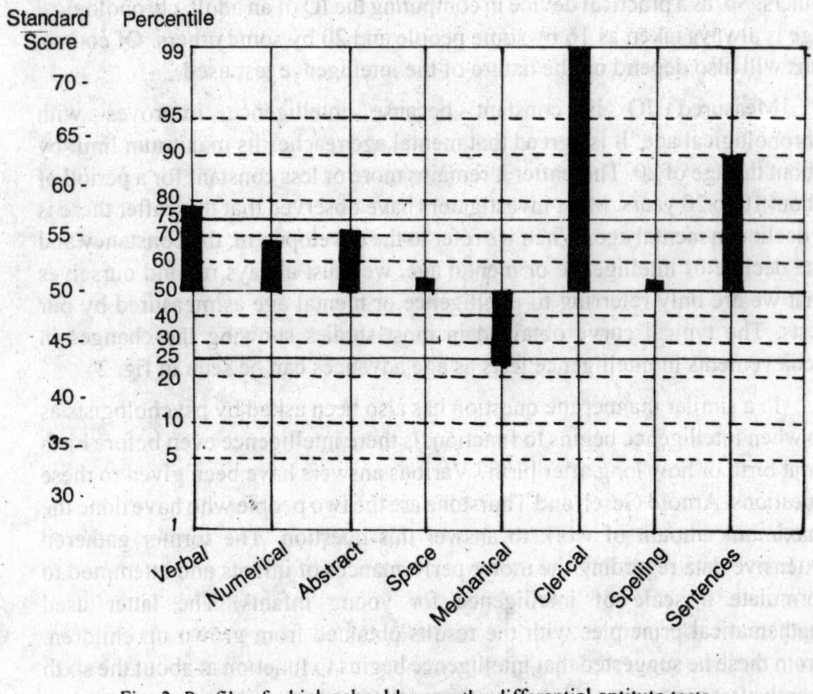

Fig. 3. Profile of a high school boy on the differential aptitute tests.

X.15 Educational Implications of Intelligence Tests

The knowledge of intelligence as mental ability has wide implications in the fields of education. Because, with the help of psychological tests of intelligence we in education can derive the following uses:

1. Classification of Students. Intelligence is one of the basis of classification. Intelligence is positively correlated with educational activities. It is the capacity of learning. Classes can be formed by testing the intelligence level of students and making their categories. Some students are superior in intelligence but they are in lower school standards due to certain reasons. If these students get the opportunity of studying in higher grades, they can pull on very well.

In a large school, often there are many sections. These sections are not formed on certain bases but arbitrarily. The sections should be according to the level of intelligence. The students who are very high in their intellect must form a separate section as their rate of learning is greater than others. Similarly there can be separate sections of dull and normal students.

2. Educational Guidance. Now-a-days, there are numerous courses of studies such as agriculture, commerce, technical, science, literature etc. Besides it, there are elective and optional subjects. Students face a great difficulty while choosing them. Some subjects are easy, whereas others are difficult. If the students choose difficult subjects but their level of intelligence is low, there are chances of educational maladjustment. In order to save the students and to fight out the problem of general backwardness, educational guidance is needed for which intelligence tests are essential.

3. Vocational Guidance. This is a recent concept which is very important in the modern democratic set up where everybody is expected to do something. Every job has different demands. One of the main qualities which is to be measured in connection with vocational fitness and adjustment is level of intelligence. If a person goes for job which needs higher level of intellect than he has or his level of intelligence is superior to the job, in both ways, there is danger of vocational mal-adjustment, the consequences of which may be far-reaching.

Vocation is most important and essential. A person is really lucky who relishes his job. A misfit may pick up quarrel with colleagues, employer, shirk work, may not show progress and thus may not get the promotion. Sometimes, vocational misfitness leads to neurosis and psychosis. In order to save the young persons from vocational mal-adjustment, vocational guidance is very much needed. Intelligence test is the most useful tool in the hand of counsellors.

4. Vocational Selection. As it has been shown that different jobs need employees, such tests can be usefully employed. All the military service selection boards use intelligence test to select the suitable candidates. Similarly, intelligence test can be used for admission purpose to various professional colleges such as medical college, engineering college etc.

5. *Use in Clinics.* Intelligence testing is an essential instrument to know about the diseases of the patients. Now-a-days, there are intelligence tests which have a great diagnostic value. They give certain useful tests to find the maladjustment and its causes in school and at home.

6. *Research.* Research in various problems of education and psychology requires the use of accurate measuring instruments. A good intelligence test is such an instrument, the use of which has great practical value for several research topics.

7. *To diagnose Backwardness.* To know whether the child is retarded or backward in education, there is use of intelligence test. Low level of intelligence is one of the causes of backwardness in class. Intelligence test is also useful to know whether a student is progressing according to his capacity or not. In several cases students are intelligent but their educational attainment is not good. By testing their intelligence we can find such children and suitable measures can be taken to reform.

X.16 Role of a Teacher in Promoting Intelligence

If we accept the analysis of cognitive-field psychology on the matter of intelligence, what can a teacher or a counsellor do to promote intelligence among students? The main avenue for achieving this aim is, of course, reflective teaching and counselling. Reflective teaching is to be successful, certain conditions should prevail. We list several concerns which Combs and Snygg think should be taken into consideration to set the educational stage for reflective teaching. (We have made additions and deletions and we take full responsibility for departure from Combs and Snygg's treatment.)

1. *Improving Perception:* Studies have shown that improvements in health may lead to marked gains in I.Q scores as well as in capacity for steady intellectual growth. Of especial importance is the problem of faulty sensory equipment. The quality of perception is closely related to how well one's senses are functioning. A child with impaired vision or hearing may appear stupid, with necessary correction, he may make startling gains.

2. *Meaningfulness of Learning Material:* Make certain that students have maximum opportunity for achieving new and higher quality perceptions. Perception occurs only when a meaning is grasped. If a learning situation is meaningless because of its nature, it can hardly be expected to lead to gains in

intelligence. We treat the problem of meaning in connection with "understanding level".

3. Increasing Sense of Responsibility: Development of a sense of responsibility of the student by a teacher ultimately activates the mental ability to perform a work accurately, speedly and fastly of a student. This ultimately is attributable to the increase in his responsibility—his greater need to do well. However, college counsellors, on the basis of interviews with students, seem inclined to attribute part of the gain to the simple fact that with marriage satisfaction of a student's heterosexual desires ceases to be a time consuming distraction.

4. Development of Self-Concept: Teachers should do what they can help children to achieve adequate concepts of self. This may well be the most important of the recommendations we can make. To a large degree a person's achievement is limited to what he thinks he can achieve. Virtually everyone eventually develops definite ideas about his limitations. Furthermore, it seems likely that, more often than not, people underestimate their abilities. Parents or teachers often act as if they think children are lazy and dull. If this happens frequently enough, children come to accept this evaluation of their abilities. As Combs and Snygg ask, "What differences in the richness and variety of perception might result from a generation of people with 'I can' rather than 'I can't' conceptions of themselves?"

5. Relaxed to work: Teachers and counsellors should make every possible attempt to relieve threat whenever it is suspected that a child is handicapped in his perceptions by it. By "threat" we are not referring necessarily to the threats a teacher might hold over students: "If you don't learn your six lessons by Monday, I will keep you after school." Rather, we mean anything in a child's life space which he sees as endangering his self-respect, or the integrity (inner harmony) of the inner-personal area of his life space. The most pressing threats, in this sense, are ideas which appear to jeopardize present self-structure. Awareness of an inconsistency in one's beliefs is often threatening; in this case, feeling of threat can be relieved only by achieving some reconciliation of the incompatible beliefs.

Obviously, any situation calculated to produce serious reflection contains some degree of threat to established convictions. Otherwise, why bother to reflect? What we are referring to in this section, however, is threat of such magnitude that all child's efforts must be devoted to combating it. Threat of this kind is often quite irrelevant to the learning task before a child. It may reflect a family situation or inadequate relations with peers. A child who carries too heavy a burden of threat usually displays a rigid, defensive mind-set. Consequently, he finds it virtually impossible to be openminded about anything.

X.17 Learning Exercises

1. What do you mean by intelligence. Discuss its nature?
2. Describe different theories of intelligence and which one you feel most important.
3. Discuss the history of development of intelligence tests and describe uses of intelligence tests.
4. Describe different types of intelligence test used to assess intelligence.
5. What in I.Q. and explain the reason why I.Q. is consistant?
6. Differentiate between I.Q. and mental age.
7. What are the educational implications of intelligence tests?
8. Discuss the role of teacher in promoting intelligence among his students.

XI
Creativity

It has generally been realised today by all nations, whether big or small; developed or developing; communist or capitalist, that their mere survival very much depends upon how effectively they can conserve and utilise their most precious human resources—their gifted children. "The greatness of a nation", says Emerson, "Varies with the number of geniuses it produces and the honour in which it holds them." This dictum, in fact, is very old and goes back to the days of Greek philosophers. However, it may be pointed out that, whenever in the past efforts were made to identify and nurture the gifted children, attention was paid to the intellectually superior children only. Nevertheless, it has been gradually realized that it is not merely intelligence but creativity which is solely responsible for the progress of mankind or society. In simple words, it has been observed that all that has come to pass in modern civilisation is the result of creative thinking done by intelligent men and women. The progress that man has attained in the world of art, literature, philosophy, science, commerce, etc. has been due to the lofty thinking done by the gifted and genius. One of the important functions of modern education is to train young minds in the art of creative thinking.

XI.1 Meaning and Definitions of Creativity

The term "creativity implies the production of a totally or partially novel identity". The term creativity has been defined by number of psychologists as a result it is difficult to give a single definition of creativity. However, Shan (1994) has tried to present the definition of creativity in historical perspective that:

"Creativity may be defined in many ways. From (1959) holds that creativeness is that basic need of man which drives him to transcend himself as creature and to overcome the passivity and accidentalness of his existence. Rhodes (1961) has referred to four kinds of definitions as the "Four P's of creativity", *i.e.*, Person, Process, Press and Product. In order to combine these four approaches, he defines the word creativity as "A noun, naming the phenomenon in which a person communicates a new concept (which is a new Product)". Thurstone (1952) argued that an act is creative if the thinker reaches the solution in a sudden closure which necessarily implies some novelty for him. To him the idea might be artistic, mechanical or theoretical, and administrative, if it solves an organisational problem.

Stein (1953), on the other hand, insisted that creativity may be defined in terms of the culture in which it appears. To him, "novelty" or "newness" means that the creative product did not exist previously in the same form. It may involve a reintegration of existing material or knowledge, but it must contain new elements and the work must be accepted, as tenable or useful or satisfying by a group in time.

In general, creativity has been seen as contributing original ideas, different points and new ways of looking at problems. Selye (1962), in his definition, requires that basic discoveries or creative contributions possess to a high degree and simultaneously three qualities. He states that they are true not merely as facts but also in the way they are interpreted, they are generalizable and they are surprising in the light of what was known at the time of the discovery. Also, a number of approaches have been suggested by those who have studied creative thinking as a mental process. Spearman (1930) thought of creation purely as a process. For him creative thinking is the process of seeking or creating relationships with both conscious and subconscious processes operating. Barchillon's (1961) definition also includes the process of creation. Barchillon further believes that thinking process involved in creation is of two kinds viz.; cognito, to shake and throw things together; and intelligo, to choose and discriminate from many alternative possibilities and then synthesize and bind together elements in new and original ways. Barchillon has taken broad-based view than that of Spearman. Spearman (1930) emphasised only mental functioning, whereas Barchillon defined the process clearly of its both functions for the product which must be unique, otherwise the process can not be creative.

Guilford conceptualises creativity in terms of the mental abilities involved in creative achievement. Guilford in his well known 'Structure of Intellect', reflects creative thinking is clearly involving what he categorised as divergent production. He defines divergent production as the generation of information from given information, in which the emphasis is upon variety of output from the same source (innovation, originality, unusual synthesis or perspective). The factors of fluency, flexibility, originality and elaboration are included in divergent thinking category. However, he is of the view that creative thinking can not be equated with divergent thinking. He further believes that the redefinition abilities and sensitivity to problems are also important in creative thinking. The redefinition abilities involve transformation of thought, reinterpretations, and freedom from functional fixedness in deriving unique solutions. Sensitivity to problems seems to be essential in getting the creative thinking process in motion.

Taylor (1959) sought to reconcile some of the apparent differences in opinion concerning creativity by suggesting creativity in terms of various levels: (*i*) expressive creativity, (*ii*) productive creativity, (*iii*) inventive creativity, (*iv*) innovative creativity, and (*v*) emergentive creativity. He points out that many people have this fifth level in mind when they talk of creativity. Since this fifth level of creative behaviour is so rare, only the lower levels have usually been involved in most of the investigations concerning creative behaviour.

Torrance (1965), while reviewing the classification of all these definitions into the categorization "Person, Process, Product and Press", argues that:

> It is true that some definitions emphasize one or the other of these categories, but almost all somehow spill over into more categories. Thus, it seems inevitable to me that a thorough understanding of creativity must involve the study of all four aspects of creativity (person, process, product and press). It is obvious that an investigator must at any one time focus on one aspect and then on another, always been alert to the other three aspects of creativity. As the focus of thinking, I have chosen as process definition, but in the experiments described in this volume the focus of investigation has been on the "Press" or environment. If we define creativity as a process, we have then to ask what kind of person one must be in order to engage most successfully in the process, what kind of environment he needs in order to function most successfully and what kind of products result from the process.

Thus Torrance describes that creative thinking takes place in the process of sensing difficulties, problems, gaps in information, missing elements; making guesses or formulating hypotheses about these deficiencies; testing these guesses; revising and retesting them; and finally in communicating the results.

A review of the definitions of creativity and view-points regarding it leads us to the conclusion that creativity is a phenomenon described variedly by the researchers. However, it is the pioneering work of Guilford and Torrance which has been followed by researchers all over the world to define the term creativity and identify it among individuals from school children to adults and to the aged.

XI.2 Characteristics of Creativity

Duric. L (1990) describes the characteristic of creativity based on the Guilford model of intelligence. A concise analysis of the model of intellectual structure proposed by the founder of the psychology of creativity, J. P. Guilford, will also be helpful in this respect.

The model (Figure 1) has the form of a rectangular solid with three edges of varying lengths. All intellectual abilities are arranged according to three dimensions. They are: (a) intellectual operations; (b) intellectual contents; (c) intellectual products.

Intellectual operations are as follows:

1. Cognition (discovery or recognition of something).
2. Memory (preservation of what has been acquired or discovered).
3. Divergent thinking (thinking in various directions and searching for different solutions).
4. Convergent thinking (leading to a unique solution in the only way).
5. Evaluation (the best, or the most correct, thought, approach, image, conclusion, etc., is determined).

The intellectual contents of the Guilford model are:

1. Figural (they reflect the size, the shape, the colour, the structure of an object thereby leading to visual perception).
2. Symbolic (expressed in numerals, letters or agreed symbols, as in mathematics).
3. Semantic (expressed in language and images, as in literature).
4. Behavioural (they reflect so-called social intelligence, social relations, intellectual communications, etc.).

Intellectual products represent the outcomes of the preceding two dimensions viz.

1. Units (shapes, symbols that have been produced).
2. Classes (formed from product units).
3. Relations (formed between units and classes).
4. Systems (originating as outcome of the structure composed of units, forming a firmly organized whole).
5. Transformations (meaning changes, modifications of information).
6. Implications (conclusions and forecast inferred from other information).

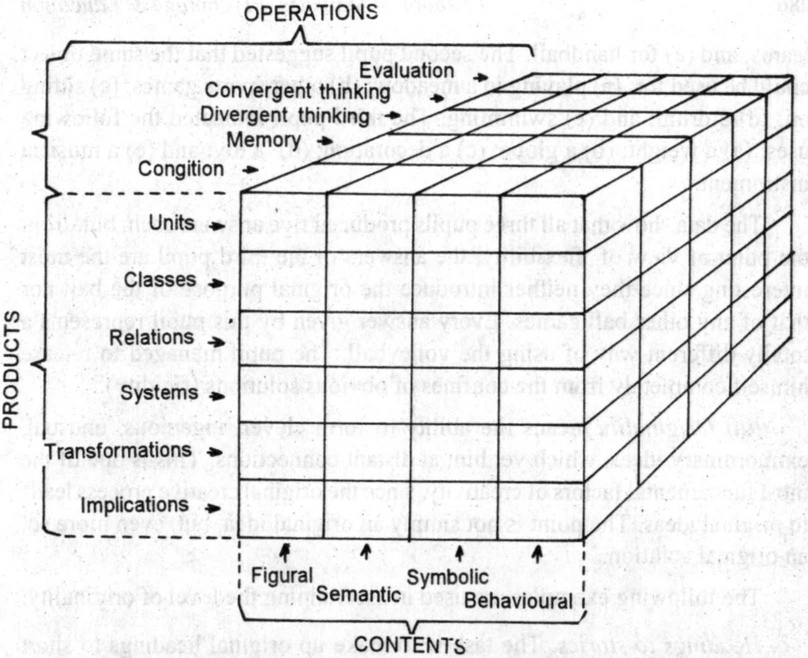

Fig. 1. Model of intellectual structure according to J.P. Guilford.

In the model shown in Figure 1, which has undergone further modifications, the individual influences on the three dimensions can mutually intersect and thus form as many as 120 small cells, each of which corresponds to one hypothetical elementary ability with three characteristics. This ensures the uniqueness of an elementary ability, determined by one kind of operation, one kind of content and one kind of product. In this way, for example, the memory (operations) of symbolic (contents) classes (products) may arise.

The basic faculties of creativity include fluency, flexibility, originality, sensitivity, redefinition and elaboration.

(i) Fluency means the ability to form with facility as many psychic products as possible of a certain kind (words, ideas, figures, symbols, etc.) in a given time.

(ii) Flexibility is the ability to come up with various solutions to problems and to overcome rigidity in thinking. Pietrasinski [5] introduces examples of flexible thinking from his own experiments. The pupils were given the task of writing (or saying) as many uses of a volleyball as possible in three minutes. On the basis of their answers he chose from among his subjects three typical cases. The first pupil proposed that the volleyball may be used for: (a) volleyball; (b) for basketball; (c) for football, (d) for any ball game with two

teams; and (e) for handball. The second pupil suggested that the same object could be used for: (a) playing in a meadow; (b) other sports games; (c) sitting on; (d) a drum; and (e) swimming. The third pupil indicated the following uses: (a) a weight; (b) a globe; (c) a decoration; (d) a toy; and (e) a musical instrument.

The data show that all three pupils produced five answers each, but, from the point of view of flexibility, the answers of the third pupil are the most interesting since they neither introduce the original purpose of the ball nor that of any other ball games. Every answer given by this pupil represents a totally different way of using the volleyball. The pupil managed to release himself completely from the confines of obvious solutions (rigidity).

(iii) Originality means the ability to form clever, ingenious, unusual, extraordinary ideas, which yet hint at distant connections. This is one of the most fundamental factors of creativity, since the original creative process leads to original ideas. The point is not simply an original idea, but, even more so, an original solution.

The following examples are used in ascertaining the level of originality:

Headings to stories. The task is to make up original headings to short events or stories. For example : 'There is a boy living in a countryside who is only 3 years old, but he can read, count and play the piano.' The ingenious (original) headings to such a story may be: 'a puzzle for the scientists'; 'a new Einstein'; 'boredom at school'; 'does he know how to play?', etc.

Inventing original consequences of unusual events (tests of consequences). These events should be of the most fantastic character, e.g. 'What would happen if people suddenly acquired the ability to pass through walls without hindrance?' Tasks for ascertaining originality are similar to those for ascertaining the level of ideational fluency (readiness) and certain kinds of flexibility. However, they differ on the point that the answers should be unusual with ingenious but distant associations; they should transform the conceived story and point out a different interpretation of the information contained in the story.

(iv) Sensitivity to problems is the ability to notice and perceive the problem before others notice it or see it. Here is an example of sensitivity in mathematics : one side of the triangle is 12 cms. long; give the lengths of its other two sides so that it would be impossible to construct the triangle, and demonstrate why! There are several possible answers, among which are (a) = 12 cms, (b) = 6 cms, (c) = 5 cms; or (a) = 12 cms, (b) = 9 cms, (c) = 2 cms and so on. The proof is that (b)+(c) should be greater than (a)!

Another example from mathematics: construct a triangle when angle $< \alpha = 90°$, angle $< \beta = 45°$ and angle $< \gamma = 50°$. The pupils who is sensitive to problems will immediately notice that there is no solution since the sum of the inside angles of the triangle does not equal 180°.

The level of sensitivity can be measured by tests, e.g. the test of apparatuses, consisting of two parts, each part containing ten apparatuses (the time available is seven minutes). The task is to suggest two ways of improving each apparatus. For example ; 'In what way would you improve the telephone?' A sensitive answer: by mounting a device on it that would tell you who is calling before the receiver is lifted:

(v) Redefinition. By *redefinition* (restructuring, reformulation) we mean the ability to transform the purpose of objects or their parts, to use them in different ways, to free oneself from customary ways of problem solving.

The tasks set before pupils may include the transformation of purpose. For example: there are five objects (a ruler, a glass-pipe, a stick, a pencil and a lighter). Which of these objects may be used for producing a musical note? The glass pipe can be used to this purpose if we close it at one end and blow across the open end.

In order to develop creative ability for redefinition it is possible to use the method of relating objects, i.e. two different kinds of objects are brought together and their juxtaposition leads to the production of a new object. For example, a nail and a stick may give rise to a waste-paper picker, a fishing rod, a javelin, a boat hook, a personal weapon, etc. Many tasks of this kind may be invented.

Joining words also represents a suitable way of developing the ability to redefine. For example, the task may be to write a story based on ten given words; club house, village, fruit, square, meeting, quickly, grass, sweet, voluntary worker, garden. There are many possible combinations.

(vi) Elaboration. Elaboration in creativity is conceived as the ability to propose elements of solutions to complete a certain whole. For example, a chain of associations suggested by the initial and the final words must be completed to form a sequence : 'work, —, —, —, an orange'. The three missing words may be 'earnings', 'money', 'food', for example.

Another kind of exercise may require that a very simple drawn line should be complemented by other lines to form a certain whole.

In addition to Guilford's model describing the creativity we have another approach of Luck A. N. (Russian Psychologist) who points out that creativity depends upon thirteen groups of abilities such as : (a) perseverance in searching for problems; (b) the ability to condense thinking operations; (c) the ability to transfer experiences; (d) the ability to perceive the whole; (e) the ability to associate concepts; (f) readiness of memory; (g) flexibility of thinking; (h) the ability to evaluate and sum up the situation; (i) the ability to integrate and dissect; (j) the ability of easy generalization of thoughts; (k) the ability to anticipate; (l) fluency in speech; (m) the ability to complete the activity.

In brief, as we have introduced six groups of Guilford's and thirteen groups of Lck's abilities which form the basis of creative thinking. Let us consider now the abilities of Guilford (fluency, flexibility, originality, sensitivity. redefinition and elaboration) in relation to individual phases of the creative process. For example, for the *preparatory phase*, sensitivity and then flexibility and originality are inevitable. For the *incubatory phase* fluency and flexibility are important. The *intuitive phase* requires sensitivity, fluency, flexibility, but especially originality. For the last phase of the creative process, i.e. the *evaluatory phase*, perhaps the factor of redefinition (oral or written interpretation) is the most significant.

XI.3 Principles of Creativity

Creativity is special mental ability which is governed by certain principles such as:

(i) Every mentally healthy individual exhibits of a certain level of creativity. However, levels of creativity differ.

(ii) Creativity (creative thinking), in common with psychic phenomenon, develops through activity (play, learning, work). Play is dominant for pre-school-age children and forms a foundation for the development of their creative potential. The principal activity of pupils and students in school is learning, therefore their creativity may be most efficiently developed through the educational process during learning under the guidance of teachers and educators.

(iii) Inculcating creativity or creative thinking in pupils and students forms an integral part of educating the whole personality.

(iv) The psychological objectives of creativity education should conform to the general educational objectives aimed at bringing forth an all-round and harmoniously developed personality. Within this prespective, the psychological objectives of creativity education may be considered as contributing elements.

(v) The global educational-psychological purpose of developing creativity in pupils and students is represented by the formation of a creative personality in the sense of being able to work in an efficient manner, displaying acceptable and progressive social behaviour, but especially taking responsibility for one's own self-education.

(vi) Those principally involved in developing creativity in pupils and students are teachers and other educational staff who have been trained for this activity at teacher training institutions and/or in various post-graduate courses.

XI.4 Theories of Creativity

There have been various attempts to understand the cause of creative behaviour ranging from purely literary and speculative shades to scientific and empirical attempts. In understanding the creativity we needs to study various theories of creativity. Prof. Dutt in this regard discuss the theories of creativity as:

i) Creativity as Divine Inspiration—According to Plato, a creative writer no longer remains in control of himself but becomes an agent of higher power. Tagore too writes in Gitanjali, that I am a dead reed, but you make it a flute by blowing various tunes through me over vales and hills. Most of the creative artists, especially poets and singers have experienced such feelings where they perceive that they are simply puppets in the hands of some higher power which is squeezing out the best from them and probably will throw them out like a juiceless lemon. Being a highly subjective experience, it is not open to scientific analysis.

ii) Creativity as Madness—According to Nietschze, there must be chaos within to give birth to a dancing star. Even Plato could not distinguish well between divine visitation and madness. Van Gogh was dancing on the razor-edge of sanity and insanity all his life. The sociologist Cesare Lombroso cited many creative men who were insane. Freud maintained that an artist was one who found in art a means of expressing innner conflict that would otherwise issue in Neurosis. Creativity was therefore taken to be a sort of emotional purgative that kept man sane and healthy. Freud's beautiful definition of an artist befits here, 'A neurotic is an artist san art,' *i.e.*, a neurotic is that artist who has not created art. His entire psycho-analytic technique was based on this theory where Catharsis played a very important role. This, however, is a very negative view of creativity. It means given no conflicts and frustrations, there would be no creativity.

iii) Creativity as Intuitive Genius—According to the viewpoint, creativity is a highly developed form of intuition. The creative person a rare specie, intuits directly and immediately. It cannot be said for definite whether this mysterious force like Intuition is a form of insight or not. The idea of the genius originated in the late Renaissance, when it was applied to explain the creative powers of such men as da Vinci, Vasari and Telesio, etc. Kant in his classical work 'The Critique of Pure Reason' says that the creativity is natural, and therefore cannot be taught. But we see now that creativity is more developable than intelligence.

iv) Creativity as a Cosmic Life Force—Darwin's theory of Evolution points out that human creativity is the manifestation of creative force inherent in life, in organic matter. This continually brings forth new species, unique, unprecedented, unrepeatable, irreversible.

As a step further, human creativity has also been seen as the expression of a universal creativity. According to A. N. Whitehead, creativity is rhythmic or cyclical, for the world consists not of a stream of single events, but rather of events that constitute actual entities, which are born, develop and die. The process of education should reflect the creativity of the universe as a whole. Thus education should be rhythmic, moving in cycles, each of which should pass through its own stages of Romance (the first encounter with the subject), Precision (in which order and system are introduced) and Generalization (where abstract principles are derived). Thus education is an inherent need of the learner, not something to be forced from outside. Therefore, the best of education is that which responds faithfully to the cosmic creative force itself. The teacher should, therefore, weed out foreign matter and prune undesirable growth. A ruthless definiteness is essential in education.

v) Creativity as Association—During the 19th century, the dominant school of Psychology in both England and America was Associationism, whose roots go back to John Locke. Still it occupies an important place in behaviourism. According to it, thinking is the association of ideas, governed by the laws of frequency, recency and vividness. New ideas are manufactured from older ones by a process of trial and error. Hence more association, more ideas and more creativity. But there can be no prediction in creativity whereas Association theory presupposes prediction. Also Associationism hardly fits in the known facts of creativity. In his book "The Sleepwalkers" a study of the great scientists of Renaissance, Arthur Koestler emphasizes again and again the seemingly irrational slips and errors that actually helped Copernicus, Kepler and Galileo in formulating their theories. The new ideas thus emerged, not from past connections, but by breaking the past connections, from probably the unconscious mind which is not determined by past connections.

vi) Gestalt Theory and Creativity—Creativity is a restructurization of patterns or Gestalts that are structurally deficient. Creative thinking begins with a problematic situation. In the absence of a given problem, the creative thinker starts with an envisaged or imagined problem. But this theory still leaves unexplained the origin, both of the envisaged Gestalt and of those original questions not directly suggested by the facts at his disposal.

vii) Psychoanalysis and Creativity—As already mentioned, according to Freud, creativity originates in a conflict within the unconscious mind. Sooner or later, the unconscious produces a solution to this conflict (also referred to as incubation). If the solution is ego-syntonic (*i.e.,* if it reinforces an activity intended by the ego or conscious part of the personality), it will issue forth in creative behaviour. If not, it will be repressed and shall emerge as Neurosis. Thus neurosis and creativity are siblings, have the name roots. The creative person thus accepts the free-rising ideas of the unconscious. One aim of Psychoanalytic therapy is to help the patient to regress of relax his ego voluntarily without fear that he will succumb to his unconscious.

viii) Neo-Psychoanalysts and Creativity—The Neo-psychoanalysts, however, reject the view that the creative person has to be emotionally disturbed. Whenever we find neurosis and creativity in the same person, we can explain that such persons create despite their neurosis, not because of neurosis. The correlation between the two may not be positive and high. Also it has been found that persons creative in the fields of Sciences, Engineering, Medicine and Agriculture, etc. are emotionally stabler than those who create poetry, literature, music, paintings and sculptory.

Also Freudian view that creativity is a recapitulation of early childhood experiences is much resented to by the existentialists like Jean Paul Sartare, Rollo May, and eclectics like J. W. Allport. So far in Freudian view, creativity like all other activities is a tension-reduction-process. But according to a more recent school of thought including E. G. Schachtel and C.R. Rogers, creativity though partly perhaps drive-reducing, is also sought as an end in itself. The person seeks not only rest but also activity; not only avoids tension but also courts it. It is more a positive view of creativity.

The main contribution of the Neo-Freudians is that Creativity is the product of the Pre-conscious, rather than the Unconscious. Creativity is a regression permitted by the ego in its own interest, and a creative person is one who can draw on his pre-conscious more freely than other people. Yet it seems that imagination, which is a very rich component of creativity, though especially strong in pre-conscious is present in some degree at all levels of mental activity. J. Krishnamoorti's saying that 'stillness of mind' and 'choiceless awareness' are most essential for becoming creative. Stillness of mind is possible only in trace, attained through hypnotism or yoga, where the ego is suspended in the foreconscious (also termed as semiconscious) for long. Ordinarily when we are awake, the ago is in the conscious sector of our mind. When we fall asleep, the ego regresses to unconscious. While awake, the unconscious cannot be talked to easily, because we can communicate only with the conscious. When asleep, the ego cannot be contacted. Thus it is only in the foreconscious state that ego can be approached and the unconscious can be tapped since it is so near the foreconscious. It is also opined that highly creative persons are those who can perform autohypnosis on them and suspend their ego in the foreconscious for long in order to communicate effectively with their unconscious. That is a state of extreme suggestibility, extreme concentration and extreme relaxation. There are a number of studies indicating that certain behavioural changes can be brought about only by making suggestions in the state of 'trance' where ego is suspended in the foreconscious, Foreconscious is the most fertile ground where creativity can grow abundantly.

ix) Creativity as Biosociation—Arthur Koestler points out creativity involves multifarious processes which share a common pattern of *Biosociation* which is the connecting of previously unrelated levels of experience or frames of reference. In creative thinking a man thinks simultaneously on more than one plane of experience, whereas in routine thinking, he follows the path set by past associations. However, this viewpoint is also open to controversy because creativity is one of the Psychological issues which is yet to be finalised finally understood and interpreted.

XI.5 Assessment of Creativity

Since the Concept of creativity is growing and the assessment techniques are similarly in the growing stage. However in assessing creativity we involves personality assessment and intelligence techniques. Although Torrance believes that no satisfactory personality instrument suitable for use in guiding creative development has been developed, he lists a number of already well known instruments that have proved helpful to teachers and counsellors of creative children. They include the Strong Vocational Interest Blank, the Allport-Vernon-Lindey Study of Values, and the Minnesota Multiphasic Personality Inventory.

Most of the present instruments available for measuring creative thinking are developed after Guilford's conception of divergent thinking, which involves, fluency, flexibility, originality, sensitivity, redefinition and elaboration. Thus, Guilford used tests which measure fluency, flexibility, redefinition, elaboration and sensitivity to problems. One test of fluency asks the examinee to produce items of information in responses to given information as rapidly as he can, such as to list as many things as he can that are white, gift and edible, or to generate a list of four moral sentences; or to combine figures like a circle, a rectangle, a triangle and a trapezoid to produce more complex objects.

Flexibility is measured through an unusual test in which the examinee is to see new and unusual uses for old objects and methods. Each usual use of a newspaper such as to swat flies, to light a fire, to line shelves, stuff packages or to wrap garbage, reclassifies it according to some particular property and the flexibility is shown in reality going one class to another.

The ability to elaborate is measured through planning Elaboration Test, "possible jobs" and "Decoration." The first test calls for elaboration of a plan, for which only an outline of a major step is given. The second test involves giving of a relatively simple but realistic picture such as setting a sum to which the examinee is to respond by lasting occupations on groups of people for which that may serve as a symbol.

Redefinition is measured through tests which involve shifts of meaning on uses of objects, "which of the following objects could be most reasonably used in making a needle: among book, fish wheel, pansy? The bone of a fish, when given an eye, would serve the purpose. Here an object on part of a subject must be modified in order to use it in some new way.

For measuring sensitivity to problems, one test asks the examinee to give things that are wrong with such common devices as telephones, refrigerators of electric irons. Another asks what is wrong with social institutions such as divorce and tipping. Being sensitive to the defects and deficiencies is the apparent quality involved.

Gatzel and Jackson adopted some of Guilford' tests with innovations here and there, thus, the measure used by them is word association in which the examinee is required to give as many associations as possible of a family common word such as 'stock' 'ball'. A second measure is 'Uses of things'. This includes giving of original use of a common object such as a brick or tooth pick.

A third measure is Hidden Shapes. The examinee is shown a card with a simple geometric figure on it. He is then required to find that figure in a more complex pattern or form.

A fourth measure is 'Fables'; here the examinee is to suggest three different endings to incomplete short fables; a 'moralistic' one, a 'humorous' and a 'such' one.

In addition to the above four measures which were adopted from Guilford, Gatzel and Jackson constructed one of their own; 'Make up problems'. The examinee is required to make as many mathematical problems as he can on the basis of information given in a complex paragraph. Scores depend upon number, appropriatness and originality of the problem.

Torrance and his associates also adopted some of Guilford measures in their Minnesota. Tests of creative thinking. Torrance have developed;

The Product Improvement test'. In this case the subject is handed a toy and is required to suggest improvements in it.

In the Ask and Guess Test, the subject is given a picture about which he is to ask questions that cannot be answered by examination of the picture and to formulate hypotheses about possible causes and consequences of the pictured behaviour.

In the just suppose Test, the subject is to, imagine all the things that elaboration.

Wallack and Kogan have objected to the work of Gatzel and Jackson and also that of Torrance. Their main objection is that not only the tests of creativity used by Gatzel and Jackson or by Torrance correlate significantly with the traditional tests of intelligence, but also are not highly correlated with one another. As such their tests do not highly correlated with one another. As such their tests do not seem to measure a pure or unitary cognitive dimension called creativity.

Wallack and Kogan therefore devised methods of asessing creativity which did not have the above defects. These methods are based on the number and uniqueness of associational responses given by pupils. They include:

1. Instances: The pupil is asked to generate possible instances of a class concept, e.g. "Name all the sound things you can think of".
2. Alternate Use: "Tell me all about the different ways you can use a shoe."
3. Similiarities between two specified objects, e.g., "tell me all the ways in which a cat and a mouse are alike".
4. Pattern Meanings: "I shall show you some drawings after looking at each one, tell me all the things you think each complete drawing could be."
5. Line meanings: "I am going to show you some lines and after you have looked at each one I want you to tell what the whole line, not just a part of it makes you think of."

Baron and his associates at the University of California have developed a battery of tasks for asessing originality among college students and adults. Among the tasks described in the literature are: Mosaic Constructions, Anagram test, Drawing completion, Figure preference test, and Ink Blot test.

Torrance Test: Torrance has also developed some non-test ways of identifying the creativity gifted. For example, the students may have self rating or the teachers may rate them—on Torrance's check-list containing eighty four characteristics. Some of these are inquistive, non-conforming, full of ideas, experimental and so on.

XI.6 Conditions Responsible for the Promotion of Creativity

The creativity is such an important psychological phenomena which can revolutionise the world. As a result psychologists are making sincere efforts to identify the concept of creativity and the conditions which may promote the creativity. The existing literature reveals that conditions promoting creativity can be studied as:

i) Content material which makes for creativity lies within the conceptual ability of the child. (In the absence of more precise definition and classification of the concept involved the difficulty level of the language demanded by the material may be taken as indicating difficulty level. If the subject can be expressed in language appropriate to the age level, it can be for the time being assumed that conceptually, it can be handled by the child.) Material which is too difficult, and too verbal, decreases creativity.

ii) Material which lends itself to being manipulated, preferably not only in the physical sense but also in the 'mental' sense, makes for creativity. Material which can be presented in concrete form e.g, science or nature study material lends itself well to this purpose, while material which is merely verbal is less suitable.

iii) Material should be related to day-to-day needs, interests, and activities of the child. It should arise from real life situations.

iv) Overemphasis on drill, memory work, simple repetition of skills, over discipline, excessive direction, and conformity pairs creativeness.

v) Creativity requires adequate time to develop. But in school days programmes the time is short periods (15 to 20) minutes creativity can hardly flourish. Creative work often requires longer periods of time to initiate and carry through lines of action.

vi) Excessive time-stress upon a child reduces creativity which often calls for an unhurried tempo in the day's affairs.

vii) Some sort of balance is needed between input and output— between impression and expression. The child must come in contact with problem situations (i.e., stimulations of an intellectual kind) and there must be interaction or feedback between the problem situation and the child's creative productions aimed at its solution, which, if successful, terminates the problem situation.

viii) Emphasis on creative work implies an appropriate set of standards by which the child's productions are to be judged (rewarded). This involves respect for the child's efforts, a flexibility in our judgements, and possibly a departure from the traditional, fussy and pedantic attitude of many teachers with an unreasonable demand upon neat work.

ix) Subject-matter which is verbal-conceptual, which cannot be expressed and presented in tangible concrete form or in practical activities, is more appropriate to the later levels of education. In the Piagetian sense much of literature, grammar, and history are quite 'mature', more mature than some branches of science.

x) Priority should be given to content material and to activities which foster and promote creativity—particularly content which is capable of being 'manipulated' and to activities which are related to current needs and which avoids 'time-stress.'

Similarly Ladislav Duric has described the following conditions to be created by a teacher for the development of creativity. The conditions can be described as:

Selection and discription of learning material. The selection and description of learning materials that would enhance the learner's creativity. There are many psychologists who deal with this problem, but more particularly in the out-of-school context and not so much in connection with pupils learning directly during a lesson in the classroom.

Learning Medium

Learning materials in mathematics and the language of instruction have received maximum attention from psychologists and educators. In modern teaching the pupils, under the guidance of the teacher, act with considerable freedom and are able to handle objects and teaching aids with liberty. Even though not result in uniformity. The uniformity of education (disliked by highly creative pupils) occurs when the relation between the individual and the community is wrongly conceived and carried out in practice; and there are times when this still happens.

XI.7 Role of a Teacher and Creativity

Psychologists are of the view that role of a teacher in developing creativity can hardly be ignored. As the teacher encourages the contious promoting creativity in following possible ways:

a) -the creative pupil participates in the activities of class, assuming a significant position or collaborates actively;

b) -the sincerity and broad interests of the creative pupil are used to advantage by his classmates;

c) -the creative pupil should be aware that the strong desire for self-expression can only be tolerated in a healthy community;

d) -the creative pupil, full of practical jokes and wit, may evoke a happy atmosphere in the whole community, thus suppressing the tension and anxiety present in other pupils, and contributing to the joyful solution of problems;

e) -the enterprising spirit of the creative pupil and his activity may in many cases be profitable for the community as a whole;

f) -acceptance on the part of his classmates reinforces the creative pupil's personality, even though this may not be the principal motivation towards further creative activity;

g) -the independent judgement, intellectual abilities and independent opinions of the creative pupil may serve as an example for other, less creative members of the class.

In brief, we refer to the statement that a good community of pupils should not normally be disrupted by the creativity and creative thinking of its individual pupils. If there are some contradictions, they must be conceived dialectically as a driving force of development by creative individuals in favour both of themselves and of the whole class.

In connection with the education of people who think and act creatively in both the interests of the community as well as their own, there are still some psychological and educational problems which have not been entirely resolved. This is perfectly comprehensible since the psychology of creativity is a new, young discipline, while we already know more about the psychology of education in the community, though even here there are still plenty of opportunities for further research. In connection with creative education or education of a creative and community-oriented personality, the following issues deserve attention: (a) the relation between creativity and the community; (b) the possibilities of adjusting education for creativity with education for the community.

XI.8 Role of Community to Promote Creativity

Community education and creative education in school represent two aspects of one and the same thing. i.e. the whole complex of education. Further development of society requires the education of both social and creative people. Of course, the level of creativity and creative thinking of every pupil is not and cannot be the same.

It is interesting that pre-school-age children manifest both creativity and a community spirit. We can observe their creative play in the group of their companions. What games can they make up together? What 'philosophical' questions can they ask and how can they answer them together?

In school the pupil becomes a member of a formal group within which informal sub-groups may arise and, only later on, under the influence of the teacher and the youth organizations, a proper community is formed. Until that time conflicts may occur between highly creative pupils and the others. These conflicts may be provoked by certain personality traits of highly creative pupils not shared with other less creative, but more social, pupils.

Possibilities for the Creative and Collective Education of Pupils

The development of a collective feeling or a social ethic passes through certain natural stages. For example, we know that the infant is more likely to conform than the adolescent. With the small child the acknowledgement of adults is of great importance, often greater than the fulfilment of the task itself. The adolescent is in general more non-conformist: he/she longs for independence, is discontented, is critical towards adults, etc. But even at this stage of development the role of education is decisive.

In properly conceived social education there is no conformity. When there is respect for individual characteristics and when differing levels of creativity and creative thinking among pupils are tolerated, then social education will their activity is guided, they are encouraged to discover new knowledge and formulate it by themselves. Teaching of this kind provides them not only with factual knowledge, but also helps them to familiarize themselves and to take note of objects and phenomena, to approach problems without fear, in fact, to seek them out and to solve them. They are taught to feel joy in solving the tasks set them, and to be curious and open. Their interest is aroused. Besides intellectual development, social relations among the pupils are also fostered. Pupils get to know their abilities and compare them with their school mates, they gain self-confidence, have no fear and learn to learn from their mistakes. Instruction of this kind influences the development of a pupil's personality as a whole, not only on an intellectual level. Therefore one of the main tasks of psychologists is to help with the creation of new textbooks, so that they contain as many different tasks as possible.

XI.9 Developing Creative Environment

Learning aimed at the development of creative abilities requires a special psychic atmosphere. Even here the principle of interaction between personality and environment is in force. This means that the more creative the atmosphere of the milieu in which the pupil learns and is educated, the better the conditions for the development of his/her creative abilities and vice versa.

Traditional schools did not make it possible even for creative teachers to cultivate a creative atmosphere in the school, the class or during lessons. Modernization of the school system should cater for this aspect. However, these are only resources. Their utilization for the development of creative thinking among pupils, with the aim of setting up a creative atmosphere in the school, requires a change in the approach of teachers, school administrators and educational authorities.

Education for creativity and the proper encouragement of a creative atmosphere in school necessitates the inclusion of the *psychology of creativity* into the curricula of all teacher training institutions, within post-graduate training courses for teachers, and refresher courses for educational managers. Literature on this subject is already available in the majority of countries.

The Creative Pupil in the Classroom

One of the basic tasks of the school is to educate creative personalities, creative workers for every field of economic, cultural and social life. The power of an individual lies in being a member of the community, and the power of the community is ensured by the activity of the greatest number of socially oriented and highly creative individuals.

Steps Involved in Creativity Development

Helmholtz stated that creative thinking passes through a series of well defined stages. Further, Walter gave the names to the stages of creative 'thinking': viz; 'Preparation', 'Incubation', Illumination,' and 'Verification'. By these terms they are known even viz; today.

a) Preparation: It is the stage, when the problem-solving becomes acquainted or familiar with the various features of the problem and begins to assemble the ideas. Such preparation may, however, also involve the gathering of new data or information bearing upon the problem. We also take stock what resources we already have in our stock and many associations are involved. Certain suggestions are accepted and certain suggestions are discarded. Gradually, more definite attitude is taken.

b) Incubation: Then second stage of creative thinking is known as Incubation. In this phase, the problem is allowed to drop for the time being and the mind is directed to some other channel. And then a renewed attention is paid to problem which results in promoting solution. This stage of incubation varies greatly in nature and duration.

c) Illumination: This is exactly the stage, when we hit upon the solution. Though this stage comes after intellectual passivity, it may be added that we do not actually drop the problem but we think creatively during that rest period or gap, as we are to go ahead.

d) Verification: This is the last stage of creativity. The proposed solution is worked out in a more specific way and may be applied and tested.

XI.10 Educational Implications of Creativity

Now the question is how to train the minds of the students for creative thinking, reasoning and problem solving? Although there is no simple formula for improving thinking, it will be worthwhile to look at some of the conditions of effective and creative thinking. All of us would like to make efficient use of our thought processes in order to solve problems better and make better adjustment in the society.

Creativity can be Implied in Education in the Following Ways

1. *Remoulding and Reshaping the Contents of Education.* The society is dynamic in nature. It is ever changing. This changing nature of the society results in the changing demands, which make the society more complex. And when the distance between the countries of world is shrinking day by day, it becomes all the more complex. So the outdated curriculum based on the traditional system of education is needed no more and hence the need for remoulding and reshaping the contents. So the entire content of Indian Education be remoulded and reshaped. It must have various problems in it. These problems must be well-graded and in accordance with the intelligence level or mental make up of the children. It should be related to life as well to provoke thinking and reasoning creatively.

2. *Attitude of the Teacher:* The attitude of the teacher must help and make the children to think creatively. He should not believe in spoon-feeding. He must have patience and self control and be able to provide opportunities to the students to think for themselves and encourage them to present some novel and appreciable ideas. The teacher must be a thinker himself and he must give suitable praise to the student-inventors.

3. *Scientific Spirit:* Scientific spirit need to be inculcated in the students to provide them with good habits, which result in scientific approach to teaching-learning process.

4. *Methods of Teaching:* Methods of education should be changed. The contents of education must have scientific facts and the student should learn by doing and through experiences. Modern methods like problem solving, project methods, learning through experience must be encouraged.

XI.11 Distinction Between Intelligence and Creativity

J.P. Guilford distinguishes clearly between the intellectual operations of *divergent thinking* (which includes characteristics of fluency, flexibility and foresight) and *convergent thinking* (which represents the kind of abilities often measured by a standard intelligence test).

The characteristics which all IQ test items have in common, are that they all have *one* correct answer and they result in a conversing of the problem under consideration to *one* appropriate response.

So too is the operation of convergent thinking. In any situation that provokes thinking, the person has the tendency to find the *one* most appropriate idea agreeing with existing social norms. In contrast to this, the creativity "test items stress the importance of many answers. Indeed, one of the criteria for successful performance on these tests is the number of answers given. Such factors as originality and flexibility are also scored by evaluating the quality and direction of responses to such questions as, "How could we improved a toy dog?"

As the new tests of fluency, flexibility and foresight have been put into greater use, it has been discovered that students who score very high on these tests are not the same as those who score high on IQ tests. The difference between these students encompasses not only their school performance and behaviour, but extends through family attitudes and values, their self-concept, their attitudes towards school and education and their projected future.

If we make a correlation table of Creativity *vs* Intelligence over a representative sample of student population, the latter appearing at the X-axis then we find some vacant cells and low frequencies in the top left corner, but not in the bottom right one. It means that the highly creative are usually intelligent (above IQ 115 to 120) but *vice versa* may not be true. In brief, Creativity represents a higher level of man's intellectual abilities than intelligence. The difference lies in the fact that creative ability means being familiar not only with new problems, with selecting ways of resolving them, with the transition from one situation to another, with the mobilization of previous experience (as is the case with intelligence), but principally with the 'invention' of new, original and unusual solutions, and, what is more, with the identification of new problems. This represents the divergent way of thinking, which can be measured by tests of creativity (creative thinking).

Creativeness is noted for original processes and original products. Intelligence measured by intelligence tests requires the very opposite, namely an identical response from all who set out to solve the set task correctly. In classical tests of intelligence there is no scope for originality, for perceiving things in new ways, for independent observation of problems and the formation of new problem situations. Tests designed to measure the level of creativity are quite different. They are constructed with the idea of provoking divergent thinking to a maximum degree.

As a matter of fact both the creativity and intelligence are mental abilities but we can not say with confidence that there is any definite relationship between them.

Howeven, in trying to resolve the relationship between creativity and intelligence, the authors agreed in distinguishing four basic groups: (a) a high level of creativity and of intelligence: (b) a high level of creativity and low level of intelligence; (c) a low level of creativity and high level of intelligence; (d) a low level of creativity and of intelligence.

While it is generally accepted that high intelligence may be combined with a lower level of creativity, a high level of creative thinking does not usually occur in combination with a very low level of intelligence. In brief, it can be said that creativity is the ability to create where as intelligence is the ability essential to create some thing.

XI.12 Learning Exercises

1. Discuss the meaning and definitions of creativity
2. What are the important characteristics of creativity and discuss how these can be developed?
3. Describe the principles of creativity.
4. Describe theories of creativity.
5. Discuss the techniques of assessment of creativity.
6. Discuss the role of teacher and community in the development of creativity among our students.
7. Discuss the educational implications of creativity in education.
8. Discuss the suitable conditions for the promotion of creativity.

XII
Exceptional Children

XII.1 Meaning and Definitions

The term exceptional is misunderstood to refer only to gifted or talented individuals. Swanson and Willis reports that we can clarify the term through the following definitions. The study of exceptionality involves all children and youth who possess conditions that constitute significant departures from the societally defined average, or norm, in (1) intellectual, (2) educational, (3) emotional, (4) Social, (5) Sensory, or (6) Physical or health capacities. As a consequence, special knowledge and services are required to aid the exceptional children in realising their maximum potential. Exceptional children are : (1) The intellectually different (whether mentally retarded or gifted), (2) The societally neglected, (3) The learning disabled, (4) The emotionally disturbed, (5) Those adjudged to be delinquent, (6) Those with speech and language problems, (7) The hearing disabled (whether deaf or hard of hearing), health disabled.

Jitender Mohan points out that an exceptional child is one who deviates intellectually, physically, socially or emotionally so markedly from what is considered to be normal growth and development, that he cannot receive maximum benefit from a regular school programme and requires special class or supplementary instruction and services.

Panda is of the view that the term "Exceptional Children" refers to children whose needs are very different from those of the majority of children in society. These children deviate from average children to the extent they cannot receive classroom instruction in regular schools. Panda further points out that exceptional children are handicapped in one extreme and of the gifted at the other.

Kirk points out that exceptional child is he who deviates from the normal or average child in mental, physical and social characteristics to such an extent that he requires a modification of school practices or special educational services in order to develop to his maximum capacity, or supplementary instruction.

Barbe has stated that exceptional children are those children who differ from the average to an extent that their differences warrant some type of special school adjustment either within the regular classroom on 'in' special classes.

Similarly, Crow and Crow say: "exceptional is applied to trait or to a person possessing the trait if the extent of deviation from normal possession of that trait is so great that because of it, the individual warrants and receives special attention from his behaviour responses and activities are thereby affected." Crow and Crow further clarified the exceptional children as they are having exception in three fields:

Exceptional Children

(1)	(2)	(3)
The physically handicapped	*The mentally retarded*	*Creative and gifted*

From the above definitions, it is evident that children could be called exceptional who have special abilities or unusual limitations and who are in the need of special methods and programmes for their training and education. In other words, it be said that exceptional children are those who differ from the average to such degree in physical or psychological characteristics. That school programmes designed for the majority of the children do not afford them the opportunity for all-round adjustment and optimum progress and who therefore, need either special instruction or in some cases special ancillary service or both to achieve a level commensurate with their respective abilities. Study of exceptional children is so vast that it include even children with mild learning and behavioural disparities who may present some problems to some teachers in the class and who may like these disturbing children to be sent to special teacher in a school or to a special school. Therefore, it can be said that exceptional behaviour of exceptional children has different types of exceptions. To deal and each type of exceptional behaviour of a child, a teacher first of all requires to identify the types of exception and has to prepare a programme for teaching the type of exceptional child's behaviour.

XII.2 Types of Exceptional Children

Different authors have classified exceptional children into different types. Prof. Udey Shankar (1976) reports that there are 12 types of exceptional children *viz.;* (1) gifted, (2) educable mentally retarded (3) the trainable retarded, (4) the socially maladjusted, (5) emotionally disturbed, (6) speech impaired, (7) deaf, (8) partially deaf or hard of hearing, (9) blind, (10) partially blind, (11) cripled and (12) the chronic health cases.

Similarly, Panda (1997) reports that there are fourteen categories of exceptional children such as :

1. The educable mentally retarded,
2. The trainable mentally retarded,
3. The profound or severely mentally retarded,
4. The visually handicapped,
5. The hearing handicapped,
6. The emotionally handicapped,
7. The disabled learner,
8. The physically or neurologically handicapped,
9. The speech and language handicapped,
10. The slow learner,
11. The gifted,
12. The creative,
13. The multiple handicapped,
14. The socially handicapped.

Crow and Crow has tried to categorised the behaviour of exceptional children in to three broad categories *viz,* physical, mental and gifted. They further reported that each category of exceptional behaviour has number of manifestations which can be studied as :

Exceptional Children

Physically Handicapped	Mentally Handicapped	Creative and Gifted

The classification of exceptional children can be further sub-classified in to different sub categories. However, the details of each category of exceptional children can be studied as:

Physically Handicapped Children

Physically Handicapped children are those exceptional children who have physically exceptions. In other words, an individual who is afflicted with a physical impairment that, in any way, limits or inhibits his participation in normal activities may be referred to as physically handicapped. In other words, we can say that any person having a disability is called handicapped. A disability consists of the objectively defined impairment of structure or function. For example, the loss of vision in one eye or the hearing in one ear is a disability.

The extent to which any disability handicaps its possessor always depends upon circumstances. There are some disabilities which do not operate really as a handicap. For example, colour blindness is a handicap for a navigation officer at sea, a car or train driver on the road or rail. But it is not a handicap in securing a job not requiring colour vision. A stammerer cannot be a good orator. Therefore, he a stammerer can not be a good lawyer. But he may be a good scientist. Of course, some of the disabilities can be mitigated with the aid of sophisticated instruments like hearing aids for hard-of-hearing and self-propelled chairs for parapalgies.

As a rule, a handicap is partial disability. In handicapped children the disability usually affects one organ, sense or system, the rest remaining unimpaired, or being even better than average. The handicap does not necessarily reduce all the power and abilities, though it does restrict their range. For example, a blind child may have strong legs, but he will find it difficult to walk in unfamiliar places. It is important to note that some disabilities can produce secondary handicaps. For example, a child with normal speech organs but with other severe defects is likely to have speech defects.

Handicappedness impairs the functioning abilities of individuals. There are different types of physical handicappedness which impairs the behaviour of exceptional children. Let us study various forms of physical handicapped exceptional behaviour of children influencing behaviour:

1. Visually Handicapped Children

Blindness is regarded as the most severe and traumatic of the physical handicaps. The visually handicapped have always been the favoured group compared to those with other types of disabilities. Social and educational provisions have been made considering them as the most important group. Special rights and privileges are given to them. This group has attracted more public concern than any other category of the handicapped.

Blindness is caused by certain environmental an genetic agents. These etiological agents include infections, diseases, accidents, poisoning, tumours and cancer. However, much of the incidence of blindness is attributed to prenatal factors. The blinds are easily identified, but the partially sighted require a detailed examination. Total blindness is an obvious condition, easy to recognise and define, but partial blindness is rather difficult to recognise and define. Blindness is viewed from different angles. There is "educational blindness", "legal blindness", "medical blindness," "occupational blindness", etc.

The professionals and the authorities have two important objectives: *(i)* to prevent blindness and other types of visual impairment by finding the causes: diseases, malformations, accidents, etc. and *(ii)* to make adequate provisions for those already affected.

Children, with a defective vision, may be classified into two categories educationally. These are *(i)* The blind, whose vision is so defective that they cannot be educated through visual methods; they have to be educated through channels other than vision; *(ii)* The partially shighted are able to utilise vision in acquiring educational skills. Partially sighted children are those who have defective vision even after correction. Adaptation of the visual materials and special methods of instruction are required for them. While a partially sighted child can utilise vision as an important channel of learning, a totally blind child must rely on other approaches, primarily auditory and tactual. For this reason, a distinction between normal vision, partial sight and blindness is made on the basis of visual equity.

Studies reveal that we do find exceptional children who have vision and audition is impaired. Education to such children is a problem. Here the role of a teacher becomes very complex. He often becomes a friend to the handicapped child and provides him constant social contact. In the first stage, education is directed at establishing contacts with the external world and arousing interest in learning. For this purpose, special educational programmes for the blind have been devised. Here the emphasis is placed on the individualisation of instruction and formation of small groups. That means the class must consist of four children only. Here the special educational needs of the blind are learning of braille, extensive use of auditory, tactual and kinesthetic experiences and special mobility training. With the help of large springs and magnification, the partially educated children are educated. Now-a-days, sheltered workshops are playing a vital role in vocational training and employment of the blind. Previously, the vocational emphasis at these workshops was almost exclusively on things like brooms, rugs and brushes. But now, the workshops often subcontract for various industrial concerns. In Bombay, one such workshop has been set up at Worli. It imparts good vocational training and employment to visually handicapped individuals.

2. Aurally Handicapped Children

Verbal communication and speech development through hearing are major sensory pathways for a human being. If a child hears imperfectly, there is every possibility that he will speak incorrectly. Hearing also influences learning and other aspects of maturation. If a hearing impairment is detected in early childhood, there is every chance of its being corrected. If detected late, there is every chance of the child developing a functional disability.

Auditory defects can be found in either one or both ears. Sometimes children have partial auditory impairment or no power of hearing at all. Some terms are used to denote auditory impairments. These are: "deaf", "hard of hearing", "partially deaf" and "deaf mute". However, no classification has been found totally correct. Some of the major variables are the degree and type of hearing loss and age of its onset.

The term "deaf" is applied only to a person who has never had hearing or who lost his hearing before he learnt to speak. A person who loses his hearing after he has acquired speech is known as "hard of hearing". Deaf children have a profound hearing loss. They have to be educated through a sense modality other than the ear. These children can be placed under separate categories according to the onset of the hearing loss. Children born deaf are known as "congenitally deaf" and children who are born with normal hearing but later lose it are called "adventitiously deaf". "Hard of hearing" children have slight, marginal and moderate losses. They are educated through the auditory channel.

Types of Hearing Defects

Hearing impairment has its various manifestation. Each type of impairment of hearing has its special effect in developing a type of behaviour rather a pattern of life. The aurally handicapped children are subdivided according to the organic hearing loss. These are as follows:

(a) Conductive Hearing Loss. This is the most common hearing impairment among children. In this case there is reduction in the loudness of sound so that its clarity is distorted. This often results from pathological changes in the middle ear due to congenital or acquired defects of the ear. If it is mild, then a surgical or medical therapy is sufficient to cure it. Proper and timely treatment of actual infections in the middle ear and the prevention of chronic infections of the ear will often greatly reduce the incidence of hearing defects. Hearing aids and sound amplification systems are also conducive to mitigate conductive defects.

(b) Sensori-neural Hearing Loss. This abnormality is generally caused by defects in the inner ear or in the auditory nerve. Medical or surgical therapy is of no use in curing it. Hearing aids employed for the amplification of sound are also of no help. Here, the sound is conducted without any difficulty, but the problem lies in analysing or perceiving its property.

The most important therapy for children suffering from sensori-neural defects is educational. Hearing aids, auditory training, lip-reading and language training can help children having moderate defects. However, special schooling is needed for children with profound hearing impairments.

(c) Psychogenic Hearing Loss. Psychogenic hearing impairment is purely psychological. Exaggerated symptoms of hearing impairment are often shown by the child. Very often, there is a history of ear infection which appears to act as a shock organ for localisation of the psychic symptom. Sometimes, under a stressful situation, the child may unconsciously develop hearing loss as an escape from what according to him is an intolerable situation. It is a very difficult job to distinguish between organic defects and psychogenic losses. Appropriate audiological techniques and meticulous observation can often help to bring out a correct diagnosis.

(d) Central Auditory Defects. Central auditory defects impairs the listening ability of a child. The nature of the defects are extremely complex. Their causes and pathogenesis are not known. Children having them seem to be aware of sound but are unable to get its meaning. So they cause severe communication problems. During early infancy, use of certain life-saving drugs can also affect the auditory system.

Besides, some children even during early age have hearing problems due to genetic reasons. It has been observed that some hearing defects are caused by disease, trauma or accidents for instance, measles, mumps and scarlet fever etc. cause hearing defects. Defects in the auditory mechanism are also found to have been caused by typhoid fever and pneumonia. In early childhood, deafmess is caused by encephalitis ormeningitis. Chronic middle ear infection (*oitis media*) is another etiological factor contributing to deafness. Certain traumatic experiences, lack of oxygen at the time of birth and accidents are known to cause deafness. Studies reveal that psychological and emotional factors are also responsible for deafness. Very often psychogenic deafness is confused with malingering. But it can be detected by audiological tests.

To educate the hearing impaired children special type of schooling. In educating the hearing impaired children normal type of curriculum selected. By adequate educational and training, persons with hearing defects can be helped and later employed in all types of jobs not requiring much hearing capacity. At present, they hold semi-skilled and unskilled jobs. They often work as tailors, clerks, painters, typists and carpenters.

Sometimes, we show a lack of interest in and sympathy for aurally handicapped children. We become impatient towards them. Children having mild hearing defects often give the impression that they are inattentive, mentally retarded, clumsy and unmotivated.

3. Speech Handicaped Children

Clear speech is considered important for communication. The communication is an essential feature of interaction. Human interaction involves language. Most people confuse 'speech' with 'language'. As we see, quite a wide range of speech patterns is considered normal. When the speech of an individual differs significantly from that of others and it affects communication, it is diagnosed as a speech defect. The number of children suffering from speech defects is much more than the number of those having any other handicap.

Development of speech and language depends upon the speech mechanism and the psychological environment in which the child lives in. There are physical, social and psychological conditions which greatly affect the normal development of a child. These conditions can disrupt the development of the speech and language skills of the child ultimately.

Defective speech results impairment in communication. Impairment in speech because of speech defects which are of different type. The speech defect may be categorised according to such major symptoms as articulation disorders, voice disorders, delayed speech, stammering and disturbances of rhythm. Another typology is based on the cause according to which it may be organic or functional.

Organic causes include speech handicaps due to palatal defects, dental irregularities, paralysis, tumours in the larynx and brain damage, etc. results to cause the following speech defects among exceptional children:

(a) Disorders of Articulation. The symptoms of this type of disorder include distortion, omission, addition or substitution of speech sounds. Very often it includes the mispronunciation of an entire word or words. This is a defect which is most commonly found among children. Statistics reveal that 70 to 80 per cent of speech defects are of this kind. In young children, this defect appears as immature speech. However, a good number of children soon outgrow it.

(b) Disorders of Voice (Phonation). This type of disorder is found more often in adults than in children. It includes marked deviations in terms of loudness, quality, pitch or intensity of sounds. In addition, some other anomalies like breathiness, huskiness, nasality and hoarseness are also found. The causes may be emotional, vocal abuse, overuse or infections. Tension and shocks in life are also contributory factors.

(c) Delayed Speech. Among children, the frequency of delayed speech is much higher than any other defects in communication. The chief causes of delayed speech are hearing loss, mental retardation, cerebral dysfunction, emotional disturbances and environmental deprivation. Very often, children are not able to speak at the usual age due to lack of motivation. Professional help should be sought for the treatment and diagnosis of delayed speech.

(d) Stuttering and Stammering. Stuttering is a type of repetitive speech. Very often stuttering is confused with stammering. These are most serious forms of speech disorders. They are chiefly caused by emotional difficulties,

fear of failure, fear of authority, anxiety, frustration, insecurity, hostility, overprodding by adults, etc. Ridiculing the children will aggravate the situation.

Stuttering is often considered a disorder of rhythm. In stammering, there appears to be a difficulty in producing any speech sound. A stutterer can articulate, but he is unable to enunciate the first consonant letter of a word. He, therefore, says : "g-g-garden". The situation becomes embarrassing for both the sufferer and others with whom he desires to communicate and this tends to intensify the difficulty.

In both the cases, the affected children need to be treated by a specialist. Studies reveal that stammering does not cause any handicap in intellectual capacities. Many persons reach high position in spite of the fact that they are stammerers. It has been found that between the ages of 2½ and 3½, stuttering is often due to a lack of correction between thought and language. In grown-up children it appears as a result of poor vocabulary, over-protective, dominant and overanxious parents.

(e) Disorders Associated with Cerebral Palsy. Children who suffer from cerebral palsy, *i.e.* spastics, as well as athetoid and ataxic children develop speech defects. In spastic children, articulatory deviations are found. The athetoid child shows slurring in rhythm. The cerebral palsy children often lack the motivation to speak.

Studies reveal that more male children than female children develop speech defects. The etiological factors accounting for this speech disorders include anatomical defects, disturbed feelings, attitudes and emotions. Faulty language habits due to social pressures and unsatisfactory speech models are other contributory factors. Further, it has been reported that speech defects are not seriously taken care of in the developing countries whereas, in developed countries the speech defects among children is well taken care off.

Mentally Retarded Children

The second category of exceptional children is mentally retarded children. The term mentally retarded means deficiency with respect to mental ability of mental function. Generally, we consider mental retardation as a disease. Earlier some people described it as a 'condition'. At one time mentally retarded children were rejected by society as they were thought to be possessed by demons. Now a days, there is greater acceptance of and awareness about them among the general public. Certainly, mental retardation is a very complex medical, social and educational problem. It presents a strong challenge to our sophisticated society. It is a condition of arrest or in complete development of mind existing before the age of 18 years.

Hebber (1962) was the first to attempt a standard definition of "mental retardation" taking intelligence adaptive behaviour and developmental level into consideration. A more adequate definition was developed by the American Association of Mental Deficiency (AAMD) in 1973. It states: "Mental retardation refers to significantly sub-average general intellectual functioning existing concurrently with deficits in adaptive behaviour and manifested during developmental period." This developmental period includes the life span from birth to 18 years of age.

The study of mental retardation began with the work of Itard, a French physician. He tried to develop his ideas while studying the case of "The Wild Boy of Aveyron". Latter, Seguin focussed on the appropriate educational placement of and provision for the low intelligent group of children.

Mental retardation implies impairment in intelligence from early life and inadequate mental development throughout the growing period. Studies have shown that 75 per cent of the retarded have no physical disability. They have sensori-defects, language disorders and neuro-muscular impairment.

The above discussion regarding mental retarded behaviour of children makes us to understand that mental retardation means the declining/deficient mental abilities of an individual . The decline in mental abilities are of different types. Each type has its own implication in training the behaviour of a child. Mentally retarded children are of four types *viz.* Mild retarded, Moderately retarded, Severely retarded and Profoundly retarded.

XII.3 Needs of Exceptional Children

Exceptional children are the children with exceptions in their physical, mental and psychomotor abilities. It is evident that exceptional children would be having exceptional rather special needs. Practically speaking that these children have special educational needs and the term special needs children is also used simultaneously for exceptional children. A brief discussion on this point is imperative.

The concept "children with special educational needs" is of British origin. Prior to 1944, provision of education was made on the basis of a specific handicap *i.e.,* visual and hearing impairment, essentially through charitable initiatives. The emphasis was more on training than on education. Originally, provision for children with sensory and physical disabilities and mental handicaps were made, and subsequently extended to those with emotional and behavioural problems.

Behaviour of exceptional children need special education services. To organise special educational service for exceptional children we need to depend upon the following factors:

(a) In institutions where special educational programmes are to be taken up, trained professional personnel should be appointed by the authorities. They should include teachers, teacher educators, administrators, consultants, psychiatrists, psychotherapists, psychoanalysts, speech therapists and physiotherapists.

(b) Special courses of study suiting different areas of exceptionality should be prepared by experts. Depending on the severity of the problem, specialised courses should be undertaken for mental retardation, giftedness, deafness blindness, orthopaedic handicaps, cerebral palsy, etc.

(c) Exceptional children should be provided greater facilities than normal children. These should include special building features, equipment, materials and crafts.

Above all exceptional children need a careful, planned education by a specialised teacher in a specialised teaching learning situation. Therefore, exceptional children are to be taught in special classrooms, study courses should be taught by experts. Recently, stress has been laid on special education programmes development for exceptional children as a part of the general education. Earlier, special education was confined to those exceptional children who were assigned to special classes. Now special programmes laying emphasis on separate special classes is discharged as much as possible.

XII.4 Objectives of Education for the Exceptional Children

Chintamani, points out that exceptional children are special type of children. Each exceptional child has its own type of problem which needs to attended carefully. In dealing with the problems of exceptional children we need to follow the below mentioned objectives of special education:

(a) The most important goal of special education is to reach the maximum level of effectiveness in school subjects.

(b) Both physical and mental hygiene of the handicapped school children are to be considered.

(c) Preparation of curricular matter that strategically determine effective living for a particular type of handicapped children.

(d) Development of motivational patterns in the exceptional children which produce achievement in the school.

(e) Interest in the handicapped for participation in the activities of the non-handicapped is to be created.

(f) Priority to be given to the development of a realistic self-concept in handicapped children.

Principles of Education for Exceptional Children

Educational psychologists have formulated a set of principles on which the total edifice of special education stands. These can be enumerated as follows:

(a) Every child in this world is unique. First, each exceptional child is a child. He has the same right to acceptance and understanding as other children. So he should get the same educational privileges.

(b) Studies reveal that there are wide individual differences among children in each domain of exceptionality.

(c) Early screening, identification and placement in special educational programmes are essential because exceptional children make optimal progress in educational institutions.

(d) In order to have proper placement, a team approach is essential. The team should consist of psychologists, educational specialists, psychiatrists and medical personnels.

(e) Since the team requires well-trained and competent persons, programmes should not be augmented till these personnel are available.

(f) A special curriculum should be prepared to match the needs of exceptional children.

(g) The domains of exceptionality will determine the quantity and nature of materials required.

(h) Emphasis must be placed on the fact that education for exceptional children should form an integral part of a total educational programme.

(i) To ensure progress, there should be continuous reassessment of exceptional children. Sometimes, revaluation of institutional programmers is also necessary.

(j) The school must take the responsibility of placement assistance for each student.

(k) When clarification is sought by the public and parents, special educational programmes should be interpreted lucidly.

(l) For promotion of research activities, selection of teachers and training programmers, the central, state, and local agencies should have joint responsibility.

Education For Exceptional Children

The process of educating the exceptional children is a specialised area in which maximum efforts are made to make exceptional child to respond normally. Therefore, exceptional children is a special type of education. The special education mostly revolve around 'normalization'—which is the popular belief that every exceptional child should be provided with an education and living environment as close to normal as possible. Educating the exceptional children Jitender Mohan points out that there are mainly two issues of special education. These issues are closely related with normalization of exceptional child *viz.* main streaming and deinstitutionalization. Two questions closely related with these issues are:

1. Are special classes effective in promoting intellectual and social growth?

There are conflicting findings on this question. There is some evidence to indicate that regular classes may be better than special class placement for both the academic and social growth of certain exceptional children *i.e.* mildly retarded children. (Budoff and Gottlieb, 1976).

2. Is labelling a child as retarded, disturbed gifted *etc.* somehow detrimental to his or her welfare?

Research evidence indicates that most people tend to view a labelled person differently from a non-labelled one. People are therefore more likely to expect deviant behaviour from labelled individuals. (Herson 1974; and Foster et al. 1975). However, labelling has been retained because of its possible advantages. Labelling a population helps professionals to communicate, abolishment of the present labels may lead to evolving a new set of labels and labelling helps to spotlight the problem for the general public (Hallahan and Kauffman, 1978). But according to Lindgren (1976) labelling is more a hindrance than a help.

Main Streaming. Mainstreaming is a belief which involves an educational placement procedure and process for exceptional children, based on the conviction that each child should be educated in the least restrictive environment in which his educational and related needs can be satisfactory provided. Mainstreaming involves *(i)* integration *(ii)* education planning and programming and *(iii)* clarification of responsibilities. Mainstreaming requires special teachers and charges in school policies, techniques and physical layout. Modifications of the school facilities are also often necessary: ramps for wheelchairs, elimination of curbs, redesigned toilet stalls and drinking fountains and removal of obstacles that might harm the blind or partially sighted; classrooms may need to be modified to provide more open space so that teachers can form several sub-groups, yet keep everyone in view, materials should always be visible; parental involvement is a prominent feature of mainstreamed schools and finally the cornerstone of dealing with handicapped pupils is an individualized education program (Storm and Bernard, 1982).

Research studies show that mainstreaming benefit both handicapped and non-handicapped children (Molloy, 1975; Reynolds and Birch, 1977; Guralnick, 1978; Allen, 1980).

Deinstitutionalization. Hand in hand with the mainstreaming movement has come a trend towards depopulation of large residential institutions. The trend is to move exceptional individuals into closer contact with the community and the home *i.e.* exceptional individuals should have as nearly a normal life as possible. Research has revealed that institutionalization can result in a lowering of cognitive abilities, possibly because social reinforcement is missing and thus motivation is lowered. (Butterfield, 1967; Zigler, 1973; and Balla, 1976).

Non-categorical Special Education. Since the late 1960s and early 1970s there has been a trend towards what has come to be called as non-categorical special education. Some consider, it to mean that all exceptional children, except the gifted, have common educational needs, and thus separate classes are not needed for each area: for instance Zigler, 1973; Kirk and Elkins, 1975; and Kauffman, 1977. However, many believe that children who have certain exceptionalities, such as vision and hearing impairments and some physical disabilities require specialized material, equipment and teaching techniques and so cannot be taught effectively in the same class, (Blackhurst, 1977). Consequently the widespread implementation of a non-categorical approach awaits further research. However, the main objectives of special education is to prepare the exceptional child to behave/respond as a normal human being. For this purpose exceptional child is educated in special environments outside regular classes in the following ways:

1) Residential Schools

Exceptional rather mentally retarded children are educated in special type of residential schools with two purposes viz.:

(a) The residential schools are primarily meant to provide 24 hour comprehensive education and care.

(b) In certain cases where the care and management of the severely disabled child poses problems, it is necessary to send disabled children to residential institutions. In this case, the aim is not education. It is just a residential facility for care. Education is an adjunct to the total programme.

The children of either category are permitted to have as much contact with parents as possible, either by home visits, parental visits or both. But the greatest disadvantage of residential institutions is that they deprive children of a chance to mingle with normal children.

2) Home Bound or Hospitalised Instructions

The instruction is provided to children in Home/Hospitals in case they

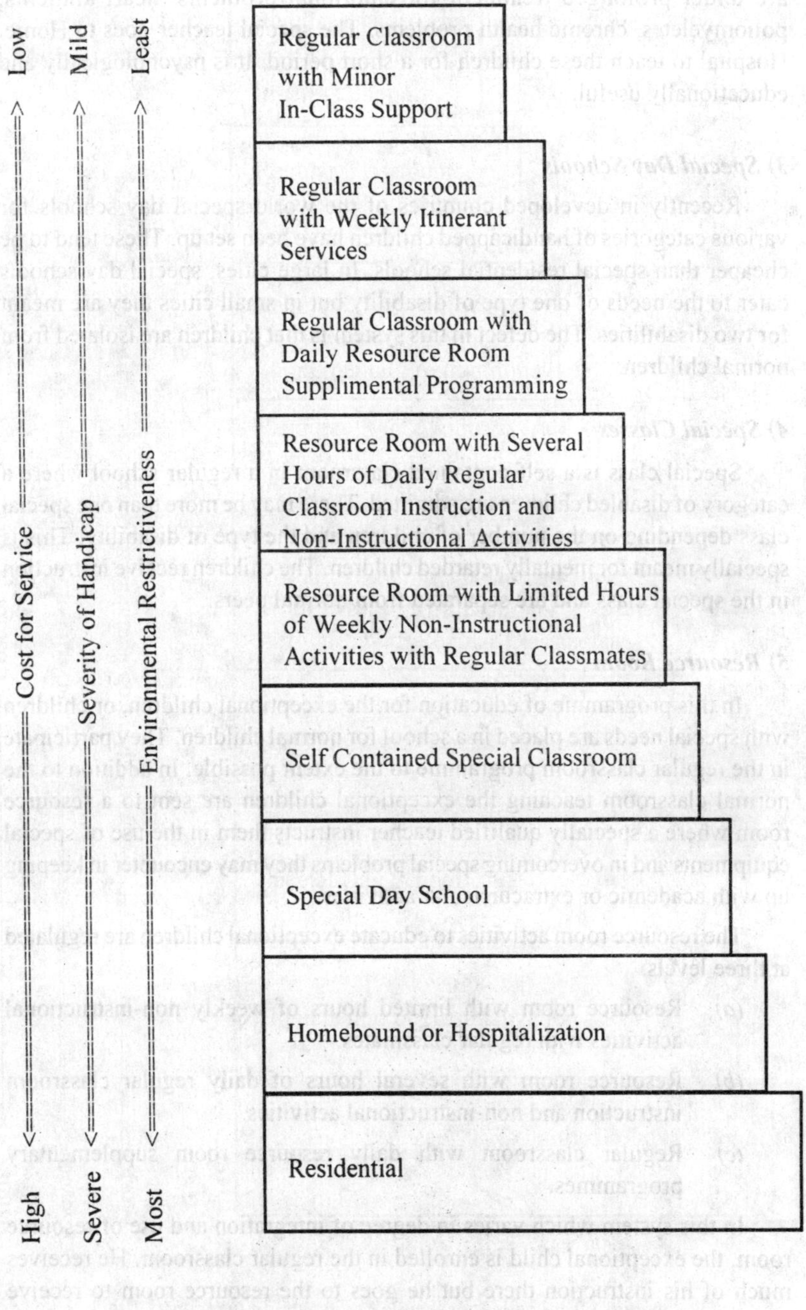

Fig. 1 Continuum of Education Services for Exceptional Children.

are under prolonged treatment for emotional problems, heart ailments, poliomyeletes, chronic health problems. The special teacher goes to Home/ Hospital to teach these children for a short period. It is psychologically and educationally useful.

3) Special Day Schools

Recently in developed countries of the world special day schools for various categories of handicapped children have been set up. These tend to be cheaper than special residential schools. In large cities, special day schools cater to the needs of one type of disability but in small cities they are meant for two disabilities. The defect in this system is that children are isolated from normal children.

4) Special Classes

Special class is a self-contained classroom in a regular school where a category of disabled children are admitted. There may be more than one special class depending on the number of children and the type of disability. This is specially meant for mentally retarded children. The children receive instruction in the special class and are separated from normal peers.

5) Resource Room

In this programme of education for the exceptional children, or children with special needs are placed in a school for normal children. They participate in the regular classroom programme to the extent possible. In addition to the normal classroom teaching the exceptional children are sent to a resource room where a specially qualified teacher instructs them in the use of special equipments and in overcoming special problems they may encounter in keeping up with academic or extracurricular activities.

The resource room activities to educate exceptional children are regulated at three levels:

(a) Resource room with limited hours of weekly non-instructional activities with regular classmates.

(b) Resource room with several hours of daily regular classroom instruction and non-instructional activities.

(c) Regular classroom with daily resource room supplementary programmes.

In this system which varies in degree of integration and use of resource room, the exceptional child is enrolled in the regular classroom. He receives much of his instruction there but he goes to the resource room to receive specialised instruction and use specialised equipments.

This plan is suitable for any type of child who can succeed in regular classes when provided with extra assistance. The resource room is well equipped with staff and equipment. The child becomes integrated with normal children academically and socially, in addition to his physical integration.

6) Regular classroom with weekly itinerant specialist

Regular class with weekly it-inerant specialist services of education to exceptional child make it possible to provide general and special education by respective teachers in the respective institutions. In this system of special education exceptional child attends the normal school and special education institution. It is because of the fact that disabled children are often widely scattered and it is not feasible to organise a resource teacher programme in every school. In such a situation it is advisable to have a travelling teacher assisting handicapped children in resource rooms in different schools. These schools should not be located at great distances from one another. It is quite similar to the resource room programme. Regular classroom teachers may also be trained to handle exceptional children in the regular class itself with more support from the special teachers.

XII.5 Creative Children

One of the important exception among the exceptional children is intellectually superiority. The attribute of intellectual superiority give us an idea that some exceptional children are productive thinkers. There productive thinking ability is based on four major components viz; Flexibility, Originality, Elaboration and Fluency. Studies reveal that flexibility is a measure of the ability to change from one form of thinking to another originality indicates the uniqueness of a response. Elaboration is a measure of the number of ideas used to build the basic response. Fluency is the number of relevant responses given within a specified time.

The great majority of the studies done in this field have been on intellectually gifted children. It seems that most investigators have not considered the possibility that children of below average intellectual functioning may exhibit some degree of productive thinking ability. Productive thinking is directly related with creative ability.

Creativity is said to be a complex and multifaceted phenomenon of human behaviour. Besides, the creativity is the ability which is most valued in all societies. Creativity was believed to be a gift of God/nature for long to be found in highly talented people. Creativity has fascinated all—scientists, educators, philosophers and layman. It is believed that a creative person has inborn talent. However, the receipt research indicates that creativity is not an extraordinary gift of God possessed by some, but a basic ability of all human beings. Like intelligence, creativity is found to exist in some measure among all people. Helvetius (1758) first psychologist who advocated that creativity is not as a divine gift but as a human quality. The traditional concept of creativity relates creativity to bringing something new into existence, literally creating something new. It was considered the ability to bring something novel and original that enriches the social and cultural life. Common use definitions also relate creativity to inventiveness and seem to view creativity primarily as the making of a product. But, today it is recognised that creativity is much more than mere production of something new. Theories explaining creativity have ranged from those that define it as the innovative combination of knowledge and imagination applied to the solution of problems to those that view creativity as an 'unconscious process through which libidinal or aggressive energies are converted into culturally sanctioned behaviours' (Freud, 1924).

Creativity has been defined by different people in different ways. There is no universally accepted definition of creativity, because, creativity has been studied from several points of view. Mac Kinnon (1978) rightly observed that one should not seek to choose from the several meanings for the best single definition of creativity, it is a concept that carries all of the meanings that have been offered and will likely carry many more as investigations continue. Current positions on the meaning of creativity suggest a holistic view, as Clark (1983) has observed, none of the theories provide a complete picture. Her rationale for organizing the various theories into four areas of human functioning—thinking, feeling, sensing and intuiting is based on her perception that none of the theories provide a complete picture. The position she takes is that each perception may only be a fragment of the total. In the following paragraphs, we shall attempt to review some of the definitions as proposed by different people. Gowman (1972) has noted five different approaches to an understanding of the concept of creativity :

1. Cognitive, rational and problem-solving aspects.
2. Personality trait; family and environmental origins.
3. Mental health, psychological openness and self-actualization.
4. A Freudian view, and
5. Existential, psychedelic and irrational aspects.

The creative process, product person and environment are the vantage points from which creativity is most often discussed. Campbell (1960) observes that creativity is neither unusual nor mysterious. The creative process is the forming of new combinations or associative bonds out of the thought elements available to the individuals. Wallas (1926) described the process as consisting of four stages: Preparation, Incubation, Illumination or inspiration and production/verification. Torrance (1970) defined the process as 'One of becoming sensitive to be aware of problems __________ bringing together available information __________ searching for solutions __________ and communicating the results".

According to MacKinnon (1963), creativity is a process extended in time and characterized by originality, adaptiveness and realization'. Barron (1969) opines, 'creativity is the ability to bring something new into existence. Since human beings are able to make something out of nothing, the human act of creation always involves a reshaping of given materials whether physical or mental. The new form is something made by the reconstitution of or regeneration from something old'. Dellas and Gaier (1970) list independence, manifested in attitudes and social behaviour, dominance, introversion, openness to stimuli, wide interests, self-acceptance intuitiveness and flexibility as characteristics associated with creativity. Torrance (1974) who developed tests of creative thinking observes that creativity can be defined in terms of product (inventory or discovery), process or characteristics of the individual who is considered to be creative.

Kirk and Gallagher (1979) view creativity as the production of a unique product (from the child's point of view) from the available data or information. Creative products may be ideas, work of art, scientific theories or even building designs provided certain criteria are met. MacKinnon (1978) suggests that these criteria should include originality or novelty and relevance to a problem, situation or goal. Creativity, according to Clark (1983) is 'the highest expression of giftedness'. Kauffman (1986) refers to creativity as the ability to express novel and useful ideas, to sense and elucidate novel and important relationship and to ask previously unthought of but crucial questions.

Creativity is a key component in most definitions of giftedness and hence can also be conceptualized as the ability to generate novel solutions to specific problems. However, the debate regarding the nature of the relationship between creativity and intelligence has not been conclusively resolved. A number of research studies have been conducted to study the relation between intelligence and creativity and most of the studies show that these are not the same. However, there is some underlying basic relation. The studies have shown that even though creative individuals have above average intelligence yet the abilities of highly creative and highly intelligent, persons are so different that they can easily be discriminated. It is not necessary that more intelligent persons are more creative also and vice-versa. Kitano and Kirby (1986) contend that "an individual can be extremely bright but uncreative, or highly creative but not necessarily intellectually gifted." Creativity, as measured by creativity tests is independent of intelligence, but when evaluated by teachers is related to intelligence. Generally the teachers visualize creativity in terms of intelligence. Though, some overlap between giftedness and creativity is generally recognised, but the degree of overlap and the practical importance of differences between students who are creative but not particularly gifted and those who are gifted but not particularly creative remain to be further investigated. Besides, creativity and personality also bear some relation. The creative person is more comfortable with and tends to prefer cognitive complexities. White (1969) recognizes the need for competence as the most important factor in creativity. Whereas Matty (1965) identifies the need for novelty and need for quality. According to him creativity is born out when both these needs are strong.

Taylor (1960) added that creativity exist at five levels with each level involving different psychological processes that may change the steps in the process. The five levels are:

1. Expressive creativity (a form of spontaneous expression without reference to originality and quality of the product).
2. Technical or productive creativity (where the emphasis is on skill rather than spontaneity and novelty).
3. Inventive creativity (with an emphasis on the new use of old things).
4. Innovative creativity (where new ideas or principles are developed).
5. Emergentive creativity (which describe creativity formulation using the most abstract ideational principles or assumptions underlying a body of art or science).

The basic psychological explanation of creativity is sublimation of unsatisfied needs, the urge for self-development, urge for communication, curiosity, novelty, change and order. The cognitive factors important in creativity are sensitivity, attentiveness, memory and imagination. The social factors important to creative thinking are unconventionality originality, willingness to be alone, a certain scepticism (Anderson, (1959). The environmental factors can be stimulating, supporting or hindering factors.

XII.6 Characteristics of Creative Children

From the above discussion, it is evident that creativity is a special type of mental ability which is mainly responsible to think productively. Mangal reports that the process of creative ability has the following attributes:

Creativity is universal. Creativity is not confined to any individual, groups of individuals, caste, colour or creed. It is universal and is not bound by the barriers of age, location or culture. Everyone of us possesses and is capable of demonstrating creativity to some degree.

Creativity is innate as well as acquired. Although many research findings and incidents favour the suggestion that creativity is a God-given gift and natural endowment, the influence of cultural background, experiences, education and training in the nurturing of creativity cannot be ruled out. Therefore, one's creativity may be correctly said to be a function of natural endowment as well as its nurturing.

Creativity produces something new or novel. Creativity denotes the ability of a person to produce something new or novel, but this novelty or newness does not necessarily imply the production of a totally new idea or object which has never been experienced or has never existed before. To make a fresh and novel combination of existing separate elements or to reshape or rearrange the already known facts and principles or to reform or modify previously known techniques, are as much acts of creative expression as the discovery of a new element in chemistry or a new formula in mathematics. The only precondition for naming an expression as creative is that it should not be repetition or reproduction of what has already been experienced or learned by an individual.

Creativity is adventurous and open thinking. Creativity is a departure from the stereotyped, rigid and closed thinking. It encourages and demands complete freedom to accept and express the multiplicity of responses, choices and lines of action. It is a kind of adventurous thinking, calling a person to come out in the open to express himself according to his will and to function unrestricted by routine or previous practice.

Creativity is a means as well as end in itself. Creativity as an urge inspires and persuades the individual to create something unique and thus acts as an impetus for expression. This creative expression proves to be a source of joy and satisfaction to the creator. No one other than the creator can experience the warmth, happiness and satisfaction which he receives through his creation. Creation is a source of happiness and a reward in itself. The creator expresses himself as fully as possible through his creation and has his own perceptions about his creation. It is, therefore, not essential that a creative work would arouse the same feelings or give the same joy and satisfaction in others as is experienced by the creator himself.

Creativity carries ego involvement. There is complete involvement of one's ego in the creative expression. One's individuality and identity are totally merged in one's creation. One's style of functioning, philosophy of life and personality may be clearly reflected in his creation be it a work of art, or a piece of writing, etc. The creator takes pride in his creation and hence makes ego involved statements like, "it is my creation", "I have solved this problem", "it is my idea", etc.

Creativity has a wide scope. Creative expression is not restricted by any limits or boundaries. It covers all fields and activities of human life, in any of which one is able to demonstrate creativity by expressing or producing a new idea or object. It is not restricted to scientific inventions and discoveries or the production of works of art but covers multifarious human accomplishments like the composition of poems, writing of story and plays, performance in the fields of dance, music, painting, sculpture, political and social leadership, business, teaching and other professions, as also the mundane activities of daily life.

Creativity and intelligence do not necessarily go hand-in-hand. Research findings and observations have demonstrated that there is no positive correlation between creativity and intelligence. One is not the essential or necessary prerequisite of the other. Those found scoring high on intelligence tests may demonstrate little or no signs of creativity whereas individuals performing poorly in intelligence tests may sometimes create something very original.

Taking a consolidated view of the researches conducted on this issue, we may conclude that although intelligence and the creativity component of one's personality can function independently, a certain minimum level of intelligence is a necessary precondition for successful creative expression. Were it not so, a person of below average mental ability like a moron or an idiot could also be creative; but in actual-life situations we hardly come across any such instances. Conversely, although creative people generally tend to be relatively intelligent, beyond a certain level, a higher I.Q. does not necessarily predict creativity. In other words, as Kitano and Kirby (1986) state : "an individual can be extremely bright but uncreative, or highly creative but not necessarily intellectually gifted". Therefore, no clear relationship has been seen to exist between intelligence and creativity.

Creativity rests more on divergent thinking than on convergent thinking. Divergent thinking involves a broad scanning operation, enabling a person to evolve a general impression of new idea. The ability to converge broader aspects to create something new is an important attribute of creative children.

Torrance (1979) has given its own model of creativity and has also developed a list of twenty-three characteristics that indicate creativity in children. Few children may exhibit all of the characteristics, while many of them in combination may suggest creative promise in children.

1. Intense absorption in listening, observing or doing.
2. Intense animation and physical involvement.
3. Use of analogies in speech.

4. Tendency to challenge ideas of authority.
5. Habit of checking many sources.
6. Taking a close look at things.
7. Eagerness to tell others about discoveries.
8. Continuing in creative activities after scheduled time for quitting.
9. Showing relationship among apparently unrelated ideas.
10. Following through an idea set in motion.
11. Various manifestations of curiosity and wanting to know.
12. Spontaneous use of discovery or experimental approval.
13. Excitement in voice about discoveries.
14. Habit of guessing and testing outcomes.
15. Honesty and intense search for truth.
16. Independent action.
17. Boldness of new ideas.
18. Low destrctibility.
19. Manipulations of ideas and object to obtain new combinations.
20. Penetrating observations and questions.
21. Tendency to seek alternatives and explore new possibilities.
22. Self-initiated learning.
23. Willingness to consider or toy with new ideas.

XII.7 Assessing Creative Children

A number of psychologists, including Getzels and Jackson (1962), Wallach and Kogan (1965), Torrance (1962), and Guilford (1965) have designed tests that support to measure creativity. One of the leaders in developing tests is J.P. Guilford, who earlier (1959) had proposed the concept of *convergent* versus *divergent* thinking. The first type, which usually leads to one right or best answer, is more often included in current intelligence tests; the second type is represented in the mental processes that search in many directions to produce wide-ranging responses, and is more often involved in creative productions.

Torrance (1962), the originator of the Minnesota Tests of Creative Thinking, has included over twenty-five different kinds of tasks in his battery. A number of them are usable with young children. Torrance's have been the most commonly used tests for assessing creativity, since all of his tasks require the production of divergent solutions. (A revised manual for administering and scoring the tests was published in 1974).

In their research with a gifted group, Getzels and Jackson (1962) utilized some of Guilford's ideas to develop their own measures of creativity. They devised five special tests: completing tables, making up problems, finding hidden shapes, word association, and listing uses of things. For example, in the test on uses of things, the subject is asked to give as many uses as he or she can imagine for some well-known object, such as a brick. The answers are then scored for both originality and the number of uses given.

Marsh (1964), in his re-analysis of the Getzels and Jackson data, believes that the conventional IQ score is the best single criterion for identifying creative persons. Burt (1975), too, takes issues with Getzels' and Jackson's assumptions that a test of creativity requires the answers to diverge and should measure the person's ability to deal inventively with either verbal or numerical symbols or with object-space relations. Burt suggests his concepts of *useful creativity* which he maintains "must involve the ability to deal, not only inventively but also rationally, with the material involved".

Most researchers in this area take the view that *some* relationship between creativity and intelligence certainly does exist but that these factors are not mutually inclusive. Most researchers are also likely to believe that some minimum intelligence seems essential for most creative productions, but beyond that the relationship between the two constructs appears to be low. Guilford, however, who first proposed the hypothesis that the relationship between IQ and many types of creativity is low or moderate (1950), has since modified his earlier view and now believes that there is a place for creative thinking abilities and functions within the broad realm of intelligence, suggesting a closer relationship between the two concepts (1975).

Despite controversy surrounding how best to define (process or product), and how best to test and measure, the concept creativity is part of the current understanding of giftedness. As a term, it is probably the best synonym we can apply to describe those human behaviours we consider original, outstanding, and desirable. It is currently believed that we can enhance creative thinking by proper educational treatment (Guilford, 1975), and that we need not all be creative in similar ways.

Some additional light on how the creative process in children may be enhanced is provided by MacKinnon (1962) in his now-famous study of creative architects. He found that the home environments of these architects provided many opportunities and encouragements for them to develop their talents. Also, the mothers of these men played a very important role in providing continuous opportunities for their intellectual growth. Finally, the families themselves did not adhere strictly to the narrowly defined sex-role standards of the males as breadwinners and the females as homemakers. In fact, most of these mothers had interests and careers of their own.

No one can seriously doubt the importance of creative persons in any society, since this feature shows itself in so many different ways—in scientific discoveries, in musical, artistic, and literary products, in technological advancements and inventions, in athletics, and in social and political innovations. Creativity in any form must come from within the person, but then it is up to society to provide the climate in which all types of creative behaviour may flourish. Fostering and nurturing any kind of intellectual and creative performance is the responsibility of everyone—parents, teachers, educators, psychologists, and all others who may come in contact with growing individuals.

XII.8 Developing Environment for Creative Abilities

Creativity is a special type of productive ability within an individual child. This productive ability can be promoted if a teacher provide adequate environment to a child. Therefore, facilitating the development of creativity is the teacher's responsibility and therefore, requires both an accurate general concept of the nature of creativity and some specific ideas and skills. A number of research findings suggest that we can stimulate creativity by establishing a classroom climate that encourages, self-confidence, self expression and individuality. The teacher in the classroom has to identify the creative potential, reach for it and provide a warm, friendly and congenial atmosphere that promotes creativity. With conscious effort to look for creativity and continuing attention to the behaviour of individual students, the class teacher can become a facilitator of creative efforts in the classroom. Although, facilitating creativity is a challenging task. This has to be done both at home and school. Different studies dealing with the problem of education for creativity indicate that the development of creative ability can be encouraged by suitable educational learning milieu {Torrance (1962); Permes (1964); Tumin (1962); Suchman (1961); Garden (1961); Hilgard (1959); Russel (1956).}

To encourage creative abilities among the children a teacher is supposed to follow certain principles of creative thinking. In this connection Torrance (1965) identified six such principles for encouraging creativity in children. These principles are as follows:

1. Be respectful to unusual questions.
2. Be respectful of imaginative, creative ideas.
3. Show pupils that their ideas have value.
4. Occasionally have pupils do something 'for practice' without the threat of evaluation.
5. Tie in evaluation with causes and consequences.

6. Encourage self-initiated learning and evaluate it.

Similarly, Klausmeier and Ripple (1971) enunciate three principles for encouraging the creative behaviour among children as:

1. Expressing oneself by figural, verbal or physical means is essential for the production of novel forms or ideas.
2. Experiencing in successful creative efforts is associated with a high level of creative expression.
3. Thinking and behaving in divergent ways is essential to creativity.

Klausmeier's study make us to recall that divergent thinking is a component of creativity—it involves fluency, flexibility and originality. To stimulate these elements, different tasks can be applied by the teachers. For example, the teachers can present any unreal or "contrary to fact" situation before the students and then ask them about what would be the results. Then there might be many things that can be improved/made better. The teacher can provide incomplete beginning to create pictures, stories, designs etc. New uses to common objects may be sought. Alternate titles or endings for a story or picture or any situation may be asked. Another practice for encouraging fluency is brainstorming. Brainstorming is a technique in which a group of people discuss a particular problem, trying to come up with as many solutions as possible.

Doorlag and Lewis (1987) have suggested that creative abilities among children can be assimilated into most school subjects as soon as basic skills are acquired by them. However, novelty should not be accepted when accuracy is the goal. **Fluency** can be developed with brainstorming sessions. **Flexibility** should also be encouraged. Flexibility also involves the ability to change one's perspective. The students should list solutions to a school problem from their own point of view and then adopt the viewpoint of the teacher, the principal, the school board or their parents. **Originality** the creation of new solutions, can be developed by providing opportunities for its occurrence. The solution should be new to its creator and not necessarily to society. Various problems can be suggested to the students and they can be directed to come up with novel solutions. In elaboration, students, can be given practice in elaborating thinking by presenting simple statements that they must expand and asked to expand the idea to include directions for implementation, ways of evaluating effectiveness, potential advantages and possible disadvantages.

Appreciating the importance attached to nurture creativity, it becomes an important goal of the school to foster creativity in the pupils. The child may be given opportunities for original expression in different media-music, poetry, art, etc. The divergent production abilities (fluency, originality, flexibility) develop over a period of many years. Thus, teaching for creativity must follow a continuing programme. In young children these abilities manifest in the form of free expression in playing, singing and other activities. To facilitate creativity, the teacher should reward all original efforts of students. A creative child is found to be sensitive, independent, self-confident and unconventional, thus, the environment of the school should be open, where the child is able to think and express himself.

Callahan (1978) in a study of the role of teacher and creativity development among children reports that a teacher can stimulate creativity in children by establishing a classroom climate that encourages self-confidence, self expression and individuality by:

(a) Providing a non-threatening atmosphere. The classroom environment should be structured in such a way that students' ideas and opinions are respected and questions are encouraged.

(b) Don't be the judge of the worth of all product in the classroom. The students should be encouraged to develop criteria to judge their own work and that of their peers. An open attitude on teacher's part allows more freedom for divergent thinking and evaluative skills.

(c) Model creative thinking as much as possible or introduce others who can illustrate the creative thinking process for the students.

(d) Provide stimuli for as many of the senses as possible. A number of stimuli encourage students to look at a problem from different perspectives. It also enhances the sense of openness and psychological freedom.

Here, in the end, are given some tips to teachers to bring out creativity in pupils. On the whole the role of teacher can hardly be ignored for the development of creative abilities among children. A teacher while promoting creativity among children can develop stimulating creative atmosphere in the behave and class in the following ways :

1. Encourage self-expression in spontaneous as well as planned activities.
2. Provide incentives and reforcements of creative efforts.
3. Make available and tell students where to find sources of ideas.
4. Value creative thinking.
5. Make children more sensitive to environmental stimuli.
6. Encourage manipulation of objects and ideas.
7. Provide a congenial classroom atmosphere.
8. Encourage creative criticism.
9. Develop adventurous spirit.

XII.9 Gifted Children

Many philosophers and scientists from Plato and Aristotle to the present day have recognised that a nation's most precious assets are its gifted population. Therefore, it is essential for a society to take special care of the gifted children.

For this purpose the educators should realize that given proper training, the gifted have the most probable potential for becoming effective problem solvers. Also if one considers that the primary aim of education is to help children develop their potentialities to the fullest—it is clear that the gifted too need special education. One must remember that it is equally frustrating for the intellectually gifted child to slow down the pace of his learning to that of the average member of his class as it is for the mentally retarded child to attempt to meet standards that are continually beyond his reach.

XII.10 Concept of Gifted Children

The concept of giftedness has always been changing with the times. At different historical periods giftedness was said to be based on birth, power or material wealth. Intellectual superiority gained recognition quite late. But, even then, so many factors entered into the definition of giftedness that it became difficult to determine the normal distribution of giftedness in any population at any given time.

Though giftedness may show itself in different ways, it has most frequently been defined through a score on an intelligence test. It may also be defined, sometimes, in terms of special abilities and capacities but more often it is defined in a normative or statistical fashion.

Galton was the first person to attack this problem through scientific methods—systematically collecting, comparing and analysing the available data. He set out to show that a man's natural abilities are derived by inheritance, under the same limitations as the physical form and features of the rest of the organic world. He wrote that for the genius, three main elements are essential—ability, zeal and readyness to work—but the decision factor is the gift of high ability. He recognized two kinds of abilities, a single general ability, entering into all we think or do, as well as a number of special aptitudes of a strictly limited range. The former, he said, was far more important. According to him, the high achiever differ from the average in degree rather than in kind, in quantity rather than in quality. While defining the average genius he estimated his ability to be one and two-thirds of that of an average man.

In 1905, at Galton's suggestion the anthropological section of the British Association appointed a Committee to plan and carry out a new anthropometric survey of the British Isles which was to include mental as well as physical measurements; special attention was to be paid to be subnormal and supernormal children of school age. Binet , the great admirer of Galton's work, adopted Galton's scheme and popularized his distinction between what he preferred to call general intelligence and partial aptitudes. Thorndike, on the other hand, recognized only a number of limited abilities or talents and denied the existence of general intelligence. In this he was followed by Brown and Thurstone, while Spearman denied the existence of innate specific aptitudes.

Thus, different theories have led to corresponding differences in the definition of the term gifted. Anastasi points out that British writers have put the main emphasis on a general factor, while American psychologists have focussed on group factors and regard '*g*' as non-existent.

Terman, in his pioneer investigations, accepted Galton's assumptions of "general ability" and therefore, based his definitions of the gifted on the IQ as assessed by tests intelligence. Actually, the psychological study of the gifted was undertaken only after intelligence tests had been developed by Binet and his successors. Leta S. Hollingworth also took general intelligence as the criterion for the selection of the gifted. She defined the gifted as children who are in the top 1 per cent of the juvenile population in general intelligence. "General Intelligence" according to her is "the power to achieve literacy and to deal with abstract knowledge and symbols". She was convinced that general intelligence was positively correlated with nearly all mental abilities, and that scholastic success depended upon it.

DeHaan and Havighurst describe "Intellectual Ability" as composed of several parts, sometimes called primary mental abilities. These constitute the basis of certain "Areas of Talents"—Verbal, Mathematical skill, Spastical imagination, Science, Art, Literature, Leadership, etc. Accordingly, they define the gifted as one who is in the top 10 per cent of his age group in one or more of these areas. They say the aim should be to discover as wide a variety of talent as possible with the help of the Differential Aptitude Tests and the Individual Profile Cards.

A.O. Heck describes the gifted as a child with a high intelligence quotient. Regardless of how talented a child may be along a particular line, if he does not have a high intelligence quotient he is not considered to be gifted. In addition he recognizes a group whom he calls "specially gifted". They may be only average from the point of view of academic ability but exceptionally endowed with poetic, musical or mechanical talent.

XII.11 Definitions of Giftedness

Giftedness is a special ability which is unequally distributed. The term giftedness has been defined by different Psychologists as:

Fleigher and Bish. The term gifted encompasses those children who possess a superior intellectual potentiality and functional ability to achieve academically in the top 15 to 20 per cent of the school population; and/or talent of a high order in such special areas as mathematics, mechanics, science, expressive arts, creative writing, music and social leadership and a unique creative ability to deal with their environment.

Witty. The term gifted or talented stands for those whose performance is consistently remarkable in some potentially valuable activity.

Prem Pasricha. The gifted child is the one who exhibits superiority in general intelligence or the one who is in possession of special abilities of a high order in the fields which are not necessarily associated with a high intelligence quotient.

Marland report. The gifted are those who possess outstanding abilities or potential in the area of general intellectual capacity, specific academic aptitude, creative or productive thinking, leadership ability, visual or performing arts and psycho-motor activity.

Havighurst. The talented or gifted child is one who shows consistently remarkable performance in any worthwhile line of endeavour.

Tannenbaum. The term giftedness denotes their potential for becoming critically acclaimed performers or exemplary producers of ideas in spheres of activity that enhance the moral, physical, emotional, social, intellectual, or aesthetic life of humanity.

Analysis of the above definitions shows that giftedness need not be necessarily associated with high performance on some general intelligence test. A person who shows outstanding or remarkable performance in other spheres of activity regardless of his average I.Q. or lower scholastic achievement may also be termed as gifted. This feature has been repeated in almost all the other definitions as well. However, while adopting demonstrated social performance as a criterion, these definitions have clearly stated that in order to qualify as an indication of giftedness, a person's performance must be consistent, outstanding, distinctive, remarkable and clearly above the average performance of others in the group. It should, at the same time, be useful and worthwhile and should contribute towards the welfare of society and also of humanity at large.

From the above discussion regarding the giftedness, it can be concluded that gifted children have the following recognising attributes:

1. The gifted child is essentially an exceptional child.
2. In comparison to children of his own group, he is superior in some

ability or group of abilities.

3. In most cases, the gifted child invariably exhibits superior performance only in the area or areas of his giftedness.
4. The appellation 'gifted children' is applicable to not only the academically talented but also to those who show promise in other spheres such as
   (a) music, dance, drama, painting, sculpture, writing and other creative arts,
   (b) mechanical work,
   (c) social leadership and human relationships,
   (d) creative scientific experimentation and exploration,
   (e) physical activities like games, sports and gymnastics.
5. A gifted child need not necessarily possess a very high intelligence quotient (I.Q.).
6. If a gifted child receives proper attention and opportunity for self-expression and development, the gifted child can make a noteworthy contribution to the welfare of society, the nation and humanity at large.

Characteristics of the Gifted

There is no doubt that an intellectually gifted child shows his talent by his remarkable performance in any undertaking worth his while. Such children are generally identified in schools by their teachers who are able to do this be observing their performance.

A number of misconceptions are found among laymen regarding the characteristics of very superior and gifted children. From the caricature and "folklore", people get the idea that they are physically small in stature and poorly developed. They also have a strong notion that the intellectually superior people are "qeer", "unstable", "one-sided" and socially-rejected persons. Most of them turn out to be average adults as far as intelligence and achievement are concerned.

However, none of the above notions are correct. For more than two decades, groups of exceptional children have been thoroughly screened. The following are their major characteristics revealed in these researches:

(i) Physical Characteristics

Different studies on gifted children reveal that they have above-average physical development. These children are taller, heavier built and well developed. Their general health is above average and continues to be so into adulthood. Incidents of mortality and insanity are found to be low in case of gifted children. They have good coordination and control of the muscles. In a study, Baldwin conducted body measurements of 594 children of Terman's gifted group (in which I.Q. was in the range of 130 to 189). These children appeared to be physically superior to the group they were compared with. In 1925, Terman obtained the following details of gifted children:

(a) Gifted children have greater weight at birth.

(b) They walk and talk earlier.

(c) They have earlier pubescence.

(d) They are prececious.

(e) They have better than average nutrition.

(f) The gifted children have more height, weight, strength of grip, shoulders, superior motoring ability, less defective hearing, mouth breathing, less stuttering etc.

(ii) Development and Intellectual Characteristics

Studies reveal that gifted children are found to have superior development in all respects. Their learning to talk, walk and even to read, is discernable early.

They are enlowed with many qualities of personality and intellect. Case studies of intellectually gifted children have shown that they possess better standards than average children. Their reactions are quick and their progress is conspicuous. At an early age, they enter school and at school, they are much ahead of their class. Their activities in the classrooms are wide and varied. Their interests are also very diverse.

As reported by Kirk, gifted children are more interested in abstract subjects such as literature, debate etc. and less interested in procedure subjects like penmanship and manual training. They are found to be less sociable. Different research works reveal that on the social plane of play interest, the majority of gifted children fall in the lowest quartile as compared to average children. Kirk also has confirmed that the gifted children are rated above average on character and maturity tests. Most of the gifted children are found to be aware of their talent and their utilisation. Their cognitive processes are very rich. They form creative ideas easily, are able to sense gaps in problems and bridge the missing elements intellectually.

(iii) Personality Characteristics of Gifted Children

Different research works confirmed that there is positive and intimate relationship between giftedness and personality. No doubt, gifted children are more desired, better known, more ambitious and hardworking. Usually they have a strong desire to explore and create. They are able to sustain frustration better than anybody else.

Some psychologists have found that gifted children are impulsive and self-confident. They are very much interested in aesthetic expression and reflective thinking. They have a high degree of motivation. Normally, they are sensitive, resourceful, flexible and enthusiastic. Various studies on gifted children tell us that gifted or creative behaviour is seen as a continuation and substitute for the play of childhood. The creative thoughts are derived from the elaboration of the freely rising fantasies and ideas related to day-dreaming and childhood play. Gifted children accept freely rising ideas whereas non-creative persons suppress them.

(iv) Family Background and Social Characteristics

Generally, intellectual children come from parentage of the educated and professional class. They also belong to the higher occupational group. Their environment at home also provides a stimulating atmosphere. They are gregarious and sociable. Studies reveal that these children are very popular and they are much sought after by the elder children. Besides all the above characteristics, they have a good sense of humour.

Some experimentalists also opined that these children are shy and lovers of seclusion. They segregate themselves from the group. Very few children have interest in the opposite sex.

These children are socially more mature than other children of their age. Usually they are rated higher by their teachers on the social and emotional plane. They always prefer games which require reasoning and judgement. These children play games that are favoured by children older than them. They are neither eccentric nor unpopular.

(v) Learning and Education

These children learn to walk and talk earlier than the average ones. Their vocabulary is very good. They possess a wide vocabulary which they use to accelerate their language development. They also have a retentive memory. They are superior in their achievements in school subjects. Unevenness is rarely noticed in their achievement because they work hard and devotedly. Near about fifty per cent of gifted children have learned to read before entering school. After entering school, they develop a keen interest in more abstract school subjects. They rank well above their individual grades.

XII.12 Identification of Gifted Children

Giftedness is a concept of nineteenth century. The history of development of the concept of gifted children reveals that the recent trend of speaking and writing in favour of intellectual excellence reflects a new profile of goals as much as a change in the level of expectations. This change of attitudes has been greatly influenced by urgent military needs and the rapid scientific advances which depend on sophisticated technology and a more highly developed intelligence. As the Commission on Human Resources has stated, "The brains of its citizens constitute a nation's greatest asset. From these minds will come the future scientific discoveries, future works of art and literature, future advances in statesmanship, technology and social organization, in short, all future progress".

The development of a nation depends upon the vision and insight of a relatively few exceptionally able people. When people have no vision they perish. Much of the vision necessary for the promotion of human welfare must come from our gifted boys and girls, who have been educated for worthwhile leadership and productivity in a democracy. High grade leadership is essential in a democracy more than in any other form of government. Democracy will be realised in its richest sense by recognizing the full range of ability in our total population and also by giving full recognition and adequate opportunities for the maximum development of the gifted and talented.

Apart from this, there is even greater necessity for developing in the gifted an awareness of their responsibility not only to develop their gifts fully, but also to use their abilities constructively in the interests of democracy. Today, we have to recognize the gifted child as a person who has much to contribute to all and also as one who deserves the good life in accordance with his personal needs, ambitions and hopes.

Efforts to identify the gifted start from two assumptions. Firstly, the emergence of talent is not inevitable. Individual promise needs the incubator of an education which challenges and motivates a pupil to develop his or her capacities to the fullest. A high level of ability can become a liability, if it is not understood, appreciated or accepted. If the education is not stimulating the child attempts to retain a kind of self-respect by rejecting the material which is not worthy of his attention. Association with other gifted is very important for the exchange of ideas and for sharing of aspirations as well as for the reason that they might not go through school hardened by a feeling of loneliness. It should never be forgotten that the superior child also has the fundamental needs of comfort, love, challenging and creative activities and a helpful and encouraging environment within which to grow. The second assumption is that the assessment techniques and procedures exist to uncover great potentials for attainment in individuals who will not profit from custom-tailored educational experiences.

Modes to Identify the Gifted

More than twenty-four centuries ago Plato pleaded for the identification of the able to act as guardians of his ideal state. He wrote, "We must watch them from their youth upward and make them perform actions in which they are most likely to forget and to be deceived; and he who remembers and is not deceived, is to be selected and he who fails the trial will be rejected."

Educationists are trying to give the identification procedure a scientific turn. The procedure which is geared to discovering a large portion of all existing talent must include systematic testing and observing, and the tests and observations must cover an inclusive range of intelligent behaviour. Besides the performance in tests of intelligence and achievement, the individual's physical, emotional and social characteristics and his pattern of behaviour, as observed day by day in many different situations, should also be included in the identification procedure, Anecdotal records, photographs, etc. are helpful in studying the child's potentialities and needs.

XII.13 Assessment of Gifted Children

There are different ways by which the gifted may be identified and assessed. At present the most prevalent and accepted method is the one adopted by Terman, which takes the score on an Intelligence or Mental Test as the criterion, though other ways are still being studied. These methods can be studied as:

(i) Mental Tests

Mental tests are based on individual differences in innate abilities to acquire, arrange and use facts as objectively as possible. An intelligence test score is a numerical appraisal of mental abilities required for performing a task that depends on the exercise of intelligence. The IQ is conditioned to the test itself, to the cultural limitations, to the person who is administering the test and to the child's attitudes as well as his physical and emotional conditions at the time. At present the reliability of the best current tests of intelligence is between 0.90 and 0.95. While current tests of intelligence will not pick out all the mentally gifted children in a group, they are probably the most effective single instruments available for selecting such children.

(ii) Aptitude Tests

Today the term "gifted" child has become synonymous with the expression

"A child with a high IQ", thus blinding us to other forms of excellence. The American Association for Gifted Children some time ago recommended that qualities other than IQ be included in the conception of giftedness and defined the gifted individual as "A person whose performance in any line of socially useful endeavour is consistently superior." This definition includes those who are talented in art, music, drama and mathematics, as well as those who possess a high level of mechanical and social skills or high abstract verbal intelligence.

Though aptitudes are being given due importance, even today there is a controversy among psychologists about the existence of aptitudes, their exact limits, their nature, and whether they are innate or acquired. For identification, at present the tendency is to use such aptitude tests as are available to throw some light at least on the nature of the abilities of the gifted. The value of the tests depends on the training of the interpreter. It is necessary today to have more and more aptitude tests because the gifted with special abilities cannot be discovered readily through the use of the intelligence tests.

(iii) Reports of Parents

While parents are likely to be biased in estimating the intelligence of their children, their reports are often of considerable value in identification. No one can hope to have as intimate a knowledge of a child's behaviour over as long a period of time as his parents. In a report on gifted children in California, Terman and Oden have stated that early indications of superior intelligence most often noted by parents are quick understanding, insatiable curiosity, extensive information, retentive memory, large vocabulary and unusual interest in such things as number relations, atlases and encyclopedias. Early walking and talking and acquiring the ability to read without training during the pre-school period have also attracted the attention of parents of these children. Moreover, gifted children are likely to have parents who are themselves gifted or at least who are superior in intelligence, so they are likely to have more insight into the ability of their children. But it cannot be denied that some parents are oftCn biased and inaccurate in their observations.

(iv) Reports of Teachers and other Professional Workers

The American Association for Gifted Children reports that many investigations have shown that teachers fail to identify the gifted; only 15.7% of the children nominated by 6000 teachers, each as the most intelligent in his class, were found to qualify as gifted. Teachers fail because they are often inclined to evaluate a child in terms of his school achievement. Few gifted are as educationally advanced as their ability warrants. Unchallenging school work, many times, develops poor habits of work and of thinking in the gifted. Teachers also tend to overlook the factor of chronological age. A reaction to the personality of different children may influence the teacher's evaluation of ability. Besides some teachers do not have adequate standards of child development by which to judge the gifted child's status and hence to estimate his ability. In most foreign countries teachers are now being given criteria for recognising deviations from physical and emotional health in school children. Ability to detect giftedness has become an important part of the teacher's training in observation, in some countries. In addition to teachers, physicians in general practice and school nurses also come into contact with the gifted. Recreation leaders and religious teachers may also recognize the gifted child.

(v) Age Grade Status of the Gifted

Terman and Oden state, "If you are allowed only one method of locating the highest 9 in a classroom, your chance of getting the right child is better if you merely look in the class register and take the youngest rather than trust the teacher's judgement". The method is useful. Recently there has been an increasing tendency in many American school systems to group children for instruction largely in accordance with their chronological age and to provide appropriate opportunities for the gifted within the group. Instead of acceleration in school there is an increasing tendency to enrich the curriculum for the gifted.

(vi) School Accomplishment and Achievement Tests

The belief that outstanding ability may invariably be reflected by superior accomplishment in school is wrong. Teachers' estimates and school achievement can often be inaccurate. Terman and Oden have said that when school marks in the various subjects were compared with scores on reliable and valid achievement tests, large discrepancies were found. In every school grade there were children whose school achievement in one more subjects was rated average or below for the grade, but whose achievement test scores showed them to be as much as two years above their grade norms in those same subjects. Standardized achievement tests are better than school marks. Terman and Oden found that the gifted child's educational age was 44 per cent higher than his chronological age, and the gifted group had a grade progress quotient of 114. This shows the probabilities that standardized achievement tests may have a better place in identifying gifted children.

XII.14 Education of the Gifted Children

History reveals the fact that in Plato's republic, there were plans for special education for all the different walks of life. This ideal Republic was the first plan to formulate explicitly the idea of special classes for scholars, artisans, warriors and labourers. We also get a similar indication in the origin of caste system in India. The entire society was divided into few groups with particular specialisations. Brahmins were supposed to be the intellectuals in the society, Kshatriyas, warriors, Vaisyas, businessmen and Sudras, servants of the above three classes. Under these plans, some kind of screening was also implied. Talented children were to be sorted out and given the kind of training best suited to them. This was done to save human wastage and to make the best use of human resources. In our old system of education, we get ample evidence of special education.

Literature states that individuals who have been specially talented were individually coached by either their parents or tutors. Organisation of a special class or special school for the gifted is of much later origin. In 1862, the earliest recognition of the gifted in USA was indicated in the form of promotion plans in the city of St. Louis. This plan suggested that promotions should be given after every six months to start with, then at intervals of three months and still later promotion after every five weeks. It was presumed that frequent promotions would provide a chance for the gifted to get recognition for their talent. Experiments were done in New Jersey in 1886 with the different groupings within a class. Children were classified in different groups according to their abilities and talents. Each group was allowed to advance as rapidly as it could. Results revealed that this provided the opportunity for each student to achieve his maximum target of ability and potentiality. In Europe, the Cambridge plan was originated in 1891 and it was spread over the section of school extending from fourth to ninth grade.

But in India, we do not find any school planned with this specific purpose. Of course, some provisions are marked in public schools and in some boarding schools. These schools are originally meant for the students coming from the upper socio-economic status families and sometimes children from Royal families. Children for these schools are selected indirectly. The fees and expenses of these schools are significantly higher. So a few parents are able to send their children to these type of schools. Once the child is admitted to the school, he has to follow an enriched curriculum than he would in an average school. One major drawback with this type of selection is that every child in this school is not gifted. But the school provides educational facilities for the gifted ones.

Nowadays, in India, attention is being paid to the education of the gifted by State and Central authorities. By providing merit scholarships, it is possible to spot the gifted children who can be placed in these public schools at Government cost. Through this procedure many scholars emerge from middle class families.

Generally gifted children, when allowed to attend regular classes, are expected to face the problems of their own. An average class and its programme are planned for children of average ability. By admitting gifted children into this class, they are denied the opportunity they need for full development of their talents. Their education is restricted. The teacher finds himself placed in a very awkward position as to how to satisfy both the talented and the average children.

In the classroom, the average child develops a feeling of backwardness and inferiority. This often leads to frustration due to a continuous sense of failure experienced by the child. He sees that the gifted ones occupy the highest positions while he is unable to do so.

In our educational system, very often we allow double promotions which places the bright children in a senior class. It is done with the anticipation that the child will be able to find a challenge in the work of a senior class and utilise his talents. But we forget that when a child is given an accelerated promotion, he is placed out of his own group with respect to physical, social and emotional development. But it is found that when a talented child is placed with children who are higher in the developmental continuum, he may find himself out of step in other activities and interests. So it is suggested that the child should be provided with an enriched programme while he is allowed to share the experiences of children of his own level of development.

Again, it is customary in our schools to entrust more work to the gifted children. But this is a wrong step which should be realised by our teachers. It must be kept in mind that being overloaded with a mediocre type of work is not enrichment for a talented child. The work that is not challenging to him or the routine type of work may invite monotony for the gifted child. An intelligent child always wants to accomplish difficult tasks which pose a challenge to him and which he can complete independently. He derives satisfaction from the urge to investigate for himself. Enrichment includes the avoidance of repetition and drill. Backward children gain from the drill but it is monotonous for the gifted ones. Drill tends to irritate the talented children affecting their output seriously.

There is every possibility of the gifted children developing bad social habits due to lack of enrichment of educational programmes. They feel, very often, that the tasks given to them are not interesting and for from satisfying. So they engage themselves in loafing and indulging in antisocial activities for excitement. Sometimes, they invite disciplinary problems in the classroom. These problems become acute when they understand that the teacher usually plans work for an average child. Suppose a teacher anticipates that a particular task will take 30 minutes to be completed by an average child. He plans it accordingly. But when the task is given, a talented child would finish it within 20 minutes. So he gets some extra time on his hands. Then he plans to utilise it in an interesting way. But this act of the talented child may not be appreciated by the teacher. He may get disturbed by that and the classroom discipline may by the teacher. He may get disturbed by that and the classroom discipline may be affected. The talented children engage themselves in such activities because they have surplus energy and time on hand which they must spend. As a result, a conflict with the social discipline is pertinent.

Sometimes the planned curriculum is so arranged that it would miss some of the aspects of the developments of a child. A gifted child needs opportunities for an all round development of his personality. Enrichment of the educational programme, if aimed entirely on the academic side, will undoubtedly ignore the development of the social, aesthetic or emotional aspects of personality. A problem is still pertinent here. We know that each child maintains a different rate of growth and development. In the same age group, one may develop one aspect earlier and faster than others. There may be others who are slower in their general rate of growth. An ideal programme meets the demands of all these individuals so that every possibility is there that individual attention is paid to every child. The programme must be suitable for individual needs, demands and nature of development.

Programmes for bright children usually take one of these three principle forms : *(i)* Enrichment, *(ii)* Acceleration, and *(iii)* Grouping in special classes. We have discussed the first two points in detail with their advantages and disadvantages. We now discuss the points "for" and "against" special classes. Enrichment is basically a teaching procedure whether it is applied to a regular class or to a special class. But acceleration and grouping are essentially administrative techniques. Each may be used alone or in amalgamation with one or both of the other types.

Special classes and schools are universally accepted by psychologists and educationists for the education of gifted children. William Stern calls these classes as "elite-classes". Investigations revealed that it has yielded satisfactory results. Still the situation is not so simple as it is thought to be. There is a very interesting controversy about the desirability of special education for the gifted. There are some valid points raised on either side of the issue. Some of the points advanced in favour of special classes are :

(1) The work of an average child done in a class is a handicap to the talented child. Here he is restrained. But in a special class, gifted children are provided with the opportunity to work according to their superior ability. In the average class, not only the superior child moves at a slower pace, but he also does not get the benefit of superior teaching. A very pertinent fact is that through mutual stimulation, a group of gifted children have the advantage of progressing and developing more rapidly.

(2) If a gifted child is placed in an average class, he will develop some

careless habits. The tasks given to him are too easy to ------------ sometimes he refuses to -------------out. Very often such children become maladjusted and antisocial. But a special class offers opportunities to the talented ones for challenging work and develop their potentialities to the maximum.

(3) Where special classes are not available, the gifted children are often permitted double promotions. With this, they are compelled to mix with more mature and older children. But while doing so, one thing must be kept in mind that a superior child may not necessarily be superior in sociability and other aspects of development. Again, some adjustment problems are also found. The child may be superior in intelligence as far as his studies go, but that does not mean that when he is put in an absolutely new group, he may not face the problem of social adjustment. However, he can overcome this difficulty if he is placed in a special class. He has the scope for passing grades at the normal rate and the opportunity to move with his own group.

(4) Very often, talented children suffer from social maladjustment. They get plenty of time in the average class because the tasks given to them are lighter and easy. They can solve it much quicker than the anticipated time span, leaving them with time to spare till the average students finish the job. In the meantime, their alert mind is diverted to seek other outlets. Research evidences reveal that many delinquents have proved to be children of superior ability, but they left school to avoid the monotony and boredom of the average curriculum.

(5) The empirical works in this area revealed that special classes also provide opportunities to develop leadership in various arenas. In the group, there may be children specially gifted in painting, poetry, mathematics, literature and other branches of knowledge. More developed and well planned programmes become conductive for their talent and future leaders in these particular fields emerge.

(6) Henry Goddard (1933) has rightly pointed out that gifted children "are made of finer stuff than the majority". These children are more sensitive alert and quick in their thinking. If proper stimulation is not provided, they create problems in the class. When put together with the average group, it becomes a problem for the teacher. Treatment and handling of the two types of children become extremely difficult.

their talents and potentialities. But a group of psychologists and educationists strongly refuted the isolation of these children from regular schools. They have their reasons too. We take these reasons as criticisms of the movement.

(a) The potent criticism against the movement is that it is highly undemocratic. "Equal opportunity of Education" should be provided to one and all. We support this point strongly.

(b) Very often, psychologists point out that if the gifted children are taken away from regular classes, they tend to develop conceit. Again, they become conscious of their superior ability and fail to develop modesty as a personality trait.

(c) Special classes give rise to a kind of intellectual aristocracy. The isolation of gifted children and formation of special groups give rise to ideas of superiority.

(d) When gifted children are separated, an average child tends to lose. When working with the gifted, an average child gets a chance to learn many things, and becomes highly motivated. Withdrawal of the gifted deprives the average child of rich stimulation.

(e) Some educationists feel that such programmes deprive the society of superior leadership. While working with the average children, the gifted gets a chance to act as a leader and gets training in leadership. Thus, the society is provided with future leaders.

(f) The most important criticism levelled against special education is the high cost of such programmes. Particularly, in a developing country like India, this point is of special importance. Some critics argue that when there is not enough money for the education of the average child, such expensive programmes for the gifted is a little undemocratic.

XII.15 Guiding Gifted Children and the Role of Parents and Teachers

Psychologists point out that parents also play an equally important role in the proper development of the gifted children. It is very important for the parents to provide the right environment for gifted children, so that they may find scope to make good use of their intelligence. Sometimes their fundamental needs are overlooked. But parents should take note of it. The children must feel that they are wanted by their parent and their parents enjoy their company.

Gifted children need recognition. Sincere praise from their parents, teachers and friends makes them feel that they are liked. If they are denied recognition, they escape into daydreaming. Gifted children must feel that they are protected in case of need and the parents should encourage them in gaining new experiences. Every parent must think that the child seeks understanding and sympathy of his parents in his search for further learning. Parents should keep themselves well informed about many facts, so that they can answer the child's questions readily and correctly. As the child grows older, he should be encouraged to read and to find out the answers to his questions himself.

Generally children learn through observation. Gifted children are keen observers. They usually learn from examples set by their parents. These children learn good manners, correct speech habits, courtesy, neatness, honesty, punctuality at a very early stage.

Another potent factor to guide the gifted child is motivation. The motive of the gifted child should be satisfied. For them, curiosity is a strong urge. A gifted child is always eager to know "Why", "How", "When" and "Where" etc. and answering the child's questions will not only provide him the knowledge but satisfy his curiosity too.

Many parents overestimate the talent of their children. They usually insist on the child achieving things much beyond his actual capacity. Again, some parents select a certain vocation for their children without consulting a vocational counsellor. To force a child into a particular vocation is highly undesirable. Psychologists advise that no selection of a vocation should be made for a bright child before he finishes his high school. If parents have any problems in handling gifted children, they should consult with Child Psychologists or Guidance Counsellors immediately.

Role of a Teacher

Coming to the role of a teacher, the teacher for bright children must be a flexible person and dynamic. He should allow the children to make new discoveries. The teacher must be a source of inspiration, encouragement and opportunity for them to test their potentialities, to explore more avenues. Bright children always need inspired guidance. Top priority should be given to productive learning and effective living.

Creativity requires sensitivity and independence. Both parents and teachers should help gifted children to discover their potentialities. They should keep them free in gathering, assembling, comparing and exchanging ideas. Parents and teachers must try to reduce the gap of emotional distance between themselves and gifted children. It is possible by participation and understanding.

Besides all these factors, it is generally agreed that education of superior and gifted pupils should emphasize certain other intellectual objectives, in addition to the acquisition of necessary and desirable information and skills. These other objectives include: *(i)* analytic perception, *(ii)* the methods of

problem-solving, *(iii)* employing analysis, *(iv)* synthesis, *(v)* conceptual thinking, *(vi)* scientific objectivity, *(vii)* independent and creative effort, and *(ix)* encouragement of special interests.

XII.16 Learning Exercises

1. **Discuss the meaning of exceptional children and the types of exceptional children.**
2. **Describe the needs of exceptional children and need of the type of education required to the exceptional children.**
3. **Enlist the characteristics of creative children and their assessment.**
4. **Explain how we can develop environment to promote creative abilities among children?**
5. **Discuss the concept of gifted children and explain how gifted children can be identified?**
6. **Describe the techniques of assessment of gifted children.**
7. **Suggest the guiding principles to educate the gifted children.**
8. **Describe the role of a teacher in dealing with the education of the exceptional children.**

XIII

Mentally Retarded Children

In the world today mental retardation constitutes one of the most pressing problems. The history of development of the study of mental retardation has been plagued by vagueness and disagreement about definitions, classification/ diagnosis and rehabilitation measures. When intelligence tests were first introduced, designating labels such as idiots, imbeciles and morons were used. These labels had a final sound to them which was consistent with the view that there was no point in trying to educated or train such people, and that they would be better off if hidden away from society in an institution.

However, today educationists are more humanitarian and realistic to the approach of education of the mentally retarded. Hostile and negative labels have been replaced by the terms 'slow learners' or 'intellectually handicapped'. Educationists have become more optimistic and have a better idea about the causes of mental retardation. Mental retardation is more a product of social deprivation than neurological defects (Zigler, 1967). This viewpoint has made educationists more willing to work with slow learners and help them realize their best potentials.

XIII.1 Meaning and Definitions of Mentally Retarded Children

Mentally retarded is termed as mentally deficient or mental deficiency. The term has been defined in several ways such as:

Page: Mental deficiency is a condition of sub-normal mental development, present at birth or early childhood and characterized mainly by limited intelligence and social inadequacy.

Rosen, Fox and Gregory: Mental retardation refers to a chronic condition present from birth or early childhood which is characterized by both impaired intellectual functioning as measured by standardized tests and impaired adaptation to the daily demands of the individual's social environment.

British Mental Deficiency Act: Mental retardation is a condition of arrested or incomplete development of mind existing before the age of 18 years whether arising from inherent causes or induced by disease or injury.

American Association on Mental Deficiency: Mental retardation refers to significantly sub-average general intellectual functioning existing concurrently with deficits in adaptive behaviour, and manifested during the development period.

From the above definitions it can be said that mental retardation is a state of mind of a child giving certain inferences such as:

1. It is related to the sub-normal development of the mind or brain.
2. It is not a disease nor a medical syndrome with a specific cause. A number of specific identified causes involving both the inherent and external factors may be responsible for it.
3. The deficiency may be observed at birth or manifested later during the course of development, generally before the end of the years of adolescence.
4. The mentally retarded, can be identified through:
   (a) their very low scores on some standardized intelligence tests.
   (b) the observation of their behaviour in the developmental period demonstrating impaired intellectual functioning.
   (c) their inadequacy to deal with the demands of environmental or deficiency and defects in adaptive behaviour.

In brief, mental retardation has been described as a state of incomplete development of the mind without reference to the state of the individual's adjustment to his environment or the nature of his adaptive behaviour or the difficulties he may face on account of his sub-normal intellectual functioning; the other definitions try to point out both, the state of the sub-normal's intellectual functioning and its effect on his day-to-day behaviour and environmental adaptation. In the same way Page stresses inadequate social adjustment as a consequence of impaired intellectual functioning, Rosen, Fox and Gregory point out difficulties in meeting the daily demands of the environment.

American Association of Mental Deficiency (AAMD) points out that mental retardedness is due to retardation of mental development during different stages of child's stages of development. The Association (AAMD) is of the view that measurable intelligence and certain adaptative behavioural attributes of a child are responsible to make him retarded. Consequently a person cannot be designed as mentally retarded solely because of a low I.Q. A low I.Q. plus impaired or deficient adaptive behaviour originating before maturity is the essential requirement for a person to be described as mentally retarded. This definition deliberately does not consider the etiology of mental retardation simply because mental retardation may not be attributed to any specific cause or causes.

XIII.2 Identification of Mentally Retarded Children

The term mentally retarded means retardation in the pace of cognitive development of a child. The principle of balanced development reveals that any type of irregularity in the pace of development (Physical Mental Social) at a particular stage automatically influence the development of other.

It is possible to some extent, that the physical appearance of the mentally retarded may give rise to some doubt about their normal intellectual functioning. Thus, however, is not always so, and in many cases the physical appearance gives no indication of mental retardation. In fact, the similarities between the mental retardates and the intellectually normal people exceed the differences. Therefore, great care must be taken for the proper identification and detection of mental retardedness among children. In this connection. Nicholas Hobbs (1975) pointed out in *The Features of Children*, to classify children who differ in significant ways from the norm in order to plan and finance special education for them. The need for classifying children with mental retardation has been recognized by the American Association on Mental Deficiency (AAMD), which proposed this definition. "Mental retardation refers to significantly subaverage intellectual functioning existing concurrently with defects in adaptive behaviour and manifested during the developmental period" (Grossman, 1977, 1983). The American Association of Mentally Retarded applies the term **mental retardation** to individuals having IQ scores of 67 and below, and classifies those with IQ scores within that range into the following categories:

Mild retardation—IQ score between 67 and 52.

Moderate retardation—IQ score between 51 and 36

Severe retardation—IQ score between 35 and 20

Profound retardation—IQ score of 19 and below

Owing to the legal challenges to IQ testing and special class placement as well as to the trend toward mainstreaming, students classified as mildly retarded who were once separated are more likely now to be placed in regular classes. You probably will not encounter a great many mainstreamed children classified as moderately or severely retarded, because of the specialized forms of care and instruction they need. You may, however, be asked to teach for at least part of the lay one or more higher-scoring mildly retarded children.

XIII.3 Classification of Mentally Retarded Children

Identification of Mental retardation is based on measurable intelligent quotient and other acquired mental abilities. Psychological studies reveals that mental deficiency among mentally retarded children varies from one another. This mental variation can be identified with the help of standardised Intelligent tests. As you know there are many tests to measure I.Q. the range of scores obtained by the mentally retarded enable us to classify in to different groups. In this connection Chintamani Kar points out that classification mental of retardation can be studied as:

Level of Mental Retardation	*Wechsler I.Q.*	*Stantford-Binet I.Q.*
(i) Mild	(55-69)	(52-67)
(ii) Moderate	(40-54)	(36-51)
(iii) Severe	(25-39)	(20-35)
(iv) Profound	Under 25	Under 20

The educational classification of retardation taking I.Qs into account is as follows :

Level of Retardation	*I.Qs*
(i) Educable	(60-85)
(ii) Trainable	(30-60)
(iii) Custodial	Below 30

Clinical evidences indicate that on an average 2.5 per cent of children in India are mild to moderately mentally retarded and 0.5 per cent severely retarded.

Since most parents of such children in India are not educated and affluent, they do not believe that their offspring are mentally retarded. They have a strong notion that if the child is not doing well in his studies, it is because he does not work hard. They strongly resent being told that their child is mentally retarded and needs special attention. So the first thing to do is to educate the parents to accept the situation. Tests of mental ability should be applied to the children and the parents made conversant with them.

If a mentally retarded child is admitted into school, his performance is very poor. There is every chance that he will discontinue his studies or he will remain in the lower grades for a long span of time. He is unable to compete with his classmates. Others expect him to show a performance equally that of a normal child. This attitude will make him frustrated.

In the table below, UNESCO has presented the following classification of mentally retarded children:

Degree of Mental Subnormality	*Terms in Current Use*	*Approximate I.Q. Level*	*Approximate percentage in Population of School Age*	
(i) Severe Subnormality	Idiot	(0.19)	0.06	} 2.56
(ii) Moderate Subnormality	Imbecile	(20-49)	0.24	
(iii) Mild Subnormality	Feeble-minded	(50-69)	2.26	
(iv) Dull-Normal	Dull and Backward	(70-85 & 90)	10.00	

(Estimated Proportion of various Grades of Mentally Subnormal Children in the School Population)*

The above table points out that there are 2.56 per cent of children have an estimated I.Q. lower than 70. So it is essential that mentally retarded children should be given special attention. They should be taught a simple vocabulary. The reading materials for them must be written around their life interests. Also they should be provided with vocational training.

XIII.4 Causes of Mental Retarded Children

Mental retardedness is based on number of causitive factors but if we classify them we can categorise the causes of mental retardedness into three groups: *(i)* Genetic, *(ii)* Organic, and *(iii)* Social.

(1) *Genetic Factors*: For a long time, it was believed that mental retardation was the result of inherited defects. The famous Goddard story placed emphasis on inherited defects. During the American Revolutionary War, Martin married a barmaid who was considered to be mentally retarded. After the war he married again, this time an intelligent girl from his own class. Goddard (1912) traced both the lines of descendants for a number of generations. Astonishingly, he found many more feeble-minded persons among the descendants of the feeble-minded barmaid than among those of the intelligent wives. Lastly, Goddard concluded that mental retardation is hereditary. Some recent research findings reveal that 20 to 25 per cent of the cases of mental retardation are due to genetic defects.

(2) ***Organic Factors*****:** Coming to the **organic causes** of mental retardation, it can be said that this is characterised by a definite pathology in the central nervous system which is not hereditary. Such anomalies in the brain or nervous system may arise before birth, during birth or after birth. **Organic causes** also include birth injury, disease or toxic conditions. Maldevelopment of the embryo or foetus due to infection, such as 'German Measles', is another potent factor of mental retardation.

(3) ***Social Factors*****:** Social factors also play a major role in mental retardation such as adverse socio-economic conditions in which children are brought up. Children coming from the lowest social classes obviously have poor educational facilities.

Remedial Measures for Mental Retardation

Whatever preventive measures we may adopt, it is neither possible nor feasible to completely eliminate the possibility of the occurrence of mental retardation. We can neither exercise much control over hereditary influences nor can we avoid accidental hazards, and traumas. Moreover, we are also handicapped in controlling the unfavourable influences of defective socio-cultural environment and are unable to overcome the deficiency arising from psychological deprivation. Therefore, cases of mental retardation are bound to exist and we have to think out and plan the treatment and remedial measures for the mental retardates.

To treat mental retardation we should keep in our mind that complete cure for mental retardation is never possible. Because mental is based on some mental deficiency Mental retardates are essentially incurable in the sense that they cannot be given more intelligence and made normal. No amount of training or medical care can transform a mental retardate into a normal individual. The mentally subnormal should not be confused with persons who are mentally ill or suffer from a mental disease. In this connection, the observation of Wechsler (1979) is worth quoting:

Mental deficiency, unlike typhoid fever or paralysis is not a disease. A mentally deficient is not a person who suffers from a specific disease process but one who by reasons of intellectual arrest or impairment is unable to cope with his environment to the extent that he needs special care, education and institutionalization.

It will be appropriate to consider the treatment or remedial measures for the adjustment, rehabilitation and education of the mentally retarded, in the light of the above observations.

Bio-medical measures

Mental retardation, to some extent, is said to be a medical problem. The following medical measures may prove helpful in some cases:

(1) Cretinism. This mental retardation resulting from deficiency in thyroid secretion, if recognised at birth or in its early manifestations, may be corrected or controlled by the institution of thyroid therapy.

(2) Congenital syphilis. Children infected with congenital syphilis are usually found to be suffering from severe mental subnormality. Early detection and prompt penicillin therapy is found to be helpful in the prevention as well as control of many effects of congenital syphilis.

(3) Phenylketonuria. On early detection with the help of a simple urine test, Phenylketonuria a metabolic disorder causing mental retardation may be checked or controlled, to a great extent, by placing the infant on a special diet relatively free of phenylalanine found in most protein foods.

(4) Hydrocephalus. Hydrocephalus, resulting from the accumulation of an abnormal amount of cerebrospinal fluid within the cranium results in mental retardation. Surgical treatment is found to be very effective in the treatment of this disorder. It is aimed at the reduction of the normal production of cerebrospinal fluid or to the channelling of the fluid by removing the blockade or obstruction resulting from congenital malformations or post-natal infections.

(5) Epileptic Seizures. In the case of patients subject to epileptic seizures, the administration of anticonvulsant medication may prove helpful in controlling and minimizing intellectual deterioration.

(6) Controlling disturbed behaviour. The administration of tranquilizers proves useful in controlling hyperactive and disturbed behaviour among mental retardates.

Psychological Measures

To eradicate psychological based mental retardation psychological measures are adopted. Psychological treatment in the form of individual or group psychotherapy is found to be useful in providing remedial measures for mental retardation. Children can be helped in solving problems of emotional and social maladjustment and resolving their mental conflicts through psychological measures.

Parent Counselling. Parents can also help in the welfare, care as well as treatment of the mental retardates. For this purpose, there is a need for proper counselling services for them. Moreover, on account of their emotional involvement the parents do not always realize the shortcomings and deficiency of their children and waste a lot of time and money in the hope that some magic cure will be found or the deficiency will automatically disappear with time. Sometimes, they become disturbed by the responsibilities of looking after their mentally retarded child. Such disappointed, insecure and guilt-ridden parents begin to demand behaviour and intellectual achievement beyond the abilities of the child who is often abused, snubbed and punished for no fault of his. Some parents adopt an over-protective approach in their effort to shield the child from challenging situations and thus make him completely dependent by interfering with the development of whatever abilities or capacities he may possess. It is therefore essential that parents should first realize the truth about their child. They should accept the child's limitations and the mental deficiency in the sense that the child cannot be given more intelligence and made normal.

Secondly, they should be educated to behave normally with their mentally subnormal child without being over protective or rejecting the child.

Thirdly, the parents should be given training and education for handling the emotional and social adjustment problems of the retarded children. They should never compare their achievements and abilities with those of their normal siblings or other children in the home and neighbourhood. It should be seen that the retarded child is not unnecessarily criticised or ridiculed by others.

Fourthly, they should be educated to provide essential training at home to their mentally retarded child. How to train him to manage his affairs independently, how to help the child to develop and seek maximum utilization of his subnormal capacities are some of the areas where useful educational and training can be provided by the parents.

Finally, the parents should be made to realise that if needed there is no harm in sending their children to special schools meant for the mental retardates. It is the best place for their education and training.

Provision of Special Education and Training

It is a cardinal educational as well as psychological error to educate or train the mental retardates with normal children. The involved attitude of the parents at home also interferes with the development of the retarded child. The remedy lies in the provision of special education or training for them. The institutes or boarding schools meant for subnormal children serve a useful purpose in this direction. For better results, the special institutes or schools must be managed keeping the following considerations in mind:

1. There should be proper grouping and classification of the mentally retarded children on the basis of the degree of severity of their retardation.
2. The 'educable' should be educated and the 'trainable' should be

trained. Those who are neither easily educable nor trainable should be cared for and efforts should be made to train them to manage their basic day-to-day needs.

3. The schools should provide the environment essential for maximum development of the abilities and capacities of all mental retardates. Curriculum, methods of teaching, and tools for evaluation should be adjusted according to their individual needs.
4. There should be provision for specially trained teachers, able to utilize latest materials and techniques for their education or training. They should be able to deal with the special problems of these children, understand them sympathetically, and help them to grow with their deficiencies.
5. In these schools greater emphasis should be placed on cocurricular experiences and the children should be provided opportunities for learning the ways for their emotional and social adjustment, imbibing moral virtues and desirable personal habits.
6. These institutions should make provision for vocational education and training. The mental retardates should be trained for manual work, crafts and specialized vocations in keeping with their abilities.

The general attitude towards the mentally handicapped needs to be changed. They are not to be sympathized with, protected or ridiculed but to be helped in growing and developing within their strengths and limitations. Their education or training should begin at home. Thereafter special schools or institutions may be involved in their education and training. The society and the state, then, should take responsibility for their rehabilitation and adjustment.

XIII.5 Education of Mentally Retarded Children

Education of the mentally retarded children is the main concern of special education teacher. A special educator while educating the mentally retarded child firstly categorise the mentally retarded educant and then teach him as per the level of mental retardedness. Mangal suggests that a special teacher while teaching mentally retarded child follow the most accepted classification based on the I.Q. as well as adaptive behaviour criteria enumerates the four levels of retardation *i.e.* mild, moderate, severe and profound. For educational care and programmes, the mentally retarded children belonging to these four levels of retardedness can be regrouped into educable (labelled as mild), trainable (labelled as moderate) and custodial (labelled as severe and profound). Let us now consider the specific educational programmes for these types of children.

(1) Educational programmes for the educable mentally retarded (EMR)

The educable mentally retarded (EMR) are considered educable in the sense that if the instructions and the atmosphere for learning are appropriate, they can be expected to acquire the basic academic skills of reading, writing and arithmetic. However, their maximum academic achievement can be expected to equal that of the average eight to twelve year old child. Most of them can easily learn vocational skills needed for future employment preferably of semiskilled or unskilled nature. The following points should be specially taken into consideration for planning the educational programmes for them:

1. Schooling of these students may be delayed for 2 to 3 years.
2. During the earliest school years, they may be given instruction in simple arithmetical concepts, understanding of the home and community and early development of good work habits.
3. Formal reading and writing instruction must be started preferably at the age of 9 or 10.
4. The curriculum for these children should include the topics, contents and learning experiences related to basic academic skills as well as the basic skills for coping with the environment as children and as adults.
5. The school's curricular as well as cocurricular activities should lay stronger emphasis on experience than on abstraction.
6. In any case, in spite of their educability these children should not be expected to attain the level of accomplishment of the same chronological age as normal children.

(2) Educational programmes for the trainable mentally retarded (TMR)

The TMR children cannot be educated like the EMR. However, they can be trained to acquire certain basic skills so that they may lead their future dependent or semi-independent lives. The following aspects may be considered for planning appropriate training programmes for them:

1. They may be helped to acquire self-help skills like independent eating, dressing, toileting, washing and combing hair, brushing teeth, and using towels and handkerchiefs, etc. They may be gradually taught to follow directions and perform simple tasks.
2. They should then be trained to acquire social skills like greeting people, play with their companions, take turns and follow the rules of the road, observe common social courtesies and health rules, etc.
3. Necessary training should also be provided for the development of motor skills and improvement of sensory discrimination.

4. Necessary household skills like dusting and sweeping, washing of utensils and clothes, ironing, sewing, using household articles and appliances like the radio, television, telephone, and limited travelling in familiar areas etc. should also be taught to them.
5. The teaching of basic academic skills should not be started until early adolescence. The academic skills taught to them should be of very simple nature like learning to recognize common signs and symbols, learning to recognize and use coins and currencies, and telling the time to the half or the quarter hour.
6. The curriculum should then include activities for teaching unskilled occupational jobs. It should also include activities related with leisure skills.
7. Throughout their training and acquiring learning experiences, the training programme should be based on the use of concrete lesson materials rather than on any abstract thinking or lecturing (i.e. real objects rather than two-dimensional representations on paper, careful modelling rather than heavy emphasis on verbalized directions).
8. In addition to providing concrete and real experiences, the training programmes for these children must be based fundamentally on principles of reinforcement like token economy, contingency management and other concepts of behaviour modification.

(3) Educational programmes for the custodial mentally retarded (CMR)

The severely retarded (I.Q. range about 20 to 35) and profoundly retarded (I.Q. below 20) children can neither be educated nor trained like the educable or the trainable children. No public school system or voluntary organisation exists in India for their schooling and rehabilitation and such children have, of necessity, to be admitted into government or semigovernment residential institutions. Educationally both the severely retarded and the profoundly retarded have no hope and custodial treatment provided in the residential institutions is the only avenue open to them. A proper custodial programme whether run in residential institutions, day hospitals, day-care centres or boarding and nursing homes must take care of the following:

1. Educational programmes for these children must lay strong emphasis on self-help skills like feeding, toilet training, washing and cleaning of their body parts and dressing up etc.
2. They must be taught to protect themselves from health and weather hazards, harmful insects, animals, fires, etc.

3. The children suffering from behavioural problems should be helped in making their life as smooth and free of trouble for themselves as well as for others.

4. Application of the reinforcement theory, specially the principles of operant conditioning used in training lower animals may be found more suitable in teaching them the basics regarding self-help skills, household skills, performance of routine tasks involved in the residential institutional management and in some cases simple, routine unskilled occupational skills.

5. Educational Programmes for Profound Mentally Retarded children is very difficult. The teacher mainly try to develop certain basic abilities to perform elementary rather essential functions of life to this category of mentally retarded.

XIII.6 Suggestions for Mentally Retarded Children

To deal mentally retarded Children means to reform our social structure. In doing so a social scientist, a Psychologist is supposed to take the following steps:

1. As much as possible, try to avoid placing mildly retarded students in situations that are likely to lead to frustration, When, despite your efforts, such students indicate that they are close to their limit of frustration tolerance, encourage them to engage in relaxing change-of-pace pursuits or in physical activities.
2. Do everything possible to encourage a sense of self-esteem.
3. Present learning tasks that contain a small number of elements, at least some of which are familiar to the pupil.
4. Give a series of brief lessons that can be completed in short periods of time instead of comprehensive assignments that require sustained concentration and effort.
5. Build overlearning into lessons. Keep going back over material previously learned, but more drill as interesting and enjoyable as possible.
6. Try to arrange what is to be learned into a series or small steps, each of which leads to immediate feedback.
7. Devise and use record keeping techniques that make it clear that assignments have been completed successfully and that progress is taking place.

XIII.7 Learning Exercises

1. What do you understand by mental retardation and how we can identify mentally retarded children?
2. What are the causes of mental retarded children and suggest remedial measures?
3. Suggest how mentally retarded children are to be educated.

XIV
Learning Disable Children

XIV.1 Meaning and Definitions of Learning Disable Children

The riddle of young children who have learning disability is disturbing because some children are quite normal and yet at all the time display learning problems. They write 'deb' for 'bed', was for 'saw' and cannot concentrate if there is background noise. The National Advisory Committee on Handicapped Children (USA) defined learning disability as follows (1986):

"Learning disable (LD) children exhibit disorder in one or more basic psychological processes involved in understanding and in using spoken or written languages. The disorders are manifested in listening, thinking, talking, reading, writing, spelling, and arithmetic. They include conditions which are referred to as perceptual problems, brain injury, minimal brain dysfunction, dyslexia, developmental aphasia etc. They do not include learning problems which are primarily due to visual, hearing, or motor handicaps, mental retardation, emotional disturbance, or the environmental disadvantage".

National Joint Committee for Learning Disabilities (NJCLD) and Federal Interagency Committee on Learning Disability gave a modified concept of learning disability which reads as—

"Learning disabilities is a generic term that refers to a heterogeneous group of disorders manifested by significant difficulties in the acquisition and use of listening, speaking, reading, writing, reasoning, or mathematical abilities or of social skills. These disorders are intrinsic to the individual and presumed to be due to central nervous system dysfunction. Even though a learning disability may occur concomitanttly with other handicapping conditions or socio-environmental influences and especially with attention deficit disorders, all of which may cause learning problems, a learning disability is not direct result of those conditions or influences" (Lerner, 1985).

Learning Disability has been defined by Wepman Committee which states that learning disability can be defined in three dimensions such as:

(a) It is noncategorical—i.e., there is no reason why a child who is also mentally retarded or emotionally disturbed could not also be included within this definition. *(b) It does not rely upon casual explanations—i.e.*, it does not matter *how* the child became learning-disabled. *(c) It specifies that the problem is perceptual in nature.* ("Perceptual" here refers to an individual's ability to process stimuli meaningfully and not to perceptual acuity. **Perception**, thus, is the *ability to organize and interpret sensory information.* A child may have 20/20 vision, for example, but have a visual perceptual disturbance.)

The other part of definition is similar to the first two points, but is does *not* specify perceptual disturbances as the crucial criteria because the measurement of perceptual disabilities is often inaccurate and some children who have learning problems show no apparent difficulty in perceptual ability (Hallahan and Kauffamn 1975; 1976; 1977). This definition posits that a learning-disabled child is simply one who is *not achieving up to his potential.* He may be at any intelligence level. He may have a learning problem for any of a number of reasons, some perceptual and some not (*e.g.* hyperactivity, language problems). He, also, may or may not have emotional problems. Using this definition may more children are considered to have learning disabilities than would be the case using the traditional definitions of the Wepman Committee definition. The advantage of this definition is that it avoids the dilemma of looking for hard-to-detect causes such as perceptual and neurological disturbance and stress the similarities of children additionally defined as mildly retarded, mildly disturbed, and learning-disabled.

In brief Learning disability among the children has been redefined precisely by Lerner (1989). The summarised conceptual definition of Learning disability can be studied as:

1. *Learning disabilities are a heterogeneous group of disorders.* (Individuals with learning disabilities exhibit many kinds of problems. Some may struggle with an individual subject or skill like mathematics, reading comprehension, listening, and writing. Some may be seriously deficient in more than one of these areas. And some students may exhibit poor socialization skills in addition to academic deficits)
2. *The problem is intrinsic to the individual.* (Learning disabilities are due to factors within the person rather than to external factors, such as the environment or the educational system.)
3. *The problem is thought to be related to central nervous system dysfunction.* (There is recognition of the biological basis of the problem.)
4. *Learning disabilities may occur alongwith other handicapping conditions.* (There is recognition that individuals can have several

problems at the same time, such as learning disabilities and emotional disorders.)

XIV.2 Causes of Learning Disabilities

Learning disability is a complex phenomena. The learning disability among children is based on multiple causes but all these causes can broadly be categories as organic, environmental and genetic.

1. Organic

Learning disability arises because of Minimal Brain Dysfunction (MBD). The dysfunction occurs in central nervous system which consists of the brain and the spinal cord. The malfunctioning is not due to damage, but due to dysfunction which is only minimal. Minimal brain dysfunction arises due to *(a)* cerebral hemarrhage, cerebral disease because of high fever, head injury, *(b)* intrauterine environment-premature birth, anoxia, physical trauma, *(c)* constitutional-genetic-neurochemical dysfunction. It must be noted that all brain dysfunction are not associated with learning disability and all types of learning disability do not arise due to brain dysfunction. Hypoglycemia or low blood sugar is a cause of learning problem. Any factor that can cause neurological damage can learning problems.

2. Genetic

Learning problems and hyperactivity run in families. Nearly 20% of hyperactive children had one parent hyperactive. Children with Turner's syndrome have higher incidence of learning disabilities.

3. Environmental

Maternal factors known to have a negative effect include the use of drugs, the consumption of alcohol and contraction of rubella. Complications during pregnancy such as anoxia (loss of Oxygen), birth injury causing brain damage, and children who received neonatal intensive care subsequently become learning disable. Learning disability may be caused due to insufficient early experience and stimulation. It is also caused by poor or inadequate instruction.

XIV.3 Characteristics of Learning Disabled Children

The complicated deficiency of learning among the children is based on number of factors. Such factor influencing learning behaviour of a child has its impact to develop identifiable characteristics. There are a variety of characteristics that have been attributed to learning-disabled children. A national task force, recognizing the proliferation of terms and labels in this area, found ninety-nine characteristics reported in the literature (Clements, 1966). The ten most frequency found symptoms of children with learning disabilities were:

1. Hyperactivity
2. Perceptual-motor impairments
3. Emotional liability (frequent shifts in emotional mood)
4. General coordination deficits
5. Disorders of attention (short attention span, destractibility, perseveration)
6. Impulsivity
7. Disorders of memory and thinking
8. Specific academic problems (reading, arithmetic, writing, spelling)
9. Disorders of speech and hearing
10. Equivocal neurological signs and electroencephalographic (EEG) irregularities.

Traver and Hallahan has pointed out that learning disability is of various types. Each type of disability has its characteristics. Therefore, it is evident that there are number of characteristics which cause different types of learning disabilities among children. In order to simplify the complex process of learning disability among children we can categorise the characteristics causing disabilities in to different groups and that can be studied as under:

1. Perceptual-Motor, Coordination Problems

Those involved in determining the causes, treatment, and educational programs for the brain-damaged mentally retarded—the conceptual forefathers of today's leaders in the field of learning disabilities—were oriented towards looking for perceptual, particularly visual, disturbances in children. Thus it is not surprising that many professionals in learning disabilities have a similar interest in perceptual problems in learning-disabled children.

It was in the 1930s and 1940s that Heinz Werner and Alfred Strauss, at the Wayne Country Training School in Northville, Michigan, found in clinical studies and rudimentary experimental investigations that a variety of perceptual abnormalities were characteristic of some mentally retarded children. At the time, they believed that the children who had perceptual problems were brain-injured. The methodology of their studies has since been seriously questioned, and it is believed that the assumption cannot be made that these children were in fact unquestionably brain-damaged. Nevertheless, Werner and Strauss *did* identify perceptual abnormalities in some of the children, brain-damaged or not. Individuals associated with Werner and Strauss—*e.g.*, Newell Kephart—

popularized the notion that learning-disabled children also have perceptual and perceptual-motor problems.

Visual Perceptual Disable. There are many studies indicating that reading-disabled children are more likely to exhibit visual perceptual problems (problems in organizing and interpreting visual sensory stimuli) than are children who are average or above-average readers (*e.g.*, Coleman, 1968; Davol & Hastings, 1967; Leton, 1962; Lyle , 1968; Skubic & Anderson, 1970; Whipple & Kodman, 1969). While some of the studies can be criticized on methodological grounds, the "evidence strongly suggests that learning-disabled children, as a group, perform poorly on tasks designed to assess visual perceptual abilities" (Hallahan, 1975, p. 31).

Auditory Perceptual Disabilities. Although fewer in number, there have been some investigations of the auditory perceptual abilities of children with learning disabilities. (Flynn & Byrne, 1970; Golden & Steiner, 1969; Lingren, 1969). These studies as well as the visual studies, indicate that auditory perceptual difficulties are more often found in learning-disabled than in normal children. Numerous professionals have pointed out that this relationships is logical, since reading requires the individual to associate visual units with their auditory equivalents.

A Cautionary Note. Despite the empirical evidence indicating that visual and auditory perceptual skills are associated with the academic ability of reading, caution must be maintained in considering the significance of these results. The studies mentioned above are based on groups of children. In other words, not all children with reading problems have perceptual defects, and some children who have perceptual deficits can read adequately. Furthermore, we must be careful not to attribute causal status to perceptual problems. Merely because perceptual skills are correlated or associated with reading problems does not necessarily mean that they cause them. Many practitioners, unfortunately, have prescribed visual perceptual training activities for all learning-disabled children. As we will discuss in a later section of this chapter, it is questionable that perceptual training by itself will even help learning-disabled children who do have perceptual problems, let alone those who do not have these deficits.

Perceptual Motor and General Coordination Problems. It has been observed clinically that learning-disabled children often have difficulty in physical activities involving the use of motor skils. They are often described by parents, teachers, and peers as having "two left feet", or "ten thumbs". The difficulties assigned to them involve both fine motor (small motor muscles) and grows motor (large motor muscles) skills. Fine motor skills often involve the coordination of the visual and motor systems. Theories and programs concerned with perceptual-motor and physical coordination are closely related to those concerned with perceptual disabilities. The same cautions noted for perceptual training are in order for these areas.

2. Disorders of Attention and Hyperactivity

Also stemming from the work of Werner and Strauss (1941) with retarded children has been the great interest in the ability of learning-disabled children to discuss their attention and control their motor activity. Werner and Strauss found a subgroup of mentally retarded children who had figure-background problem—an inability to focus on a specific figure while ignoring irrelevant background stimulation.

The kind of experimental task they used is depicted in Figure 1. Each of these slides was presented one at a time for a very brief exposure period (about one-half second). After seeing each slide, the child was asked to tell the experimenter what he had just seen. Responses could be to the figure alone, the background alone, or both the figure and background. Werner and Strauss found that the endogenous (presumably brain-injured) children were more likely to respond to the background than were the endogenous (presumably *not* brain-injured) children. As we mentioned earlier with regard to these investigations of perceptual problems, the two groups may not have been truly distinguishable on the basis of brain injury. However, there was found to be a sizable subgroup of retarded children who had figure-background, or distractibility problems. William Cruick-shank, who at one time worked with Werner and Strauss, was instrumental in bringing the distractibility problems of the *learning-disabled* to the attention of educators.

Many investigators have documented the attentional difficulties of learning-disabled children. Both within the auditory and visual domain, there is substantial evidence in laboratory situations indicating that learning-disabled children appear to be more likely than normal children to be destractible. Learning-disabled children have also been found to be more attentative in the classroom (Bryan, 1974; Bryan & Wheeler, 1972).

Some laboratory experiments, however, have found learning-disabled children *not* to be more distractible than normal children; a few, in fact, have been found to attend *better* under conditions in which there were deliberate distractions. (For example, in some experimental situations bright lights were flashed or balloons were dropped from the ceiling.) Traver and Hallahan (1974) have noted that this may not indicate that learning-disabled children are not more distractible, but that these seemingly conflicting results may be due to any one of at least three explanations: *(a)* Some of the children may be hyporesponsive (Browning, 1967)— *i.e.* show to respond; and high-intensity distractors may serve to alert them to respond. (b) The high-intensity distractors

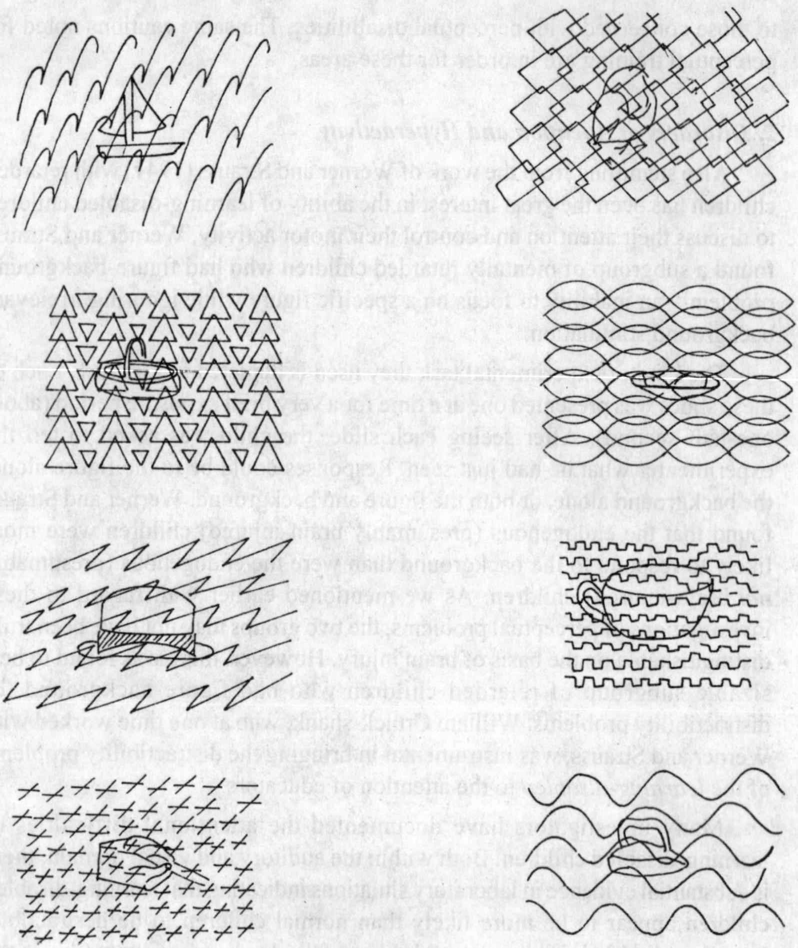

Fig. 1. Werner-Strauss figure-background slides to test pure visual perception (A.A. Strauss & L.E. Lehtinen, Psychopathology and education of the brain injured child, Vol. 1 (New York: Grune & Stratton, 1947), Reprinted by permission).

may help the learning-disabled children determine what exactly is relevant and what is irrelevant *(c)* The obvious efforts to distract the child may motivate him to attend and not be "taken in" by efforts at distraction.

Often mentioned in conjunction with distractibility, the characteristic of hyperactivity is another behaviour frequently attributed to learning-disabled children. The hyperactive child displays rates of motor activity that are too high for his particular age group. The activity must be compared to his peers of the same age, since it is normal for the very young child to be quite active. If, however, the first and second-grader is still as active as when he was 3 or 4 years old, he may be exhibiting behaviour that will interfere with his ability to learn. Teachers are very aware that the child who cannot sit still is going to have great difficulty in engaging in school work. Unfortunately, it is in those very situations in which the child is expected to be still that the hyperactive child has the greatest problems in controlling his motor impulses.

3. Language Problems

Werner and Strauss' work with the mentally retarded greatly influenced the development of the field of learning disabilities, and because they were interested in perceptual-motor rather than language problems of children, professionals in the field have tended to over-look the importance of language. Thus it is not surprising that very little research has been done on language disabilities. In keeping with the perceptual orientation, even when language problems are considered they are often seen as stemming from auditory perceptual problems (Eisenson, 1972).

Auditory perceptual problems contribute to what are referred to as receptive language disabilities, difficulties that derive from the *in-ability to understand spoken language.* Expressive language disabilities, on the other hand, are problems associated with the *inability to express oneself verbally.* Many theorists and practitioners believe that expressive problems (aside from those resulting from motor problems such as articulation difficulties) are rarely if ever present without receptive difficulties as well (*e.g.* Eisenson, 1972; Wood, 1969). While little research has been carried out on this subject, most experienced teachers maintain that receptive and expressive disabilities are closely interwoven. Johnson and Myklebust list three different kinds of expressive language problems:

1. The first group has a deficit primarily in reauditorization and word selection. These children understand and recognize words but they cannot member (or retrieve) them for spontaneous usage.
2. The second group has difficulty learning to say words, they comprehend and reauditorize but cannot execute the motor patterns necessary for speaking. There is no paralysis but they

cannot voluntarily initiate the movements of the tongue and lips because of an apraxia.

3. The third group has defective syntax. They are able to use single words and short phrases but are unable to plan and organize words for the expression of ideas in complete sentences. They omit or distort the order of words, use incorrect words, use incorrect verb tenses, and make other grammatical, syntactical errors long after such skills have been acquired by normal children.

4. Disorders of Memory and Thinking

Memory. Although the late 1960s and the 1976s have seen a burgeoning interest in the memory abilities of learning-disabled children, relatively few conclusions can be reached. The safest statement it is possible to make is that *learning-disabled children, in general, demonstrate memory deficits for both auditory and visual stimuli.*

The research is inconclusive, however, regarding the specific reasons for the memory deficit. For example, Bakker (1967, 1971) has found that learning-disabled children are particularly deficient compared to normal controls when meaningful, but not nonmeaningful, stimuli are used. Other studies, however, have not found "meaning-influences" to be a variable differentiating learning-disabled from other children. There is some tentative evidence favouring the view that learning-disabled children are especially deficient in using the strategy of categorizing to-be-remembered stimuli. *Clustering* words or pictures into conceptual categories, a strategy employed by normal children, reduces the amount of information one has to remember. But Frestorn and Drew (1974) and Parker, Freston, and Drew (1975) have found that learning-disabled children do not take advantage of this strategy. Ring (1976), however, found evidence that they do make use of another memory strategy—*temporal grouping.* Temporal grouping refers to the strategy of breaking up presentation of stimuli into groups by separating some of them by longer pauses than others. In addition, there is some evidence to suggest that *verbal* material is particularly difficult for learning-disabled children to remember.

Thinking. Thinking can be defined in a number of ways. Among other things, thinking involves the ability to "problem-solve" and to conceptualize. Since the ability to think, broadly considered, is what is generally thought of as making up "intelligence," it is not surprising that very little consideration has been given to the thought process of learning-disabled children because they are, by definition, commonly regarded as being of normal intelligence. *Concept development,* however, has been found deficient in learning-disable children as have problem-solving strategies.

Children identified as learning-disabled are likely to act impulsively and this particular kind of problem-solving strategy—impulsivity—corresponds with the characteristics of distractibility and hyperactivity. Interest in impulsive behaviour was stimulated by the work of Jerome Kagan and his colleagues (Kagan, 1965, 1966; Kagan, Pearson, & Welch, 1966; Kagan, Rosman, Day, Albert, & Phillips, 1964). Kagan has been interested in determining whether children are impulsive or reflective problem solvers. An item from the Matching Familiar figures Test he developed to assess this behaviour is pictured

Fig. 2. Matching Familiar Figures Test

in Figure 2. Each child is tested individually. He is asked to find the figure on the bottom that is identical to the one on top. If the answer is incorrect, the child is asked to choose again. There are two measures taken—the *large amount of time* the child takes to make his first choice on each of the items and the *total number of errors* he makes on all the items. Children scoring above the median (the middle score for the group) in errors and below the median in response time are classified as "impulsive" and children scoring below the median in error and above the median in response time are categorized as "reflective".

It is easy to see why impulsivity can be detrimental to learning. Rather than reflecting before responding, impulsive children seem driven to respond quickly without carefully considering the various alternatives. The frequency with which school activities require the student to select among competing choices makes it evident that an impulsive problem-solving style is a hindrance.

5. Emotional Lability

Emotional Lability, frequent changes in mood, can be viewed as a particular aspect of personality and social maladjustment. As we know that emotional immaturity, can be seriously questioned whether it is fruitful to try to differentiate emotionally disturbed from learning-disabled children. Children within the two categories have a great deal in common. The learning-disabled child frequently exhibits behaviours characteristic of emotional disturbance. He is typically not a happy child, and he may have low self-esteem.

6. Neurological Problems

We have already observed that not all children with learning disabilities show definitive signs of having neurological abnormalities. However, a larger percentage of learning disabled children show such signs than is true for the normal population. It surprises many parents, teachers, and other outside the medical profession to find that methods of neurological diagnosis are still fairly limited. The tests are not as accurate as many believe, particularly, the casc of children. Moreover, it is not unusual for an otherwise perfectly normal and healthy child to display one or more of the behavioural signs of brain damage. Called "soft signs", such characteristics:

> include poor fine motor coordination, impaired visual motor coordination, poor balance, clumsiness, strabismus [crossed eyes], chloreiform movements [uncontrollable movements], and "poor speech".......Such signs re referred to as "soft" because—unlike the "hard" signs of classical neurology paresis and paralysis, anaesthesia, and reflex changes—the "soft" signs are slight, inconsistently present and not clearly associated with localized neuro-anatomical lesions. Dysfunctions such as clumsiness may represent "normal" variation

and be totally unassociated with central nervous system pathology. (Wender, 1971, p. 27)

The greatest danger in considering the neurological aspects of learning disabilities is to attributes as "fact" the existence of brain injury based on the presence of only soft sign. This practice can be very misleading. Too many parents of learning-disabled children have become needlessly alarmed because of the ominous diagnosis of "minimal brain injury." This term convinces parents that their child's problem is frighteningly serious and engenders thoughts of irreversibility of the condition. Fortunately, learning-disabled children are far from being "beyond hope" in terms of remediation.

7. Academic Achievement

There are no disagreements among professionals concerning the presence of academic deficits in learning-disabled children. They are the sine qua non of learning disabilities. By definition, without an academic problem, a learning disability does not exist. Some children have disicits in all scholastic areas, while others have problems in only one or two academic subjects. Reading disabilities are probably the most prevalent of all of the academic problems.

Most specialists in the field of learning disabilities are primarily concerned with remediating academic difficulties. In fact, there is a strong movement to be concerned with academic deficits to the exclusion of the other characteristics we have listed, particularly perceptual and perceptual-motor problems. We will turn to this controversy in the selection of this chapter devoted to educational considerations.

XIV.4 Educational Provisions for Learning-Disable Children

In dealing with learning-disable children we can adopt number of techniques but broadly we can classify the possible ways of teaching the disabled children in the following manners:

(a) *Day school*

Where the learning disabled children receive specialised schooling using special teachers essentially on the same curriculum but with greater care and pace. This is segregated settings—

(b) Special class in a Regular School

Where LD children are given special instruction in a self contained classroom by special teacher as well as regular classroom teacher do assist in teaching subject matters. These children receive instruction on academics in these classes but for social activities etc. they are with general students.

(c) Resource Room

Since their number is large, and they do not pose organic problems or problems of low IQ, these children are integrated in the regular classroom with resource room facilities (mainstreaming/integration).

A. General Instructional Techniques

Inspite of different educational provision there are certain general techniques of instruction. The following instructional techniques have been used and recommended for use with learning disable:

(i) Use short, brief directions, large print.

(ii) Use consistent language, colour cues.

(iii) Write directions or steps on the chalkboard *i.e.* underline important words etc.

(iv) Alternate the use of colours for each step in a series on directions.

(v) Increase sound level of instruction.

(vi) Use diagrams of pictorial illustrations.

(vii) Use an overview of the lesson, ask questions, ask them to read the material, recite and review.

The learning disabled children lack structure and organisation, they have to be told to keep daily engaged in the activities; list all future events that need to be scheduled. Provide a hypothetical list to suggest possible events; and plan future events that must be planned, it is time to develop a weekly schedule. Pupils in the upper grades may find useful a schedule that provides for specific subject matter assignments on various types of activities.

(a) Thinking skills can be developed by guiding students to collect data by reading, listening, and observing; and discriminate differences on similarities in the data. Teacher questioning can be used to prod the pupil until the ability to make these discriminations improves. Ask the pupil to categories and classify the data. Labelling is important during this stage.

Have the pupil recategorise and classify the data in other ways. This continuous reorganisation and restructuring is necessary to integrate new information and new experience into the pupil's mental structures. Have the pupil make predictions based on the data. Have the pupil evaluate the alternative predictions using the same data. Have the pupil generate alternative predictions by comparing and contrasting possible outcomes and their effects.

(b) Memory ability can be improved by using certain specific techniques, visual and auditory messages can be recalled. Facial expressions indicative of certain materials can be retrieved. Cramming is to be avoided. Certain activities

can be practised to improve auditory, visual memories. For this purpose, the learning disabled children are made to follow the following:—

(i) Have pupils repeat telephone numbers and street address of emergency service facilities (police, fire, etc.)

(ii) Have pupils learn songs by listening to the words and tunes.

(iii) Play games in which the first pupils makes a statement, the next pupil repeats that and adds a statement, the third pupil repeats those statements and adds one, and so on.

(iv) Have pupils make up rhymes related to subject matter, such as, "In 1492 Columbus sailed the ocean blue".

(v) Have pupils repeat oral directions.

(vi) Have pupils resequence cartoons strips (without words) that have been cut apart. This forces them to observe details in the pictures.

(vii) Have pupils describe configurations of words that are similar.

(viii) Have pupils repeat the sequence for a recipe that they have read.

(ix) Have the pupil practice attending to larger units at one time. For instance, some try to copy one syllable at a time. Encourage the pupil to increase the length of the visual stimulus that she holds in her mind as she write it down.

(x) Help the pupil to practice internal auditorisation as an adjunct to visual memory; that is, have the pupil say the letters or words to herself while she is translating the written information.

(xi) Write every other item on the chalkboard with a different colour chalk. This helps the pupil to "find her place".

(xii) Allow the pupils to copy another pupil's work. Some of these pupils perform better with paper-to-paper copying.

In dealing the disabled children care needs to be taken by a teacher *i.e.*, teachers must be flexible in their approach to teaching reading because of the heterogeneous characteristics of learning disabled pupils. A diagnostic perceptive approach must be used. The reading programme must be matched to pupil's needs and abilities. There are several approaches having different degree of relevance.

The Basal reading approach is comprehensive, which uses controlled vocabulary in a sequential manner with adequate reinforcement. Diagnosis is done in course of teaching but it is not so advantageous for learning disabled children because of its rigidity, individualised nature and lack of provision for removing deficits.

Phonic approach has very limited use especially for those who had good auditory capacity. Linguistic training also has limited use as it does not aid comprehension.

(c) Language experience approach is most useful as it uses stories of personal experiences, child's oral language, incorporates specific skill development, language art skills and makes use of visual motor abilities. Programme instruction is also another viable technique. The other approaches to reading use multisensory approach and use of pictures. Both the methods have limitations. Because of complexities of both the reading process and learning disabilities, it is difficult to make definitive statements.

Teaching Approaches for the Learning Disabled Children

Teaching Approach	*Advantages*	*Disadvantages*
Asal	1. Comprehensive	1. Limited flexibility in teaching style.
	2. Controlled vocabulary	2. Individualized instruction not encouraged.
	3. Sequential introduction of skills.	3. Lack of depth of material necessary for skill mastery.
	4. Reinforcement of skills.	4. Lack of provision for processing deficits.
	5. Diagnostic and evaluative material usually provided.	5. No choice of analytic or synthetic phonics instruction.
		6. Subject to repetition of the same stories and methods resulting from failure.
Phonics	1. Effective decoding techniques for pupils with good auditory abilities	1. Not effective for pupils with auditory deficits
		2. May be taught in isolation.
		3. Comprehension neglected.
		4. Invariance in English language may cause confusion.

Contd.

Teaching Approach	*Advantages*	*Disadvantages*
Linguistic	1. Control for irregular spelling in initials stages 2. Gradual introduction of phonics. 3. Extensive repetition.	1. Little emphasis on comprehension in initial stages. 2. Vocabulary controlled for regular elements and does not utilize spoken language of pupils.
Language Experience	1. Motivates with personal stories. 2. Uses pupil's oral language. 3. Can incorporate specific skill development. 4. Can include language art skills. 5. Good for pupils with good visual-motor abilities.	1. May be limited by pupils language level. 2. Lacks structured systematic approach to skill development
Progra-mmed Instruction Materials	1. Small, sequential steps. 2. Immediate feedback. 3. May be boring because of consistency.	1. Lack direct instruction. 2. May be confusing format.
Multisen-sory	1. Uses more than one sensory input to get message to the brain. 2. Can use an analytical approach or a synthetic approach.	1. Lack of sequential skill development in some programmes. 2. Sensory overload experienced by some pupils.
Rebus picture	1. Uses a rebus (picture) instead of a word to simplify initial stages of reading. 2. Well structured materials. 3. Provides for transition to traditional print materials.	1. Format appearing immature for older pupils.

(d) Handwriting. Poor handwriting in the learning disabled has been attributed to numerous causes: Poor fine motor control, poor visual discrimination and memory, spatial difficulties. Manipulative exercise can be used to strengthen muscles: cutting, moulding clay games. Chalkboard practice should precede pencil and paper writing. Proper position for writing habit to develop. Paper should not be placed at a slant for manuscript writing. The writing instrument is held between thumb and middle finger with index finger applying pressure. Graph paper is of valuable help to teach pupils with special difficulties. A creative teacher improves handwriting using certain techniques by adopting following exercises:

(i) Tape alphabet forms to the floor. Have them reproduce the form with coloured chalk.

(ii) Have pupils use a stick and their bodies to form the letters.

(iii) Write each letter in a paper with red marker.

(iv) Have pupils form letters in wet fingerpaint.

(v) Use coloured directional cues such as green arrows and red dots.

(vi) Teach manuscript letter forms that are oval and slanted slightly. This will encourage left-to-right progression and will facilitate transition to cursive writing.

(vii) Teach pupils to start all lower-case cursive letters from the line.

(viii) Help pupils to form an association for a letter they have difficulty in remembering.

(ix) Have pupils orally describe their movements as the letter is being written. This provides auditory reinforcement.

The various approaches used in teaching by the resource or specialist or classroom teacher have relative advantages and disadvantages.

(e) Spelling. Spelling errors are quite common among learning disabled children. Therefore a systematic work-study techniques is used in the following sequence.

"Look at the word—say the word—say the word—look at the word—cover the word—write the word—check your spelling—Repeat"..Some of the remedial techniques involve—writing the word on the chalk board and then trace it in fingers until it disappears tracing in sand, write the first letter of the word when one listens the word and then pronounce. Ask the children to spell the word properly and clap softly for each vowel sound, if possibly by looking at the word.

(f) Arithmetic. Ashlock (1972) made certain specific remedial instruction step for removing arithmetic errors of learning disabled children. Some of the steps are as follows:

Use manipulatives such as bottons and chips to teach number. Use visual material and give reinforcement. Use graph paper for alignment difficulties. Time line, coloured chalks, markings are helpful for attention to cues. A sample problem can be given for each assignment. The size of numbers can vary to indicate more or less. Reduce distractions as far as possible. Reduce number of examples in the assignment and eliminate copying. Use of display charts, abacus, playing cards, calculator, language master are quite useful.

(g) Curricular-Concerns.. Learning disabled children read in the class as other children. Hence, certain extra care would benefit these pupils. These concerns may relate to four areas; such as:

(i) Auditory Perception

1. Identify classmates from voice when one is blind.
2. Produce a speech sound and ask if they listen.
3. Ask whether pairs of words are same or different.
4. Start naming objects that starts with a particular sound.
5. Practice rhymes.
6. Ask them to repeat oral directions.
7. Tell a sequence of information to improve auditory memory.

(ii) Visual Perception

1. Match geometric designs.
2. Ask them to replicate a pattern.
3. Ask them to classify objects.
4. Match, sort and group word cards.
5. Start copying designs from simple to complex.
6. Tell a story with pictures. Then scramble the pictures and ask pupils to tell the story.
7. Recall letters speedily and find a series of letters in words.

(iii) Sensory Motor Development

1. Manipulation of object according to directions *i.e.* in front of, in the middle etc.
2. Use puzzles.
3. Reproduce block designs.

4. Pour water in different containers.
5. Design games.
6. Use tracing, lacing and cutting activities and visual tracking activities.

(h) Social Skills

1. Discuss different emotions through pictures.
2. Explain body language and symbols.
3. Use T.V. for explaining social encounters and social interactions.
4. Identify topics for discussion with peers, neighbours.
5. Remember key points of conversation.
6. Discuss personal experiences that have caused social difficulties.

Mildly and moderately learning disabled pupils can function satisfactorily in the regular classroom with these adjustments. The regular classroom curriculum may require little modification. These are some of the general techniques of remediation but a specific theoretical model should guide the practitioner.

The cognitive processing approach provides a way of thinking about how a child learns and offers a framework for teaching. The developmental approach emphasises sequential approach for remediation. Test related approach identifies specific area of deficiency which can be taught.

B. Specialised Instructional Techniques

The specialised techniques approach indicate that the teacher would follow the prescribed order and fashion for a specified period of time. Hierarchy of skills are to be developed in the Skill-Development approach using criterion referenced teaching. Published materials can be used for remediation of learning disability.

Behavioural Approach. Behavioural approach refers to behaviour modification approach for manipulations of environmental conditions of learning. Apply reinforcement and change behaviour. Psychotherapeutic approach should build feelings of success and establish a healthy psychodynamic relationship between teacher and student. The major cause of reading failure is dyspedagogia *i.e.*, lack of good teaching. Inadequacy in the child's teacher and the teaching environment are the answer to remediation.

Remediation of Learning Problems.	Analysis of the Child	Cognitive Processing Developmental Test related.
	Analysis of Content.	Specialised Techniques Skill Development Materials.
	Analysis of Environment Conditions.	Behavioural Psychotherapeutic Pedagogical.

The models of remediation suggested are not mutually exclusive. A teacher can use one or more of the several approaches to deal with the situations. Koppitz (1973) stated:

"... learning disabilities can not be corrected or cured by a specific teaching method or training technique. It is imperative that teachers have a wide range of instructional materials and techniques at their disposal and that they are imaginative and flexible enough to adapt these to specific needs of their pupils.

XIV.5 Role of Teachers in Promoting Learning Disable Children

The learning disable children as a group are heterogenous. As such they require a variety of techniques approaches as well as materials to satisfy their unique educational needs at different levels of development.

Environmental Approach. At the preschool level, the environment should be arranged to promote efficiency, accessibility, independence and functionality. Safety is also a factor in the preschool setting. Heavy breakable and dangerous materials should be out of reach of these children. At the elementary level children classrooms should not be noisy, visually distracting and sterile. The special educator and the regular classroom teacher should provide a less distracting environment for students who are overtly distractible and hence learning disabled. Such children can be placed in the centre of the classroom where more often teacher's attention is focused.

Individual Instructional Approach. Although small group permits individualised instruction yet have demonstrated the efficacy of peer turoring in instruction, seat work and special projects. Care should be taken to select a good regular peer.

Structure in planning the instructional programme is a must for learning disabled children. The curriculum should be organised sequential and routine based so that the LD child can attend to it carefully. For this task analysis procedure is most relevant. This enables the teacher to break the task into components and help the student at each stage.

The teacher should also provide a summary presentation after each sub-plan of teaching so that LD children can learn well in school and this will provide as an advance organiser for learning.

The equipments and materials must be ready to be used in 'dead time' when the learning disable children has nothing to do. They can not waste their time. There are a number of specific teaching procedures that have been used to remedy academic deficits or failures among LD children. One of the general approach is cognitive behaviour modification. They help children internalise efficient learning strategies by actively involving them in the learning process mostly consisting of self instruction and verbalisation.

Self-Instructional Approach. Learning disable children lack abilities for metacognition. Hence, teacher can initiate self questioning strategies for students to use while reading: finding main ideas, underline, answering questions, writing down, asking himself the purpose of reading etc. self instructional techniques have been found quite effective for LD children.

Precision teaching is a system of evaluating and improving instruction. It is direct, continuous and precise measure of student progress where the teacher records a wide range of behaviours. They help teachers on track and make accurate instructional decisions.

As regards teaching contents and materials it should be motivating, non-complex, and appropriate for child's level of functioning, and learning style. Using student's name, talents or interests is one way a teacher can make assignments more motivating. Illustrations, too much use of colours in the printed page do distract learning disabled children. Educational games capture students' attention and make learning exciting.

Multi-Sensory Approach. Multisensory approach have also been applied to teach learning disable children. Visual, Auditory, Kinaesthetic, and Tactile (VAKT) was developed by Fernald (1943) which is essentially a language experience. He selects a word and goes through feeling seeing, saying and hearing the word. Once the word is mastered the teacher helps them to write a story and then gives him feedback. In this way new words are learned. Children can be taught through association of a how a letter or word looks, sounds and feels. After he learns the works sentence and story writing begin, gradually they begin to read. There are several combinations of multisensory teaching methods.

Direct instruction which includes assessment, instruction and evaluation are used. DISTAR is one of the direct instructional system which teaching sequences are so arranged that errors are minimised, it provides ample practice, and give immediate and positive feedback. Distar includes Mathematics and reading components. DISTAR was used first with disadvantaged children and now with LD. It is a back to basics structured programme. Learning strategies are also used for helping LD children to learn. Computer assisted instruction is also being introduced in the school system for the management of IEP (Learner, 1985).

Panda is of the view that a teacher in a mainstreamed classroom has to make the classroom personalised where individual differences are accepted and valued. Teachers lead students to value and accept personal responsibility for their own learning. They should promote independence, cooperative functioning, and problem solving among all students. Specifically, they—

(a) Accept the perception of learner about classroom environment.

(b) Provide variety of options to motivate each child.

(c) Encourage independent and small group work.

(d) Increase pupil's commitment, control, and responsibility.

(e) Informal and formal conferences are held.

(f) Ongoing assessment and student evaluation are done to know the each student's progress.

To make these implementable in the regular classroom:

1. A structured programme has to be avoided.
2. Allow distractible student to sit in centre.
3. Use peer teaching and allow the LD child to be tutor.
4. Drive homework on the curriculum taught.
5. Keep close contact with parents.
6. Tailor the programme to student's needs.
7. Make task analysis and lead student step by step for learning.

Learning difficulties are quite pervasive and non-specific, which arise out of several factors and are achievement specific. In regular schools, learning disabled students can be handled well if regular and resource teachers become conscious and sensitive to the problems of these children. The various concerns expressed in the field are mentioned along with tips for relevant remedial measures.

XIV.6 Suggestions for Learning Disabilities

1. If an Instructional Educational Programme (IEP) has been prepared for a pupil with a learning disability to make sure you

understand what instructional materials are to be used how to implement the plan, and how and when to evaluate progress.

2. If a pupil has a learning disability but is not officially identified as learning disabled, prepare your own version of an IEP.
3. Refer to the suggestions for teaching students with mild retardation, presented earlier in this chapter.
4. Seek ways to help learning disabled pupils compensate for weaknesses in psychological processes as they improve achievement in specific subject areas.
5. Use systematic procedures for helping students use psychological processes more effectively.

XIV.7 Learning Exercises

1. Discuss the meaning and definitions of learning disabled children and their characteristics.
2. Describe the causes of learning disabled children and suggest remedial measures.
3. Explain the educational provisions for learning disabled children.
4. Discuss the role of a teacher to educate learning disabled children.
5. Suggest means and measures to enhance learning level of the learning disabled children.

XV
Delinquency

Delinquency is a behavioural tendency of an individual which makes an individual to violate the prescribed legal and social norms of a society. Delinquency is of various types. The delinquent behaviour of an individual is the by product of multifarious ill-conceived bio-social factors. Efforts are being made to prevent and to correct the delinquent behaviour of our fellow beings with the hope that the world may become more peaceful and livable place.

XV.1 Meaning of Delinquency

In our day-to-day life we use the terms 'crime' and 'delinquency'. These terms are legal one and their meaning varies from nation to nation even some times in the same country it differs from state to state. Therefore, delinquency some how is associated with criminal behavioural tendency of an individual. The criminal tendency to commit crime in any society of a nation, is not only found among the adults, but minor children and adolescents also. Such individuals are known as delinquents. The delinquents who are of younger age i.e., minors are called Juvenile delinquents. The delinquents are the individual who violate the law of the land and commit offences like thefts, gambling, cheating, pick-pocketing, murder, robbery, dacoity, destruction of property, violence and assault, intoxication, vagrancy, begging, kidnapping, abduction, and sexual offences. The terms delinquency has been interpreted by social scientists and social psychologists differently. A generalised concept of delinquency reveals that a child is classified as a delinquent when his anti-social activities are so serious that he becomes the object of official actions or ought to become the object of official actions. The activities of a delinquent are anti-social. They are not approved by the social order. They are against the code of society in some of their actions.

The children, who become the subject of police, are only those who are caught. There may be a good number of children who are never caught. We have no means of knowing how frequently delinquent acts are committed by children who are not caught or brought to the attention of court. The delinquents are not only those who are behind the bars for serious offences but they are also found in our homes. Actually delinquents are children who are not sharply differentiated from not delinquent or normal children. Their offences form a gradual series of acts of different degrees of social consequences from mere naughtiness to very serious crimes. The seriousness of crime is no criterion of the seriousness or extent of social mal-adjustment of the offender but total personality of actor i.e. delinquent is responsible. It has been seen that delinquents, of the same social adjustment level may commit different crimes and mal-adjustment of different levels may commit same crime. Thus, there is no positive perfect correlation between the actual crime, and social mal-adjustment. It is not simple to grasp the delinquency.

As discusses earlier delinquents show *anti-social activities i.e., the activities which are not approved by the social order at a given time.* As we look at delinquency from the viewpoint of social rules and regulations, therefore, it is not an absolute term, Society is never static. Its standard of social behaviour, its codes, rules and regulations are subject to change and they change from time to time. They also differ from society to society. In India smoking, dancing, drinking and mixing up freely of both the sexes in the adolescent period is not accepted by society at large but it may be a normal behaviour in a western country, where it is very common. In the same way, some actions or patterns of behaviour which were forbidden may be liked by the modern society of our country. Thus, delinquency is only a comparative term.

By the term anti-social, it does not mean that these delinquent children are very introvert, they live aloof and do not like the company of others. This is not the case with all delinquents. Some delinquents may be very extrovert and show varied types of interests. They can move about very comfortably in different situations. Still at times, they may show delinquent acts.

XV.2 Cause of Delinquency

Studies report that delinquency has become a global phenomena. Efforts have been made and will be made further to check the increasing tendency of the phenomena of delinquency. The nature and type of delinquency differ from country to country but it has been found that the main causes of delinquency are similar rather common. These causes causing delinquency can be studied up on the following factors:

1. Hereditary factors: The early researches held heredity responsible for delinquency. The claim of hereditarians like Henry-Maudsley, Tredgold, and Dugdale that delinquency is inherited was tested by William Healey, Cyril Burt, Conrad and Jones, Wingfield and Sandford, They concluded that delinquency is not inherited and therefore, it is unjustified to blame heredity for delinquent behaviour.

2. Physiological factors: Defective constitution or glandular systems were also thought to be the cause of delinquent behaviour. Uday Shanker observes that "poor structured, short or too big stature or some deformity which give rise to feeling of inferiority, dispose one to more aggression, as a compensatory reaction for his inadequacies." Consequently, this leads to delinquent, behaviour. Apparently this alienation seems to be well founded but it is not so, for not much scientific evidence has been reported in its support so far. However, in some cases, it may be taken as one of the causes of delinquent behaviour.

3. Intelligence factors: While earlier writers like Lombroso and Goddard emphasize that the most important cause of delinquency and crime is low grade mentality, Burt, Healey, Bronner, Merrill and others deny that delinquents are mentally retarded. In fact, a direct causal relationship between intelligence and delinquency is doubtful. High intelligence is no guarantee for good behaviour. Often persons with superior intelligence have been found to be the leaders of notorious gangs, and antisocial organisation. Sometimes it is argued on the basis of the statistics that since the majority among the delinquents possess low intelligence, defective intelligence therefore, causes delinquency. But this conclusion is not well founded. The collected statistics, in such cases, may represent an unreal picture. An intelligent individual may not be caught red handed, whereas, someone with low intelligence may always be taken in custody. Moreover, defective intelligence may lead to delinquency in one situation and may be a barrier to it in another situation. Hence, low intelligence alone cannot be held responsible for delinquent behaviour.

4. Environmental and social factor: It has been proved that delinquent behaviour is a learned reaction. Delinquents do not inherit delinquent characters from their parents or ancestors but are made so by the uncongenial environment and social conditions. Uday Shanker observes that "delinquency is not inherited: it is the product of social and economic conditions and is essentially a coefficient of the friction between the individual and the community. The most important causes of antisocial behaviour are environmental and sociological in character." It is, therefore, the uncongenial environment of the family, school, neighbourhood and society which should be blamed for the delinquent behaviour of the child since he picks up delinquent traits in such situations. We shall now see how environment is responsible for the delinquent character formation among minors.

5. Home environment as factor: A defective and deficient family environment is a fertile ground for the germination of delinquency. As a matter of fact, family life and delinquency are closely related. Findings of various studies indicate that the family environment, where the below stated conditions prevail, is most susceptible to delinquency.

(i) Broken home—where the family is incomplete due to death, desertion, separation or divorce.
(ii) Improper parental control.
(iii) Unusual jealousy and rivalry among the siblings or children within the family and reactions like, "My parents gave him more love than they gave me."
(iv) The delinquent and criminal behaviour of the parents or other family members.
(v) Domestic conflicts.
(vi) Economic difficulties and poverty of the family.
(vii) Dull, monotonous and uninteresting home environment.
(viii) Denial of reasonable freedom and independence to the youngsters.
(ix) Mal-treatment and injustice done to the youngsters.
(x) Lack of proper physical and emotional security.

In these situations and environment the child does not get the opportunity for the satisfaction of his basic needs. He becomes victim of the emotional problems like inferiority, insecurity, jealousy or being thwarted which make him a maladjusted individual and consequently turn him into a hostile, rebellious and antisocial personality. Thus, uncongenial home conditions deserve to be blamed for juvenile delinquency and in all circumstances the root cause of delinquent behaviour must be investigated in family background and home environment.

6. Uncongenial social environment: Whereas, home provides the roots for the delinquent behaviour, the social environment outside the home nourishes it by supplying some substitute for the satisfaction of unsatisfied basic needs and urges. For example, the peer-group or gang presents itself as a substitute for family love and belongingness. It also satisfies the need for recognition and gives an individual the opportunity for self-dependence and adventurism. Delinquent acts of peer-group lead him to delinquent behaviour and engage in delinquent acts. Neighbourhood and the places of social contracts and situations where the elder members of the society engage in antisocial activities, or the mass media like newspapers, books, magazines and cinema that acquaint children with immoral and anti-social acts, provide temptation for the youngsters to become delinquents.

7. Uncongenial school environment: Uncongenial school atmosphere contribute as an important factor in promoting delinquency, unconducive school environment in school breeds serious mal-adjustments and consequently increases the probability of delinquent character formation. Such environment may involve the following elements:

(i) Defective curriculum.

(ii) Improper teaching methods.

(iii) Lack of cocurricular activities.

(iv) Lack of proper discipline and control.

(v) Slackness in administration and organisation.

(vi) Antisocial or undesirable behaviour of the teachers.

(vii) Maltreatment and injustice done to the child.

(viii) Failure of backwardness.

8. Giftedness: It may be pointed out that sometimes very intelligent gifted children become delinquents. The reason is that their intellect or self-worth is not properly recognised. Sometimes, they are altogether neglected. Gifteds, being in minority, do not mix up with normal students and the other class-fellows may tease them in different ways. So there are dramas; they take a revenge from the society at large who has not respected their self-worth in way of committing several types of crimes.

Thus, parents and teachers should be very careful in handling the children. If the home atmosphere is not good, the children should be sent to other places with some affectional relation or in a good boarding house. Bringing up of children is great art. Science can give us only the broad principles but using the principles depends upon the nature of child, his needs and age. As no two children are like and their environment is not the same, therefore, it is very difficult to give the specific problems and their cause. As every child is unique to himself, so every delinquent child is unique, his problem and cause is different from others either in quality or in quantity or in both.

It is further accompanied with opportunity, freedom and joy. Children must play. The form of play is not so important. If suitable facilities are not available, let them play with mud, earth etc. Stealing will go low if opportunity of play is provided to all students.

Besides, all the above mentioned courses, there may be other contributory factors which help the children or stimulate them to steal. This is encouragement from elders or a bad company of children.

XV.3 Remedial Measures of Delinquency

Delinquency, besides being a legal problem is basically a psychosocial problem. All delinquents are essentially maladjusted personalities and the result of faulty up-bringing and maltreatment. The solution of the problem can be studied as:

(A) Preventive Measures

Prevention of delinquency involves the improvement of the social or environmental conditions which thwart the satisfaction of the basic needs of the individual. Some of the following suggestions may work well in this direction to prevent delinquency by the following preventive measures:

1. *Parental education:* Parents should be aware of the psychology of delinquency so that they can treat and handle their children with understanding and provide them an environment for the satisfaction of their basic needs and urges. It requires parental education which may be provided through guidance services, clinics and voluntary social services.

2. *The child's company:* Parents, family members and school authorities should keep a close watch on the activities and social environment of the children and take care so that they do not fall in bad company. Antisocial elements and criminals often seek out youngsters for their own purpose. Attempts should be made to save the children from them and they should be educated in keeping away from such elements.

3. *Substitute environment:* It is difficult to bring a change in the defective family environment or the influences of the neighbourhood and peer group. In such circumstances children should be removed from their original environment and placed either in foster homes or well-managed reformatories and special schools so that they may be provided with healthy environment for their emotional and social adjustment.

4. *Rectifying school education and environment:* School environment should be healthy and congenial. The curriculum, methods of teaching, discipline, class-room behaviour of the teacher and the social atmosphere of the school should be rectified so that children do not involve themselves in emotional and social maladjustment problems. The attitude of teachers who impose their authority on children and do not understand their basic needs should be changed. The headmaster as well as the teachers should be familiar with the psychology of individual difference and delinquency.

(B) Curative Measures

In order to cure the delinquents we need to adopt the following measures to check delinquency by adopting reformative measures. Delinquents require rehabilitation and re-education for which special legal provisions should be made. The legal dealings with the juvenile delinquents have been changed in the progressive communities of the world. The "Children's and Young Person's Act".

U.K. can be adopted with some modifications in India. The act suggests the following measures to check delinquency:

(i) Establishment of special juvenile courts with trained magistrate to deal with the juvenile delinquents.

(ii) Appointment of trained social workers or probation officers for taking charge of delinquents cases.

(iii) Taking help from clinical psychologists and pychiatrists for understanding the delinquent behaviour of children.

(iv) Establishment of special schools where the education, correction and rehabilitation is possible.

(v) Provision of keeping the children in the custody of responsible persons or social agencies.

(vi) Establishment of remand homes where juvenile delinquents are placed while they wait for their trial or for approved school placement or for being given to the custody of responsible persons or as asked by probation officer before employment on being discharged from the approved schools.

The provision of 'special schools' needs specially trained staff. Special schools need to work on the flexible curriculum to be established which provides opportunities for self expression, recreation, manual work and learning of useful crafts. Provisions are made to satisfy the basic needs and urges of the children and thus they are helped in their social and emotional readjustment. In this way the children are helped to rid themselves of the delinquent behaviour and learn to respond meaningfully to social situations and conditions.

Change in the Attitude Towards Delinquency

The attitude towards delinquency in our country is also changing. It has now been realized that children who are called delinquents are ill primarily in their inability to conform to the social milieu. Consequently, in most of the states, the Children Act has been enforced and some have gone ahead in the work of rehabilitation and re-education of the young offenders. Separate child welfare boards for dealing with the problem of delinquency have been established and approved schools have come into existence. Some states encourage voluntary organisations to take custody of the delinquent children. Provisions for the care of the neglected and destitute children are also made so that they do not become delinquents. Some states have started foster care programmes which envisage the court giving custody of a child to a responsible person. There is, however, the need to arouse public consciousness on this problem. No government can solve a social problem without public cooperation. Therefore, there is a need for a change in our attitude towards delinquents so that they may be helped in their readjustment and rehabilitation.

XV.4 Learning Exercises

1. What do you understand by delinquency?
2. Discuss the causes of delinquency.
3. Describe the remedial measures in checking delinquency.
4. Describe factors causing delinquency.

XVI

Mental Health

Modern age is the age of information highway technology during which we are aware of the national and international tensions and wars, on the contrary we are ignorant about the Mahabharat going on within the Psyche of a man which takes away such a big chunk of humanity. In the same way, we are also aware about the social, economic and political structures based on mutual exploitation, cut-throat competition, spiralling individualism and disoriented morality which are responsible for looting our mental peace. Meaning thereby, that a healthy individual is supposed to be physically healthy but is also supposed to be mentally healthy. The latest concept of mental health extends beyond the proper functioning of the body which includes a sound, efficient mind and controlled emotions.

XVI.1 Meaning and Definitions of Mental Hygiene

The term mental health is used to describe how well the individual is adjusted to the demands and opportunities of life. In other words the term mental health is recognised as an important aspect of one's total health status. The factors that contribute to the maintenance of physical health as well as social effectiveness.

Mental health is a normal state of well-being, and in the words of Johns, Sutton and Webster, 'is a positive but relative quality of life. It is a condition which is characteristic of the average person who meets the demands of life on the basis of his own capacities and limitations." By the word 'relative' we imply that the degree of mental health which an individual enjoys at a time is continuously changing. Similarly Hadfield defines "mental health is the full and harmonious' functioning of the whole personality". It is a positive, active quality of the individual's daily living. This quality of living is manifest in the behaviour of an individual whose body and mind are working together in the same direction. His thoughts, feelings and actions function harmoniously towards the common end. In other words, we mean that mental health is the ability to balance feelings, desires, ambitions and ideals in one's daily living as well as ability to face and accept the realities of life. It connotes such habits of work and attitudes towards people and things that bring maximum satisfaction and happiness to the individual. But the individual gets this satisfaction and happiness without any function with the social order or group to which he or she belongs.

From the above discussion, one can conclude that mental health has two important aspects. It is both individual and social. The individual aspect connotes that the individual is internally adjusted. He is self confident, adequate and free from internal conflicts and tensions or inconsistencies. He is able to adapt himself to the new situations. But he achieves this internal adjustments in a social set up. Society has certain value systems, customs and traditions by which it governs itself and promotes the general welfare of its members. It is within this social framework that the internal adjustment has to be built up. Only then, the individual becomes a person who is acceptable as a member of society.

It is an undesirable fact that social forces are in a constant flux. They are constantly moving and changing. Similarly, our internal adjustment is also affected by various stresses. As such, mental health is a process of adjustment which involves compromise and adaptation, growth and continuity. Because of the significance of individual and social aspects, some psychologists have defined mental health as the ability of the individual to make personal and social adjustments.

It will be pertinent here to explain the word "adjustment". If one can establish a satisfactory relationship between himself and his environment, between his needs, desires and those of other people, or, if one can meet the demands of a situation, he has achieved adjustment. Adjustment results in happiness because it implies that emotional conflicts and tensions have been resolved and relieved.

Other definitions of mental health refer to such abilities as of making decisions of assuming responsibilities in accordance with one's capacities, of finding satisfaction, success and happiness in the accomplishment of everyday tasks, of living effectively with others and of showing considerate behaviour. Generally, a mentally healthy individual has some insight into and an understanding of his motives and desires, his weaknesses and strong points. He can evaluate his behaviour objectively, and can accept his short-comings and weaknesses. He can give and accept love, can form friendships which are satisfying and lasting to give him a feeling of belongingness. He has developed a philosophy of life that gives meaning and purpose to his daily activities. This philosophy belongs to this world and discourages the tendency to withdraw or escape from the world. It makes him to do something concrete about his problems as they arise. He does not evade responsibility or duty. Such a person has developed a capacity to tolerate frustrations and disappointments in his daily life. He shows emotional maturity in his behaviour. This means that he is able to regulate such emotions as fear, aggression, love, jealousy and expresses them in a socially desirable manner. He does not go to pieces as a result of his fears, anger and worries." He has a variety of interests and generally lives a well-balanced life of work, rest and recreation.

XVI.2 Importance of Mental Hygiene

Brown describes the importance of mental hygiene as the application of a body of information and technique taken from the science of psychology, child study, education, sociology, psychiatry, medicine and biology to solve the problems of preservation and importance of the mental health of the individual and community and the problems of prevention and cure of minor mental diseases and defects of mental, educational and social mal-adjustment.

As a matter of fact, mental hygiene is not concerned with mal-adjusted people. It does not study only the problems of mal-adjustment. It is as much concerned with normal children and adults as backward, retarded, sensitive, social, feeble-minded, gifted, handicapped children and people as well as persons suffering from serious mental disorder. It aims to remove the trouble of the troubles and also to raise the standard of mental efficiency of normal children and normal adults.

Mental hygiene is not only concerned with the mind of an individual or with attitude towards other people and objects but is also concerned with creating a favourable background or atmosphere that may promote the adjustment of individual with others. Adjustment is a great word in mental hygiene. Mental hygiene gives us the positive approach to adjustment of ourselves in the different situation of life. Broadly speaking, the secret of life is adjustment.

Life itself is a continuous adjustment of an individual with his environment. Adjustment is responsible for our existence. If adjustment is of better order, we live and happy in this world, otherwise we have miserable time in our feel. In order to avoid the miseries we have to make life pleasant in its real sense, there is need of healthy adjustment between individual and environment.

Adjustment is a two-way traffic. Sometimes, we dominate over the environment and make it a tool to get our aims. At others we may not be able to master the environment, but the environment may overcome us. In other words, we are defeated. It may be pointed out that defeat is also a form of adjustment. The problem is how we take our success and failure and what our attitude towards success and failure is. Mental hygiene teaches us the desirable attitude under the different conditions.

Mental hygiene provides a positive approach to become a whole some personality at each and every stage of life of an individual. In other words, mental hygiene strengthens our personality by improving the different needed qualities.

XVI.3 Criterion of Mental Hygiene

Mental health depends on certain criteria which can be studied under the following heads:

1. Adequate feelings of security: Adequate feelings of security are essential for the growth and development of well integrated personality. Physical security is indispensable for life. Feeling of security means to feel at home. The mentally healthy individual radiates poise and emotional confidence. The first duty of home is to educate the child in acquiring emotional security. The home must be a mental trust. The child must feel that he is among the wanted members of the family. He is needed by his relatives. Parents should see that children must feel at home and secure. Whatever adds to one's feelings of security, adds mental hygiene. Security of child depends on certain basic needs of children. They should be adequately satisfied. It is seen that in broken homes or where the parents are step-parents, the children are not satisfied and they feel insecure. They do not get the share of love, recognition and praise which are their natural needs. On the other hand, they are treated very badly. The mental health of the children suffers and they may become problem children and in their life, they may become criminals.

2. Adequate feelings of personal worth: Everybody is gifted with some talents, lusterous qualities and assets. This personal worth of an individual must be recognised by himself. One should explore himself to know it. It would be natural and normal to feel proud ofsuch qualities. This adds to one's self-confidence which is an important factor for each and every success. Without being be littled, adequate feelings of personal worth, the child will feel himself. It will make him small in his own eyes. Thus he will have feeling of inferiority and be victim of neurotic conflicts and indecision.

3. Adequate understanding of self: It is very easy to know about others, but it is very difficulty to know one's ownself. Sometimes, we deceive ourselves. Self-knowledge is a great knowledge. In order to achieve self realization which is one of the most important and fundamental aims of education, knowledge of one's ownself helps a lot by way of adjustment. It serves a great purpose in rationalization. It resolves and prevents the conflicts and aids to meet the challenge of life situations with greater force and insight.

4. Adequate understanding of others: We do not live alone. Man is a social animal. In order to have healthy adjustment with social environment or with other persons, there is a need to understand others. Adjustment needs two objects i.e. self and others. Unless we do not know as what is not of interest, aptitude, temper, temperament, attitude and value others have, we may not be able to make adjustment with others. Therefore, knowledge and understanding of other people is very much needed for good mental hygiene.

5. Emotional maturity: A good personality is always emotionally matured. He does not live on extreme and is very sensitive. He is not a tool in the hands of his emotions but emotions are under his control. Ordinarily he does not worry over trifles or about his future or about the things which cannot be helped at all.

6. Adequate integration of personality: The person should function as whole. He should be an organized unit. His thoughts, processes and his emotions are harmonious and compatible. He does not hesitate long in his attempt to solve his problem or allow emotional tension to build up inhibitions which reduce him to maturity.

7. Adequate basic harmony: A person achieves fundamental harmony with his environment when his own ambitions do not conflict with his ability to satisfy them or with rights and desires of others.

In addition to the above mentioned criteria for optimum mental health there are also other factors which contribute towards healthy mind. They are, such as: desirable attitude towards life, sound philosophy of life, self-confidence, achieving most of the aims and getting satisfaction in many activities usually achieving the goals that one seeks , social efficiency, normal desire to work or to play, beneficial habit patterns and a good nervous system.

Thus from the above discussion, it is very clear that mental hygiene aims at healthy adjustment. It concerns with all and at all times. This is not limited to children only. It is interested in all. Education is harmonious development of personality to adjust one-self adequately with the environment. The aim is the same. Mental hygiene has a specific field to work and thus it aids to achieve the educational aims by strengthening the minds of people to tackle the problems of life intelligently and boldly.

XVI.4 Factors Influencing Mental Hygiene

Mental health of an individual depends upon the following factors:

(1) Heredity factors.

(2) Physical factors.

(3) Fundamental social factors.

(4) Satisfaction of fundamental needs.

(1) Heredity. It provides the raw material of the individual. Heredity sets the limits for his mental health. What the individual inherits is the potentialities in relation to growth, appearance, intelligence and the like. The development and utilisation of these potentialities is determined, to a large extent, by the environmental opportunities. Investigations have shown that heredity may predispose a person to the development of a particular type of mental illness when he is placed under excessive stress. Even in psychoneuroses and psychopathic personality trends, heredity factors may play some role. In the production of number of the mentally defective and feeble-minded hereditary factors are quite prominent. In the words of Wallin, "defective heredity may furnish a fertile soil for the development of mental and nervous diseases but so far as minor personality maladjustments are concerned, heredity supplies only a predisposing condition."

(2) Physical Factors. Physical factors make a significant contribution to mental health of an individual. An erect posture, a winning smile, colour in the cheeks, a feeling of exhilaration promote a sense of personality security and have a marked influence on other people. People with greater strength, better looks and robust health enjoy a social advantage in the development of personality characteristics. An individual with a feeling of physical well-being ordinarily enjoys a good disposition and is enthusiastic and intellectually alert. He has a desire to live, to achieve and to be happy. No body can deny that physical health improves mental vitality in as much as it increases motivation and drive. It has been observed that continued hunger, overwork or sleeplessness produce fatigue, and that may affect our mental health adversely. Sick people find it more difficult to make adjustments to new situations than healthy people. Vitamin deficiencies have been found to be the causative factors in many personality difficulties. In pernicious anaemia, for example, there occurs a deficiency of red corpuscles and this produces characteristic symptoms of apathy, irritability, depression and anxiety.

Again, person suffering from serious defects may have problems of adjustment, on account of inferiority feelings which they have not been able to deal with adequately. Positively speaking, the individual who follows a hygienic regimen, pertaining to food, drink, elimination, bathing, physical activity, work, sleep, rest, relaxation, prevention of disease and correction of defects, is more likely to have good mental health.

(3) Social Factors. Social factors pertain to the individual's society in which he lives, the interactional process, and his social functioning with other persons. The social environment shapes the knowledge, the skills, interests, attitudes, habits, values and goals that he acquires. Every individual is born into a society which influences the content of his behaviour. Of the social

factors, which influences the mental health of an individual are the *home*, the *school* and the *community*.

(i) Home: Parents who give affection and security to their children contribute to their mental health. Parents who are nervous, tense or self-centred, over-protective or rejecting, dominating or inconsistent in disciplinary practices or who are partial in dealing with their children are laying the foundations of mental inadequacy or ill-health. On the other hand, parents who share their life and time with their family and children, who show interest in the development of their children, play with them or work with them help them to develop mentally healthy attitudes.

Broken homes or unstable homes where parents are in constant conflict produce a large percentage of children with adjustment problems. A good home, on the other hand, where there is a harmonious relationship between parents where parents understand the needs and interests of their children and where there is an atmosphere of happiness and freedom contributes greatly to the mental health of every member.

(ii) School: The school can also develop a sense of personal worth, social growth and social competence, if its experiences are satisfying and if they evoke affectional responses. A good school provides an atmosphere in which each pupil is respected as an individual. It provides a curriculum enriched by activities, meeting the needs and interests of pupils co-curricular activities such as dramatics, athletics, debates which promote the physical and emotional development of its pupils. Such a school plays positive factor in the development of sound mental health.

(iii) Community: The community provides the frame work and climate within which the family lives and develops. It ought to provide, therefore, a healthy atmosphere and a well-organised network of public and private community services of the highest possible quality. These services, will satisfy the needs of love and affection, and will give to its members a feeling of belongingness, and will provide opportunities for group anticipation and for emotional release. Some of these community services could be libraries and reading-rooms for the general public, social education centres. Well round recreational programmes, vocational and educational guidance bureaus for youth, child-guidance clinics, *Bal-bhavans*, hospitals for the mentally and physically ill, arrangements for family counselling like family-like institutes, maternity and child welfare centres in the urban and rural areas.

(4) Satisfaction of Fundamental needs. Mental health in childhood and in later depends very much on the adequate satisfaction of our fundamental needs. These are physical as well as emotional or psychological. The organic or physical needs are to be satisfied for maintaining physical well-being.

Physiological Needs : Hunger, thirst, fatigue, lack of sleep, physical pain, exercise, heat or cold and the like set up certain tensions in the individual which must be relieved for sound mental health of an individual.

Psychological Needs: In addition to the biological needs the Psychological or emotional needs are considered essential for mental health. These needs are also called 'ego needs' which must be satisfied to maintain 'self'. They are as important as the organic needs. There are two main ego needs. Firstly, we have the need for a sense of security through love and affection of those who are important to us—our parents, our friends and our fellow men. We wish to have a warm and satisfying relationship with other people. This feeling of security mostly comes through love which consists of such elements as understanding, trust, cooperation and overt affection. The child feels secure which he is assured that his parents care for him, wants him and accept him as he is. Accepted in this way the child can establish healthy relationship with the world outside. To the person with a feeling of security, the world is a friendly and safe place. Such a person likes people and feels comfortable with them.

The second type of Psychological rather the ego need is for recognition or regard as a person of worth and importance. The adequate satisfaction of this need gives a sense of adequacy, a feeling of self-enhancement. In order that this need is satisfied in the child, parents and others have to demonstrate their affection and their approval and evince in what the child does. Once the child has a feeling of adequacy and importance, he will be able to cope with, and if possible, solve the problem which confronts him.

Other needs besides these two are the need to grow independently, the need to play and the need to belong to a group. The need to grow independently is often not properly satisfied in our homes. Our parents are mostly over-protective. They find satisfaction in their children remaining dependent on them for ever. Generally, the youngsters are not allowed to think and decide for themselves. On the whole it can be said that Psychological, Sociological and Physiological factors play vital role for mental adjustment of an individual. The level of mental adjustment therefore reflects the level of mental health.

XVI.5 Mental Health and Role of Teacher

The aim of mental hygiene is not different from the aim of education. It means that mental hygiene can go a long way to attain the aim of education. The question is how to do it. We can accomplish the task in the following ways:

1. Develop Free Atmosphere. First of all, the teacher should see atmosphere of class and school very encouraging. That is free atmosphere inside as well outside the class-room. Because students want to express themselves. A teacher equipped with useful knowledge of mental hygiene will always encourage the students to come out with their ideas and opinions. Somehow or the other, the teacher will show that he likes the self-expression of students. He will listen to the view-points of students and give them due appreciation. Self-expression is a great means to develop the personality. If self-expression is checked and curbed, the students will not feel secure. Adequate feeling of security is very important for mental hygiene. The child without feeling of security will feel that he is not wanted in the class and therefore his self-expression has been checked. It may injure his feeling. He will be seeing himself small and little. He will be thinking it over and again and thus feeling of inferiority will develop. Gradually feeling of insecurity will change into inferiority behaviour. This feeling can be removed by a wholesome atmosphere in the class.

2. Democratic Attitude. The attitude of teacher should be very democratic. The children are very sensitive. If due attention is not given or the teacher attends to a child without any special reason, the children may cast their small finger towards this sort of inequality. All sorts of rivalries, jealousies or preference may threaten the security of young students. If the teacher acts like a friend and establishes social contact with them, calls them by name and mixes up with them without showing the dominant attitude, the students will feel more secure. To feel safe is to feel at home, provided the expression gives us feeling of affectionate security. Mentally healthy child is he who feels at home in school, home and street.

Since the role of a teacher for the healthy development of students is considered important as a teacher having a sound knowledge of mental health would guide to develop mentally healthy students by discharging the following roles:

School is a specialised environment to foster the growth and development of children. Thus teacher must build up a child's feeling of security and perhaps next to parents, this is his most important duty. As far as possible, the teacher should love all the children alike and equally. Equality of opportunity and treatment is a good principle of mental hygiene. This means that dirty, ugly, backward and retarded children are not to be ignored but due attention should be paid to them. These children have their special difficulties and our negligence towards them will increase their trouble. No student should get a chance to say that teacher has a grudge against him. Strictly speaking, the principle of equality cannot be carried on. In the class there are students of different variety. There are bright students and dull students. There are children of different temperament. There are children who always sit on the back benches. There are students who are physically or mentally backward. Therefore, certain students may need more attention than others. Moreover, the teacher is a human being. He is not a machine. Therefore, he cannot do away with all his likes and dislikes. It needs tactful handling on the part of teacher to satisfy all the students so as to avoid feelings of resentment, disappointment and frustration. It has been seen that the morale of students goes up if there is democratic atmosphere in the class. Common sense, analysis and clinical expression show that dominant attitude of teacher causes frustration among students which results into several behaviour problems.

3. The Teacher Must Pay attention to Abnormal pupils: In every school we may get children who do not show normal behaviour. They may be shut in personalities. These children do not mix up with others. They remain aloof. They dare not to ask questions in the class. If ever they stand up to ask some questions or to clear some points, they feel nervous and their movements are awkward. There are other students who study much. Still they do not do well in the examination. Some children are emotionally upset. Some children are anti-social in their behaviour. They steal the things of others. They are aggressive towards other class-fellows or they are in the habit of telling a lie. Some students may indulge in various serious mischiefs. The teachers have to mend them. They must solve their difficulties. Such problems are not solved adequately and so there is faulty adjustment. In order to re-educate these children, the teacher must be very sympathetic and kind towards such students. He must win their confidence and their lost confidence must be restored. The teacher can talk to them after the class or after school hours. He can find the trouble and the cause. Positive suggestions with follow-up programme and vigilant observation would treat the several cases. If need be, the teachers can arrange meeting with their parents to study the life of child at home. The problem, and its cause and cure can be determined by discussing with the parents or guardians. If the home conditions are not favourable, the parents may be advised to change the home atmosphere. Sometimes there will be a need to change the school or place of the child.

4. Use of Clinics: Mental Hygiene clinics must be utilised. Mental hygiene clinics are becoming more and more common. This is a remarkable achievement. Problem children who cannot be treated or reformed by parents or by teachers are referred to the clinics. These clinics are well equipped with the needed apparatuses. They interview the child and try to find the trouble. For the complete diagnosis, there is physico-medical examination of the child by the medical doctor. The case-history of the child which tells the story of his development and growth, is also prepared by the social worker. The psychologist applies several mental tests in order to know about the intelligence, personality, aptitude, interest and other traits of personality. After the diagnosis is done, the child is treated by psycho-therapy. This is a great contribution of mental hygiene towards education.

5. Knowledge of Individual Differences: Mental hygiene recognises the individual differences of the students. No two individuals are exactly alike. They may differ in qualitative or quantitative aspects of personality. This means that the needs of students are different. In order to meet the individual differences. The curriculum of school must be such as to satisfy the various interests and aptitudes of students. The courses may be of different types and of different standards. There should be numerous optional and elective subjects. Let the children have their selection. In the same way the co-curricular activities should be available in the school. All the students should take part in one activity or the others so that their mental needs are cared to. The co-curricular activities should include some criterion of mental health. The students who are dull or backward in scholastic attainment may be encouraged to show themselves in scouting, games, sports, athletics, dramatics, community work, cooking, art and craft, fine arts and such other activities. Such sort of compensation is essential in order to maintain the balance of life.

6. Organisation of Co-curricular Activities: Co-curricular activities are extremely useful to understand one's own self, thus the students may come to know what their assets and difficulties are and what aspect of personality or trait is more developed than other. They may compare themselves with others in order to evaluate themselves. Such a self-appraisal is needed to understand oneself. This sort of insight is quite helpful in setting and achieving the aims. Self-understanding, self-concept, self-confidence and adequate feelings of self-worth can be obtained through these co-curricular activities. Social efficiency and knowledge of others is gained. Moreover, co-curricular activities do not have rigid discipline. Therefore, students are accompanied with joy, freedom and spontaneity. Students are interested. In such activities encourage the students to take more active part. Such sort of hobbies or play-way occupations are very healthy as the pent-up of bottled up energy is let off in the form of some useful behaviour.

7. To Work As Model: Mental hygiene of teacher should be of high standard. Teacher is a model for students which should be of high standard. Students copy the teacher consciously or unconsciously. This model must be worth copying otherwise the idiocyncrasies and the prejudices of the teacher which are not worthy of coping will be taken by the students and as such they may become problem for themselves. The teacher must be perfectly mentally healthy.

8. Developing High Morale: Mental hygiene is very much concerned with the general morale of children. If the students are in high spirits and they do not lose their heart in difficulties and failures and do not evade the reality but face it like bold persons, then they have good mental hygiene. Students can pick up these things in class-room and at the play-ground and the teacher can help a lot to inculcate such spirit of high morale, strong determination and firm resolution.

XVI.6 Mental Health and Role of Family

Family plays vital role in the development of mental health of a child. For sound mental health of a child family plays its role in the following ways:

1. Family the basis of adjustment. The family is the first and probably the most significant agency which determines the adjustment of an individual towards successful living. All the basic needs are provided at home and the child begins to learn through the social interaction at home. It is at home that the child gets a sense of security, physical as well as psychological. Family determines the attitude of child towards these. All these things are learnt by the child from the parents and other elder members of family. The atmosphere of family and the standard and the traditions of family are borrowed by the child. It is a sort of family code that a child learns from the parents. So it is upto parents to determine the social and moral code. The super-ego of child is directly related with the standards prevailing in the family, because the child has to identify himself with the elder members of the family who meet all the needs of the child.

2. Love and security. In a well organized and hygienic atmosphere, the child gets the proper attention of the parents and other elder members of the family. He is well looked after by others. So he feels secure. Whenever, there is any sort of danger, the child runs towards parents or towards home. For him, father and mother are great authorities to make the complaints of others. This shows that child feels at home and safe in his family. This sense of security is the first need of child. If the child does not feel at home, he will fail to adjust himself adequately out of home. Family gives the first opportunity of adjustment. This is specially helped by the atmosphere of love and affection. If the child fails to get love and affection from the parents, it would become very difficult for him to get love or to be successful in getting love and affection in his future life. As the child is refused his due and natural share of love, his attitude towards home or parents is changed and later on this attitude of child may be reflected in his problems when he is declared as a problem child.

To give love is equally as important as to get love. Parents should not only love the child but they should also be the objects of love of the child.

3. Social Recognition. Social recognition is another point of home life. Family is a primary social group. He is member of the group and is aware of his membership. Thus his membership should be well recognized by his parents. If he is ignored or neglected, he would mind it and feel that he is not wanted in the family. Such feelings of the child may show some sort of resentment and dis-appointment which may be reflected in his later life.

4. The Present Homes. Unfortunately, the number of homes where the relationship between child and parents is harmonious in the real sense is very small. No doubt parents are often well wishers of their development, yet they do not know it well as how to go about. The parents do not realize that even their children are entitled to get respect as individuals. They do not care for individuality of the child and think it too much of their property. Some parents over-protect the child while others neglect him.

Unfortunately the joint family system and the real home atmosphere is disappearing. In the advanced countries the home life is broken and shattered. Clubs have replaced the homes. The progress of mechanical invention and the change in the mode of living and the modern mechanical life has taken away the home life of individual which is the fundamental structure responsible for the healthy adjustment. Perhaps this is the reason that as a good family life is vanishing and the cases of neurosis and psychosis are increasing in number.

5. Need for parents in place of teacher. No doubt there are infant schools and nursery classes for babies. In such schools diet is given and child is nicely looked after by lady teachers. Still a teacher cannot be a substitute for mother. Mother pays individual attention to her child accompanied with love and affection. This is the greatest wealth of humanity which is being wasted. There is no need to teach the child in a formal way by sending him to the school when he is very young. Create the atmosphere of love and affection, security and freedom, self-expression and recognition and the child picks up unconsciously all that is good. Ladies can serve the nation more by rearing the needful children and satisfying their natural needs in a natural atmosphere than attending offices and schools. Nothing can be more precious and more useful than the human wealth. The development of human child depends largely on the atmosphere of family.

XVI.7 Mental Health Hazards Inadequate Schooling and Family Climate

Adequate environment is most essential for healthy growth and development of mental health of a child. Inadequate climate in school and the family causes the following hazards among our future generations:

(a) Hazards due to Inadequate School Climate:

(1) *Lack of Friendliness.* The teacher when he acts as strict disciplinarian prevents a genuinely friendly atmosphere in the school.

(2) *Competition.* A competition between groups and individuals where there is the possibility of success on the part of all concerned provides a good

motivation. Competition which is friendly and co-operative, which minimizes jealousy and suspicion is also good. But a competition becomes a mental hazard when it is between unequally matched individuals. For example, scholastic competition between slow learners and bright children leads to feelings of insecurity, inferiority and frustration, etc., among children.

(3) *Uniform Grades.* The grading or marking system is not proper. Every child is graded for memorizing the text. This is undesirable since some have good memory and some bad. Also in the type of examinations we have, the same teacher is liable to award very different marks on the same answer on different occasions or to the similar answers of the students. This discrepancy is all the more alarming when the teacher knows the boys. 'Halo effects' act here. A good student in the opinion of the teacher gets high marks though his answer may be poor.

(4) *Promotion Practices.* A number of students fails in the examination. It often happens because of stresses on the mind of the student during the examination period. Moreover, failure makes them dejected and they begin to feel that they are not good students.

(5) *Fear of Failure.* Many students develop psychotic tendencies only because they are afraid that they will fail in the examination.

(6) *Homework.* When the teachers give very heavy home-work the pupils fail to do so much.

(b) Hazards Due to Inadequate Family Climate:

The duty of parents has to know problems and solve them. Sometimes, instead of solving the problems the parents create problems for children. These problems are as follows:

1. Broken homes.
2. Divorces.
3. Un-happy matrimonial life.
4. Step children or step parents.
5. Death of one or both the parents.
6. Emotional and drunkard parents.
7. Illegal Children.
8. Unwanted children.
9. Economic crisis in family or poverty.
10. Un-educated parents.
11. Low moral and social standards of family.

In all the above cases, the development of children suffers. Parents attitude towards children should be favourable. The needs of children are not satisfied. There is some check on their budding personality. This may result the development of aggressive behaviour on the part of the children. Children show resentment and like to get revenge from their parents but they are weak and helpless. Later on the formation gets its outlet while showing aggressive behaviour towards brothers, sisters, friends, in the street or class-fellows in the school. If parents and teachers do not see the problems of their children and fail to make them understand, such children may become delinquents and later on criminals. They take revenge from the society at large which was due towards parents.

As a matter of fact, knowledge of mental hygiene is extremely useful for parents. The art of mental hygiene is based on the sound principles. These principles show us the path and serve the parents as guiding directions. It is true that parents cannot control the heredity but the social and mental environment of family is not less important than heredity in the growth of development of young children. The early childhood is the most impressionable period of life. It is a base and serves as fundamental structure of the personality. Thus home life should be very pleasant and the parents should respect the children.

XVI.8 Role of Different Agencies Promoting Mental Health

There are three main agencies which play vital role to promote mental health. Out of these three the school and home are considered most effective agencies promoting mental health of a child. These agencies work in the following way to promote and develop mental health in the following stages:

(1) Group Dynamism: In schools simply we are not dealing with the relation between one teacher and one child. We must take account of group factors, and this means that we have to broaden and reinterpret the basic notions of security—insecurity, dependence—independence, ambivalent feeling and sibling rivalry, in terms of the interrelations of individuals within groups and with relationships between groups. In coming to schools for the first time the child is faced with two new sets of demands. He has to form many new relationships with other children and with other teachers on the basis of the relationships he has already established within his family and immediate community. He has also to meet new experiences, acquire new skills and has to conform to the new standards of behaviour and achievement expected of him.

Teachers too are members of the special group within the school. They are also member of a profession with a particular status and special duty. Also they have private lives as men and women. They have thus to maintain a complex series of relationships and to perform a variety of tasks within a special kind of community, which has its own structure of authority and rules of conduct. The school itself is a part of a larger educational structure and is in constant relationship with the rest of the adult community. All these considerations affect the mental health and behaviour of teachers, and are thus relevant to the mental health and to the development of the pupils. Care should be taken that no newcomer in the school should receive a shock from the group or groups in which he is expected to move. It does not mean that every student should find groups ready-made to his tastes. He should be expected to understand, analyse and strive for adjustment with the groups. In fine, the overall tone of the group should be of acceptance and encouragement, which is possible only in a democratic structure and not in an autocratic one. The moral of the members of a democratic group has been found to be always higher than that of the members of an autocratic group. The morals is a sure index of mental health.

The school is itself a community and is made up of several groups. There is the staff group and there are groups of children according to their ages. Sociogramic studies reveal that there are individuals in leadership roles and often there is a hierarchy of leaders among both staff and children. Some structure of authority is essential for the welfare of community, but authority may be exercised through a more or less strict authoritarian regime, *i.e.*, in a more or less tyrannical way, or it may be used to create and protect a generally permissive atmosphere in which those invested with authority take the lead as required but in which all other members also contribute to the enrichment of the common life. The first category of group is known as autocratic and second one as democratic. We have already mentioned this issue earlier in this chapter but it should be remembered the issue involved is at the philosophical level determining the nature of order and freedom, but in practice and in psychological terms the conditions for ordered freedom obtained through democratic group dynamism concern the minimising the anxiety and aggression in the exercise of leadership and authority and maximising the security and purposeful participation among the members of the school community. There is no single issue in education which can better repay our schools and universities than honest examination of the relations between their exercise of authority and mental health and achievement of their members. It is suggested that some of the techniques of group discussion where an acknowledged common problem is taken up and the therapeutic component is implicit, not explicit could very well be utilized by staff and students, groups for self-examination. To be effective, such groups should be led by someone with a deeper understanding of the issue involved than most of the other members. For this the majority of the principals and headmasters of schools are not as yet well prepared and there is much to be said for special orientation and training courses for all prospective heads, which would include some experience of quasitherapeutic group discussion. There should also be selection of heads on personality grounds. Some teachers are charged with to much anxiety, though not always of the unconscious type that they are quite unable to exercise authority except in an authoritarian way. It is important to note that it is right here that the real answer to most of the problems of undisciplined is to be found in an institution where there is an orderly and actively permissive atmosphere and which is trying to face up to its own internal problems through the conscious use of its own group resources, and which consequently has a high morale, the majority of behaviour requiring special and severe punishment are not likely to occur often. There is a close and positive relationship between permissive but efficient leadership, high morale, absence of anti-social behaviour and effective achievement. They are all indices of good mental health and are found together like a syndrome. An educational institution is essentially a part of the wider community. In some cases the relation may be one of apathy or even of thinly veiled hostility. Our schools and university campuses do reflect this hostile relationship between an educational institution and society periodically. It looks that the educational world and the societal world in our country are thriving practically independent of one another. According to the famous economist Myrdall, school education can be and should be positively related to social and economical development in a developing society, where the university education tends to become not only superfluous and useless but also an instrument in the hands of the vested interests for further exploitation. There is a considerable scope for the improvement of mental health in schools and universities through the improvement of their relations with the community, whether in the form of parent-teacher associations or the interpenetration of school and occupational life or enrolling the active cooperation of students in the academic and administrative life of the institution. Such developments are difficult and slow, and success will be largely dependent on the degree to which teachers and heads can become aware of and learn to manage successfully the latent anxieties, rivalry and pride which inevitable motivate much of the behaviour shown by both sides in such relationships. In a wider context it can be suggested that school education in India should become terminal and production-oriented for inducing sound mental health in the society. At present it prepares students for university education which is tangentially related to the life and aspirations of the community.

(2) Adjustment to Institutional Stress: In our school system there are two or three points at which children have usually to make an abrupt change from one environment to another. They have to give up sets of established relationships and attitudes to learning, and form new sets, often they are ill-

prepared for such changes and more often than not, nothing tangible is done to help them to make a smooth transition. These points are from primary to secondary schools and from secondary to higher educational institutions where they are required to exercise their choices for various options. Curriculum should not be rigid but flexible to suit individual differences. At the same time individual differences should not be over-stressed or over-exploited to produce individual snobs or group rivalry, or for exploitation by vested interests. Guidance and counselling services are a must in school where it should be attempted that vocational aims become clear to the students. Hence these services are intimately influenced by the employment opportunities in the society outside.

(3) *The Mental Health of Teachers and Parents*: For a student, a teacher is a second parent, and parent is a second teacher. Mental health, in student-teacher and ward-parents relationships, is highly contagious. As the psychology of abnormal behaviour points out, the pattern of behaviour in an individual tends to become more and more rigid and inflexible with age. Therefore, it is always advisable to take more prophylactic steps to avoid the development of some disorder, rather than curative therapy.

There are three purposes of teacher-training, the development of proper knowledge skills and attitudes. In our training colleges the development of attitudes is least attended to and this is well-known that the mental health of a teacher is related to his proper attitudinal development. A teacher is expected to respect and recognize the personality of a student. A student who is neglected and recognized simply as a cog in the machine or as a non-effective member of the group, is likely to develop the feelings of worthlessness and inferiority. Once a child begins to develop such feelings of worthlessness, unwantedness, inferiority, lack of sense of belongingness and consequent insecurity, the foundation-stone of some category of neurosis, delinquency or even some more serious disorder is laid. The teachers are known to remember or call their students by their roll numbers or at the most by the colour of their dress. They refuse to see something else in the student, his name, parentage, intelligence and a host of other personality variables. The role of a teacher, of a mother and of a gardener is basically of encouraging growth and development, though they may have to prune off the unnecessary growth around. The practice of calling the students by their first names and the knowledge on the part of the teacher regarding the family circumstances of a student are likely to keep a student disciplined and gives him a sense of belongingness, worth and orientation towards a particular goal. Somebody humorously defined army 'as a group of serially-arranged brainless patriots'. This definition is too unbearable for an army, what to speak of a roomful of energy, comprising of hopeful, optimistic and aspiring youngsters. A student not properly recognized home or at school feels aggressive. If he happens to be timid, the aggression will be internalized resulting in psychoneurosis. If he happens to be adventurous and outgoing, the aggression will be externalized on society through various acts of delinquency and indiscipline.

Also the role of competition and cooperation at homes as well as in school life should be carefully planned. Undue comparisons, stressful competitions and a shamed conduct should be replaced by cooperation which is a natural urge of man. 'The survival of the fittest' in 'the struggle for existence', so dear to Darwinians may be well applicable on the lower forms of life. The homosapien is quite intelligent for he knows that competition should gradually be replaced by cooperation. The dire competition generated by a capitalistic order hits at the roots of the mental health of an individual. Some competition contained by an overall cooperation as postulated by a socialistic order guarantees integrative adjustment, creativity and corporate life. The belief that stimulation through competition will keep an individual growing is not very correct, for life in its true form does not need much stimulation from outside to grow. The human organism cannot sustain stress beyond a certain point. Too much emphasis on efficiency and speed by teachers and parents produces a lot of tension in a child, which tends to impair the finer tissues of his body. Lin-Yu-Tang, the Chinese philosopher, says that had the Chinese Society been 'efficient' like that of America, it could not have survived for more than five thousand years of high blood pressure. A perfectionistic attitude on the part of the parents and teachers 'that the child should top in each subject and win a colour in each activity' is irrational and produces undue anxiety in the child.

As already mentioned, anxiety is contagious and there is transference of anxiety from parents and teachers to children. A father suffering from inferiority complex as he could not get a lucrative job himself would constantly enquire about his son's progress at school. He wants to live through his son and wants him to become what he could not be himself. This is ethically not undesirable but the ambition regarding the future of the son should be in consonance with his abilities and propensities. That sort of constant enquiry about his progress evokes an anxious response in his mind, since he beings to doubt himself. Sometimes parental conflict also grows into the child's life. Gates mentions in his book 'The Improvement of Reading' an interesting case of a boy whose parents had a conflict between themselves. The father was not in favour of sending the boy to that school, but the mother wanted it as that enhanced the social prestige. Whenever the boy would come home, the father would put him somewhat difficult questions to prove that he is not progressing satisfactorily. On the other hand, the mother would ask him relatively simpler questions to prove otherwise. The boy unconsciously began to exhibit a queer behaviour in his academic achievements. In one class test he would do brilliantly and in the next he would fail. Thus, trying to please both the parents. Later on, this unconscious conflict began to sap his energy and his academic achievements fell consistently. There are cases where daughters doubted by their parents later developed paranoid suspiciousness in their married life. Usually the childhood pattern tends to grow in adult life, though adults do help themselves out of this psychic determinism through the process of self-analysis, self-insight and self-drive. Sometimes children grow rebellious as a reaction to the over-domineering fathers. They retaliate and defeat their parents by earning a disgraceful failure at the school. Extremist attitude on the part of the parents on the continuum of love has also been established to be harmful for the mental health of the children. Watson found that over-protected children become very anxious. Ribble, on the other hand, found that the over-rejected children become anxious adults. Both are right. The true virtue lies between the two extremes. Parents should not over-indulge with their children to the extent that their ego is unnecessarily inflated and they always wish to be the focus of attention wherever they go. Also the parents should not deny due love and care which their children deserve, otherwise they would develop persecutory paranoid feelings of unwantedness, rejection, jealousy and suspicion.

Usually there have been recognized four types of maladjusted teachers; the aggressive, the megalomaniac, the sycophant and the pseudo-psychologist. The aggressive teacher is a bully and often resorts to physical and mental torture, insult and reproof. The students grow anxious and might develop masochistic or sadistic tendencies. The megalomaniac is a self-advertiser who goes on praising himself before the students. Some of the students begin to take themselves to be inferior, while others as a reaction might develop a sort of hatred for the teacher. Both these situations are undesirable. The sycophant teacher is weak enough to stand up on his own legs in the class. He needs the support of at least some strong students in the class and goes on praising or cajoling them in order to enlist their support. This produces a tension in the otherwise peaceful and normal class group. The 'chosen' student or few students become the target of the rest of the class. The pseudo-psychologist is the most interesting category who having read some of Freud's work, or attended some therapeutic group-discussions, or undergone a hyponotic session, or undergone some personal analysis behaves as a member of some mysterious and chosen elect, in possession of some priceless secret knowledge which he or she is often only too willing to divulge in an aggressive way. Life to such a psychologist then becomes an endless stream of interpretations. Such people are a menace to themselves and to the mental health and happiness of their friends and acquaintances. Perhaps we shall always have to put with a few of them for the sake of discussing with the majority some of the basic facts about human behaviour and personality. A little knowledge is not always a dangerous thing; and in many fields this is all that most of us will ever be able to have. It is people and the use they make of knowledge who are dangerous, not knowledge in itself. It must be emphasized that no responsible psychologist ever gives direct personal interpretation of behaviour outside a therapeutic relationship. Teaching is in some respects necessarily a therapeutic relationship, but the therapy required in largely that of spontaneous, intuitive understanding. That should be the goal of the education of teachers for mental health is the classroom, not an extensive academic knowledge of the more intricate parts of the dynamic psychology, or a quack skill in discovering unconscious meanings in everyday life.

In Hindu view, one should try to reform only himself. The world will automatically be reformed. This should be the guiding star of a teacher interested in his mental health as well as the mental health of his students.

(4) *The Creative Learning*: Learning that is healthy is creative, and whatever is creative is healthy learning. To make every act of learning a spontaneous joyful discovery is the dream of every idealist in education, and perhaps the great majority of teachers have some experience of the vision becoming reality. It is such an experience that sustains our faith. The whole activity movement in education has this as its aim, although the aim is much older than the movement. The techniques of inducing creative learning have been ranging from the inspiring example, through expressive activity to the subtleties of the art of Socratic interrogation. The activity movement has been supported both for its therapeutic possibilities as well as its strictly educational ones. The key lies in the notion of the creative function of fantasy within emotional relationships. From the older point of view of mental hygiene, activity methods of learning and free expression through music, drama and arts were encouraged because they were supposed to give an outlet for repressed tendencies. The child was encouraged to express his difficulties in the interests of a rather aimless catharsis. It is now realized that the essentially therapeutic element in play is that through the child learns to control in fantasy, impulses which are as yet for him to control in reality. In this kind of situation the participation of other children and of the teachers is often a vital factor.

In creative learning, the therapeutic and the educational aspects are almost indistinguishable. It emphasizes that there is a continuity in the child's relationships with things as there is in his relationship with people. Just as our later personal relationships contain echoes from our relations with our parents, so our adult interest in the world of things are impregnated by our infantite interests in our bodies, in the products of our bodies and the bodies of our parents. There is also a continuity of development between the magical omnipotent wish of the child (according to anthropologists, of the primitive adult too) and the controlled imagination of the poet and the reasoned argument of the scientist. We have to see all learning as primarily motivated by unconscious phantasy. An education which does not allow the constant interplay of the inner and the outer is a violation of our natures, and does not provide the nurture essential to healthy growth to maturity. We develop our innerselves through the exploration of the adult world of activities and ideas. As children we invest the world with value and it is the job of education to return our investment our interest. Education has to enable us to remain in active touch with our feelings and to use them freely in relationships and creative imagination. Creative learning is essential to all these aims. Formal instruction is only an instrumental techniques in necessary parts of a larger whole. Alone it is the ally of authoritarianism, of slavish, unassimilated and uncriticized knowledge, and of mental ailments.

(5) *The Role of Religion and Values*: The idea of the emotional significance of subject and activities is not new, but recently there has been an important shift in the psychologist's vision of the relation of passions to learning and to cultural achievements like values, religion, art and science. This shift in view point and its significance for mental health and education is most clearly evident in connection with religion. Under the influence of the early Freudian idea of sublimation, school subjects and other cultural activities were thought of as outlets for primitive instincts. Love of God, for example, was merely a socially useful substitute for biological sex satisfaction—a handy safety valve. Religion was thought to serve as one of the best lines of activity for the expression of ungratified desires. In contrast to this view point the modern anthropologists tell us that religion is pragmatically necessary to the individual's life if he is to overcome his shattering anticipation of death, disaster and destiny. Socially, they say, religion is the core of civilization and the main spring of moral values, one of the prime integrative forces in society. Even this pragmatic evaluation of religion is not sufficient. It is in fact through these basic structures of religion, art and science that we acquire any experience of meaning of values, any perception of what human mutuality entails and hence any real self-knowledge. These achievements in art, science and religion have a basic component of biological urges and are capable of a vast variety of pathological expression, like all other human activities. This does not mean that religion, art or science are in themselves neurotic activities. It does mean, however, that their social stability and integrative power for the individual depend on specially favourable forms of integration of these same basic biological urges. It is through education in its broadest sense that this integration takes place and the school necessarily carries a great deal of responsibility. Success in this process spells mental health and educational achievement; failure, mental ill-health and educational disaster. A true religion in its core, not the ritualistic and formal form of it, would entail value like courage, truth, brotherhood,

altruism, faith, etc.; so essential for human maturity, the aim of mental health and education. We should remember, the aim of mental health and education. We should remember that values are not taught, but caught. Here at least, example is always better than precept.

(6) *Social Structure*: This is an overall factor which determines the level of mental health of a large number of individuals in a society. When this goes wrong, all the attempts by educationists, psychologists and psychiaratrists to preserve and strengthen the fabric of mental health turn futile as we are seeing in the present societies of the world, where the sources of production and distribution lie in the hands of few, where a large majority works simply as a nut and a bolt in the huge socio-economo-political machine, where true workers lose their sense of identification with the above-mentioned machine and ultimately with their family and immediate community, where for the sake of efficiency. Life is turned so fast, impersonal and impassioned, unconcerned and without a sense of direction that the human psycho-physical system tends to break down under stress. In the wake of Industrial Revolution, large scale production and unbanization long with the development of a capitalistic structure in the then European society, Karl Marx propounded his thesis of socialism (where every source of production is owned by the workers) and ultimate communism (where even to state withers) to save the society from the disastrous process of dehumanization. Marx gave his theory taking it for granted that urbanization and large-scale industry are inescapable. His solution of the riddle of dehumanization should be viewed in this background. But Mahatma Gandhi went one step ahead and suggested cottage industry and a go-back-to-the-village movement. He had clearly seen that Raj-satta (the Governmental power) should gradually be replaced by Lok-satta (the people's democracy), where every body will feel himself belonging to all sources of production and distribution. He had dreamt that in that Ram-Rajya there will be no exploitation, no yawning gap between the haves and have-nots and consequently people will be happy and healthy. It is in the larger context of such a structure of the society that a sound mental health can be insured and mental hygiene movement can be deeply rooted. Probably this is the reason that there is comparatively less incidence of crime, neurosis, suicide, alcoholism and drug-addiction in the socialist countries than in the capitalist ones. It looks that education is subservient to the giant social structure of either category. But can't we lay the foundation of a new egalitarian, exploitation-free and democratic structure in our classrooms? We know that only a highly committed leadership can do so. But can't we lay the foundation of such leadership in our corridors and laboratories? If we are able to achieve this aim, we shall be planning for sound mental health of the society in much subtler and deeper way.

There are at least two more very important implications of the principles of mental hygiene in school practice, the Relaxation Therapy (the art and science of reducing tension and inducing relaxation) and Sex Education. We intend to devote more space to these topics.

XVI.9 Learning Exercises

1. Discuss the meaning and importance of mental health.
2. Define mental health and discuss the criteria of good mental health.
3. Discuss the factors considered important for mental health of a student.
4. Discuss the role of different agencies of mental health.
5. Discuss the role of a teacher in promoting mental health of his students.
6. Discuss important mental health hazards due to defective home atmosphere and inadequate Schooling.
7. Describe the role of different agencies promoting mental health.

XVII

Elementary Statistics in Educational Psychology

Modern age is the age of science and technology. The advancements in the field of science and technology basically depends upon the development of quantitative methods. The science without quantitative methods gives crude observation and classification. With the use of scientific techniques we can collect informations. This information can give us refined conclusions. For instance, people know that stones fall when they are dropped, but therefore, Physics made little progress as a science until its early scientists began to measure how fast stones falls, how far a stone falls in a given period of time and whether a stone falls faster as compared to an apple or a leaf. The use of quantitative methods helps us to understand complex phenomena of life. When we use quantitative methods the use statistics.

XVII.1 Meaning and Definitions of Statistics

The term statistics has been derived from the Latin word "status" which means the political status. The term statistics in early biblical times notations was used to denote to provide information regarding the population, birth rate, death rate, income and expenditure etc. The description of the data in terms of number was known as statistics. Statistics in the words of Horace Secrist means "The aggregates of facts, affected, enumerated or estimated according to a reasonable standard of accuracy, collected in a systematic manner for a predetermined purpose and placed in relation to each other." Similarly, Baron J.F. Von Bidfeld describes statistics as "The science that teaches us what is a political arrangement of all modern states." Baron's definition appears to be too narrow when we see statistics in its modern setting.

Modern definitions of statistics

(1) W.G. Sutcliffe. "Statistics comprises the collection, tabulation, presentation and analysis of an aggregate of facts, collected in a methodical manner, without bias and related to a predetermind purpose."

(2) Ferguson. "Statistics deals with the collection, classification, description and interpretation of data obtained by conduct of surveys and experiments."

In brief statistics is an applied science which enables us to collect facts to analyse and interpret in numerical form.

XVII.2 Functions of Statistics

Important functions of statistics can be studied as:

1. The first function of statistics is 'collection' that means the foremost function of statistics is to collect the facts (data) regarding the problem under consideration.
2. The second function of statistics is 'classification.' That means to classify the collected data in a desirable manner, so that it comes before our eye in a condensed form.
3. The third function of statistics is to tabulate the classified data in order to give it such a shape that our mind can easily comprehend.
4. The fourth function of statistics is 'analysis'. Analysis is made on the basis of tabulated data by using various techniques of statistics (which will be discussed later).
5. After analysis the results are interpreted, described and presented in a simple manner so that any one could comprehend the conclusions very easily.
6. To compare different facts and problems.
7. To establish relationship between different facts.
8. To examine old formulations and theories.
9. To establish new formulations and theories.

XVII.3 Importance of Statistics

Modern age is the age of globalisation, free flow of information in the form of statistics is essential. As a result almost every aspect of natural phenomenon and of human and other activity is now subjected to measurement in terms of statistics which are then interpreted. Keeping this rational in view the importance of statistics can be studied in the following areas:

(1) *Importance of statistics for a teacher.* The scientific movement in education is an important step in the improvement of educational system. The teacher is to play a definite role in the development of this programme. He is to conduct research connected with the classroom, with the students and with the school. Statistics helps the teacher to study character, ability, health and interests of the pupils.

The teacher use different kinds of educational and psychological tests for evaluation of the development of the pupils. The construction of these tests for interpretation of results needs a teacher to be statistical minded.

(2) *Importance for students.* Importance of statistics for the students is that, it gives a clear view of the interests and abilities of the students and thus helps in knowing the individual differences among the students. With this the students can be guided in the choice of their educational and professional career.

(3) *Importance for evaluation.* Statistics is used in the evaluation of the results of various tests such as intelligence tests, achievement tests and diagnostic tests etc.

(4) *Importance for school.* Statistics can help to givebetter explanation of the achievements of school in various school activities.

(5) *Importance for research and educational activities.* Knowledge of man is increasing very fast. Under the effects of this fast increasing knowledge, education is to be changed with respect to time and place. For this purpose, various experiments are to be conducted and research is to be done, the results of which are better explained and analysed with the help of statistics.

Importance of statistics can hardly be ignored because both the teacher and the student apply, it to arrive at a conclusion. So, we can say that a teacher without an adequate knowledge of statistics may do more harm than good to the development of his pupils.

Without the knowledge of statistics we cannot make any significant judgement from the scores as they are obtained from the tests administered on a class of 40 or 60 students. For having a clear cut view of the results obtained from the tests, we have to group the data (obtained scores) into a frequency distribution. In other words, the knowledge of statistics enables us to develop a scientific approach to measure a phenomenon. Therefore, it can be concluded that statistics leads to scientific measurement of facts.

The importance of statistics in education described by Guilford pointout that importance of statistics can hardly be ignored in modern age because:

(a) Statistical techniques permit the most **exact kind** of description of a phenomenon.

(b) Statistics forces us to be definite and exact in our procedures and in our thinking.

(c) Statistics enables us to summarise our results in meaningful and convenient form.

(*d*) Statistics enables us to draw general conclusions.

(*e*) Statistics enables us to make predictions.

(*f*) Statistics enables us to analyze some of the causal factors out of complex and otherwise bewildering events.

XVII.4 Measurement in Statistics

To understand the statistics let us try to know operational terms of measurements. Measurements may be of various kinds and may be taken to various degrees of precision. When people or objects have been ranked or arranged in '*ordinal*' series with respect to some traits or attribute, it is a simplest type of measurement. School children may put in 1, 2, 3 order of marks on an examination or regularity of school attendence. This type of measurement is known as '*Rank Order Scale*'. It is sometime used in educational statistics, but it is not a reliable measure.

When the scores are expressed in equal units they constitute an '*Interval Scale*'. Standard Psychological Tests are usually interval scales as they have equal units, but they do not possess a true zero. Scaled test scores may be added or subtracted, but we cannot say that a score of 40 is twice as good as a score of 20, as neither is taken from a zero of just no ability.

When measures are expressed in equal units and are also taken from a true zero they constitute a *Ratio Scale.* Examples are c.g.s. scales found in physical sciences. In this scale a score of 40 is twice as good as a score of 20. This type of scale is rarely used in Psychology and Education. Measurements of sensory functions may be expressed in ratio scale, but mental and social traits must generally be represented in interval scale. To assess the psychological attributes we can use scales. The scales to assess the psychological attributes which are continous and discrete in nature.

XVII.5 Discrete and Continuous Series

Series which exhibit real gaps are called *discrete series.* Families in India may be called to consist of 2 or 3 childrens. There is obviously a real gap between two children and three children.

A Continuous Series

Continuous series is that which can be subdivided to any degree of subdivision. In refined methods of measurements we may get an I.Q. of 108.8 or even 108.83. Physical measures as well as score are represented in continuous series within a given range any score may exist and have meaning. The meaning of scores in a continuous series are considered as distances along a continuum rather than as discrete point. "*A score* in a mental test is a unit distance between two limits." A score of 130 upon an intelligence test, for example, can be represented as an interval from 129.5-130.5. The exact mid-point of this interval is 130, as is shown below:

129.5 130 130.5

DRAWING UP A FREQUENCY DISTRIBUTION

Data collected from tests convey little meaning to a specialists and the layman until data has been classified in some systematic way. This leads to a grouping of the scores into classes. Rules for classifying scores into frequency distribution may be laid down as follows:

(a) Determine the range or gap between the highest and the lowest.
(b) Decide the number and size of the grouping to be used. Common grouping intervals are 3, 5, 10 units in length. The number of intervals can be determined approximately by dividing the range by the grouping intervals tentatively chosen.
(c) *Tally* the scores in their proper intervals.

Keeping in view, the rules for classification of scores into frequency distribution let us make an exercise from the score of 25 students on an achievement test and tabulate them into a frequency distribution:

72	81	67	83	61
75	78	82	71	67
77	65	76	63	84
67	86	76	72	69
72	73	70	72	64

After the tabulation of score we need to decide range. Range = Highest Score–Lowest Score = 86 – 61 = 25. If the length of the interval be 3 then the No. of class interval = 25/3 = 8 (approximately) + 1 = 9. Let the Ist interval begin with 60.

I *Class Interval*	II *Tallies*	III *Frequencies (f)*
84-86	||	2
81-83	|||	3
78-80	|	1
75-77	||||	4
72-74	|||||	5

69-71	|||	3
66-68	|||	3
63-65	|||	3
60-62	|	1
		N=25

In the first column the class intervals have been listed serially from the smallest score at the bottom to the largest score at the top. Each class interval covers 3 scores. The first class interval begins with 60 and ends with 62 thus including the scores 60, 61 and 62. Second class interval starts with 63 and ends with 65 including 63, 64 and 65. Similarly, all class intervals include 3 scores each.

In column II are marked 'Tallies', the separate score have been listed opposite their proper intervals. The first score of 72 is represented by tally placed opposite the intervals 72-74 and second score of 81 is represented by a tally placed opposite to the interval 81-83 and so on the remaining scores have been marked.

When all the tallies have been marked, the total number of tallies (*i.e.* frequencies) is written in the column (3). The sum of the (4) column called the number (N). When all this is done our 25 test scores have been arranged into a frequency distribution.

XVII.6 Finding the Mid-point of an Interval in a Frequency Distribution

There is a definite limit of scores in every class interval, such as 3-5-10, etc. If we want to represent all these scores within a class interval by a single value we can do this by finding the mid-point and making it the representative of all the values within a class interval. For example, in the interval 72-74 above, all three scores upon this class interval are represented by the score 73 the mid-point of this interval. The method of finding out the mid-point is as under :

$$\text{Midpoint} = \frac{[\text{Lower limit of the class interval} + \text{upper limit of the class interval}]}{2}$$

In this class interval lower limit is 71.5 while the upper limit is 74.5. Hence, by applying the formula we get:

$$\text{Mid-point (Mpt.)} = \frac{71.5 + 74.5}{2} = 73$$

The assumption that the mid-point is the best representative value, is more reliable when number of scores in a distribution is very large, and when intervals are not too broad. This may be made more clear with the help of following Table:

Class intervals	*Exact limits of the class intervals*	*Mid-points*	*Frequencies fs.*
84-86	83.5-86.5	85	2
81-83	80.5-83.5	82	3
78-80	77.5-80.5	79	1
75-77	74.5-77.5	76	4
72-74	71.5-74.5	73	5
69-71	68.5-71.5	70	3
66-68	65.5-68.5	67	3
63-65	62.5-65.5	64	3
60-62	59.5-62.5	61	1
			N=25

XVII.7 Graphic Representation

Graphic representation of data is a technique of classification of data which may convey worth while meaning of the population from which the data has been collected. Statistical data used in tabular form reveals different kinds of facts to the reader. If this data is presented in graphic form, it makes everything clear on the first sight and holds the attention. Different data are compared easily with help of the graph.

Graphs are also utilised as visual aids which are more effective than complex numerical presentation. School teacher can also make use of graphic methods in presentation of the progress of pupils in various school subjects and may compare the two or more sections of a class with respect to various abilities, achievements, and personality traits, etc.

General Principles of Graphic Representation

The presentation of data collected by a psychologist or a teacher dèmands certain principles to be adopted. For the presentation of data we need to follow the Algebraic principle underlying all graphic representations. Graphing is done with reference to two lines or *co-ordinate axis* the vertical axis is known as '*Y*' axis and the horizontal axis as '*X*' axis. These two lines are perpendicular to each other. The point where they interest 'O' is called the origin of the graph or curve. Figure 1 represents the system.

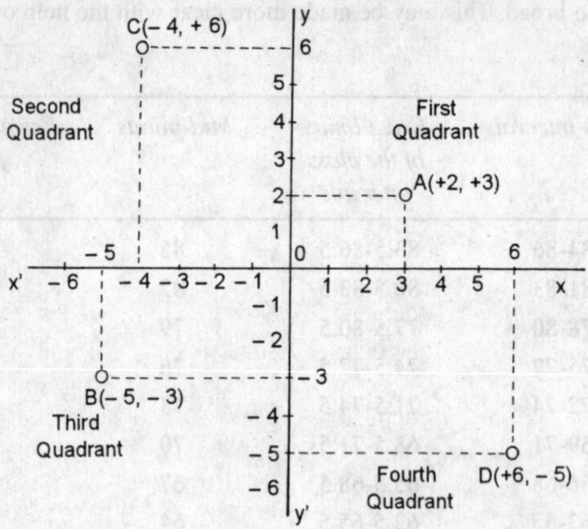

Fig. 1. Showing the General Principles of Graphic Representation.

On both these axes certain equal distances are taken which represent the measures of behaviour in terms of unit distance. Distance along the '*X*' axis to the right of '*O*' or called positive and to the left is called negative. Similarly distance along the '*Y*' axis above '*O*' are positive and below '*O*' are negative.

By the intersection of these two axes, four quadrants are formed. Now we see in quadrant (1) both the co-ordinates are positive (+, +), in quadrant (2) one negative and one positive (–, +), in quadrant (3) both are negative (–, –) in quadrant (4) one positive and one negative (+, –).

The distance along '*X*' axis is known as '*abscissa*' and distance along '*Y*' axis is known as *ordinate.* In order to locate the point '*A*' whose co-ordinates are $x = 3$ and $y = 2$, we move three steps on '*X*' axis toward the right of '*O*' and 2 steps upwards from '*O*' on '*Y*' axis. Similarly, we can locate any point whose co-ordinates are known. Thus by locating any number of points on the two axes and by joining them the graphs are drawn for representing any frequency distribution.

XVII.8 Methods of Graphic Representation

There are four different methods of graphic representation of frequency distribution which are generally used in educational statistics. They are:

(1) Frequency Polygon,
(2) Histogram,

(3) Cumulative Frequency Graph,
(4) Cumulative Percentage Curve, or O give.

1. Frequency Polygon

Before we proceed to draw a frequency polygon, we must be clear about, what we mean by it. By *Polygon* we mean many sided figure, thus a "*Frequency Polygon* will mean to us a figure which have many sides representing the frequencies."

Now comes the question how we draw a frequency polygon. It is not a simple process. Various systematic steps are to be kept in mind while drawing a frequency polygon.

Steps to be followed in constructing a frequency polygon

Step 1. Draw two straight lines which are perpendicular to each other. The vertical line (*OY*) is drawn on the left side of the graph paper and horizontal line (*OX*) near the bottom. Thus *O* is the point of intersection.

Step 2. Lay off the mid-points of each class interval, at equal distances on the '*X*' axis. While plotting the class intervals, we should begin with the interval next below the lowest in the distribution, and end with interval next above the highest.

Step 3. Successive units of '*Y*' axis are marked off to represent the frequency on the different intervals. Units of *Y* axis are so chosen that the height of the polygon be approximately 75% of its width.

Step 4. At the mid-point of each interval on '*X*' axis find the point on the '*Y*' axis equal to the number of frequencies on that interval and place the points on these locations.

Step 5. Join these points with straight lines so as to give the shape of the figure.

Example. Draw a frequency polygon from the following distribution:

Class Intervals	*Frequencies*	*Mid-Points*
56-59	0	57.5
52-55	1	53.5
48-51	0	49.5
44-47	5	45.5
40-43	10	41.5
36-39	20	37.5

Contd.

Class Intervals	*Frequencies*	*Mid-Points*
32-35	12	33.5
28-31	8	29.5
24-27	2	25.5
20-23	3	21.5
16-19	4	17.5
12-15	0	13.5

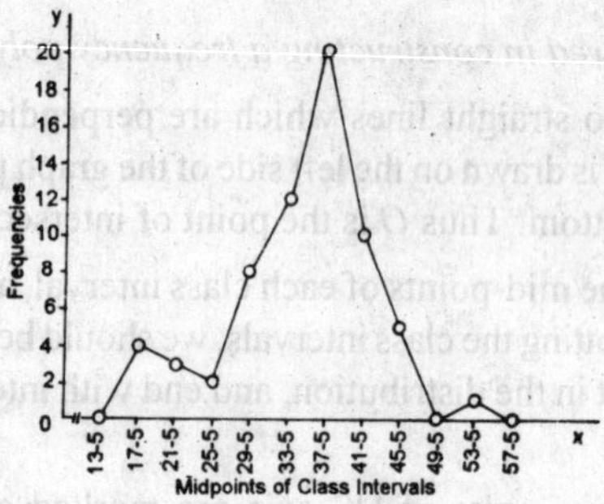

Fig. 2. Showing the Frequency Polygon of 65 Achievment Scores.

2. The Histogram and Bar Diagram

"A Histogram of or Column diagram is a bar graph of a frequency distribution". Bar graph is the most simple method of graphic representation of data.

Construction of the Histogram

Both, the frequency polygon and the histogram, are constructed almost in the same way. There is a little difference in the process of construction. In frequency polygon all the scores within a given interval are represented by the mid-point of that interval, while in histogram the scores are assumed to be spread over the entire interval.

In histogram frequencies are shown by a rectangle the base of which is the length of the interval and the height of which is the number of scores within the interval.

While constructing histogram base line is labeled with the exact limits of score interval. Figure 3 shows the histogram and we can clear about the method of drawing it.

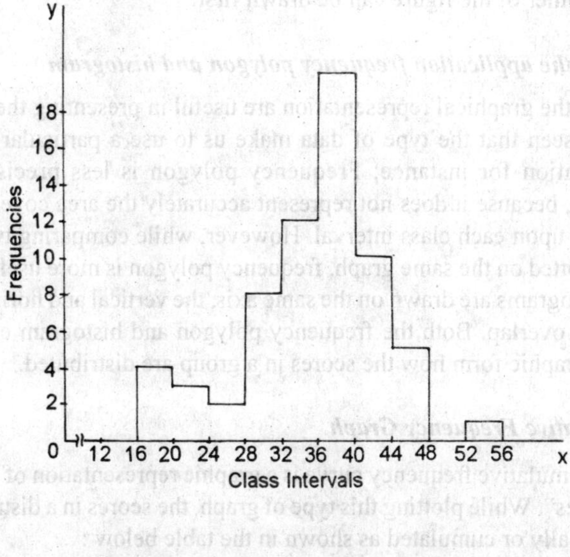

Fig. 3. Histogram of 65 Achievement Scores.

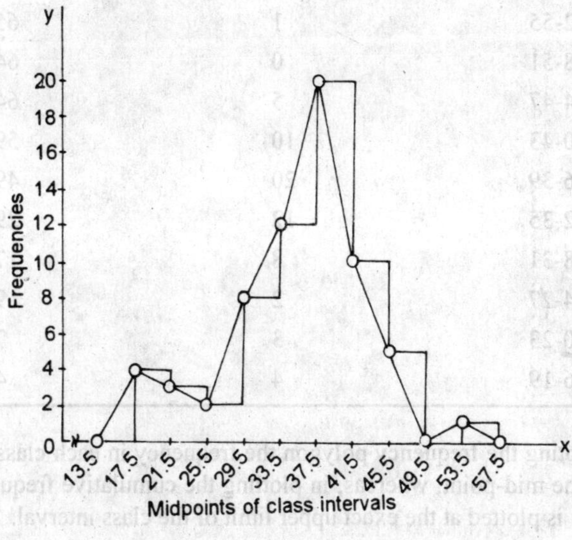

Fig. 4. Superimposition of Frequency Polygon on Histogram

Sometimes, we need to draw both histogram and frequency polygon on the same graph. This type of drawing is helpful in comparison of the two figures. Either of the figure can be drawn first.

Deciding the application frequency polygon and histogram

Both the graphical representation are useful in presenting the data but it has been seen that the type of data make us to use a particular method of representation for instance; Frequency polygon is less precise than the histogram, because it does not represent accurately the area covered and the frequency upon each class interval. However, while comparing two or more graphs plotted on the same graph, frequency polygon is more useful, because if two histograms are drawn on the same axis, the vertical and horizontal lines will often overlap. Both the frequency polygon and histogram enable us to show in graphic form how the scores in a group are distributed.

3. Cumulative Frequency Graph

"A cumulative frequency curve is a graphic representation of cumulatied frequencies". While plotting this type of graph, the scores in a distribution are added serially or cumulated as shown in the table below :

Ciass Intervals	*F*	*Cum. F.*
52-55	1	65
48-51	0	64
44-47	5	64
40-43	10	59
36-39	20	49
32-35	12	29
28-31	8	17
24-27	2	9
20-23	3	7
16-19	4	4

In ploting the frequency polygon the frequency in each class interval is taken at the mid-point, whereas, in plotting the cumulative frequency curve frequency is plotted at the exact upper limit of the class interval.

4. Cumulative Percentage Curves or Ogive

This type of curve differs from the cumulative frequency curve in the sense that the frequencies are expressed in cumulative percentage of the *Sample (N)* on the *Y* axis. Here we change the cumulative frequencies into percentage of the *N* as shown in the table below:

Upper Limits of Class Intervals

Class Intervals	*F*	*Cum. F.*	*Cum. % F.*
52-55	1	65	100.00
48-51	0	64	98.56
44-47	5	64	98.56
40-43	10	59	90.86
36-39	20	49	75.86
32-35	12	29	44.66
28-31	8	17	26.18
24-27	2	9	13.85
20-23	3	7	10.77
16-19	4	4	6.15

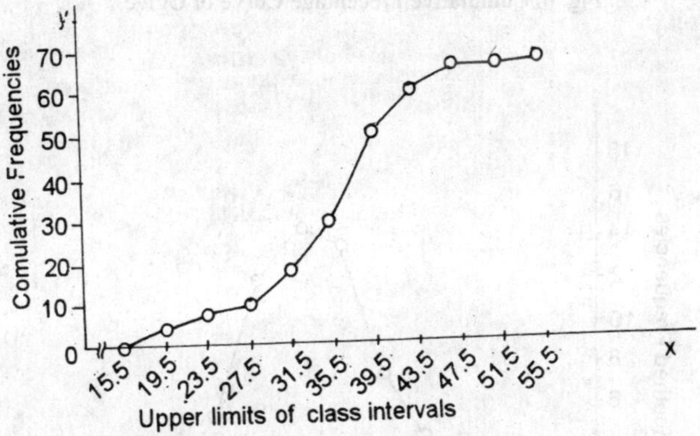

Fig. 5. Cumulative Frequency Graph of 65 Achievement Scores.

Smoothing the Frequencies

Sometimes the shape of the curve is so irregular that it does not convey any sense if we look at it. To remove this drawback we smooth the frequencies and then draw the curve. The method of smoothing the frequencies is given below.

First we add the *f*s on a given interval with the two adjacent intervals and then we divide the sum by 3. For example, in the above distribution the first class interval is 16-19 and possesses the frequency of 4. We assume one class interval below having a frequency of zero and one on the upper side which has a frequency of 3. We add these three frequencies and divide it by 3 thus we have

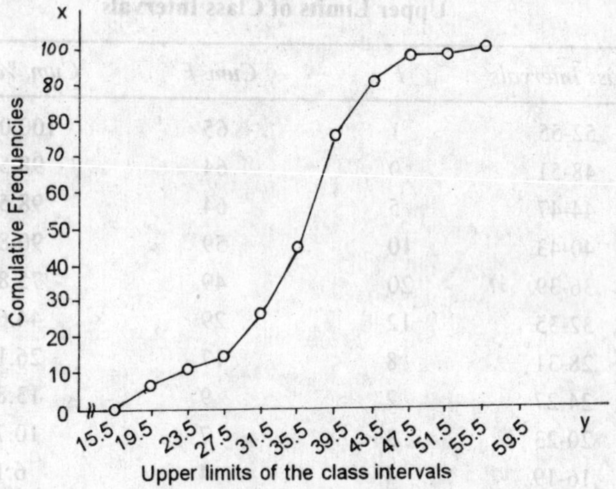

Fig. 6. Cumulative Precentage Curve or Ogive.

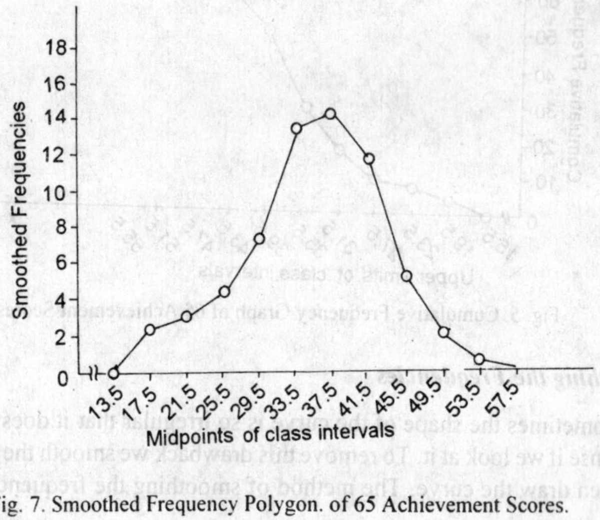

Fig. 7. Smoothed Frequency Polygon. of 65 Achievement Scores.

have $\frac{0+4+3}{3} = \frac{7}{3} = 2.33$ as the smoothed frequency for class interval of 16-19. In the same way smoothed frequency for the class intervals 20-23 will be $\frac{4+3+2}{3} = \frac{9}{3} = 3$, thus, we calculate the smoothed frequencies for all the intervals as shown below:

Class Intervals	*Frequency*	*Smoothed frequency*
52-55	1	0.33
48-51	0	2.00
44-47	5	5.00
40-43	10	11.66
36-39	2	14.00
32-35	12	13.33
28-31	8	7.33
24-27	2	4.33
20-23	3	3.00
16-19	4	2.33

For practice let us draw a graph from these smoothed frequencies.

In the same manner cumulative percentages can also be smoothed and a smoothed Ogive can be drawn and also smoothed cumulative frequency curve.

XVII.9 Learning Exercises

1. Discuss the meaning and importance of statistics.
2. What is measurement in statistics describe its various types.
3. What is the importance of graphic representation of frequency distribution?
4. What are different methods of graphic representation?
5. Describe the principles of graphic representation.

XVIII

Measures of Central Tendency & Dispersion

As discussed earlier that the data consisting of scores of 25 students on achievement test were organised into frequency table (table 1 to 7). The frequency distribution and its graphical presentation gave us information about the performance of the students on an achievement test.

Suppose we draw the students from two or more classes and schools appeared in the achievement test and we want to compare the performance of the classes and schools on achievement test. Seondly, we are interested in comparing the performance of the same class after some coaching over a period of time. When making these comparisions, it is not practical to use the full frequency distributions, however compactly these may be presented. Therefore, for such a statistical analysis, we need a single representative value that describes the entire mass of data given in a frequency distribution. The single representative value is called central value, or an average around which individual values of variables cluster. The central value or an average is frequently called measure of central tendency.

> *Definition of Central Tendency.* According to C. V. Good, the tendency of the observations in a distribution to cluster about a point on a scale, is known as the central tendency.
>
> *Measures of Central Tendency*—These measures are useful for two reasons:

(1) They provide an average which represents all the scores made by a group and thus provide a precise description of the performance of the group as a whole.

(2) They enable us to compare two or more groups as regarding their performance on a particular test of achievement/ability or personality.

Types of Measures of Central Tendency. There are three types of the measures of Central Tendency which are generally used in psychology. They are:

(1) The Arithmetic Mean or Mean;

(2) The Median; and

(3) The Mode.

XVIII.1. The Mean

1. The Arithmetic Mean. The Arithmetic mean which in short is known as mean denoted by capital (*M*). It is the simplest measure of central tendency which is calculated by adding all the scores and dividing the sum by the number of scores.

"Statistically mean is defined as a point on the distribution on which or around which the maximum number of cases lie or tend to lie".

Calculation of the mean from the Ungrouped Data.

When the number of scores is less we calculate the mean by a very simple formula, *i.e.*,

$$M = \frac{\Sigma X}{N}$$

where:

M denotes the Mean;

Sigma (Σ) denotes the sum of scores;

X denotes the scores; and

N denotes the number of scores.

This means that we add the scores and divide the sum by the number of scores.

This will be clear from the example given below:

Problem. *A test of English Vocabulary was administered on a group of 15 students of VIII Class. The number of correct responses given by them is as follows:*

8, 6, 11, 7, 18, 13, 9 14, 12, 10, 9, 12, 7, 13, 16

Find out the mean of the correct responses.

Solution. First we add all the scores arithmetically and get:

$\Sigma X = 8 + 6 + 11 + 7 + 18 + 13 + 9 + 14 + 12 + 10 + 9 + 12 + 7 + 13 + 16 = 165$

$N = 15$

$$\text{Mean (M)} = \frac{\Sigma X}{N} = \frac{165}{15} = 11$$

Thus, the mean of the above group on the above test is 11.

Calculation of the Mean From the Group Data

When the obtained scores are grouped in a frequency distribution the mean is calculated in slightly different manner. Two methods are adopted to calculate the mean from the grouped data They are: (1) Long Method, (2) Short Method.

Calculation of Means by Long Method (when data is grouped)

Let us calculate the mean by using long method from the following data:

I *Class Intervals* *(C.I.)*	II *Frequencies* *(f)*	III *Mid-Points* *(X)*	IV *(fx)*
52-55	1	53.5	53.5
48-51	0	49.5	00.0
44-47	5	45.5	227.5
40-43	10	41.5	415.0
36-39	20	37.5	750.0
32-35	12	33.5	402.0
28-31	8	29.5	236.0
24-27	2	25.5	51.0
20-23	3	21.5	64.5
16-19	4	17.5	70.0
	N=65		Σ*fx*=2269.5

The *first* step in long method of calculation of mean is to calculate the mid-points of all the class intervals which are denoted by X. In the *next* step we multiply the *X*'s with the frequencies given in col. II, corresponding each mid-point in col. III, and thus obtain the fx in col. IV. In the *third* step we add all these values in col. IV and thus obtain the value of Σfx.

Now we apply the formula for getting the value of Mean which for long method is as below

$$M = \frac{\Sigma fx}{N}$$

By putting the values from the table above we get

$$M = \frac{2269.5}{65} = 34.9.$$

There fore, Mean = 34.9.

Calculation of Mean by Short Method

For the calculation of mean by short method we need to work out the middle value of some class interval is assumed as mean, which is denoted by A.M. (Assumed Mean). There is no strict rule for this assumption but generally the A.M. is taken in the middle of the distribution or the mid-point of the class interval which has the highest number of frequencies.

The method of calculating the mean from the assumed mean is described below in detail :

I	II	III	IV	V
C.I.	*f*	*X*	*x*	*fx*
Class Interval	*frequency*	*Mid-point*	*Deviation from A.M.*	*(frequency × devations)*
52-55	1	53.5	+4	4
48-51	0	49.5	+3	0
44-47	5	45.5	+2	10
40-43	10	41.5	+1	10
36-39	20	37.5	0	0
				24
32-35	12	33.5	−1	−12
28-31	8	29.5	−2	−16
24-27	2	25.5	−3	−6
20-23	3	21.5	−4	−12
16-19	4	17.5	−5	−20
	N = 65			−66

$\Sigma fx = -42$

A.M. = 37.5

Formula for calculating Mean from the Assumed Mean is:

$$M = A.M. + C \times i$$

where:

A.M. = Assumed Mean

C = Correction

and i = length of the class interval.

Now formula for finding out the value of correction (C) is:

$$C = \frac{\Sigma fx}{N}$$

Now formula for Mean becomes

$$M = A.M. + \left(\frac{\Sigma fx}{N}\right) i$$

Substituting the values in the formula we get

$$M = 37.5 + \left(\frac{-42}{65}\right) \times 4$$

$$M = 37.5 - 2.60$$

$$M = 34.9$$

In this method, if we see the table above, first three columns are the same as in the long method, the fourth column is changed. In fourth column we have taken the deviations of the class scores from the assumed mean, which is taken as the mid-point of the interval 36-39, *i.e.* 37.5.

This class interval is almost in the middle of the distribution and has the largest frequency, *i.e.* 20. So the deviation of the midpoint 37.5 from the assumed mean is 0 (zero). The next mid-point of 41.5 is having a deviation of + 1 as it is at a distance of one unit from the A.M. on the upper side and the mid-point of 33.5 has a deviation of –1 as it is at a distance of one unit on the lower.

Similarly, the other deviations of +2, +3, +4, and –2, –3, –4, –5, are taken. Then the product of *fx* is taken in the V column and Σ*fx* is calculated and by applying the formula discussed above and the value of mean is calculated.

XVIII.2 Median

Definition: When the scores are arranged in either ascending or descending order, the median is exactly the central point of that series. It divides the series into two equal parts. Exactly half of the cases fall below this point and half above it.

According to *Tate*, "The median is that central point below which one-half of the cases lie and above which one-half of the cases lie.

The formula for finding the median of series of ungrouped score is:

$$\text{Mdn} = \left(\frac{N+1}{2}\right)^{th} \text{ measure in order of size}$$

Example. We have a series of 9 scores, *i.e.* 7, 8, 11, 12, 14, 16, 17, 19, 20. The median of this series is:

$$\text{Mdn} = \left(\frac{9+1}{2}\right) th \text{ measure} \qquad = 5^{th} \text{ measure.}$$

As the fifth measure in the distribution is 14, hence the median will be 14.

Calculation of Median from the Grouped Data

When the scores are grouped into a frequency distribution, the median is defined as 50%[th] point in the distribution. Therefore, to find out the median we take N/2 of our scores and count into the distribution until the 50%[th] point is located. The formula for finding out the median from the grouped data is:

$$\text{Mdn} = l + \left(\frac{\frac{N}{2} - F}{fm} \right) \times i$$

where:
- l = lower limit of the class interval in which the median lies.
- N/2 = one half of the total number of scores.
- F = Sum of total scores below l.
- fm = Number of frequencies within the class interval in which the median lies.
- i = length of the class interval.

To illustrate the use of the formula an example is solved below:

CI (*Class Interval*)	*f* (*frequency*)	*Cum. f* (*Cumulative frequency*)
52-55	1	65
48-51	0	64
44-47	5	64
40-43	10	59
36-39	20	49
32-35	12	29
28-31	8	17
24-27	2	9
20-23	3	7
16-19	4	4
	N = 65	

$$\frac{N}{2} = \frac{65}{2} = 32.5.$$

As we see the 32.5[th] frequency of the total distribution is complete at a point which lies somewhere in the class interval of 36 to 39. This class interval is assumed as containing the median.

Now by applying the formula we get:

$$\text{Mdn} = l + \left(\frac{\frac{N}{2} - F}{fm} \right) \times i$$

l = 35.5, *i.e.* the lower limit of the class interval in which the median lies.

N/2 = 32.5.

F = 29, *i.e.*, total frequencies below the class interval in which the median lies.

fm = 20, i.e., number of frequencies of the interval in which the median lies.

i = 4, *i.e.*, the length of the class interval.

Let us put these values in the formula stated above

$$\text{Mdn} = 35.5 + \left(\frac{32.5 - 29}{20} \right) \times 4$$

$$= 35.5 + \frac{3.5}{20} \times 4$$

$$= 35.5 + .70$$

$$\text{Mdn} = 36.20$$

XVIII.3 The Mode

In a simple ungrouped series of scores the 'crude' or empirical mode is that single score which occurs maximum number of times, *e.g.*, in the series 7, 8, 8, 9, 10, 10, 10, 11, 11, 12, 13, 13, the most frequently occurring score is 10. Therefore 10, will be the crude mode.

When the data is grouped into a frequency distribution the mode is generally taken as the mid-point of the class interval which contains largest frequency. However, in calculating mode from a frequency distribution we differentiate between true mode and crude mode.

The True Mode is the point of greatest concentration in the distribution the formula for calculating the true mode is:

$$\text{Mode} = 3\ \text{Mdn} - 2\ \text{Mean}.$$

Now for example let us find the Mode after same distribution of which we have calculated Mean and Median earlier.

Mean of that distribution is 39.4

Median is 36.20

Mode $= 3 \times 36.20 - 2 \times 34.9$

$= 108.60 - 69.8$

$= 38.80$

Conditions Required for the use of Different Measures of Central Tendency.

Mean. We use mean when the scores are distributed symmetrically around the central point because mean is the centre of gravity. This central tendency has the greatest stability and thus it is more useful. Many statistical calculations may be based upon mean and thus in higher statistical calculations it may be utilised.

Median. Median is calculated when the exact mid-point of the distribution wanted or when there are extreme scores, which would markedly effect the mean.

Mode. Mode is calcuated when a quick and approximate measure of central tendency is required and when the measures of central tendency is the most typical value in the distribution.

XVIII.4 Importance of the Measures of Central Tendency

The importance of various methods of central tendency can be studied with respect to their merits/demerits such as:

Mean

(1) It is most stable measure of central tendency.

(2) It provides the best estimate of average.

(3) It makes the comparison of two different groups easy.

(4) It is a more reliable measure in comparison to other measures of central tendency.

Median

(1) It is more reliable because it is clear and fixed.

(2) It is easy to understand and thus can be utilised easily.

(3) It is more useful when there are extreme deviations of the scores.

Mode

(1) It is the most modern index of central tendency.

(2) It is most easy to determine.

(3) It gives the quick estimate of central tendency.

XVIII.5 Measures of Dispersion

A measure of central tendency is a single representative value for a set of observations or a frequency distribution. But the central value or an average alone cannot describe the distribution adequately. For example, consider the scores of two groups of students on the same test:

Scores of 1st group : 45, 57, 24, 41, 68, 84, 55, 62, 90 and 74

Scores of 2nd group : 57, 60, 63, 68, 70, 52, 50

Here both groups have the same mean score of 60. But a close examination reveals that the two sets of scores differ widely from one another. The scores in the first group range from 24 to 90 while that in the second range from 50 to 70. This difference in range shows that the students in the second group are more homogeneous in scoring than those in the first. They seem to have nearly the same ability because their scores are less scattered from mean score of 60 as compared to the scores of students in the first group. Thus, the scores in a class consisting of individuals of nearly the same ability fall around the same point on the scale and the *variability*, *dispersion* or *scatter* of scores is relatively less.

Meaning of Dispersion. In previous pages we have discussed about the measures of central tendencies which are points to represent generally the whole of the distribution. But if we want to compare two different distribution on the basis of their means we shall not be able to make any accurate judgement, as the two distributions may have the same central tendencies, but they may cover a wide areas. For example, two samples of 50 N may have their means as 37.5 each, but sample (*A*) may have its scores ranging from 15-65 and sample (*B*) may have scores ranging from 23 to 58 now, if we judge them on the basis of mean we can say that both the groups are of same ability. But when we see the range of scores we find that group, (*B*) is definitely better than group (*A*), as the range of group (*B*) is shorter than the range of group (*A*), which shows that the group (*B*) is more homogeneous than group (*A*). Most of its members have the same ability.

Hence, to know more accurately about the abilities of two different groups on a certain test, we must know the spread of their scores.

The statisticians have derived different measures to give us the indices of spread of scores in a distribution. These measures are known as the *Measures of Variability* or Measures of dispersions. There are four different Measures of dispersion which are given below:

1. Range,
2. Quartile Deviation,
3. Average Deviation, and
4. Standard Deviation.

XVIII.6 Calculation of the Measures of Dispersion

1. Range

Range may be definded simply as the interval between the highest and the lowest scores of the two distributions. It is the simplest measures of dispersions which gives us a rough estimate of the spread of scores.

Because this measure takes account of extreme scores it is not more reliable in such cases where N is very small and large gaps (*i.e.*, zero *fs*) are present.

2. The Quartile Deviation

The quartile deviation which is denoted by 'Q' in the one half of the scale distance between the 75th and 25th percentiles in a frequency distribution. The 25th percentile or first quartile or 'Q_1' is the point on the scale below which the 25% of the cases lie and 75th percentile or third quartile or 'Q_3' is the point below which the 75% of cases lie. These two points are calculated almost in the same manner as the median, (which is the 50th percentile) of the distribution. The formulas for Q_1 and Q_3 are:

$$Q_1 = l + \left(\frac{N/4 - \text{Cum. } f_v}{f_q} \right) \times i$$

$$Q_3 = l + \left(\frac{3N/4 - \text{Cum. } f_b}{f_q} \right) \times i$$

l = The exact lower limit of the C.I. in which the quartile falls.

i = the length of the class interval.

Cum f_b = The cumulative frequencies below the C.I. in which contain the quartile.

f_q = The number of frequencies within the class interval which contain the quartile.

After finding these two points, *i.e.*, Q_1 and Q_3 we can find out the Q, *i.e.*, the quartile deviation, by substituting in the formula.

$$Q = \frac{Q_3 - Q_1}{2}$$

Example:

Class Interval	*Frequency F*	*Cumulative F*	
52-55	1	65	
48-51	0	64	
44-47	5	64	
40-43	10	59	
36-39	20	49	Q_3
32-35	12	29	
28-31	8	17	Q_1
24-27	2	9	
20-23	3	7	
16-19	4	4	

$$Q_1 = 27.5+\left(\frac{16.25-9}{8}\right)\times 4$$

$$= 27.5+\frac{7.25}{8}\times 4$$

$$= 27.5 + 3.6.$$

$$Q_1 = 31.1$$

$$Q_3 = 35.5+\left(\frac{48.75-29}{20}\right)\times 4$$

$$= 35.5+\frac{19.75}{20}\times 4$$

$$= 35.5 + 3.95$$

$$Q_3 = 39.45$$

$$Q = \frac{39.45-31.1}{2} = \frac{Q_3-Q_1}{2}$$

$$= \frac{8.35}{2} = 4.18$$

$$Q = 4.18$$

The distance between Q_1 and Q_3 is known as the interquartile range and Q which is one half of the middle 50% between Q_1 and Q_3 is known as the semi interquartile range. Because Q is the measure of the average distance of the two quartile points from the median it is very good index of score density

at the middle of the distribution. If the scores are concentrated closely the quartiles will be near one another and the value of Q will be small.

3. The Average Deviation

The average deviation of A.D. is the mean of the deviation of all the scores in a series taken from the mean of the distribution. In order to find A.D. the signs are not considered and all the deviation are taken as positive.

An example below will make the above definition clear.

Suppose we want to know A.D. for the following set of scores 4, 6, 8, 10, 12, 14, 16. The mean of these scores is 10. Now let us take the deviations (which are denoted by x) as below –6, –4, –2, 0, 2, 4, 6. Some of these deviation without the consideration of signs is 24. Now we apply the formula for A.D. which is A.D. = $\frac{\Sigma|\times|}{N}$. The two bars arround X denotes that we have added them without the considerations of signs. Hence the A. D. will be

$$\text{A.D.} = \frac{|24|}{7} = 3.43$$

Calculation of A.D. From the Grouped Data

Though the A.D. is rarely used in modern statistics as its use is often found in old experiments. If we want to calculate A.D. from the grouped data we can do it with the help of the formula:

$$\text{A.D.} = \frac{\Sigma|fx|}{N}$$

Class Interval	*f*	*Mid-point X*	*Devation (X-Mp)=x*	*fx*
52-55	1	53.5	18.6	18.5
48-51	0	49.5	14.6	0.0
44-47	5	45.5	10.6	53.0
40-43	10	41.5	6.6	66.0
36-39	20	37.5	2.6	52.0
32-35	12	33.5	–1.4	–16.8
28-31	8	29.5	–5.4	–43.2
24-27	2	25.5	–9.4	–18.8
20-23	3	21.5	–13.4	–40.2
16-19	4	17.5	–17.4	–69.6
	N = 65			Σ*fx* = 378.1

Mean = 34.9

$$A.D = \frac{\Sigma|fx|}{N}.$$

Substituting the values we get

$$AD = \frac{|378.1|}{65} = 5.82$$

$$AD = 5.82.$$

4. The Standard Deviation

The standard deviation is defined as the square root of the mean of the squared deviations taken from the mean of the distribution. The standard deviation or S. D. is the most stable measure of dispersion and is frequently employed in research work. While calculating A.D. we discard signs but when we calculate S.D. the difficulty of signs is removed by squaring the deviations. Deviations in calculating S.D. are always taken from mean and never from median or mode.

The Calculation of S.D. from Ungrouped Data

To illustrate the calculation S.D. from the ungrouped data we may take the same 7 scores which were used in calculating A.D.

Scores = (X) 4, 6, 8, 10, 12, 14, 16.

Mean (M) = 10.

Deviation from the mean (X – M) x = –6, –4, –2, –0, 2, 4, 6.

x^2 = 36, 16, 4, 0, 4, 16, 36.

$$\Sigma x^2 = 112$$

$$S.D. = \sqrt{\frac{\Sigma x^2}{N}} = \sqrt{\frac{112}{7}} = \sqrt{16}$$

$$S.D. = 4$$

Calculation of S.D. From Grouped Data

The process of calculating S.D. from the grouped data is same as that of from the ungrouped data. For this purpose we apply two different methods, *i.e.*, short method and long method.

1. Short Method. The formula for calculating S.D. by short method is

$$\sigma = i\sqrt{\frac{\Sigma fx^2}{N} - c^2}$$

The method will be clear from the following example:

Class Interval	*f*	*x*	*fx*	*fx²*
52-55	1	4	4	16
48-51	0	3	0	0
44-47	5	2	10	20
40-43	10	1	10	10
36-39	20	0	0	0
32-35	12	–1	–12	12
28-31	8	–2	–16	32
24-27	2	–3	–6	18
20-23	3	–4	–12	48
16-19	4	–5	–20	100
	N = 65		Σ*fx* = –42	Σ*fx*² = 256

$$C = \frac{\Sigma fx}{N} = \frac{-42}{65} = -.65$$

$$\sigma = i\sqrt{\frac{\Sigma fx^2}{N} - c^2} = 4\sqrt{\frac{256}{65} - (-.65)^2}$$

$$= 4\sqrt{3.94 - .42}$$

$$= 4\sqrt{3.52}$$

$$\therefore \text{S.D. } (\sigma) = 7.52$$

Long Method of Calculating S.D. From the Group Data

They only difference in calculating S.D. from the grouped data, by long method is that here the deviations are taken from the actual mean, whereas in short method deviations were taken from the assumed mean. Let us explain it with the help of an example below of the same distributions.

I	II	III	IV	V	VI
Class Interval	*f*	*x*	*x*	*fx*	*fx²*
52-55	1	53.5	18.6	18.6	345.96
48-51	0	49.5	14.6	0.0	00.00
44-47	5	45.5	10.6	53.0	561.8
40-43	10	41.5	10.6	66.0	435.60
36-39	20	37.5	2.6	52.0	135.20

32-35	12	33.5	–1.4	–16.8	23.52
28-31	8	29.5	–5.4	–43.2	233.28
24-27	2	25.5	–9.4	–18.8	176.72
20-23	3	21.5	–13.4	–40.2	538.68
16-19	4	17.5	–17.4	–69.6	1211.04
	N = 65				fx^2 =3661.80

Mean = 34.9.

$$\text{S.D.} = \sqrt{\frac{\Sigma fx^2}{N}} = \sqrt{\frac{3661.80}{65}} = \sqrt{56.30}$$

S.D. = 7.50

In the above example we have taken the deviation (x) in the forth column by subtracting the mean (M) from the mid-points (X) and then in column (V) we have taken the product of f and x. For getting fx^2 we have again multiplied fx by x and hence we got column (VI) and all values are positive. Then we took the Σfx^2 and by applying the formula S.D. (σ) = $\sqrt{\frac{\Sigma fx^2}{N}}$ we got the S.D. = 7.50.

XVIII.7 Conditions Required for the Use of Various Measures of Dispersion

Use of Range:

(a) When data are too scattered or too much concentrated so as to justify the computation of a more exact measure.

(b) When the knowledge of total spread is only requirements.

Use of Q:

(a) When the median is the measure of Central Tendency.

(b) When scores are so spread to influence the S.D. disproportionately.

(c) When the concentration around the median is the basic interest.

Use of A.D.:

(a) When the deviation of extreme nature would influence S.D. unnecessarily.

(b) When we wish to weight all deviations from the mean according to their size.

Use of S.D.:

(a) When the statistic having the greatest stability is sought.

(b) When extreme deviation have proportionally greater effect on dispersion.

(c) When other higher statistics are to be computed.

Merits & Demerits of Various Measures of Dispersion

Merits and demerits of Range

1. Range is the simplest measure of dispersion. It is easy to calculate and rigidly defined.
2. Its computation is based on only two extreme observations which may be purely accidental.
3. It is not capable of being handled algebraically as its computation is not based on all the observations.
4. Its value, being based on extreme values, is highly affected by extreme observations.
5. Its value is highly affected by fluctuations of sampling in most of the cases.

Due to these demerits the range is an unreliable measure of dispersion but it may be used frequently in situations where we are interested in roughly comparing two or more sets of observations for variability.

Merits and demerits of A.D.

1. Mean of average deviation is easy to interpret.
2. It is easy to calculate and rigidly defined.
3. Its computation is based on all the observations.
4. Since A.D. is calculated about mean or median, it has all the merits and demerits of these central values.
5. It is less effected by the extreme observations as compared to S.D.
6. It ignores the positive and negative signs of deviations and, therefore, is not amenable for further algebraic treatment.

Due to certian inherent drawbacks the mean deviation is also not a common measure of dispersion. But it is very useful when extreme deviations influence standard deviation unduly.

Merits and Demerits of S.D.

1. It is rigidly defined but comparatively difficult to calculate.
2. Its value is based on all the observations.
3. It is capable of further algebraic treatments.

4. It is not much affected by sampling fluctuations.
5. It gives greater weight to extreme observations.
6. Standard deviation is based on arithmetic mean, therefore, it has all the characteristics of this central value.

Since, standard deviation possesses most of the properties of a good measure of dispersion, it is widely used in statistics. Standard deviation plays a vital role in sampling and correlation theory.

XVIII.9 Learning Exercises

1. Discuss the meaning and types of measures of central tendency.
2. Describe the conditions required to use different measures of central tendency.
3. Explain the importance of measures of central tendency.
4. Discuss the merits and demerits of different measures of central tendency.
5. What is dispersion describe its different measures?

XIX

Percentiles, Percentile Ranks & Correlation

XIX.1 Percentiles and Percentile Ranks

(a) Meaning of Percentile. According to Guilford the percentile is often called the centile point. Percentile is a value on the scoring scale below which are given percentage of cases. For example, the 90th centile is the point below which are 90 per cent of the scores, and the 25th centile is the point below which are 25 per cent of the scores falls. In other words percentile is inverse of Percentile Rank.

(b) Meaning of Percentile Rank. Percentile rank (PR) of a given point on a score scale is the percentage in the whole distribution that are below the given point. For instance, if a 4th grade student makes a score of 52 on a reading comprehension test and if this score has percentile rank of 65, then we know that the pupil's score was better (in the sense of being higher or larger) then the score of 65 per cent of the pupils taking this test. Raw scores (usually the number right) on most educational and psychological tests have little, if any, absolute significance—they do not mean very much when considered alone. Thus, we did not learn very much when we read that the fourth grade student scored 52 on the reading comprehension test. But as the above example shows Percentile Ranks, (PR's) can be useful aid to the interpretation of a raw score value. Such interpretations are often referred norm-reference interpretations, since the meaning of the Percentile Rank is derived by reference to some norm group.

XIX.2 Calculation of Percentiles

Garrett says that "the median is that point in a frequency distribution below which lie 50% of the measures or scores; and that Q_1 and Q_3 mark points in the distribution below which lie, respectively, 25% and 75% of the measures or scores. Using the method by which the median and the quartiles can be found, we may compute points below which lie 10%, 43%, 85%, or any per cent of the scores. These points are called percentiles, and are designated, in general, by the symbol P_p the p referring to the percentages of cases below the given value. P_{10} for example is the point below which lie 10% of the scores, P_{75}, the point below which lie 75% of the scores. It is evident that the median, expressed as a percentile, is P_{50}, also Q_1 is P_{25}, and Q_3 is P_{75}."

The method of calculating percentiles is essentially the same as that employed in finding the median. The formula is

$$P_p = l + \left(\frac{pN - F}{f_p}\right) \times i$$

(percentiles in a frequency distribution, counting from below up)

where p = percentage of the distribution wanted, e.g., 10%, 33%, etc.

l = exact lower limit of the class interval upon which P_p lies.

pN = part of N to be counted off in order to reach P_p.

F = sum of all scores upto interval below l.

f_p = number of scores within the interval upon which P_p falls

i = length of the class interval.

Table 1

Calculation of Percentiles in a Frequency Distribution

Scores	*f*	*Cum f*
195-199	2	50
190-194	2	48
185-189	3	46
180-184	3	43
175-179	5	40
170-174	7	35
165-169	8	28
160-164	6	20
155-159	4	14
150-154	4	10
145-149	3	6
140-144	2	3
135-139	1	1

Calculation of Percentile Points

10% of 50 = 5	$144.5+\frac{5-3}{3}\times 5=147.83$
20% of 50 = 10	$149.5+\frac{10-6}{4}\times 5=154.50$
30% of 50 = 15	$159.5+\frac{15-14}{6}\times 5=160.33$
40% of 50 = 20	$159.5+\frac{20-14}{6}\times 5=164.50$
50% of 50 = 25	$164.5+\frac{25-20}{8}\times 5=167.62$
60% of 50 = 30	$169.5+\frac{30-28}{7}\times 5=171.23$
70% of 50 = 35	$169.5+\frac{35-28}{7}\times 5=174.50$
80% of 50 = 40	$174.5+\frac{40-35}{5}\times 5=179.50$
90% of 50 = 45	$184.5+\frac{45-43}{3}\times 5=187.83$

In Table 1, the percentile points, P_{10} to P_{90} have been computed by formula $P_p = l+\left(\frac{PN-F}{f_p}\right)\times i$ for the, distribution of score made by the fifty college students. The details of calculation are given in Table 1. We may illustrate the method with P_{70}. Here pN = 35 (70% of 50 = 35), and from the Cum. f we find that 30 scores take us through 170-174 up to 174.5 the exact *lower* limit of the interval next above. Hence, P_{70} falls upon 175-179, and substituting pN = 35, F = 28, f_p = 7 (frequency upon 175-179), and i = 5 (class interval) in formula (20), we find that P_{70} = 174.5 (for detailed calculation, see Table 1). This result means that 70% of the 50 students *scored below* 174.5 in the distribution of scores. The other percentile values are found in exactly the same way as P_{70}. The reader should verify the calculations of the P_p in Table 1 in order to become thoroughly familiar with the method.

It should be noted that P_0, which marks the exact lower limit of the first interval (namely, 139.5) lies at the beginning of the distribution. P_{100} marks the *exact upper limit* of the last interval and lies at the end of the distribution. These two percentiles represent *limiting points.* Their principal value is to indicate the boundaries of the percentile scale.

Calculation of Percentile Ranks

Previous analysis shows that how the percentiles, e.g., P_{15} or P_{62} may be calculated directly from a frequency distribution. Let us refresh ourselves that percentiles are *Points* in a continuous distribution below which lie given percentages of N. Let us consider the problem of finding an individual's percentile rank (PR) or the position on a scale of 100 to which the subject's score entitles him. The distinction between *percentile* and *percentile rank* will be clear if the reader remembers that in calculating percentiles he starts with a certain percent of N, say 15% of 62. He then counts into the distribution the given per cent and the point reached is the required percentile, e.g., P_{15} or P_{62}. The procedure followed in computing percentile ranks is the reverse of this process. Here we begin with an individual *score* and determine the percentage of scores which lies below it, if this percentage is 62, say, the score has a percentile rank or PR of 62 on a scale of 100.

As have illustrated in Table 1. What is the PR of a man who scores 163 ? Score 163 falls on interval 160-164. There are 10 scores up to 159.5, exact lower limit of this interval (see column Cum. *f*) and 4 scores spread over this interval. Dividing 4 by 5 (interval length) gives us 8 *score per unit of interval.* The score of 163, which we are seeking, is 3.5 score units from 159.5, exact lower limit of the interval within which the score of 163 lies. Multiplying 3.5 by 8 we get 2.8 as the score distance of 163 from 159.5; and adding 2.8 to 10 (number of scores below 159.5) we get 12.8 as the part of N lying *below* 163. Dividing 12.8 by 50 gives us 25.6% as that proportion of N below 163; hence the percentile rank of score 163 is 26. The diagram will clarify the calculation:

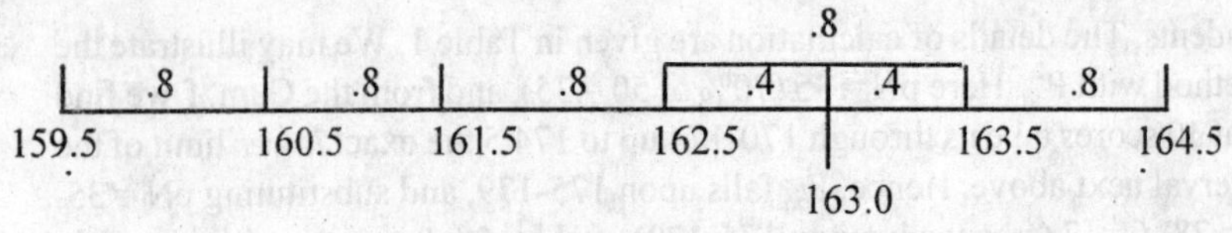

Ten scores lie below 159.5. Prorating the 4 scores on 160-164 over the interval of 5, we have .8 score per unit of interval Score 163 is just 8+8+8+4 or 2.8 scores from 159.5; or score 163 lies 12.8 scores (i.e., 10+2.8) or 25.6% (10+2.8) or 25.6% (12.8/50) into the distribution.

The PR of any score may be worked on in the same way. For example, the percentile rank of 181 is 70 (verify it). The reader should note that a score of 163 is taken as 163.0, midpoint of the score interval 162.5-163.5. This means simply that the midpoint is assumed to be the most representative value in a score interval. The percentile ranks for several scores may be read directly from Table 1. For instance, 152 has a PR of 10, 172 (median) a PR of 50, and 187 a PR of 90. If we take the percentile points as representing *approximately* the score intervals upon which they lie, the PR of 160 (upon which 159.5 lies) is approximately 20 (see Table 1); the PR of 165 (upon which 165.3 lies) is approximately 30; the PR of 170 is approximately 40; of 175.60; of 178.70; of 182.80. These PR's are not strictlly appropriate, to be sure, but the error is slight.

Calculation of Percentile Rank (PR's) From Ordered Data

In many instance, individuals and things can be put in 1.2.3 order with respect to some trait or characteristic when they cannot be measured directly, or measured conveniently. Suppose, for example, that 15 salesmen have been ranked from 1 to 15 for selling ability by the sales manager. It is possible to convert this order of merit into percentile ranks or "scores" on a scale of 100. The formula is :

$$PR = 100 - \frac{(100R - 50)}{N}$$

(*Percentile ranks for persons or objects put in order of merit*) in which R is the rank position, counting # 1 as highest and N as lowest. In our example, the salesman who ranks # or highest has a PR = $100 - \frac{(100 \times 1 - 50)}{15}$ or 97.

The salesman who ranks 5th has a PR = $100 - \frac{(100 \times 5 - 50)}{15}$ or 70; and the salesman who ranks 15th has a PR of 3.

If 100 students are ranked for average grade earned throughout the school year, each student will occupy one division on the percentile scale; Hence, the PR of the best student is 99.5 (midpoint of interval 99-100); and the PR of the poorest student is .5 (midpoint of the lowest interval 0-1). The PR of the 50th student is $100 - \frac{(100 \times 50 - 50)}{100}$ or 50.5 midpoint of interval 50-51. As a PR is always the midpoint of an interval, it follows that no one can have a PR of 0 or 100. These two points constitute the boundaries or limits of the percentile scale.

PR's *are useful when we wish to compare the standing of an individual in one test with his standing in another: the N'*s do not have to be the same. For example, suppose that Sita ranks 8th in a class of 22 in English and 18th in a class of 42 in history. How do these two "standings" compare? In English Sita PR is $100 - \frac{(100 \times 8 - 50)}{22}$ or 66; and in history, her PR is $100 - \frac{(100 \times 18 - 50)}{42}$ or 58. It is evident that relative to the members of her class, Sita is better in English than she is in history. In many schools, grades in the various subjects are converted into PR's, so that a student's standing in classes of different sizes may be compared directly.

CORRELATION

XIX.4 Meaning & Definitions of Correlation

If two quantities vary in such a way that movements in one are accompanied by movements in the other i.e, the fluctuation in the one are accompanied by fluctuations in the other such quantities are said to be correlated e.g, price of a commodity and the amount of demand or the increase in age and increase in height or the increase in rainfall and the increase in production of rice. The degree of relationship between the variables under consideration of relationship is called correlation. Coefficient or correlation index, gives in one figure the direction and degree of correlation.

Correlation analysis deals with the association between two or more variables Simpson & Kafka Conner has defined correlation in the following words:

If two or more quantities vary in sympathy so that movements in one tend to be accompanied by corresponding movement in the other, then they are said to be correlated.

Ya Hun Chou report that Correlation analysis attempts to determine the degree of relationship between the variables.

Juttle has defined correlation as is an analysis of the co-variation between two or more variables".

The study of correlation analysis is very important because it gives the relationship of two variables in one figure. correction enable us to estimate the value of one variable from the value of the other variable. Progressive development in the methods of service and philosophy has been characterized by the increase in the knowledge of relationship or correlations. In nature also one finds multiplicity of inter-related forces correlation analysis has a wide currency especially in social sciences and psychology.

Guilford reports that the coefficient of correlation is one of those summarising numbers, like a mean or a standard deviation, which, though it is a single number, tells a story. It can vary from a value of ± 1.00, which means perfect positive correlation, through zero, which means complete independent or no correlation whatever, on down to -1.00 which means perfect negative correlation.

In other words correlation points out the relationship between different variables may be positive, zero, or negative. If the correlation is positive we may say that individual getting high scores in one test is likely to get high score in the second. If the correlation is negative we may say that individual getting high score in one test is likely to get low score in the second. If the correlation is zero, that means the two variables are independent of each other and the score in one test will have no effect on the scores in other test.

XIX.5 Methods of Studying Correlation (ungrouped data)

The methods of studying correlation between two variables in the case of ungrouped data may listed as below:

(1) Scatter diagram method,

(2) Karl Pearson's coefficient of correlation,

(3) Spearman's coefficient of rank correlation.

Scatter diagram or dotdiagram is a graphic device for drawing certain conclusions about the correlation between two variables. In preparing a scatter diagram, the observed pairs of observations are plotted by dots on a graph paper in a two dimensional space by taking the measurements on variable along the horizontal axis and that on variable y along the vertical axis. The placement of these dots on the graph reveals the change in the variable as to whether they change in the same or in the opposite directions. Scatter diagrams, as an example, showing various degrees of correlation are shown on the next page.

In case all the dots are lying on a straight line of positive slope [Fig. 1 (a)], we have a *perfect positive correlation* between the two variables, i.e., r = + 1. Similarly, if all the dots are lying on a straight line of negative slope [Fig. 1(b)], correlation between two variables will be *perfectly negative* and in such case r = –1. Should the dots lie close to a straight line of positive slope [Fig. 1(c)] or negative slope [Fig. 1(d)], we have a high degree of positive or negative correlation between the two variables. If the dots do not follow a pattern along with a straight line as in [Fig.1 (e)], we have no correlation or zero correlation and conclude that no linear relationship exists between the two variables x and y. In view of the above discussion, it is now clear that the correlation between two variables, varying from –1 to +1, is a measure of their linear relationship. The greater the scatter of the dots from the straight line on the graph, the lesser the correlation.

XIX.6 Product Moment Correlation

This is also known as *Karl Pearson's coefficient of correlation or product moment correlation coefficient.* It is one of the most widely used algebraic

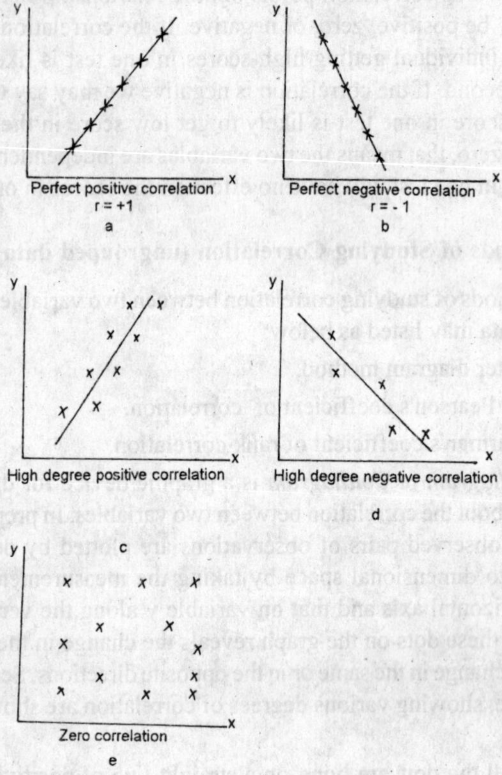

Fig. 1. Scatter diagrams showing various Degrees of Correlation.

methods of finding correlation between two variables. The *coefficient of correlation* is denoted by r, gives an exact idea about the degree of linear relationship between two variables and is defined as:

$$r = \frac{\text{covariance (x, y)}}{\sigma x \sigma y} = \frac{\text{cov}(x, y)}{\sigma x \sigma y} \qquad (3;1)$$

Again since $[\Sigma(x-\bar{x})(y-\bar{y})]/n$ is taken as a measure of covariance between x and y [cov (x, y)], we can say

$$r = \frac{\Sigma(x-\bar{x})(y-\bar{y})}{n\sigma_x\sigma_y} \quad (3;2)$$

or

$$r = \frac{\Sigma(x-\bar{x})(y-\bar{y})}{\sqrt{\Sigma(x-\bar{x})^2\,\Sigma(y-\bar{y})^2}} \quad (3;3)$$

where,

n = the number of paired observations.

Cov (x, y) = covariance between variable x and y.

σ_x = the standard deviation of variable x.

σ_x = the standard deviation of variable y.

$\Sigma(x-\bar{x})^2$ = the sum of squared deviations of x taken from mean x.

$\Sigma(y-\bar{y})^2$ = the sum of squared deviations of y taken from mean y.

$\Sigma(x-\bar{x})(y-\bar{y})$ = the sum of the products of deviations of x and y from $\bar{x}$ and $\bar{y}$ respectively.

The value of coefficient of correlation r, as obtained by using formula (3.1), (3.2) and (3.3) shall always lie between –1 and +1. When r = –1 or + 1, the correlation between two variables is said to be perfectly negative or perfectly positive. An intermediate value of r between –1 and +1 indicates the extent of linear relationship between x and y whereas its sign tells about the direction of this relationship. The value r = 0 means no linear relationship between the two variable. It is, however, wrong to say the r = 0.8 indicates a covariability which is twice that indicated by r = 0.4. A coefficient of correlation, as discussed above, is a pure number which is independent of the unit of measurement.

Karl Pearson's coefficient of correlation can be obtained by using one of the following methods:

(a) Direct method.

(b) Short-cut method.

(a) Direct Method of Calculating Coefficient of Correlation (ungrouped data)

For ungrouped data, formula (3.3) is used for calculating coefficient of correlation between two variables. This formula may be further simplified for computation purposes as under :

$$r = \frac{N\Sigma xy - (\Sigma x \Sigma y)}{\sqrt{[N\Sigma x^2 - (\Sigma x)^2][N\Sigma y^2 - (\Sigma y)^2]}} \quad (3.4)$$

Here ΣX = the sum of observations on variable X.

ΣY = the sum of observations on variable Y.

ΣX^2 = the sum of squares of observations on variable X.

ΣY^2 = the sum of squares of observations on variable Y.

ΣXY = the sum of the products of observations on X and Y variables.

It should be noted that formula (3.3) is suitable in cases where the mean values $\bar{x}$ and $\bar{y}$ are not in fractions. In case these happen to be fractional numbers, we should apply formula (3.4) from computing r. The computation procedure will be clear from the following examples:

Example 3.1. Calculate coefficient of correlation between scores of two students on five testings as given below:

Testings	: 1	2	3		
Scores of first student (x)	: 10	8	12	9	11
Scores of second student (y)	: 16	15	19	17	18

Solution

In this example, we first use formula (3. 3) for calculating r. The needed calculations are given in Table 2.

$$\text{Here } \overline{X} = \frac{\Sigma X}{N} = \frac{50}{5} = 10$$

$$Y = \frac{\Sigma Y}{N} = \frac{85}{5} = 17$$

Using formula (3.3), the coefficient of correlation

$$r = \frac{\Sigma(x-\overline{x})\ (y-\overline{y})}{\sqrt{\Sigma(x-\overline{x})^2 \times \Sigma(y-\overline{y})^2}}$$

Putting values from table, we have

$$r = \frac{9}{\sqrt{10 \times 10}} = \frac{9}{10} = 0.90$$

Thus, there is a high degree of positive correlation between the scores of students.

Example 3.2. Calculate coefficient of correlation for the data in example 3.1. Use formula (3.4)

Solution

The necessary calculations are given in Table 2

Table 2

Computation of r

S. No.	X	Y	X^2	Y^2	XY
1	10	16	100	256	160
2	8	15	64	225	120
3	12	19	144	361	228
4	9	17	85	289	153
5	11	18	121	324	198
N = 5	ΣX = 50	ΣY = 85	$\Sigma X^2 = 510$	$\Sigma Y^2 = 1455$	ΣXY = 859

Putting the values from table in formula (3;4), we have

$$r = \frac{N\Sigma XY - \Sigma(Y)}{\sqrt{[N\Sigma X^2 - (\Sigma X)^2][N\Sigma Y^2 - (\Sigma Y)^2]}}$$

$$= \frac{5 \times 859 - 50 \times 85}{\sqrt{[5 \times 510 - (50)^2][5 \times 1455 - (85)^2]}}$$

$$= \frac{4295 - 4250}{\sqrt{[2550 - 2500][7275 - 7225]}}$$

$$= \frac{45}{\sqrt{50 \times 50}} = \frac{45}{50}$$

= 0.90.

Which is the same as we obtained in example 3.1.

XIX.7 Ranks Difference Correlation or Rho (P).

While calculating the rho (ρ) we first have two sets of scores and rank them either in ascending or descending order (generally we use descending order of merit). Then the next step is to take the difference (D) between the two ranks, ($D = R_1 - R_2$). After this we take the squares of all the ranks and they are summed to get ΣD^2. Then we find out the row (ρ) by applying the formula

$$P = 1 - \frac{6\Sigma D^2}{N(N^2 - 1)}$$

The method will be more clear from the example solved below:

Example. 3.4. A group of 10 and 8th class children, was given test of achievement in English and Hindi. There scores were as follows:

English Test : 8, 10, 6, 11, 9, 4, 7, 12, 5, 13.

Hindi Test : 6, 9, 5, 12, 11, 4, 7, 10, 8, 13.

Find out if the achievement in Hindi have some effect on achievement in English.

Scores in English	*Scores in Hindi*	R_1	R_2	D $(R_1 - R_2)$	D^2
8	6	6	8	−2	4
10	9	4	5	−1	1
6	5	8	9	−1	1
11	12	3	2	1	1
9	11	5	3	2	4
4	4	10	10	0	0
7	7	7	7	0	0
12	10	2	4	−2	4
5	8	9	6	3	9
13	13	1	1	0	0
N = 10					$\Sigma D^2 = 24$

$$\rho = 1 - \frac{6\Sigma D^2}{N(N^2 - 1)} = 1 - \frac{6 \times 24}{10 \times 99} = 1 - \frac{144}{990} = 1 - 15$$

$$\rho = .85.$$

The coefficient of correlation (ρ) for the above sets of scores is .85, which is very high the positive. This show that the achievement in Hindi have a very close relation with achievement in English. A child who scores high in Hindi likely to scôres high in English.

The correlation coefficient is of great value in education and psychology as a measure of relationship between test scores and other measures. So the statisticians have designed various methods of calculating the (r) coefficient of correlation for different kinds of data. But many times it happens that the investigator does not have scores and must work with data in which difference can be expressed in ranks only or by classifying individual into of the several categories. Sometimes the relationship between two measures is non-linear and cannot be described by the product moment correlation. In such cases the method of Rank order correlation is employed.

Rank order or rank difference methods of correlation takes account only of the position of the items in the series and do not consider gaps between adjacent scores. For example individuals who scores 65, 64, 63, 52 will be ranked 1, 2, 3 and 4 although the difference between first three score is of 1 each and of fourth from third is of 11.

Therefore, accuracy may be lost in changing the scores into ranks, especially when there are number of ties. Even after such mathematical disadvantages, the rank order correlation rho (ρ) provides a quick and convenient estimate of correlation when the N is small, say below 25 or when we only have ranks.

XIX.8 Interpretation of Correlation

By interpretation we intend to point out how high is any given co-efficient of correlation is. Any co-efficient of correlation that is not zero and that is also statistically significant denotes some degree of relationship between the two variables. As regards the strength of relationship in between the two variables, the co-efficient of correlation does not give directly any thing like percentage that is indicated by an r. For instance, we can not say r of .50 indicates two times the relationship that is indicated by an r of .25. Nor we can say that an increase in correlation from r = .70 to .90. The coefficient of correlation is an index number, not a measurement on a linear scale of equal units.

There is no denying fact that correlation enable us to find out relationship between the two variables. The value of 'r' (correlation) reflects the strength of relationship between the variables.

The strength of relationship between the two variables can be described roughly as under for various r's:

Less than .20 slight, almost negligible relationship.

.20 to .40 Low correlation

.40 to .70 Moderate Correlation

.70 to .90 High Correlation

.90 to 1.00 Very High Correlation

It may be noted that the relationship i.e., correlation may be either positive or negative but in no case the value of correlation may exceed (the value of r more than) ± 1.

XIX.9 Learning Exercises

1. What do you mean by Statistics and what is its importance in education?
2. What are the functions of Statistics?
3. What do you understand by percentile and percentile rank ?
4. Determine P_{32}, P_{44}, P_{69}, P_{88} from the data shown in the table 1.
5. Find out the percentile rank of a student who scored a score of 176 from the frequency distribution shown in Table 1.

XX
Normal Probability Distribution

Introduction

During our day-to-day life we have to depend upon the number of biological, social, economic, industrial and psychological measurements where the variables are continuous in nature and as such can be adequately described only by a continuous probability distribution. One of the most important continuous probability distributions in the entire field of statistics is the normal probability distribution. It has been shown that a vast number of distributions arising in studies of natural, social and psychological phenomena conform to normal curve. The graphical expression of the normal distribution is presented in the form of *normal curve.* Normal curve is the bell-shaped smooth symmetrical curve as shown in Fig. 1.

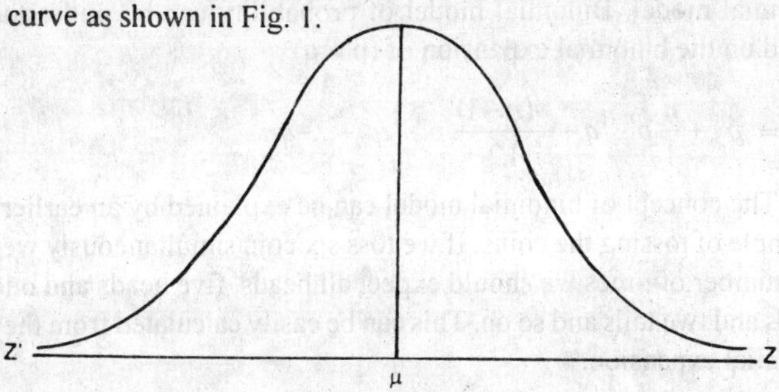

Fig. 1.1. The Normal Curve

Normal probability curve mostly show the concentration of frequencies near a central value of the distribution and the frequencies gradually taper off symmetrically on both sides. This general tendency of quantitative data, for a large number of measurements, gives rise to the symmetrical bell-shaped to the normal curve. Thus the normal curve or distribution is a general theoretical model which may be used to describe the frequency distribution of many variables.

The normal curve has its significance in different disciplines. Its wider applicability in different fields of knowledge makes us to understand the meaning, properties and applications of normal curve in education.

XX.1 Meaning of Probability

In order to understand the meaning of normal probability distribution firstly we need to know about the probability. In simple terms by probability we mean the possibility of being selected. The concept of probability can be understood by the games of chance. If we toss a coin, either we shall get a head or a tail. We say that the probability of getting a head is 1 out of 2. Similarly, the probability of getting a tail when we toss a coin is also 1 out of 2. This can be expressed as the probability of getting a head or a tail is 1/2. A cube has 6 faces, numbered 1 to 6. When we throw the cube, the probability of the face with marks 2 coming up is 1 in 6 or 1/6. Similarly the probability of getting the face marked 1, 3, 4, 5 or 6 is 1/6 each. We can apply the same principle to the drawing of playing cards. The number of favourable ways is 13 and the total number of ways is 52. Therefore, the probability of drawing a spade (any spade) is 13/52 or 1/4. There are four kings and the total number of ways is 52. Therefore, the probability of getting a king (of any colour) is 4/52 or 1/13. For drawing the queen of hearts the probability is 1/52. So is the probability of drawing any card of any colour. In brief, the probability means the possibility to be selected. The probability theory is governed by various mathematical models. Most popular model to explain the probability is binomial model. Binomial model of probability can be understood as it is based on the binomial expansion of $(p + q)^n$

$$= p^n + \frac{n}{1} p^{n-1} q + \frac{n(n-1)}{1.2} p^{n-2} q^2 + \ldots + qn$$

The concept of binomial model can be explained by an earlier discussed example of tossing the coins. If we toss six coin simultaneously we can know the number of times we should expect all heads, five heads and one tail, four heads and two tails and so on. This can be easily calculated from the following binomial expansion.

$$(H + T)^6 = H^6 + 6H^5T + 15H^4T^2 + 20H^3T^3 + 15H^2T^4 + 6HT^5 + T^4$$

Thus we shall get once all the six heads when we toss the six coins 64 times. Hence the probability of getting all the six head is $\frac{1}{64}$. The probability of getting 5 heads and one tail is $\frac{6}{64}$, the probability of getting 4 heads and 2 tails is $\frac{15}{64}$, and so on. You will observe that the sum of all the probability is one in such cases. We can draw bar diagram from the frequencies obtained by the above expansion. When there are 10 coins, there will be 11 frequencies mathematical model to represent these probabilities when N is very large is known as the Normal Probability Curve. The shape of the normal curve is given below:

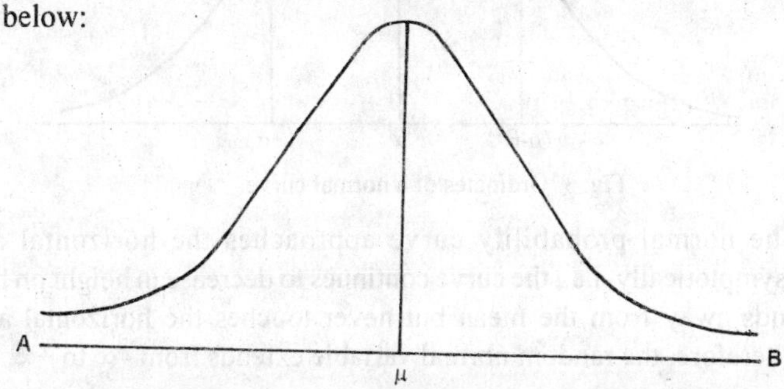

Fig. 2

You can see it is a bell shaped curve; symmetrical about its axes. The line AB is called the base line. The curve tapers off as we move towards the right or the left. The curve never touches the base line. After sometime *p-2Xit becom parallel to the base line. The curve has one side + ve and the other as negative side. The curve is divided into different classes on the basis of standard deviation. Mean, Median and Mode fall in the centre of the curve and the centre of the curve is denoted by μ (Meu).

XX.2 Properties of Normal Distribution Curve

The important properties of normal distribution or Normal curve may be described as under:

(i) The curve is symmetrical about a vertical axis through the mean μ, i.e., if we fold the curve along this vertical axis, the two halves of the curve would coincide.

(ii) As a result of symmetry, the mean, median and mode of the distribution are identical and they fall near the centre of the curve.

(iii) Since there is only one maximum point in the curve, the normal curve is unimodal, i.e. it has only one mode.

(iv) The height of the normal probability curve declines symmetrically in either direction from the maximum point. Hence, the ordinates for values of $x = \mu \pm k$, where k is a real number, are equal. For example, the heights of the curve or the ordinates at $x = \mu + \sigma$ and $x = \mu - \sigma$ are exactly the same as shown in the following Fig. 3.

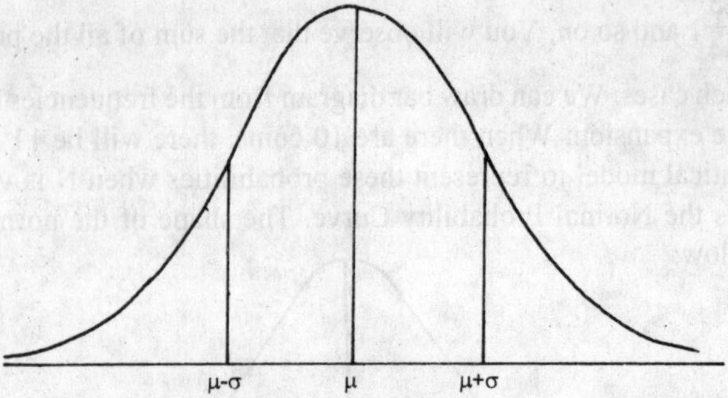

Fig. 3. Ordinates of a normal curve.

(v) The normal probability curve approaches the horizontal axis asymptotically, i.e., the curve continues to decrease in height on both ends away from the mean but never touches the horizontal axis. Therefore, the random normal variable extends from $-\infty$ to $+\infty$, i.e., $-\infty < x < \infty$.

(vi) The total area under the normal probability curve and above the horizontal axis is 1.0 which is essential for a probability distribution or curve.

(vii) Since, the shape of the normal probability curve is completely determined with its parameters μ and σ, the area under the curve bounded by the two ordinates also depends on these parameters. Some important areas under the curve bounded by the ordinates at σ, 2σ and 3σ distances away from mean in either direction are shown in figure 4, 5 and 6 given below.

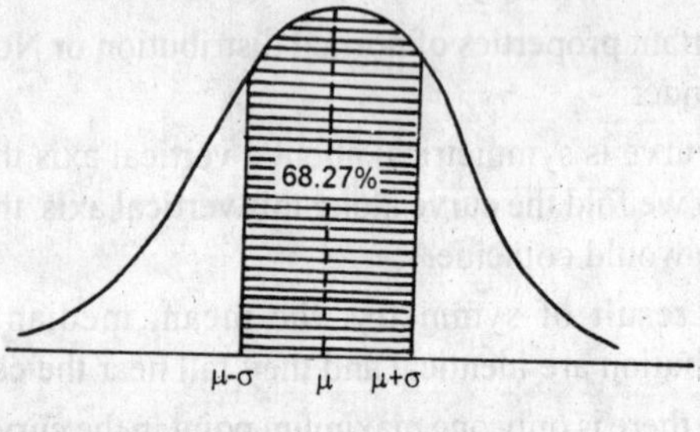

Fig. 4. Area between 1–sigma limits (68.27%).

That is:

(a) the area between ordinates at $x = \mu - \sigma$ and $x = \mu + \sigma$ is 0.6827 or 68.27%.

(b) the area between ordinates at $x = \mu - 2\sigma$ and $x = \mu + 2\sigma$ is 0.9545 or 95.45%.

(c) the area between ordinates at x = μ –3 σ and x = μ + 3 σ is 0.9973 i.e., the area under the normal curve beyond these ordinates is only 1–0.9973 = 0.0027 which is very small. Thus, practically the whole area under the normal curve lies within limits μ ± 3σ which are also called 3–sigma limits.

(viii). Normal probability distribution is the index to representative sample of a population.

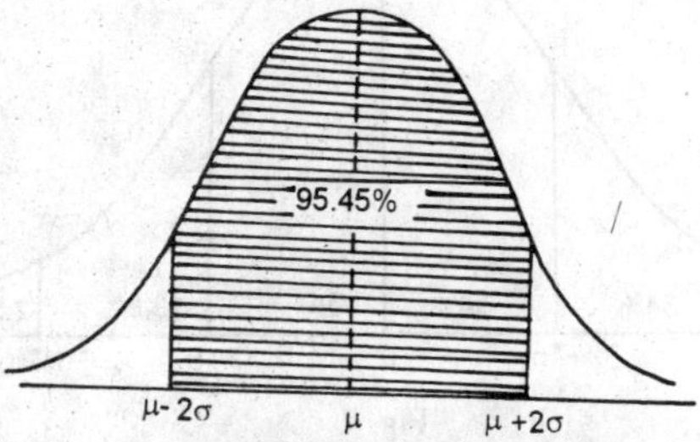

Fig. 5. Area between 2–sigma limits (95.45%)

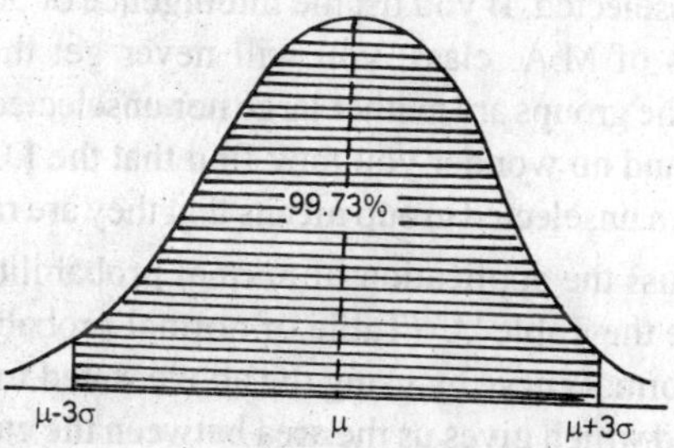

Fig. 6. Area between 3–sigma limits (99.73%).

XX.3 Applications of Normal Probability Curve

Normal probability distribution is represented in the form of normal curve. The normal distribution curve is of wide applicability in Education and Psychology. For instance, we are aware of the fact that all our traits physical, mental and social are normally distributed. Let us take mental traits as an example. All of us do not have the same I.Q., some are intelligents, some are very intelligent, some are intelligent, some have intelligence level below normal intelligence, some have much below normal intelligence level. This is what we mean by distribution. The normal distribution follows a set pattern. If the mean I.Q. is 100 and the standard deviation of I.Q.'s is 15 then 68% persons in a large unselected group will have their I.Q.'s between 85 (100–15) and 115

(100 + 15), that is between one standard deviation below and one standard deviation above the mean I.Q. 13.5% will have their I.Q. in the range 116 to 130 and the same number shall have their I.Q.'s in the interval 70–84 of the remaining 5%, 2.5% will have their I.Q.'s above 130 and 2.5% will have their I.Q.'s below 70. This is shown in the below mentioned nornal distribution curve.

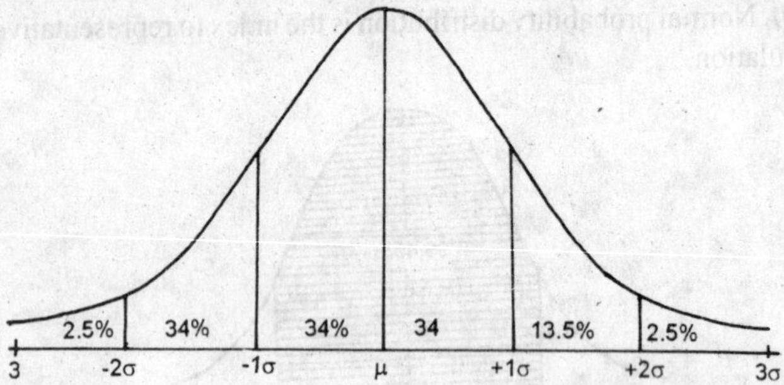

Fig. 7

The same is true of any other trait. It may be noted that the group observed must be large and unselected. If you list the intelligence of 50 students of B.A. class or 20 students of M.A. class, you will never get the I.Q.'s normally distributed because the groups are neither large nor unselected. Both the groups are highly selected and no wonder you may find that the I.Q.'s of all of them are more than 110. An unselected group means that they are randomly selected.

Before we discuss the application of normal probability curve, we need to understand to use the Table 'A' (Table of normal probability) to calculate the area under the normal curve by using the above stated formula. The Table 'A' has been prepared which gives us the area between the curve, the base line, the ordinate at the mean and the ordinate at any other point on the base line. This area is in terms of fraction having four figures. If we multiply by 100, we get the percent of the total area in that portion.

The first column is headed by $\frac{x}{\sigma}$ where x stands for the distance of the any point on the base line from the mean and σ stands for the standard deviation. In this column you find the figures from .01 to...In the first row we have numbers .00, .01, 02, 03, .04, .05, .06, .07, .08 and .09. It is very simple to read the table 'A'. Suppose we want to find the area between the ordinates at the mean and the ordinate at a points on the base line such that our $\frac{x}{\sigma}$ =.63 we shall see .60 in the first column and .03 in the first row. The figure in the cell below .03 and opposite. 60 gives us the required area. Once again it may be stated for emphasis that area in the table 'A' are given under the curve from the ordinate at the mean and the ordinate at any other point on the base line. Let us study examples to illustrate the applications of normal probability curve.

I. Application of Normal Probability Curve to determine the percentage of cases in distribution.

For instance (1): A class of a school scores in mathematics which has its mean of 12 and a σ of 4. Assuming normality, *(i)* What percentage of the cases fall between 8 and 16? *(ii)* What percentage of the cases lie above score 18? *(iii)* Below score 6?

(i) A score of 16 is 4 points above the mean, and a score of 8 is 4 points below the mean. If we divide this scale distance of 4 score units by the σ of the distribution (*i.e.*, by 4) it is clear that 16 is Iσ above the mean, and that 8 is Iσ below the mean (see Fig. 8). There are 68.26% of the cases in a normal distribution between the mean and ±Iσ (Normal Distribution Table A.) Hence, 68.26% of the scores in our distribution, or approximately the middle two-thirds, fall between 8 and 16. This result may also be stated in terms of "chances." Since 68.26% of the cases in the given distribution fall between 8 and 16, the chances are about 68 in 100 that any score in the distribution will be found between these points.

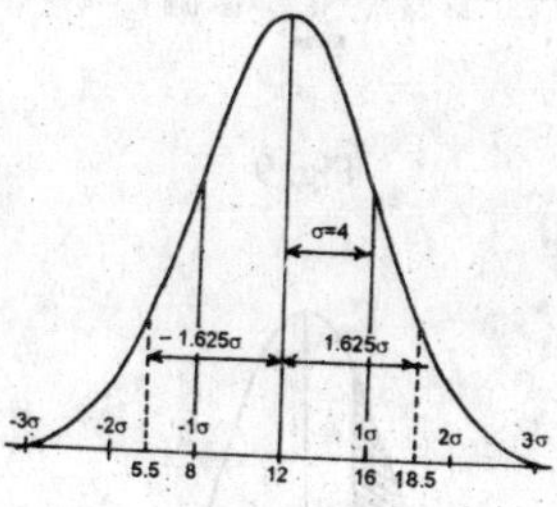

Fig. 8.

(ii) The *upper limit* of a score of 18, namely, 18.5, is 6.5 score units or 1.625% σ above the mean (6.5/4 = 1.625). From Normal Distribution Table A we find that 44.79% of the cases in the entire distribution fall between the mean and 1.625 σ. Accordingly, 5.21% of the cases (50.00–44.79) must lie *above* the upper limit of 18 (viz; 18.5) in order to fill out the 50% of cases in the upper half of the normal curve (Fig. 8). In terms of chances, there are about 5 chances in 100 that any score in the distribution will be larger than 18.

(iii) The *lower limit* of a score of 6, namely, 5.5 is –1.625 σ from the mean between 5.5 (–1.625 σ) are 44.79% of the cases in the whole distribution. Hence, about 5% of the cases in the distribution lie below

5.50-fill out the 50% below the mean-and the chances are about 5 in 100 that any score in the distribution will be less than 6, i.e., below the lower limit of score 6.

Example (2): Given a distribution with a mean of 29.75 and a σ of 6.75. Assuming normally, what percentage of the distribution will lie between 22 and 26? What are the chances that a score will be between these two points ?

A score of 22 is 7.75 score units or –1.15 σ (7.75/6.75 = 1.15) from the mean; and a score of 26 is 3.75 or –3.75 or –.56 σ from the mean. (Fig. 9) We know from Tahle A that 37.49% of the cases in a normal distribution lie between the mean and –1.15 σ; and that 21.23% of the cases lie between the mean and –.56σ. By simple substraction, therefore, 16.26% of the cases fall between – 1.15%σ and –.56σ or between the scores 22 and 26. The chances are 16 in 100 that any score in the distribution will lie between these two points.

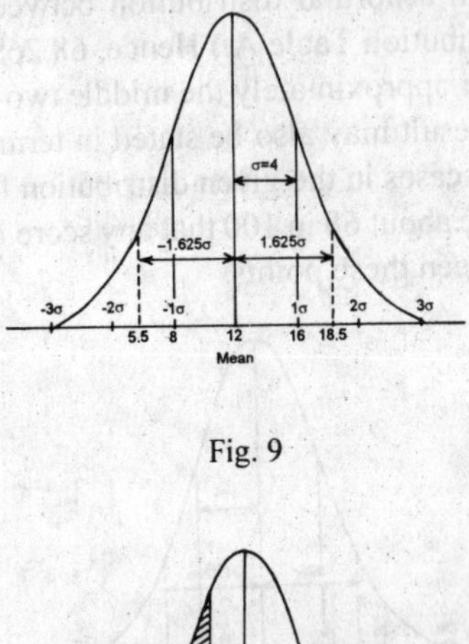

Fig. 9

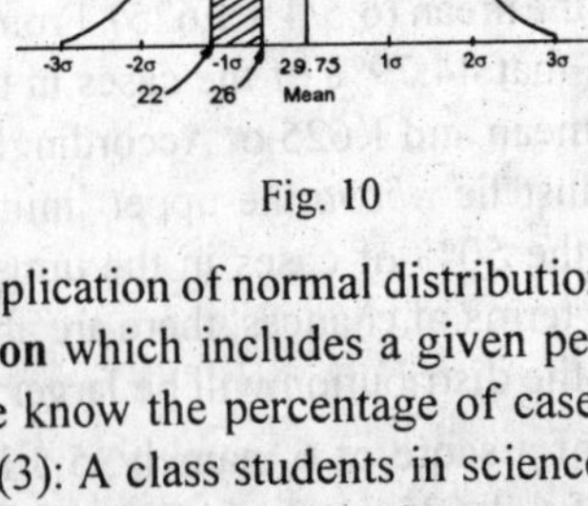

Fig. 10

II. The second application of normal distribution helps us to **find out the limits of a distribution** which includes a given percentage of the cases. In other words when we know the percentage of cases qualifying a particular subject. For instance (3): A class students in science on a distribution scores with a mean of 16.00 and a σ of 4.00. If we may assume normality, what limits will include the middle 75% of the cases?

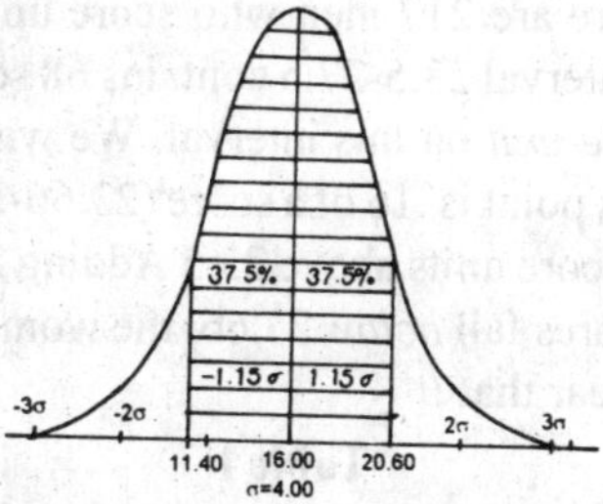

Fig. 11

Solution: As per the problem, the middle 75% of the cases in a normal distribution include the 37.5% just above, and the 37.5% just below the mean. While consulting Table 'A' i.e., normal probability table we find that 3749 cases in 10,000, or 37.5% of the distribution also fall between the mean and –1.15σ; and, of course, 37.5% of the distribution also falls between the mean and –1.15 σ. The middle 75% of the cases, therefore, lie between the mean and ±1.15 σ; or, since σ = 4.00, between the mean and ±4.60 score units. Adding ± 4.6 to the mean (to 16.00), we find that the middle 75% of the scores in the given distribution lie between 20.60 and 11.40 as shown in figure 10.

III. An important application of normal distribution is that it helps in **comparing the two groups** belonging to the same population. The comparison of two traits, types of abilities among the real or artificial group can be made for obtaining meaningful differences or similarities. For. instance, (4) : Given the distribution of the scores made on a intelligence test by 300 men and 250 women. The men's mean score is 21.49 with a σ of 3.63. The women's mean score is 23.68 with a σ of 5.12. The medians are : Men's 21.41 and women 23.66. What percentage of men exceed the median of the women's distribution?

On the assumption that these distributions are normal, we may solve this problem by means of Table A. The women *median* is 23.66-21.49 or 2.17 score units above the men's *mean.* Dividing 2.17 by 3.63 (the σ of the men's distribution), we find that the women's median is .69σ above the mean of the men's distribution. Table 'A' shows that 23% of a normal distribution lies *between* the mean and .69σ; hence 27% of the men's (50%–23%) exceed the women's median.

This problem may also be solved by direct calculation from the distributions of men and women's scores without any assumption as to normality of distribution. The calculations are shown in Table 1; and it is interesting to compare the result found by direct calculation with that obtained by use of the probability tables. The problem is to find the *number of men* whose scores exceed 23.66, the women's median, and then turn this number into a percentage. There are 217 men who score up to 23.5 (lower limit of 23.5-27.5). The class interval 23.5-27.5 contains 68 score; hence there are 68/4 or 17 scores *per scale unit* on this interval. We wish to reach 23.66 in the men's distribution. This point is .16 of a score (23.66-23.50 = .16) above 23.5, or 2.72 (i.e., 17 × .16) score units above 23.5 Adding 2.72 to 217, we find that 219.72 of the men's scores fall *below* 23.66, the women's median. Since 300-219.72 = 80.28, it is clear that :

Table I

To illustrate the method of determining overlapping by direct calculation from the distribution:

Men Scores	*f*	*Women* Scores	*f*
27.5-31.5	15	31.5-35.5	20
23.5-27.5	68	27.5-31.5	35
19.5-23.5	128	23.5-27.5	73
15.5-19.5	79	19.5-23.5	68
11.5-15.5	10	15.5-19.5	41
	N = 300	11.5-15.5	13
			N = 250

N/2 = 150 $\qquad$ N/2 = 125

$$\text{Mdn} = 19.5 + \frac{61}{128} \times 4 \qquad \text{Mdn} = 23.5 + \frac{3}{73} \times 4$$

$$= 21.41 \qquad = 23.66$$

$$M = 21.49 \qquad M = 23.68$$

$$\sigma = 3.63 \qquad \sigma = 5.12$$

What percent of the men exceed 23.66, the median of the women's ? First, 217 men makes scores *below* 23.5. The class interval 23.5-27.5 contains 68 scores; hence, there are 68/4 or 17 scores *per scale unit* on this interval. The women's median, 23.66, is .16 *above* 23.5, lower limit of interval 23.5-27.5. If we multiply 17 (number of scores per scale unit) by .16 we obtain 2.72 which is the distance we must go into interval 23.5-27.5 to reach 23.66.

Adding 217 and 2.72, we obtain 219.72 as that part of the men's distribution which *falls below* the point 23.66 (women's median). *N* is 300; hence 300–219.72 *gives* 80.28 as that part of the men's distribution which lies *above* 23.66. Dividing 80.28 by 300, we find that .2676, or approximately 27%, of the men's exceed the women's median. 80.28 + 300 or 26.76% (approximately 27%) of the men exceed the women median. This result is in almost perfect agreement with that obtained above. Apparently the assumption of normality of distribution for the men's scores was justified.

The agreement between the percentage of overlapping found by direct calculation from the distribution and that found by use of the probability tables will nearly always be close, especially if the groups are large and the distributions fairly symmetrical. When the overlapping distributions are small and not very regular in outline, it is safer to use the method of direct calculation, since no assumption as to form of distribution need then be made.

IV. The Normal Probability Distribution helps us to determine the require percentage of cases of a particular population. The probability further helps us to identify the level of difficulty of a psychological or teacher made achievement test. Besides, the application of normal probability also helps us to identify the items comprehensive level item difficulty e.g; (s) In a class if we find the student of 9th class 10% are able to solve first problem and the second problem solved by 20% of the same group; and a third problem solved by 30%. If we assume the capacity measured by the test problems to be distributed normally, what is the relative difficulty of questions 1, 2 and 3 ?

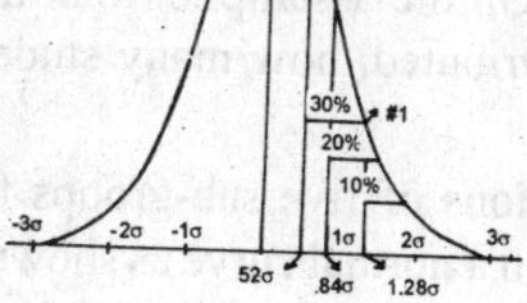

Fig. 12

To understand the application of normal distribution firstly we find for problem 1 a cut in the distribution, such that 10% of the entire group (the percent passing) lies above, and 90% (the percent failing) lies below the given point. The highest 10% in a normally distributed group has 40% of the cases between its lower limit and the mean (Fig. 12). From the normal distribution Table 'A' we find that 39.97% (i.e., 40%) of a normal distribution falls between the mean and 1.28σ. Hence, problem No. 1 belongs at a point on the base line of the curve, a distance of 1.28 σ from the mean; and accordingly, 1.28 σ may be set down as the difficulty value of this problem.

Problem No. 2, passed by 20% of the group, falls at a point in the distribution 30% above the mean. From Normal distribution Table 'A' it is found that 29.95% (i.e., 30%) of the group falls between the mean and .84 σ;

hence, problem 2 has a difficulty value of .84 σ. Problem No. 3 which lies at a point 10% the distribution 20% above the mean, has a difficulty value of .52σ, since 19.85% of the distribution falls between the mean and .52σ. To summarize our results :

Question	Passed by	σ Value	σ Difference
1	10%	1.28	–
2	20%	.84	.44
3	30%	.52	.32

The σ difference in difficulty between problem 2 and 3 is.32, which is roughly 3/4 of the σ difference in difficulty between problem 1 and 2. Since the percentage difference is the same in the two comparisons, it is evident that when ability is assumed to follow the normal curve, σ and not percentage differences are the better indices of differences in difficulty.

V. Psychologist feel that one of the important application of normal probability curve of normal curve is to help us to **understand whether the data collected** is uniformly distributed among the population. Similarly, the application ensures that the data collected for study is representative of the population or not. Besides, the normal curve helps us to separate given group into sub-groups. (b), For instance, we have administered an entrance examination to 100 college students. We wish to classify our group into five subgroups A, B, C, D and E according to ability, the *range* of ability to be equal in each sub-group. On the assumption that the trait measured by our examined is normally distributed, how many students should be placed in groups, A, B, C, D and E?

To find out the positions of five sub-groups let us draw diagram and work out the distribution on a normal curve as shown in Figure 12. If the base line of the curve is considered to extend from –3 σ to + 3σ, that is, over a range of 6σ, dividing this range by 5 (the number of sub-groups) gives 1.2σ as the base line extent to be allotted to each group. These five intervals may be laid off on the base line as shown in the figure 12, and perpendiculars erected to demarcate the various subgroups. Group A covers the upper 1.2σ; group B the next 1.2σ; group C lies .6σ to the *right* and .6σ to the *left* of the mean; groups D and E occupy the same relative positions in the lower half of the curve that B and A occupy in the upper half.

To find what percentage of the whole group belongs in A group we must find what percentage of a normal distribution lies between 3σ (upper limit of the A group) and 1.8σ (lower limit of the A group). From Table 'A' 49.86% of a normal distribution is found to lie between the mean and 3σ, and 46.41% between the mean and 1.8σ. Hence, 3.5% of the total area under the normal curve (49.86%–46.41%) lies between 3σ and 1.8σ; and accordingly, group A comprises 3.5% of the whole group.

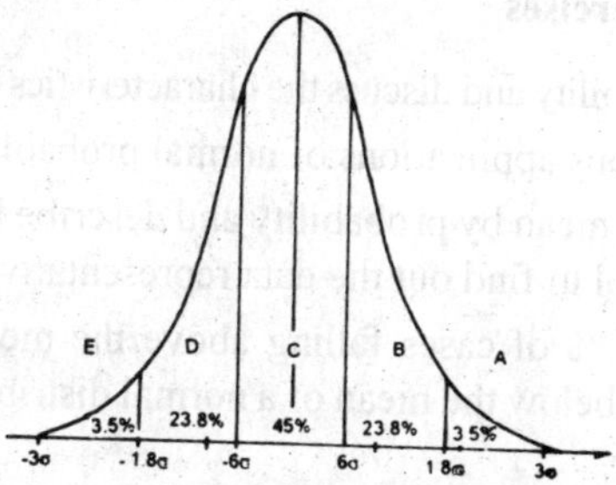

Fig. 13

The percentages in the other groups are calculated in the same way. Thus, 46.41 in the other groups are calculated in the same way. Thus, 46.41% of the normal distribution falls between the mean and 1.8σ (upper limit of group B) and 22.57% falls between the mean and .6σ (lower limit of group B), Subtracting, we find that 46.41%-22.57% or 23.84% of our distribution belongs in subgroup B. Group C lies from -6σ. above to –.6σ below the mean. Between the mean and .6σ is 22.57% of the normal distribution, and the same percent lies between the mean and –6σ. Group C, therefore, includes 45.14% (22.57 × 2) of the distribution. Finally, subgroup D, which lies between –.6σ and 1.8σ, contains exactly the same percentage of the distribution as subgroup B; and group E, which lies between –1.8σ and –3σ, contains the same percent of the whole distribution as group A. The % and number of men in each group are shown in the following table:

	Groups				
	A	B	C	D	E
% of total in each group	3.5	23.8	45	23.8	3.5
Number in each group (100 men in all)	4 or 3	24	45	24	4 or 3

On the assumption that the capacity measured follows the normal curve, it is clear that 3 to 4 men in our group of 100 should be placed in group, 'A' the "marked" ability group; 24 in group B, the "high average" ability group; 45 in group C, the "average" ability group; 24 in group D, the "low average" ability group; and 3 or 4 in group E, the "very low" or "inferior" group.

The above procedure may be used to determine how many students in a class should be assigned to each of any given number of grade groups. The assumption is always made that performance in the subject upon which the individuals are being marked can be represented by the normal curve. The larger and more unselected the group, and the better the test, the more nearly is this assumption justified.

XX.4 Learning Exercises

1. Define probability and discuss the characteristics of normal distribution.
2. Discuss various applications of normal probability curve.
3. What do you mean by probability and describe how probability curve helps as a tool to find out the data representative of a population.
4. Find out the % of cases falling above the mean and percentage of cases falling below the mean of a normal distribution when M = 25, σ = 10.
5. Find out the limits of a distribution of students scoring 45% and 25% when the mean of distribution is 20 and σ = 5.